ATTACK AIRCRAFT of the West

ATTACK AIRCRAFT of the West

BILL GUNSTON

LONDON

IAN ALLAN LTD

First published 1974

ISBN 0 7110 0523 0

Published by Ian Allan Ltd, Shepperton, Surrey, and printed in Great Britain by Morrison & Gibb Ltd, London and Edinburgh.

Contents

Foreword	7
Glossary	13
UNITED KINGDOM	
Hawker Siddeley Buccaneer	17
BAC TSR.2	38
Hawker Siddeley Harrier	69
COLLABORATION	
Sepecat Jaguar	108
AFVG	129
MRCA	151
UNITED STATES	
General Dynamics F-111	170
McDonnell Douglas A-4 Skyhawk	209
Grumman A-6 Intruder	221
Vought A-7 Corsair II	234
Fairchild Republic A-10A	249

Foreword

THIS IS the second in a series of books which tell the stories of important types of modern aircraft. The first, entitled 'Bombers of the West', deals with aircraft intended to bomb strategic targets. I included the evergreen Canberra in that volume, because strategic bombing was the mission for which it was designed, even though most Canberras have actually served in various kinds of 'attack' role. Obviously there is a need to explain the difference.

Bombers are intended to inflict damage in enemy heartlands. Some of their objectives may be what are called 'point targets'. ICBM silos demand accuracy within a matter of yards, even when attacked with a nuclear weapon, and so do large radars or any other kind of single building when attacked with h.e. The other objectives are cities, calling for a large thermonuclear warhead delivered within a circle of a mile or two in radius. Most of these strategic targets are permanent and fixed. Once you know exactly where they are, in relation to your own country, you can hit them very well with long-range missiles. For this reason most of the chapters in the 'Bombers' volume deal with aircraft designed 20 and more years ago. The penultimate chapter is concerned with a mighty bomber which tried to compete with the ICBM and failed. It is the final chapter which is the eye-opener, because this is a totally different sort of strategic bomber which is not due in service until 1978.

Attack aircraft, as a class, are more difficult to define. I could suggest they are usually employed on 'tactical' missions in support of land or sea battles and that their usual targets are enemy forces and military installations. I could also suggest the typical attack aircraft is smaller than a bomber and looks like a fighter. I could also say the class is divided into 'interdictors', which operate from good airfields far behind the front line and hit objectives deep in enemy territory, and 'close air support' aircraft which operate (or ought to operate) from small makeshift strips very close to the front line and hit troops, armour and fortifications right in front of one's own soldiers. What makes the definition more difficult is that in the past most attack missions have been flown by fighters, a class of aircraft intended primarily for aerial combat. Even the F-111, an interdictor twice as heavy as a B-17 or Lancaster, is classed as a fighter (which, as the longest chapter in this book shows, led to all kinds of trouble). Navies and Marines have appreciated that attack aircraft ought to be purpose-built. The US Army knew this before World War 2. The Swedes knew it too, even though the Lansen and Viggen were both later developed into fighters. But during the 1950s and 1960s the US Air Force, the RAF and practically every other air force has appeared to consider that clobbering a few soldiers was a rather second-rate sort of task that could be done by the nearest fighter outfit—or, better still, by a squadron of old obsolescent fighters that could not safely be used for anything else.

If you ram home a lesson often enough the penny eventually drops, even with staff officers. This is a rude thing to say, but World War 2 ought to have prepared these people for Korea, and Korea ought to have prepared them for Vietnam. What worries me is that, now that SE Asia appears to be trying a new sort of existence called peace, the lesson may still not have been learned. And what makes it much harder is that the harassed staff officer is faced with many more or less new options, such as jet-VTOL, attack helicopters, remotely piloted vehicles, and sensing systems which blanket the battle area with microwaves or coherent light. To make it harder still, inflationary prices threaten to put almost everything financially out of reach.

What does the attack aircraft have to do? It has to live in an austere place, which may have been virgin territory the previous day, yet be ready at a few minutes' notice to go and hit the enemy. Sometimes the mission is against a town, a railway bridge, a ship or some similar target which—provided the weather is not too bad—can be found and probably hit. But most battlefield targets are small, dispersed, and either hidden or moving. To find them is no easy task, even if you have half a million dollars' worth of clever black boxes to help. Five thousand men pointing their rifles at your cockpit can make life difficult; even if they all miss, they are likely to introduce an 'operational degradation factor' (better known as 'twitch factor') and if this halves your accuracy it means you need not two but four aircraft to do the work of one. Worse, today's well-equipped soldier may be able to point a little guided weapon at you that will spoil your whole day. In Vietnam, life was quite hard enough without shoulder-fired guided weapons. Attack missions by the US Air Force were generally flown either by supersonic fighters or by heavy bombers, with a cost/effectiveness that the Department of Defense just hated trying to calculate.

In place of these unsuited aircraft we have today an increasingly wide range of specially designed aircraft. Some of these are helicopters, and

I have deliberately left these for a possible future volume on this class of aircraft. One is really a well-protected STOL turbofan transport (the A-10A) which represents an intensely interesting compromise between the conflicting needs of availability, lethality, survivability and low cost. Another is the unique jet-lift Harrier. Not one is in any sense a fighter (though the Harrier has been found to have extraordinary and unplanned potential in the fighter role). Trying to choose between such dissimilar vehicles is quite difficult enough without having the added problem of deciding just what array of black boxes represents the irreducible minimum that one can actually afford to buy. Obviously this last question is strongly influenced by where the battle is going to be; in the Middle East the human eyeball does pretty well by itself. In Northern Europe few people would dispute the need for an inertial navigation system (the French are at last admitting their lack of one), a head-up display and an accurate ranging device; a modern radar is a nice extra. A further complication is that many countries want their 'attack aircraft' to be a fighter as well.

Unlike most of the so-called 'bombers', nearly all the aircraft described in this volume are very active current programmes, with the single exception of the British TSR.2. This sorry tale is by no means the only one here that is liberally laced with controversy and larded with acrimonious emotion. No other aircraft in history have generated so many ulcers as the modern attack aircraft of the West.

TSR.2 will forever be a classic example of sustained inadequacy by successive governments. At first the government of the day announced that the RAF would be unlikely to require any more fighters or bombers (or, by implication, any other 'combat aircraft'). Almost at once the RAF said it actually would like a new aeroplane, for tactical strike and reconnaissance. After prolonged argument and enforced 'shotgun weddings' between the companies to make the airframe and the engines, industry was allowed to get down to the job of creating the most challenging aircraft ever designed in Britain. As there was nothing else in the same class in Western Europe the task involved creating not only the aircraft but also a whole new range of technologies, skills, materials and other supporting services. It had an enormous and widespread beneficial effect on the technical spearhead of British industry, and every penny was charged to the TSR.2. This made it seem an expensive item in the budget and a new government was then elected which professed to loathe TSR.2 and those who strove to create it. Angrily TSR.2 was swept away—the very jigs used to make it being smashed into scrap metal along with the aircraft on the production line—and replaced by an American aircraft said to be much better and cheaper. Then this US replacement was itself cancelled and replaced by a programme started jointly with the French.

Then the French said they were sorry but they had no money for this project (and anyway they had something just like it themselves). Eventually the British managed to set course a fourth time, in partnership with Germany and Italy. And at last the result is a viable programme which is actually so good and potentially important that it is being studiously attacked by commercial rivals—the greatest compliment that could be paid to it.

Lest anyone should think my objective is merely to re-open the countless old wounds of the mournfully managed British programmes, the longest chapter tells the tale of the TFX, the 'American replacement' I mentioned earlier, which turned out to be possibly the biggest headache in the history of aviation. Despite superhuman efforts by an enormous team of talented engineers, this aircraft, the F-111, failed to sustain the giant, low-cost programme the Pentagon had planned; indeed, headlines across the nation quite unfairly called it 'a lemon', the most acidic of the Americanisms for a total abject failure. Designing and developing modern military aircraft is probably the most difficult occupation in the world. Even if the political environment is one of long-term stability and a grain or two of common sense, there is still no guarantee of complete success. And in Britain in 1957–67 the political environment was worse than anything that an enemy could have contrived.

Any nation about to embark on a large and challenging peace-time programme surely ought—unless there are peculiar and compelling reasons to the contrary—to tell its public exactly what the objectives are, how the management hierarchy has been structured, who the people are in all the key jobs (yes, name them!), and how long and costly the job is expected to be. Any change in the estimate for time and cost should be announced and explained immediately. In American parlance this would be a programme having 'a high degree of visibility'. But in Britain such a procedure seems contrary to the laws of nature. The tradition has been to reduce visibility to zero, thus setting everything up for a scandal of marvellous proportions. Often it has taken the Comptroller-General as long as ten years to drag the whole nauseating tale out from under a score or more of carpets and he frequently has to play a gramophone record complaining that the programme took twice as long as it was meant to and cost five to 50 times as much. (Hardly ever has he suggested that this may have been partly because the estimates were ridiculously optimistic in the first place.)

In 1961 in the United States Mr McNamara devised the concept of 'Total Package Procurement', in which the Department of Defense signed an astronomically large 'fixed-price' cheque with one prime contractor who thereupon undertook to deliver a complete functioning system, right down to the engineering manuals for the ground-support equipment. Unfortunately this great idea came badly unstuck with several of the largest programmes, including the F-111. But, even though in this kind of procurement the notion of a fixed price is nonsense, the giant package is still a better deal than the traditional British method of funding a programme in tiny dribs and drabs from month to month. And there used to be an even sillier British procedure (which, like the dribbling funding, has—I trust—been swept away by the big collaborative programmes). This is the attempt to save money by stretching a programme out over a longer period. It used to be an almost instinctive reaction whenever the going became really rough, yet I suppose the officials who proposed it would have known better than to try to save their own money by asking a building contractor to take twice as long to build their own house.

Aircraft, and especially the aircraft of this book, appeared to bring out strange behaviour not only in Treasury officials but also in Britain's elected rulers. In 1964–65 the British government was urgently concerned to make the British public believe than an American aircraft—the same F-111—was the greatest invention since sliced bread. Whereas in the United States its desperate technical problems were a matter of deep public concern, the officials and ministers in Whitehall either pretended these problems did not exist or else angrily shouted that they did 'not affect' the version of the F-111 they had bought for the RAF. Simultaneously TSR.2, an all-British aircraft which had completed Phase I of its flight programme with fewer problems than any attack aircraft of the post-war period, was presented to the public as a thoroughly rotten aeroplane that the nation would be well rid of. Truth became lost in a miasma of ideological emotion and people in high places lost not only their ability to manage vital programmes but also their ability to live as rational human beings.

There followed a dismal succession of investigations into the British aerospace industry, which came up with a pathetic succession of recommendations which were variously vague, blindingly obvious or wrong. One recurring recommendation was that British airframes should be made by a single company that should do little except collaborate madly with everyone it could find in other countries. Even today there are people in Parliament, of all shades of political opinion, who would be delighted if the two chief British planemakers could merge into one. In some vague way this would 'increase their combined strength' and make 'a more effective unit.' I recommend such people to read the chapter in this book on the Buccaneer, which would have been a disaster if the British industry had been such a monolithic unit. Then they can read the chapter on the A-7 Corsair. To build this outstanding American attack aircraft a company put its signature to a contract which promised to fine it $65,000 for every day it was late, and to penalise it the entire price of the aircraft if it should turn out to need more than 17 man-hours of maintenance for each flying hour—this at a time when several RAF aircraft had equivalent figures well in excess of 100. (Oooh! How wicked! I forgot such figures must be kept secret in Britain.) Why did the company accept such vicious terms? Simply because there was another chap just down the road.

This is real competition, with teeth. If you do not agree the terms, the other man gets the job. If you do agree the terms you move heaven and earth to comply with them, because the next big contract will be determined very much on past performance as well as on promises. So the Corsair was not late by a single day, and it sets new standards in trouble-free operation.

Some years ago George Schairer, a vice-president of Boeing, lectured in London on the importance of competition in aeronautics. He reported the widespread belief of the British that competition was something wasteful that they could not afford. 'Really,' he said, 'you cannot afford to do without it.' Britain's considered answer, at the moment, is to try to get the worst of both worlds by having one huge British airframe company ('Why stop there?' asks the current Aerospace Minister, 'Let's have just one airframe company in Europe!') and then planning so-called 'competitions' between 'rival' design teams in different offices. I would think this a marvellous idea, if I were a Russian—or an American.

I have no doubt that the staggering pace of technical development in the Soviet aircraft industry rests on a bedrock of intense competition of the toothed variety. Schairer emphasized how the Russians always try to have a choice of at least two design bureaux for each major job and often actually fund rival hardware—something that looks terribly 'wasteful' but to which the United States is now returning after a lapse of 30 years. Unfortunately I am again unable to include Soviet aircraft in this book, for fairly obvious reasons, but perhaps the pressures of competition will eventually become so great that they will tell me a little of how they do it. After all, this book tells them in some detail how not to do it.

Haslemere, 1974

Bill Gunston

Glossary

Like every technical subject, attack aircraft are difficult to discuss without introducing jargon that would puzzle the complete layman. In general I have tried to explain obscure terms in the text, but many of the following abbreviations occur so often that it will help to spell them out here:

AAEE Aeroplane & Armament Experimental Establishment (now the Royal Aircraft Armament EE) (UK)

ACAS Assistant Chief of the Air Staff (RAF)

AFB Air Force Base (USAF)

AFSC Air Force Systems Command (USAF)

APU auxiliary power unit carried within an aircraft to start main engines, provide ground power and, sometimes, provide emergency systems power in flight

BLEU Blind Landing Experimental Unit (UK)

Boscombe Boscombe Down, location of AAEE

BuAer Bureau of Aeronautics (US Navy)

BuWeps Bureau of Weapons (US Navy)

CA Release Release by the Controller, Aircraft, of a new type of aircraft for operational service (UK)

CAS 1, close air support; 2, Chief of the Air Staff (RAF)

CEAM Centre d'Experimentation Aériennes Militaires (Fr.)

c.g. centre of gravity

Co-In counter-insurgency (US)

COS Chief of Staff (USAF, Luftwaffe)

c.p. centre of pressure

CPIF cost plus incentive fee, type of procurement contract

CTOL conventional take-off and landing (ie, needing a long run)

c.t.p. chief test pilot

DCOS Deputy Chief of Staff (USAF)

DoD Department of Defense (US)

DTCA Direction Technique des Constructions Aéronautiques (Fr.)

ECM electronic countermeasures: investigation of enemy electromagnetic radiations, and defences against them

FAC Forward Air Control(ler)

FLIR forward-looking infra-red (attack sensing system to enable aircraft to 'see' land surface features in blind conditions)

FLR forward-looking radar

g-a general-arrangement drawing, a simplified but accurate drawing of the side elevation, plan and front view (eg, of an aircraft)

GFE government-furnished equipment, such as engines, radar and weapons (US)

HUD head-up display, cockpit instrument which projects information on to the windscreen, in the pilot's forward line of sight

ICBM Inter-continental ballistic missile

FF identification friend or foe (avionic interrogating device)

ILS instrument landing system (for safe landing in bad weather)

ISA International Standard Atmosphere

ITP instruction to proceed (UK)

LABS low-altitude bombing system

LLTV low-light TV, sensing system able to picture scenes in near-absence of visible light

Mintech Ministry of Technology (UK)

MMH/FH maintenance man-hours per flight hour

MoA Ministry of Aviation (UK) (now MoD (Procurement Executive))

MoD Ministry of Defence (UK)

MoS Ministry of Supply (UK) (now MoD (PE))

MTBF mean time between failures

MWDP Mutual Weapons Development Program (US)

NACA National Advisory Committee for Aeronautics (predecessor of NASA, US)

nape napalm, fire bomb

NAS Naval Air Station (US Navy)

NASA National Aeronautics and Space Administration (US)

NATC Naval Air Test Center (US Navy)

n.m. nautical mile (about 1·15 miles)

OCU Operational Conversion Unit (RAF)

OR Operational Requirement(s)

Pax Patuxent River, location of NATC

PCB plenum-chamber burning, method of boosting thrust of cold (fan) nozzles of vectored-thrust turbofan engine

RAE Royal Aircraft Establishment (Farnborough/Bedford/Aberporth, UK)

RAF Royal Air Force (UK)

RAAF Royal Australian Air Force

R&D research and development

RDT&E research, development, test and evaluation (US)

RFP request for proposals (US)

RN Royal Navy (UK)

RNAS Royal Naval Air Station (UK)

RRE Royal Radar Establishment, Malvern, (UK)

Saceur Supreme Allied Commander, Europe (NATO)

Saclant Supreme Allied Commander, Atlantic (NATO)

SATS small airfield for tactical support (US).

SHAPE Supreme Headquarters Allied Powers Europe (NATO)

SLR sideways-looking radar (sometimes written SLAR, side-looking aircraft radar)

SOR Specific Operational Requirement

TBO time between overhauls

TES Tripartite Evaluation Squadron

TFR terrain-following radar (linked to autopilot to command aircraft to maintain constant low height above undulating ground)

TFS Tactical Fighter Squadron (USAF, USMC)

TRE Telecommunications Research Establishment (UK) (now RRE)

TRIM Trail/Roads Interdiction Multisensor (US)

T/W thrust/weight ratio

USAF United States Air Force

USMC United States Marine Corps

USN United States Navy

VCAS Vice-Chief of the Air Staff (RAF)

VG variable-geometry (esp. variable wing sweep)

VMC visual meteorological conditions (ie, good visibility)

V/STOL vertical or short take-off and landing

YAG yttrium-aluminium garnet, one family of lasers

United Kingdom

Hawker Siddeley BUCCANEER

THE wasteland in British military aviation that followed the Defence White Paper of 1957 was not completely barren. At one place—actually a rather bleak one—there was a substantial and flourishing new growth: at Brough, East Yorkshire, a new strike aircraft was being built for the Royal Navy. Believe it or not, this aircraft, the Buccaneer, is today the only remaining type of aeroplane designed from the start for British military use that was not flying when George VI was on the throne. The Lightning was derived from a pure research aircraft built to a 1947 specification; the Harrier gradually emerged from an equally pure research aircraft as the result of the manufacturer's refusal to be disheartened by the RAF's lack of interest during the first eight years of development; and the Nimrod stemmed from the civil Comet 4 airliner. All other British combat aircraft flown since 1952 have been either cancelled or bought from the United States or an international consortium. The solitary Buccaneer has thus had to fight a rather lone battle against political incompetence, vacillation, policy changes, emotional controversy and the persistent refusal of the RAF to buy it until all the more glamorous alternatives had vanished. Unlike the 22 other types of combat aeroplanes planned for the RAF or RN that had their genesis later than 1952, the Buccaneer survived all this and has made a major contribution to the nation's armoury.

It even managed to be developed on schedule, although the schedule was so leisurely in comparison with American or Soviet timing that no British hats ought to be thrown in the air on this account. The time from the start of the design competition to the start of operational service was ten years and one month; the corresponding time for the nearest rival, the US Navy A-6 Intruder (page 221), was five years and nine months. Yet the original idea was so sound and it was pursued so enthusiastically by the contractor and the Royal Navy, that it resulted in a first-class aircraft that has never suffered from its long gestation and is likely to stay in the front line until at least 1980.

Back in 1950 both paper studies and hardware trials had shown beyond doubt that penetration of defended airspace by manned aircraft was likely to be hazardous, if not suicidal, except at minimum altitude below the effective reach of most surface-based radars. During the period 1951–58 the RAF studied proposals for a lot of interesting low-level bombers and decided not to buy any of them, but pressed ahead with trying to make its high-level V-bombers fly fractionally higher still for reasons which have always eluded me. The Navy alone took the seemingly obvious course of deciding to fly low, perhaps because in general the sea is flatter than the land. In June 1952 the Admiralty issued the exceedingly important NA.39 requirement calling for a two-seat bomber able to fly at Mach 0·85 at 200 feet altitude, carry a nuclear weapon internally (and other stores both internally and externally), be equipped with navigation and bombing radar, have a hi-lo-hi radius of action exceeding 400 nautical miles and fold up to fit the Royal Navy's carriers. I think this was a bigger challenge than B.35/46—which led to the Victor and Vulcan—had been five years earlier, yet almost every firm in the industry fell over themselves to tender for it. Maybe they hadn't read it too carefully and thought the Admiralty still wanted biplanes.

The Ministry of Supply specification sent out to industry was M.148T, dated August 1952. Responses began to come in by February 1953. Ultimately I was able to see at least a three-view of all the submissions and I recommend any politician who still clamours for a single nationalized British aircraft company to go and do likewise. In the big league, be it military or civil, the quality of aircraft a nation produces is determined to a considerable degree by the quality of the customer's procurement machine. Second only to this in importance comes the need for rival design teams, each taking an individual approach and desperately trying to win. If Britain had had a single aircraft company in 1952–55 there would never have been a Buccaneer, the NA.39 specification would not have been met and the public would have been none the wiser. None of the original submissions came within a mile of what was finally achieved and although the process of design refinement and selection took as long as three years—which under normal circumstances might be considered disgraceful—the time was well spent in turning indifferent projects into keenly competitive ones.

Initially everyone but Hawker Aircraft chose a pair of Avon or Sapphire engines, selected a big wing for carrier operation and examined the reduced field or deck length that was possible by using the jet deflection principle which the MoS were about to test using a Nene-engined Meteor. But one of the many problems facing a design team preparing a project submission is that the state of the art moves forward. A project design that looked competitive last week suddenly can be seen to be outmoded. In the NA.39 competition the state of the art was probably moving faster than at any time before or since. Aerodynamics, flying controls, propulsion, structures, manufacturing methods and every sort of airborne system were all progressing at a cracking pace and seen against this background the decision of the MoS and Admiralty to choose a design in 1955, and freeze it, begins to look not so much woefully delayed as positively courageous. The whole thing was a matter for fine judgment. To have accepted any of the submissions of 1953 would have been a grave error. To have continued the study period into 1956 or later would have brought in all sorts of tantalizing new developments, among them turbofan engines, titanium primary structure, inertial navigation, blind attack systems and variable-sweep wings. To eschew such goodies and sign a contract for hardware in 1955 was probably as fair a compromise as could have been achieved. Certainly, if the Buccaneer had been delayed until now its cost-escalation would probably have ruled the whole thing out on budgetary grounds, quite apart from the creeping paralysis of national uncertainty and timidity where complex defence hardware is concerned.

At the start there was not a great deal to choose between the rival submissions, although Sir Sydney Camm never quite convinced me why his entry had six engines. Barry Laight's team at Blackburn Aircraft was one of those favouring jet deflection, applied to a pair of Sapphire engines from Armstrong Siddeley Motors, a sister-firm in the Hawker Siddeley Group, but apart from this their initial submission was not very exciting. What saved it was that the concept of blowing hot, high-pressure air bled from the engines out of thin slits along the wings, especially ahead of the flaps, was studied more deeply by Blackburn than by any of the company's rivals. The technique was pioneered by NACA and the US Navy from 1949, the research leader being John D. Attinello. His work was aimed mainly at blowing a sheet of air at sonic speed across the upper surface of the wing flaps in order to prevent separation at large flap angles and obtain a dramatic increase in lift coefficient. The 'Attinello flap' was adopted by several US aircraft—indeed, the F-104 could hardly fly without it—and it was borrowed by Supermarine for the aircraft that eventually became the Scimitar. But Laight's team collaborated with Dr John Williams, of the National Physical Laboratory, and Lewis Boddington, Director of Naval Aircraft R&D at the MoS, in taking the American idea much further.

By 1954 model tests had shown the enormous increase in lift that could be gained by blowing right across the wing from tip to tip, immediately ahead of acutely depressed flaps and drooped ailerons. The effect was to allow the Blackburn project, the B.103, to use a significantly smaller wing. This was the crucial advance that put the company on the high road of success. The vital importance of a small wing for a low-level bomber had long been appreciated, but nobody had previously been able to reconcile such a wing with use from normal runways, let alone from aircraft carriers. By 1955 the B.103 had emerged with a wing barely 500 square feet in area, with small plain flaps and large ailerons hinged immediately behind full-span blowing slits. In addition the proposed slats were discarded and replaced by a second slit facing rearwards in the upper surface close to the leading edge (at first in the outer wings only, but in the later Spey-Buccaneer from tip to tip). These slits, only 11 thousandths of an inch wide, discharge air bled from the downstream end of the engine compressors. This air is so hot that the ducting and the slit structures had to be made from heat-resistant Nimonic alloy.

This 'supercirculation' or 'boundary-layer control' system was arranged to cut in automatically when flap was selected. At full blow, with about ten per cent of the engine airflow being expelled through the slits, the circulation and pressure-distribution around the wing was dramatically intensified, giving roughly double the lift of the unblown wing. It also had the undesired effect of quadrupling the nose-down pitching moment. Instead of making the tailplane bigger, Blackburn neatly gave this a blowing slit as well, just behind the leading edge on the underside, which allowed the area of this surface to be cut by more than half. In conjunction with a hinged trailing portion, which looks like an elevator but is actually unlocked to move upwards only when the wing flaps are lowered, this very small tailplane imparts the required very large down-load at low speeds yet is small enough not to be excessively powerful at near-sonic speed in dense air. The system works beautifully and makes one wonder why all high-speed aircraft do not have blowing slits all over. It also makes me wonder why, with the notable exception of the Viggen, they do not have foreplanes, which in the high-lift regime add to the lift, but instead have tailplanes which, in the very periods of each flight when lift is most needed, push downwards and thus add to the apparent weight?

From the start the ambitious blowing idea realized all its designers' hopes, gave rise to few really severe problems, and offered an incidental advantage in providing protection against airframe icing in all but the most severe conditions. The fire risk of the almost red-hot Nimonic pipes and valves which fed the air from either engine to every slit never caused any disasters, the system weight penalty was less than a tenth as much as the weight saved in making the wing and tailplane smaller, and the only worry was trying to ensure that the aircraft would never be in a situation such that failure of either engine could cause the lift suddenly to be less than the weight. This worry remained. Laight's men had made a real advance in the aeronautical art in using blowing to such widespread effect, but the next big step was questionable. For maximum range they wanted to use the smallest engines possible. Assuming that every take-off in service would be off a steam catapult, it seemed that the de Havilland Gyron Junior turbojet, rated at a mere 7100 lb thrust, would suffice to push the aircraft at sea level at the desired Mach 0·85 and to provide the big flow of air on the approach. Discussions at Stag Lane with Dr Eric S. Moult in 1954 confirmed this, and the PS.43 (project study 43) version of the very new 'Junior' was selected instead of the Sapphire. This gave a 35 per cent increase in range, and put the B.103 way out in front as a very attractive and significant proposal.

During 1954 another change took place in the design which was as visibly obvious as the incorporation of blowing, and it likewise rested on pioneer research by the American NACA. Richard Whitcomb's 'area rule', in which the plot of total cross-sectional area of a high-speed aircraft is made to form a smooth curve from nose to tail, with no sudden bulge due to the wing, had shown itself to be every bit as applicable to a Mach 0·85 machine as to a supersonic one. Indeed in the B.103 the introduction of area ruling not only made available a great deal of extra volume in the new bulging rear fuselage but it also substantially reduced the thrust needed for high-speed cruise, making the Gyron Junior adequate for the task. At the same time jet-deflection was abandoned. Today all high-speed aircraft are area ruled without waisted middles or bulged sterns, but in the Blackburn machine application of the rule could hardly have been more evident.

In July 1955 the B.103 was chosen by the Admiralty and MoS, and an order was at once placed for 20 development aircraft, the first to fly in April 1958. (This continued the excellent policy established a few months previously by Sir Toby Low of the MoS who, watching his minister, Duncan Sandys, wring his hands over the slow development of the Swift and Hunter, suddenly did the obvious thing and ordered 20 of what later became the Lightning.) It was a tremendous fillip for Robert Blackburn, who at once told employees and shareholders 'An important and challenging aircraft development contract, for which a number of other major firms in the industry competed, is being placed with your company.' Thus he left his firm in good shape when he died the following year and his young successor, Eric Turner, watched the programme behave like a text-book lesson on how British programmes ought to go. The Gyron Junior ran on the bench and flew in a Canberra, the breadboard blowing system exceeded expectations and the works at Brough and such people as High Duty Alloys got to grips with large slabs of integrally stiffened machined skin, huge forged spars and ribs machined all over and sizeable forgings in high-strength steel in grades unobtainable a year earlier except in small test quantities. Unlike earlier British jets the B.103, now known as the Blackburn NA.39 from the naval requirement, was fully tunnel-tested up to its design Mach number and beyond, at first in the big high-speed tunnel just opened at the RAE at Bedford and then at the company's own supersonic tunnel opened at Brough by Earl Mountbatten, then First Sea Lord, early in 1958.

By this time the task of building XK486, the first of the 20 aircraft, was practically finished. Undoubtedly it was the most unbreakable aircraft in Britain. So massive was the airframe that many of the techniques were quite new to the British industry (but usually not new to the US). In contrast to the American acceptance of difficult three-dimensional machining of skins, Blackburn found great economies in machining them flat and then bending them to the finished profile. In the mid-1950s it was obvious that future high-speed aircraft and possibly the bigger slow ones, were increasingly going to demand giant skin mills able to carve out complicated shapes from plates and slabs of light alloy and even steel. In the United States the trend had been keenly studied from 1948 onwards and the US Air Force had funded a special programme to help the machine-tool makers produce giant skin mills, stretch presses and other very large machines. In Britain such planning was conspicuously absent, so when in 1955 Blackburn tried to buy a big skin mill the best quote the company could get included a time to delivery of 2½ years. As the first B.103 was to be airborne in three years this was hopeless. Blackburn accordingly designed its own skin mill and had it running in eleven months. Subsequently the company built three similar machines, all of which have now been carving out skin panels for 18 years. Doubtless, as the British machine-tool industry could not deliver a stretch-press either, Blackburn could again have made one for themselves; but they got the MoS to import a big Hufford, as other British planemakers had done before them. When the Ministry of Technology was formed in 1964 one of its first assignments was to do something about British machine tools. I do not wholly blame the British machine-tool industry (which I believe still exists). It is easy to dismiss aerospace as a limited and specialized market for such very costly machines. But a consortium of firms might perhaps have looked beyond the end of their noses and stopped Hufford, Sheridan, Giddings & Lewis, Cincinnati and other American firms from scooping up what is actually a very big market indeed.

This business of cutting and forging airframes from solid metal is one that took a long time to learn. One of the most difficult problems in producing a low-level strike aircraft is to ensure that it will have an adequate fatigue life and not crack to pieces under the fearful buffeting and reversal of loading experienced on each mission. Blackburn knew no more than other firms when the B.103 was on paper, but their policy of avoiding sharp changes in section, small radii, scratches or any other stress-inducers or concentrators paid off handsomely. Chemical etching, careful polishing and great attention to detail have gained their full reward; I have never heard of a Buccaneer coming unglued, although it is designed to a limit factor of 12 and does have some hollow spaces inside.

XK486, like most British combat jets, could not make its maiden flight where it was built. After running its engines in March 1958 it was pulled to bits, by withdrawing large-diameter, precision-ground steel bolts and pins from precisely matching holes, covered with shrouds which didn't hide much, and trucked from the banks of the Humber to the RAE at Bedford. Here it was swiftly assembled, painted glossy white below the centreline and royal blue above, and thoroughly inspected. Then Lt-Cdr Derek Whitehead, who had joined Blackburn from Boscombe Down specially to test-fly the NA.39, climbed the ladder to the front Martin-Baker seat, positioned to the left of centre, and observer B. J. Watson took his place behind, higher up and offset to the right. There was plenty of time to meet the first-flight schedule of April 1958; three weeks of the month remained for taxying trials. But on one of these runs the harsh braking grossly overheated the main wheels and one tyre burst. This would not have been serious, but as luck would have it the rupture in the high-pressure tyre pointed straight up into the wheel well, and the violent blast of air blew the thick skin clean off the top of the wing. It was this structural damage to the strongest wing ever built in Britain that finally drove home the lesson of the devastating consequences of tyres bursting in flight. Today all advanced aircraft (except, alas, for a Caravelle lost with a full passenger load because the brakes were overheated before take-off) have special plugs which, when excessively hot, deflate the tyre safely. Repairing the NA.39 took until the last day of April. Then, as soon as the wing was pronounced sound, Whitehead and Watson fairly raced into the air, climbed straight ahead to 17000 feet and found they had a winner. In the next morning's *Daily Express* it was reported that 'The successful flight of the first prototype NA.39 on the target date represents a unique achievement.' I don't think the paper quite appreciated what a damning statement this was; fortunately it isn't true.

XK486 was an empty shell, without folding wings or any other operational gear. The next aircraft had even thicker wing skins and was subjected to exhaustive flutter and airframe resonance tests to prove the fatigue life of a representative production airframe. Extensive flutter testing was carried out in one of the high-speed tunnels at NASA's Langley Research Centre in Virginia. This was possible because the NA.39 was supported by the US Mutual Weapons Development Program in which American funds helped develop the arms of friendly nations—a policy which drew sour comments from those who paid for it when Britain began to offer hurtful competition with transport aircraft. It was the last British aircraft to receive such MWDP aid, and in addition to the NASA help the Americans contributed $13 million worth of flight-test instrumentation and data recording and analysis equipment, some of which was loaned. This brought the aircraft into direct contact with the US Navy at an early stage. Not surprisingly Blackburn and the MoS were very interested in selling some to the Americans. In view of the existence of the Grumman A2F, later called the A-6 Intruder (p. 221), shortly to fly and in exactly the same class, I think a few schoolboys might have been consulted before pressing the claims of the NA.39. I was assured by BuAer in Washington that the US Navy already knew more about the British aircraft than they were told by the British staff charged with trying to sell it to them, found that the engineering knowledge of those salesmen was invariably superficial and often faulty and that none of them had any detailed knowledge of the fast-approaching A2F. In July 1958 the Minister of Supply, Aubrey Jones, said Blackburn had been authorized to seek a US Navy order and the maker's men found that the amateur sales job attempted by the officials had killed what polite interest there might have been previously.

In fact I doubt if there was ever any chance of selling the NA.39 to the US Navy, but the exercise could have been used to instruct a skilled and sophisticated team of uniformed and civilian experts in engineering, contract financing, production and logistics in two vital subjects: how the Americans procure major weapon systems; and how major weapon systems can best be sold to the Americans and other nations. Had this been done I believe this fine aircraft would have worn the insignia of Federal Germany by 1963, and the government would have been a better and tougher aerospace customer. As it was, Britain found only one overseas customer, on whom it then placed an arms embargo, as related later.

Even this sad tale pales into insignificance beside the story of the NA.39 and the RAF. It all began, so far as I was aware, in 1957 at the time of the original OR.339 draft requirement (see TSR.2, page 38). As soon as this was noised abroad the MoS began comparing it with what might be done with a developed NA.39, which would have been politically palatable and relatively simple to get past the Treasury. Blackburn privately pointed out the range-stretch potential of the NA.39 when used in a land role and suggested that a developed form—which was obviously being proposed to meet the RAF Requirement—would be a natural replacement for the Canberra. I dared not print a word of this, but within a few days Chapman Pincher, the dean of the Fleet Street defence sleuths, announced that the range of the NA.39 was 'so short the Air Chiefs say it is useless for their purposes.' In July 1958 Aubrey Jones said there was 'also an RAF requirement' in the course of a discussion on NA.39 sales prospects to the US Navy, but would not be drawn further. Not until September 1958 did I learn some of the background, when Eric Turner said that a 'de-navalized version' of the NA.39 had been formally put forward to the MoS to meet the requirement; and, he said, 'I think there is a chance for its acceptance, as realization of a true OR.339 machine is probably some seven years distant.' He said the MoS had studied, and indicated their probable intention of ordering, long-lead parts for an RAF version of the aircraft, possibly bringing in Fairey as a major subcontractor. He put the total bill for design, development, the 20 development NA.39s, and the first 50 production machines (which had not then been placed under contract, although long-lead parts were in hand) at £40 million, a figure which would make today's governments wistful. Had the notion of a totally new OR.339 aircraft been killed at birth, which history shows might have been a good idea, I think the RAF would have done very well with the up-rated NA.39 proposed so long ago. But as long as people could see the glittering prospect of the custom-built machine, they didn't want to know. I have several suitable quotes I could use, and I will choose one from George Ward, Air Minister, dated January 1959: 'This proposed new version of the NA.39 does not begin to meet the requirement . . . it would be extremely costly, and inferior to TSR.2 . . . and we would not have got it any earlier.' But that was not the end of the story; TSR.2 just delayed the RAF Buccaneer for six years, and then the F-111 and AFVG delayed it for another three.

Meanwhile, back in 1959 Blackburn bolted together the 20 development aircraft for the Royal Navy, each a little nearer the definitive article. Whereas XK486 had left Brough on a truck, XK487 and every subsequent specimen was towed on its own wheels along 18 miles of highway to the former RAF base at Holme-on-Spalding Moor which had a 6000-foot runway. Here Blackburn set up a new flight test department, which initially, in 1958, hoped it might soon also be handling the big B.107 freighter (but the Short Belfast was bought instead). Both the first two NA.39s were at the 1958 SBAC show, when it was announced the type would be 'bought in quantity' for the Royal Navy. Eric Turner said 'At least these are additional to the first 20', because the total production run could have been very small. The contract was signed at that time, for 40 aircraft, and not in October 1959 as was later reported. This prevented any 'bathtub gap' between the 20 and the 40.

The third aircraft, flown in October 1958, introduced a colour scheme of dark grey above and light grey below which was used on the following

14 machines. No. 3 was sent to Hatfield where DH Engines put it to much-needed Gyron Junior development—and also through a row of greenhouses, which came off second-best—before passing it on to Filton after the formation of Bristol Siddeley Engines, which took over DH Engines in August 1962. The original Gyron had been a monster turbojet for supersonic aircraft which never flew in anything but the subsonic Sperrin. The two-fifths-scale Junior had an added compressor stage and two rows of variable stators, but still had a pressure ratio below the optimum for a subsonic machine such as the NA.39. With several supersonic applications in mind it was fitted with air-cooled turbine blades, and in fact had the first such blades in the world apart from Rolls-Royce ever to go into production, in 1956. Air-cooled blades were essential in allowing no less than ten per cent of the total airflow to be bled off for the Blackburn blowing system, from a large manifold surrounding the combustion chamber, without exceeding permissible turbine gas temperature. But from the start the engine seemed marginal and my personal view was that choosing it made the engine-out case in the two most critical flight conditions, full-load take-off (free or accelerated) and landing with maximum blow, unnecessarily hazardous. The official line was that failure on the approach was 'not serious on a good airfield if recognized in time', which speaks for itself. Coupled with the wing loading of over 100 lb/sq ft, the ratio of thrust to weight of 0·25 caused the aircraft to have one of the most protracted free take-offs since Stirlings towed gliders to Arnhem. I once timed one—without any weapon load—at 46 seconds, a scarcely credible figure, and Cdr 'Spiv' Leahy, RN, delicately commented 'events on take-off occur frequently enough to avoid feelings of boredom.' Hardly surprising that XK488 overshot through the greenhouses.

Subsequent machines introduced folding wings and a hook, the internal weapons bay with rotary door, full electrics and avionics and all sorts of other gear. Amongst the latter was a folding flight-refuelling probe ahead of the windscreen on the starboard side. Writing in *Flight International* I described this as 'much neater than the clumsy afterthoughts carried by most British operational aircraft.' It was a real pleasure to see a neat folding probe in Britain, and you can imagine my disgust when it was exchanged for a crude fixed one. The problem was oscillation of the drogue round the Buccaneer's nose. Aerodynamics can still play funny tricks, and although the front end of a Buccaneer looks much like that of, say, a Jaguar, the airflow round it demanded that the probe should be extended further and further outwards and upwards until it could no longer be retracted. The production probe is at least detachable, but pilots seem to get so used to having it blocking their vision that they are afraid to have it removed in case they find they cannot put the horizon in the right place. RAF Germany have no FR commitment, yet I have never seen them fly with the probe off.

The public were first allowed to walk round an NA.39 at the 1959 Paris Salon. Previously the dimensions had been closely guarded; so closely that one of my favourite artists who specializes in three-view drawings was a whole six inches out in the length and four inches in the span. The NA.39 was (I hope) the last time officials had taken immense pains to keep the dimensions secret by never releasing 'a photograph from which the aircraft could be scaled by comparing it with a known object'. According to A. J. Jackson, writing in *Blackburn Aircraft since 1909* (Putnam), this even extended to photographs 'with personnel in the vicinity'. I am sure the Kremlin possess the vital statistics of all Blackburn and RN personnel. To confuse the enemy further, the roundels on the first three aircraft were all made different sizes. Yet anyone could have measured the thing when it left the factory by road. My artist colleague preferred to use known yardsticks such as probes, aerials, Martin-Baker seats, jet nozzles and major bits of hardware which had been publicly displayed. The British official mind loves secrecy; maybe it imparts a sense of power?

At the SBAC show in September 1959 XK490, the armament trials machine, performed thunderous toss-bomb attacks, only to suffer an unexplained in-flight emergency the following month while being flown from Boscombe by American civilian William Alford of the US Office of Naval Research. Both he and his Blackburn observer were killed as they ejected while the aircraft was upside-down low over Hampshire, near Lyndhurst. This was the first aircraft to be lost, but it was by no means the last; nine of the original 20 crashed, although the operational record of the production aircraft gave less cause for concern. Time and again the cause of disaster to the early machines was basically attributable to lack of thrust.

Carrier trials from *Victorious* in the English Channel in January 1960 went well, despite extremely changeable weather. The two aircraft involved showed they could be taken up and down the deck elevator without scraping anything, even though the clearance on length (from the hinged nose radar, turned right round to face aft, to the big air brakes opened to 90° on each side behind the tail) was a mere two inches. The folding ends shortened the aircraft by almost twelve feet. The Rank-Cintel head-up display was not ready for these trials, but the deck-landing index was and so was the definitive pilot panel with new tape and roller-blind instruments. Another new feature was the liquid storage of crew oxygen. In August 1960 it was announced the NA.39 would henceforth be called the Buccaneer S.1 (S for strike, used previously only for the Wyvern) and RNAS Lossiemouth, on the beautiful coast of Scotland's Morayshire, prepared to receive the formidable new machine. Leahy was given command of 700Z Flight, the Intensive Trials Unit, which eventually received the last six development aircraft, the final three having the all-white livery of anti-nuclear-radiation paint then in vogue. My colleague Humphrey Wynn, an experienced service pilot, was impressed by his bumpy trip round the Scottish highlands testing the Ferranti nose radar in the terrain-clearance mode, and he can vividly recall the close proximity of mountains, seagulls and waves at Mach 0·85.

Between then and 1964 three squadrons of Buccaneer S.1 aircraft were formed, worked up and deployed, 801 aboard *Ark Royal* and then *Victorious*, 809 at Lossiemouth and 800 aboard *Eagle*. These made a dramatic difference to the Royal Navy's strike capabilities, even though their aircraft were operated at restricted weight and sometimes needed flight refuelling from 'Buddy' packs carried either by Scimitars or by other Buccaneers. Much of their time was spent in distant waters, and trouble spots abounded. Revolutions in East Africa, troubles in the Far East and enforcement of the oil embargo on Rhodesia all called for Buccaneer squadrons which steamed up in a way that Britain will find not so easy when she has no carriers. There is nothing like operational service for sharpening the interest of possible customers, and throughout its early years of service the Bonn government was genuinely interested in the Buccaneer for use by shore squadrons of the Kriegsmarine which were eager to replace Sea Hawks and not wholly happy at the prospect of the F-104. Unlike the case of the SR.177 mixed-power interceptor, where Britain pressed an unwanted product on the Germans and said 'We want you to buy this, but we don't want it ourselves', the Buccaneer could at least claim some home patronage—even if the RAF did steadfastly refuse to show interest (it was at this time that an officer of Air Rank said to me in explanation 'My dear chap, the RAF has *never* bought a Fleet Air Arm aircraft'). Despite the limitations of the S.1 and its distressing attrition rate, the Buccaneer was clearly a first-rate modern strike weapon, capable of considerable further development; indeed, it cried out for it. The enthusiasm of Hawker Siddeley was not merely commercial but genuine and echoed by the RN customer, so the Bonn government spent almost three years conducting a very careful evaluation.

I believe the Germans would have bought the Buccaneer if British officials had possessed about twenty times as much expertise and dynamic enthusiasm. The Germans were well placed to judge the British approach and compare it with the enormous intensity and depth of the studies that would be made by the United States in clinching a deal of this kind.

Right at the very start the 'Men from the Ministry' set the ball rolling in the approved manner. The Chief of German Naval Staff asked for some brochures which, as they were classified, had to travel via the MoA and thence by diplomatic bag to Bonn. Many weeks later, when the Admiral in Kiel complained he was still waiting, Hawker Siddeley found that the brochures had languished some time at Bonn waiting for a British official to take them personally to Kiel. When it seemed that nobody was going to go to Kiel, an official decided the best thing to do would be to return them to London. The MoA in turn merely took them back and told nobody.

Bonn's 'nein' could have been the end of the road for this basically great aircraft. Its salvation lay in the rather distant fact that in May 1959 BEA had made de Havilland cut down the size of the new Trident airliner. The one good result of this monumental error was that it made Rolls-Royce scale their fine new turbofan engine to a size that fitted the Buccaneer perfectly. At once this could be seen to make the aircraft everything it wanted to be; but merely removing the thrust-induced limitation of the S.1 would have cut no ice with the Treasury. Fortunately the Navy wanted more Buccaneers anyway, and the Rolls engine, known as the RB.168, offered a substantial improvement in range. Outwardly this was because of its better specific fuel consumption, but I think an equally good reason is that the much greater installed thrust enabled the Buccaneer to take off with maximum fuel as well as weapons. Not having the Gyron Junior's double-datum fuel system, the new turbofan lost thrust when blowing was selected, but as 70 per cent of the loss was recovered through the blowing slits the net loss was cut from 15 to only five per cent. Calculations showed that the re-engined aircraft could be launched eight knots slower than the S.1 and approach 2 knots slower, besides having a considerably higher flight performance. At one stroke the critical emergency situation following engine failure on take-off or landing was swept away and from that time on the Buccaneer has been an effective, safe aircraft.

Having revealed in May 1961 that the Buccaneer S.2 would have what is today known as the Spey engine—perhaps because the *Daily Express* had revealed it the previous November—the MoA placed a production order in January 1962, before the first S.1 had joined a squadron. To speed the programme two of the original development NA.39 aircraft were re-engined with the first military Speys to be cleared for flight, although these were not fully representative of the definitive RB.168-1A Mk 101, which was rated at 11100 lb minimum thrust, an increase of more than 55 per cent over the S.1. As the much bigger airflow through the Spey needed deeper oval-section intake ducts and fatter jet pipes, conversion of the two aircraft meant a total rebuild with new machined forgings to carry the wings. Eventually Derek Whitehead got the first rebuild, XK526, into the air on 17 May 1963. Meanwhile the production machines were fast coming through the Brough plant. They had much more than just new engines. Perhaps the chief improvement was that each Spey drove a 30 kVA alternator through a constant-speed drive to feed a proper a.c. electrical system. The S.1 had an odd sort of arrangement, most of the aircraft being d.c. but with raw a.c. for de-icing being generated by a turbo-alternator in the rear fuselage spun at 24000 rpm by hot bleed air. In the S.2 the inner wing was fully blown for the first time, and another change was the extension of the span from 42 ft 4 in to 44 ft by adding slanting glass-fibre tips. At the same time the continuing fatigue-test programme on the primary structure reached 20000 hours, with no significant failure.

Whitehead flew the first production S.2, XN974, on 6 June 1964. By the end of the year four had flown, and carrier qualification on *Ark Royal* had been completed in one week instead of two. It all seemed the proverbial piece of cake and I wondered at Hawker Siddeley's dogged insistence to the MoA that this was a very new and difficult contract and should be priced accordingly. Costing complicated industrial processes is not a subject to be dealt with in a slick, simple way, but to a layman like me this seemed to be a case of the contractor running rings round the customer. Briefly, the MoA began the horse-trading by offering a unit price of X plus £32000, where X was the baseline price. Hawker Siddeley asked for more, claiming that manufacture, assembly and test for each S.2 would take 208,000 man-hours. The MoA studied S.1 figures and calculated an S.2 could be made in 176,500 man-hours. After more investigation, with the company enjoying the strange position which at that time was traditional in British industry of hiding its figures from the government, the MoA came to the conclusion the firm was planning to make each aircaft in only 135,600 man-hours. Yet, after further study of the company's labour and overhead rules the officials came to the main pricing meeting in October 1964 empowered to make a generous offer of X plus £48000 per airframe. The firm rejected this and asked for cost plus ten per cent. 'The Department considered that there were no grounds for allowing so high a rate of profit on a non-risk contract and suggested a target-price arrangement. This was rejected and the meeting ended without agreement.' Thus runs the record in the Civil Appropriation Accounts (Classes I–V) 1964–65. Ultimately the Ministry, which had just said it was a no-risk job, agreed a price of X plus £63000, 'having regard to the uncertainties inevitable in the manufacture of advanced aircraft.'

The tradition of screwing the lid down on every possible fact is so dee - ingrained in British official circles that there are still some in Whitehall who blink at the thought that since 1968 there have been new pricing clauses and a Review Board for Government Contracts which at least allows the government, as customer, to discover the costs incurred by the contractor. But the taxpayer most certainly may not know. When this chapter was being checked, Hawker Siddeley told me 'the extra £15000 the company negotiated out of the Ministry could, if expressed as a percentage of the total price, certainly be counted on the fingers of one hand' and they added 'It is not for us to disclose the price which was agreed, nor would the Ministry allow us to do so.' To which as good an answer as any is 'Why not?' The Americans seem to get by without any troubles on this score; indeed, as I write, the Pentagon tells me 'Even if the Congress voted this way, which is inconceivable, neither the Department of Defense nor, I suspect, its industrial suppliers would wish hardware costs to be anything other than a matter for the public record.' So we in Britain can look forward to years of interesting reading (on matters of ghastly history) in the Civil Appropriation Accounts. It is our choice, and we must stop grumbling as the horror stories unfold.

Certainly I do not wish to knock the Buccaneer on grounds of cost or mismanagement, because, as British programmes go, it is one of the happier experiences. There even were a few real 'uncertainties', and in 1964 one of these was the rocket installation intended to boost the take-off of a special Buccaneer variant for the Republic of South Africa. In January 1963 Hawker Siddeley had been extremely happy to sign a contract with the RSA for 16 aircraft called the S.50. The RSA had for a long time been wondering how to replace its Venturas and Sunderlands and equip the SAAF Maritime Command with a modern strike and reconnaissance aircraft to keep open the vital sea routes round the Cape—routes which, with the closure of the Suez canal in 1956, had become of crucial importance to the whole world and which under the terms of the Simonstown Agreement were the responsibility of the RSA. As events transpired it may be that a specialized ocean-patrol aircraft, such as the Nimrod, would have been more suitable, but the Buccaneer had the advantage of being available in 1963. The SAAF Buccaneer S.50 was bought with a deck hook and folding wings, for anticipated collaboration with RN carriers, although the hydraulic wing-folding system was deleted. In the bottom of the rear fuselage was hinged a neat pack containing a Bristol Siddeley BS.605 twin-barrel rocket engine, adding some £20000 to the price but giving much better 'hot and high' field performance by imparting an extra 8000 lb thrust for 30 seconds, at the cost of some £60 worth of kerosene and high-test peroxide (quoting prices like this will land me in trouble!). Gross installed thrust was in excess of 30000 lb, compared with 14200 lb for the original S.1 aircraft.

Blackburn flew the first S.50 on 9 January 1965, and trials with the rocket engine and four Nord AS.30 guided weapons went well. Aircraft not engaged in trials went to Lossiemouth for SAAF crew training, and on 27 October 1965 eight S.50s set off on their long delivery flight in loose formation, first stop the Canaries. One aircraft suffered control failure after being violently popped out of the top of a giant cu-nim cloud and crashed into the sea some 500 miles south of the Canaries, but the crew was picked up by a Dutch ship. As a result of this loss the other eight aircraft were towed the 18 miles from Holme back to Brough, 'cocooned' and shipped from Hull as deck cargo. In the RSA the aircraft have been well looked after and in 1966 the CO of 24 Sqn made a flight over 5000 miles involving two refuelling contacts with the buddy-pack of another Buccaneer. But the Labour government elected in Britain in 1964 took a poor view of shipping arms to South Africa, on the grounds that they could be used to suppress the non-white population. In fact I think the arms embargo imposed by Harold Wilson on 20 November 1964 was the result of heat overcoming light. The £1 million Buccaneer was designed to fulfil very difficult duties destroying well-defended major targets and the non-white population of the RSA could in no conceivable circumstances offer such targets. However much one may detest the second-class status of non-whites in the RSA, the situation was really one in which the UK government could have shown that, contrary to popular belief, it did know a little about aircraft. It could have agreed to supply the RSA with the second batch of 20 aircraft requested, and spelt out in simple terms how completely irrelevant the Buccaneer was in terms of repressing civil populations—while, if it wished, pointing out in equally clear terms how highly relevant to such duties were the many helicopters being bought from France and the Macchi light jets about to go into production in the RSA under an Italian licence agreement. As it was, the embargo would not even permit the replacement of the aircraft lost on its delivery flight.

It seems strange in retrospect to recall the hatred of the British aircraft industry by the government of 1964, which was based on the belief that the industry, in fulfilling its government orders, had taken the public for a ride. The fact that disallowing the overseas sale of 20 Buccaneers hurt the industry actually seemed to cause pleasure in Whitehall. The fact that planemaking combined the value-added levels of high-quality watches with a big tonnage product never entered into the debate at all. If the public had really been taken for a ride, the blame surely rested on the customer and on his dreadful tradition of secrecy, but this was likewise ignored in the search for a ready whipping-boy that could be 'sold' to the public. The curious dislike of British planemakers replaced the Hawker Siddeley P.1154 by the Phantom, the HS.681 by the C-130 and the TSR.2 by an option for the F-111. Clearly the government was not just against planemakers in general, but only British ones. So when TSR.2 was axed, nobody wanted to know about the British Buccaneer.

This was soon made abundantly evident to the British industry as it tried to offer something a little more home-grown than the F-111 from Texas. While BAC offered a Spey-Mirage, Hawker Siddeley cooked up some new Buccaneer options, with special emphasis on a not greatly altered model called Mk 2*. This was to have more powerful Spey engines, of about 13000 lb thrust each with water injection, and a lot of special RAF equipment including many of the TSR.2 systems, soft-field landing gear, an optional fuselage gunpack and the BS.605 rocket. Other options would have had a longer fuselage, reheat and the full range of TSR.2 devices including the Ferranti radar, Elliott inertial guidance and the multi-sensor reconnaissance pod. In fact one Buccaneer had since May 1963 been busily test-flying the TSR.2 radar up at Edinburgh with a remarkably small amount of bother. (Indeed I believe the RAF's serious interest in the Buccaneer dates from the effortless way in which the trials aircraft held 500 knots at 100 feet in these extended missions, without cracking or running out of fuel.) While admitting that the Buccaneer could not begin to meet the OR.343 requirement and was very much a second-best compared with TSR.2, Hawker Siddeley did think their proposal might receive serious consideration. They could point to the fact that it was cheap, available and a known quantity. To help drive the point home two RN officers from Boscombe, Cdr G. Higgs and Lt-Cdr A. Tayler, flew an S.2 back from trials at NAS Pensacola, Florida, non-stop across the North Atlantic from Goose to Lossiemouth without flight refuelling on 4 September 1965.

The government's reaction was predictably adverse; indeed there was no public reaction whatever. A Ministry of Defence spokesman said confidentially in October 1965 that the 'Buccaneer is really not cost/effective for the RAF because its high-altitude payload for a fifteen-hundred-mile radius of action is less than half the 16000 pounds of the F-111', and he added that the RAF had 'urgent need of a high-altitude supersonic reconnaissance capability.' In fact at that time the RAF seemed to have an urgent need for everything the F-111 could do, or rather was meant to do, and for nothing else. By December Hawker had offered the souped-up Buccaneer Mk 2**, with modifications already noted, which Roy Jenkins parried with a barrage of arguments. While admitting it would have 'a reconnaissance capability, and a nav/attack system broadly comparable with that proposed for the F-111 or Spey-Mirage' he suggested that the claim it would cost 'half as much as an F-111' was no advantage because 'we should need twice as many'. Warming to his task he insisted 'It will need a hard runway . . . it is not supersonic . . . it would be later than the F-111. It would incur a really massive R&D cost, and would get mixed up with the vital AFVG on timing.' According to Hawker Siddeley the R&D would have been 'miniscule', whatever that meant. Things were getting just as warm as they had been a year earlier, and in February 1966 the poor Air League thought it could pour oil on troubled waters by arranging special briefings for Members of Parliament by the three prime contractors, General Dynamics, Hawker and BAC. February 7 was set aside for Capt Lewin and John Stamper to come down from Brough and put across the 2*, or 2**, or maybe by then it was the 2***. At the eleventh hour Hawker Siddeley chose to send them both on an urgent overseas assignment. I'm sure it didn't matter where they went.

It was evident to anyone able to read a newspaper or switch on the TV that Britain was suffering from the F-111 disease. One of the symptoms was that anything that couldn't swing its wings and fly at Mach 2 was automatically judged obsolete. To show how it affected people, the air correspondent of the *Daily Telegraph* reported on 11 December 1966 that 'Mr Healey, Minister of Defence, may try to force on the RAF an obsolete sub-sonic bomber . . . as replacement for its V-bomber fleet in 1975. . . . Acceptance of the plane would make the RAF the world's only air force operating a sub-sonic bomber.' In fact the variant of the Buccaneer by then being proposed was GLARE, an acronym derived from Ground-Level Attack, Reconnaissance and Electronics and equivalent to a Buccaneer 2 with a few more asterisks. It was still subsonic, but a lot of people seemed to forget that, in the low-level strike role, so was almost everything else. Even the F-111 could only just exceed the speed of sound in the clean condition; carrying any respectable external load it was (and is) slower than the Buccaneer with four 1000 lb bombs in its weapon bay. The Mach 2·4 Phantom likewise comes across its target somewhat slower than the clean Buccaneer in a ground attack mission (the Brough engineers, who are sister firm to McDonnell Douglas in supporting the Phantoms in UK service, know only too well the performance of a Phantom carrying full external stores). And the notion that other air forces do not operate subsonic bombers is almost unbelievably wide of the mark. The attack aircraft built in the greatest numbers for the US Air Force is the subsonic A-7 Corsair, while the even more subsonic A-10 (p.249), is to enter the USAF inventory in the mid-1970s. The A-10 is 200 mph slower than the Buccaneer, but back in

1966 it was fashionable to pour scorn on the Buccaneer because it could not fly at Mach 2.

By this time I think everyone connected with British Aviation knew that black is white, good is bad (and vice versa) and that a little standing on the head before breakfast is a good idea. As if none of the past had happened, the Ministry of Defence blandly announced on 11 July 1968 that the Buccaneer was to be 'ordered for the RAF to replace the F-111 aircraft' (and the AFVG, and the TSR.2). Thus, 16 years after the specification was written, 11 years after it was proposed to the RAF and ten years after the first flight, the Buccaneer finally took off its sea boots and came ashore. And to make sure it did, it was announced at the same time that, with the run-down in the fixed-wing Fleet Air Arm, all remaining Buccaneers would be transferred to the RAF. Pity it took so long for the RAF to get the Buccaneer, which was finally accomplished by the simple process of eliminating all the alternatives.

Probably today's RAF would consider that they would be most short-sighted to criticise *any* possible hardware, no matter how unsuitable they may regard it for their own requirements, because they may well end up having to use it. In January 1970 Sir Peter Fletcher, then VCAS, commented that, when the RAF lost the prospect of either TSR.2 or the F-111 'it was essential that the Buccaneer should possess similar qualities of range . . .' He went on to announce how the RAF Buccaneer, with a new fuel tank of 425–440 Imp gal capacity clipped externally under the rotary bomb door and highly efficient Spey engines 'will extend the Buccaneer's range to meet our target requirements.' This seemed a rather unnecessary face-saving exercise. The extra fuel tank and fan engines had been options for the previous eight years. Furthermore, as the fuel tank was not used except for ferrying and took the place of the reconnaissance camera pack, it did not appear to play a major role in Buccaneer operations. In any case, to suggest the Buccaneer should possess 'similar qualities of range' to TSR.2 and F-111 is simply nonsense, unless one interprets 'similar' in a way I would describe as 'dissimilar'.

In RN service the S.2 did very well. First aircraft joined the service on schedule in March 1965, formed a new Intensive Trials Unit called 700B Flight and then went on to equip 800, 801, 803 and 809 Sqns, which at times have been embarked in *Eagle*, *Victorious* and *Hermes*. In May 1966 Lt K. B. Cross and Lt-Cdr G. Oxley of 801 were catapulted off *Victorious* in the Irish Sea, performed a splendid simulated low-level toss of a nuclear weapon on the airfield at Gibraltar, and then flew straight back to their ship, a round trip of 2300 miles. In the following month a second batch of S.2 aircraft was ordered, and the first S.2 to be lost, XN979, was recovered from the remarkable depth of 360 feet after diving into the

Channel off the Lizard on 9 June. Possibly the most public assignment ever given a Buccaneer unit came on 28 March 1967 when some of 800's aircraft, temporarily detached to Brawdy, Pembrokeshire, attacked the giant tanker *Torrey Canyon*, fast aground off Lands End and spewing 115000 tons of crude oil, with live 1000 lb bombs to destroy the hulk and ignite the oil. A total of 42 bombs were dropped, 30 scoring direct hits. Further attacks, backed up by bombs, rockets and napalm from Hunters, were made on subsequent days. My chief reaction was how startlingly well the tanker stood up to it. Not to be outdone, the SAAF sank the *Wafra* off Cape Town, using AS.30 missiles, and in 1972 six SAAF Buccaneers polished off the 20000 ton *Silver Castle* in six minutes using bombs. Both vessels were abandoned and leaking crude oil. I do not believe any other aircraft has sunk three ocean-going tankers, and certainly not in peacetime!

Today, as the proud strike squadrons of the Royal Navy run down for ever, the Buccaneer has transferred to fixed runways with the RAF. The RAF has just completed its force of 90, 26 of them new aircraft contracted for in July 1968 and the other 64 ex-Navy. The RAF began to learn at an OCU formed at Lossiemouth in 1968 using old S.1 aircraft and then formed the first operational squadron, No 12, at Honington in 1969. The RAF machines are camouflaged green and grey, with off-white underside and a fin flash, whereas the RN machines had since 1967 been dark sea grey all over. The first RAF aircraft, XV350, was rolled out in January 1969 and photographed carrying four of the new HSD/Matra Martel guided weapons, identifying it as a Buccaneer S.2B; ex-RN machines not equipped to launch Martel are designated S.2A. To confuse the picture, the AS.30, bought in quantity for the RAF in 1963, is used only by South African Buccaneers, while the Sidewinder installation seen on an RN aircraft in 1967 has never appeared since.

Nevertheless, the RAF S.2B is the most capable Buccaneer of all. Confounding the ministerial critic of 1965, it *can* carry an ordnance load of 16000 lb by fitting each wing pylon with a triple-1000-lb ejector or 6 × 500 lb ejector, with only minor restrictions on the flight envelope. The weapon-bay door can carry 4000 lb of stores, or a 440 gal (528 US gal) tank, or a reconnaissance pack with a big F97 and six F95 cameras or Linescan or other gear. Surprisingly the S.2B has no inertial unit, the main navaid being a doppler radar. By the time this book is published the RAF will have six S.2A and S.2B squadrons, four at Honington assigned to NATO (three of them with maritime responsibilities in support of Saclant) and two in Germany replacing Canberras in the strike/recce role for Saceur. They have kept their hooks, and cables on their runways—at Honington, Laarbruch and elsewhere—can pull them up in 1000 feet, which I would find comforting. So far the fatigue programme has gone beyond 30000 hours, still with no bothersome cracks, clearing the aircraft for an excellent 3000 hours in the high-lo profile. I doubt if my frame could take 30 minutes. Basically, the concept of a near-sonic (instead of Mach 2) attack aircraft, structurally capable of standing up to low-level operations and with a big internal weapons bay, is just what everyone wanted and nobody else built.

BAC TSR.2

The most nerve-wracking, frustrating, emotional and politically fraught programme in the history of aviation was that for a manned bomber for the RAF, begun in the year the government said the RAF would need no more manned bombers. In this single project was to be gathered together the fruits of a thousand new technical advances, in systems, techniques, materials and knowledge, to provide the RAF with a modern multi-role aircraft to fill what had become a yawning chasm in British defence. No programme ever seemed so vital to a nation as did TSR.2, both in terms of national defence and in industrial capability. And no programme was ever torn to pieces and destroyed by its own government with such venom. TSR.2 served as the watershed that separated the days when Britain could do anything—or thought it could, which is almost the same thing—from a new and harsh world in which the nation's self-confidence in aerospace evaporated, so that it became afraid of embarking on a major programme without overseas partners who were supposed to reduce the risks and the costs.

Going back to the start of TSR.2 is not very long in years, but it is to a different world in which the needs of the RAF were exclusively and unfailingly met by an industry comprised of some 20 proud and long established British companies. In 1957 there was scarcely a man in those companies who did not have vehement views on the lately published *Statement on Defence*. About half thought the Minister's belief that the RAF would be unlikely to want any more fighters or bombers was quite right; missiles were the coming things, although perhaps the Minister ought to have pursued a 'belt and braces' policy for a little longer in case the marvellous new missiles failed to work. Almost all the other half thought the suggestion stark lunacy and pointed to the United States where a full clutch of missiles was being backed up by a complete spectrum of manned aircraft. Similar arguments went on in the RAF, although it is not done for a serving officer—whatever his rank—to question the decisions of Ministers of the Crown. Junior aircrew generally echoed the younger brother of a friend of mine: 'Most of us have felt that aircraft were eventually going to give way to missiles, but now that it's about to happen we can't really believe it. It has come so suddenly it has been quite a jolt. No doubt we shall all be assured it won't affect our careers, but it looks as if we've only got a few more years of flying.'

Whatever may have gone on in Whitehall, there was little public debate on the startling new policy except by the uninvolved commentators of the mass media, who sought in vain for a furious air marshal. In fact the air marshals had begun to prepare a draft outline Requirement for what was essentially a new bomber two years before the White Paper appeared. During 1956 it had become apparent that the Avro 730, planned as a supersonic bomber as well as a reconnaissance aircraft (its primary role), might never see service. A great deal of new ground was explored investigating (largely on paper) jet VTOL, variable sweep and zero-length rocket launch techniques to see to what extent heavily loaded strike aircraft could be made to operate from shorter and rougher platforms than a 9000-foot concrete strip. It was deeply worrying to the NATO air forces that all their combat aircraft were tied to the fine long-runway bases that had been built at such immense cost between 1951 and 1954 and which, apparently to everyone's surprise, had suddenly been transformed into sitting ducks for missiles. Soon SHAPE was to issue the NATO Basic Military Requirements for strike fighters and transports having V/STOL capability. The UK Air Staff, like the US Air Force, while participating in these specifications, considered it had a rather different global role that called for different aircraft.

Early in 1957 their views began to crystallize into a little seven-page document called General Operational Requirement 339. To get a new aircraft past the Treasury it had to be a direct replacement for something and the aircraft it was to replace was the Canberra. At that time the Canberra was still in production (indeed, the PR.9 had yet to fly in production form), but its ancient conception made a replacement seem not unreasonable. Indeed many grandiose Air Staff savants had never regarded this aircraft as anything more than an interim design (after all, it had only two engines). Unfortunately this replacement could not have come to the boil at a worse time, and much of 1957 was spent partly in making GOR.339 seem as unlike a fighter or a strategic bomber as possible and partly in simply waiting for the White Paper to be forgotten by Fleet Street. By mid-year it was clear there had been private discussions to see what could be done to erase the prevalent mental picture of a Minister telling the RAF it could have no more manned aircraft. Sandys himself was very forceful on this point, perhaps because he had nagging doubts about what the White Paper said. At an off-the-record luncheon he stressed that the document merely reflected what the RAF thought it would need.

The crucial wording was 'unlikely to require' and, in his view, 'if the RAF find they now have a requirement for a new fighter or bomber there is absolutely no reason why it should not be put forward and discussed.' It would have seemed sarcastic to ask him if the Air Staff knew this.

In fact at this time GOR.339 was probably well known to him, and I suspect there had already been preliminary talks to see what horse-trading could be done. From very early in the programme the government had realized that, like the new short-haul jet for BEA, it could be used as a carrot to bring about mergers and thus reshape the aircraft industry into the desired smaller number of stronger units. But I did not notice any leakage into the public domain until in December 1957 Sir Matthew Slattery, chairman of Bristol Aircraft and Short Brothers & Harland, revealed there was 'a new military aircraft in view' which would be 'so complicated that no single firm could tackle it.' Any company wishing to tender, he claimed, would 'have to find a partner to do half the work.' Soon afterwards the Minister of Supply, by this time Aubrey Jones, privately confirmed there was indeed such a project, but said that it was not fantastically complicated; the development estimate was 'under £40 million'. (I recall that my immediate reaction was that this was a substantial sum. So it was by earlier standards, but it is less than the amount by which the Concorde development bill rose in 1971 due to inflation alone.) In the same month, December 1957, newspapers reported that English Electric and Vickers had 'reached agreement concerning their aircraft interests'. Both denied this, but stated they had been discussing 'the question of possible co-operation.'

Early in 1958 it was clear that most of the major firms in the industry were working on the Requirement and talking about partnerships (always of course, without losing their full independence and identity). It was also obvious that the Treasury was hostile and going to need some convincing; in fact I heard the view expressed that the Treasury still shared the popular misapprehension over the meaning of the 1957 White Paper and professed to be surprised at a new aircraft programme. It was partly because of Treasury reaction that the 1958 *Report on Defence* announced that the naval NA.39 (see Buccaneer chapter) was 'being considered' for the RAF. Soon the designation OR.339 was appearing in public print, something I believe had never before happened at so early a stage in a programme. One report in July 1958 said OR.339 was to produce a low-level tactical bomber for service in 1965–70; it would be a STOL machine, VTOL having been considered and rejected. A partnership between English Electric and Short was said to be the favoured team.

Rumour piled on rumour until at last, on 17 December 1958, the Secretary of State for Air, George Ward, made the first official statement:

'It has been decided to develop a new strike/reconnaissance aircraft as a Canberra replacement. This will be capable of operating from small airfields with rudimentary surfaces, and have a very high performance at all levels.' In fact there was still argument over just how small an airfield ought to be the design target. For a while 500 yards was held to be the maximum, but by 1961 TSR.2 had grown much too heavy for this and the V/STOL P.1154 was on order as the V/STOL tactical support machine, with a V/STOL transport to complement it. The history of TSR.2 is one of ever increasing demands by the customer service. Whereas in the 1957 draft outline it was put forward as a small tactical machine, by 1961 it had gradually developed into a strategic bomber to enable Britain to fulfil its supposed role as a great global power. Stress had been lain on achieving the furthest possible radius of action, exceeding 1000 nautical miles on most mission profiles with various weapon loads, and with a ferry range which ultimately reached 3700 n.m. to enable it to hop across great oceans, while accentuating the rough-field STOL capability.

In view of the extraordinary political circumstances prevalent at the time it might be thought that the RAF knew what they wanted all along and simply had to take a circuitous route to getting it. In fact I believe this was not so, and the continual growth of the aircraft reflected genuine and unpremeditated upgrading in the requirement. GOR.339 was in 1958 being translated into Air Staff Operating Requirement 343, and OR.343, a document describing in detail what the proposed weapon system would comprise and what its performance would have to be, was in turn translated into the Ministry of Supply Specification RB.192D (nothing to do with Rolls-Royce, despite the ambiguity!). This was the basis of the contractual documents and all negotiations with suppliers. The designation TSR.2 arose early in the programme as a quick appellation that even politicians could remember. I never heard why it was not TSR.1, although I secured a letter from the MoS saying that 'as far as can be discovered' TSR.1 was 'a designation applied to the Canberra when the question of its replacement arose.' It was a sharp break with tradition not to give the new aircraft a name.

The designation TSR.2 was made public on 1 January 1959, when Aubrey Jones announced that the aircraft was being procured for the RAF. He said its development 'will be undertaken jointly by Vickers-Armstrongs and English Electric, the work being shared on a 50-50 basis. A joint project team drawn from both companies is being established at the Vickers works at Weybridge . . . engines will be undertaken by Bristol-Siddeley Engines, the new company formed out of Bristol Aero-Engines and Armstrong Siddeley Motors. Both these engine companies have indicated that they are now proceeding to a complete financial integration.

. . . The TSR.2 is a tactical support and reconnaissance aircraft. The specification was originally based on GOR.339. It has been found possible to incorporate in the final OR modifications which will greatly increase the usefulness of the aircraft in limited operations and for close support of the Army, particularly by reducing the length and strength of runways required for take-off.' This statement left everyone thinking the initials TSR, which between the wars always meant 'Torpedo Spotter Reconnaissance', now signified 'Tactical Support and Reconnaissance'. Yet in every subsequent document the middle word is changed to 'Strike' and this may fairly reflect the way the basic role changed from battlefield support to strategic strike deep in enemy territory.

It was hardly to be wondered at that Fleet Street gave the 1 January announcement front-page treatment under such helpful headlines as 'VICTORY FOR THE AIR MARSHALS'. The MoS seemed embarrassed and at once issued a statement confirming the necessity of the programme. It pointed out that the development bill would be 'between £25 and £50 million', and stated that a 'substantial number' of production aircraft would be needed, at a cost of 'up to £200 million'. To the suggestion made by some commentators that a few NA.39s ought to be bought for the RAF anyway, to indoctrinate aircrew into transonic attacks at low levels, the MoD asserted 'It would hopelessly delay things if we did this; we have to get ahead with TSR.2.' I wasted many hours trying to discover how training on the NA.39 could cause delay, and eventually, in March 1959, was told 'The RAF is totally uninterested in the NA.39. It is quite unsuited to the need. It would waste time because it is quite different from TSR.2 and there is no point in using it to help train TSR.2 crews.' Fortunately today's RAF has Buccaneers, not NA.39s.

This sort of assertion made it clear that TSR.2 was going to be quite something. Before the end of January 1959 there were straws in the wind that led one to believe it would fly most of the missions of a V-bomber and this was long before the aircraft had reached the end of its growth process. So the Minister of Supply conceived the notion that he ought to squash such an improper idea once and for all. On 25 February Mr Jones explained, 'The TSR.2 is not a deterrent weapon. It is not a bomber in the conventional sense of the word but an aircraft intended to give strike support to ground forces. The reason for the delay in deciding on it was the redesign of the aircraft to make it suitable for limited war contingencies overseas.' One couldn't even be bothered to enquire how such an obvious part of the requirement happened to have been overlooked, apparently until the aircraft had actually been 'designed'. The whole tone of Mr Jones' statement played down the TSR.2, so that one conjured up mental images of STOL propeller aircraft and of jet trainers with bombs under their wings. It certainly did not prepare me for the entirely opposite view put out by George Ward a few days later, on 5 March: 'The radius of action will be at least 1000 miles. This implies flight at high level for at least a part of the time, and to survive at high altitude the aircraft must fly at high supersonic speed. At the same time it must also be able to fly at around the speed of sound at low altitude . . . TSR.2 will take off on an operational mission using as little as 600 yards of runway. . . . It will carry the navigation and bombing equipment to enable it to find and attack accurately tactical targets by day and night in all weathers.'

Newspapers began to call it the 'all-singing all-dancing TSR.2'. Versatility is surely commendable, but from that point onwards the mass media seemed to consider TSR.2 variously (1) unbelievable, (2) too good to be credible, (3) grossly extravagant, and (4) British, therefore to be scorned. The 1959 Defence White Paper, *Progress of the Five-year Defence Plan*, even disclosed TSR.2 would 'be capable of carrying air-to-air missiles.' After a lot of cross-checking I came to the conclusion this was simply a mistake, unless the official who wrote it was thinking of Sidewinder, which clips on to anything. As for the suggestion that high supersonic speed made aircraft safe at high altitude, suffice to say the reason escaped the missile designers.

It also eluded the College of Aeronautics at Cranfield, where the 1958 design study project was for nothing less than a low-level bomber. The Department of Aircraft Design told me the consensus of opinion among all who had studied the problem was that one might as well forget about high-flying bombers entirely, except for ferrying and for the part of each mission that lay through airspace 'known to be friendly', a choice of words that I liked. In their view hostile airspace could not be safely entered at any speed within the practical limits attained by manned aircraft, except at or below the nominal height limit of 200 feet. So their bomber came out with a tiny, high-mounted wing loaded to 300 lb/sq ft for a gust-response so low that Mach 1·5 could be sustained at 200 feet. Inside the wing were three turbojets (scaled RB.108s) on each side, discharging through an almost full-span jet flap along the trailing edge. Tests with a model made in Nimonic 75 showed extremely high lift at 60° flap deflection using 750°C gas. Tunnel testing of the model bomber showed it to be unstallable, but indicated some sort of rocket or catapult take-off system would be helpful.

This technically interesting study was for a sort of aircraft more radical than TSR.2, and more difficult to introduce and maintain in service. To me, the most remarkable thing about TSR.2 was its supremely straightforward design. It did not contain a single feature that was not flying on US aircraft in operational service; indeed, a surprising number were to be found on that splendid pioneer design, the Vigilante.* But this did not prevent its R&D costs from inevitably galloping away from the ridiculous estimates. And, before there was any public inkling that this was going to happen, in June 1960, the Treasury urgently called for 're-assessment by the Chief of the Air Staff and Minister of Defence' to find out whether the role of TSR.2 could not 'be fulfilled by a cheaper aircraft developed to an earlier timescale.' As one heard no more, the answer was probably 'no.'

Vickers and English Electric received a full design study contract in June 1959, a fact unearthed by Austin Albu in the Commons just ten years later. GRE (Sir George Edwards) said the 'one-year run-in period' of the original 50-strong project team had proved 'most valuable' and that it had 'paved the way at the working man's level' for the formation of British Aircraft Corporation (by the two companies plus Bristol and later swallowing Hunting as well) in February 1960. He said he was 'quite sure the two teams have hammered out an extraordinarily good aeroplane.' He spoke of two teams because initially there had been two quite separate project studies. English Electric's outstanding P.17 was later illustrated mounted on top of the Short PD.17 flat-rising jet VTOL platform, doubtless triggering off the suggestion that these two firms were going to get the joint contract. In fact, as GRE confided, at one time the 'Vickers STOL study and the English Electric machine with a tiny low-level wing had seemed irreconcilable', but during 1959 the two projects were somehow made to yield a single optimized TSR.2. The splice came at the trailing edge of the wing box: Vickers did the very long fuselage with pilot, navigator and almost everything else in tandem, while English Electric retained their excellent wing, tail and rear fuselage. During 1959 and part of 1960 the main project centre for the Vickers team was the former Supermarine design office in the once fine mansion at Hursley Park, near Winchester, to which English Electric designers from Lancashire sometimes commuted. Both Vickers and English Electric had missile divisions which made helpful contributions. GRE asked Brigadier John Clemow, his chief engineer (weapons), to prepare a schedule of TSR.2 electronic systems and weapon equipment, fulfilling an early MoS idea that the maximum use should be made of existing hardware. Not until late 1960 was the full weapon system idea applied, in which everything is integrated with the minimum of compromise. In the event there must have been a large element of luck involved, because everything went remarkably smoothly.

What sort of aircraft was TSR.2? I consider it one of the severest and yet most successful compromises I know in aircraft design. In September 1967 B. O. Heath, then VG project manager at Warton, explained the

See companion volume Bombers of the West, *Ian Allan, 1973.*

one big question regarding the original design: 'We looked very hard at variable sweep. . . . We did a very thorough data search. We couldn't find any information on large, heavily-loaded, slow-moving and intermittently-moving bearings. There just didn't seem to be enough to go on to guarantee the performance and the timescale, so—possibly quite wrongly—we didn't put a VG wing on TSR.2. Today at BAC we have the data we then lacked, a lot of it at Warton based on Ministry-funded research at Weybridge.' But in 1958 TSR.2 took the irrevocable path of caution, with a non-VG wing, despite the fact that specially designed VG wing bearings were a major concern of Sir Barnes Wallis at Weybridge since the mid-50s. He had been researching fail-safe bearings, primarily with civil SST applications in mind, while the TSR.2 team wanted a rather different bearing based on a guaranteed safe life. Pity they couldn't have got in touch a bit sooner.

One could write reams about British VG work and its perfect mistiming, but the odd fact here is that it all boiled up just as TSR.2 was being planned yet apparently with no connection between the two. Throughout 1958 there were ceaseless scurryings to and from Wallis's den at Weybridge, with Richard E. Horner, Assistant Secretary (R&D), US Air Force; P. A. Hufton, chief superintendent, RAE Bedford; John Christie, Air B2 Assistant Secretary, MoS; and a team from the newly formed NASA, including John Stack, all rushing about in the cause of variable sweep. By January 1959 the Minister of Supply said there was likely to be 'a joint research programme' (I don't think it was meant as a pun), and on 24 February he announced 'a series of tests and engineering studies . . . partly at Vickers, partly at the RAE and partly with American government research facilities to prove the potentialities and practicability of the concept.' The following day, in the Defence debate, it was announced that 'The Swallow (VG) aircraft . . . was cancelled in 1957 because it was related to the supersonic bomber. It was a post-SSB. The case for having (VG) in the research programme now is that we shall have to study its applicability to the strike role. . . .' Aubrey Jones had in 1958 told Vickers the 'proposal in the form they had couched' [*sic*] could 'no longer rank high on the list of priorities'. Off the record he said 'The very last thing we can do is announce a new bomber aircraft; I doubt that we shall ever do so again. But this idea of variable sweep clearly has something in it and my department are anxious it should not be abandoned.'

This is all a digression from the main thread of TSR.2, but it serves to show the almost incredible facts that: the MoS wanted to use VG but dared not announce a new bomber; in TSR.2 they announced a new bomber without using VG; the research tempo, aimed specifically at the strike role, reached a climax as TSR.2 was being planned; yet those designing TSR.2 had inadequate VG data and were forced in consequence to use a non-VG wing. As the world knows, the centre of gravity of VG research swiftly moved across the Atlantic and by 1962 the F-111 had been planned with a VG wing, yielding an aircraft that by 1965 was being bought for the RAF in place of TSR.2. The only consolation in the extraordinary tale is that the RAF's change of aircraft had much more to do with price than with wing design.

The wing chosen for TSR.2 was a 60° delta, with a consequent aspect ratio of 2, with 700 square feet of area and a t/c ratio of 3·7%. The outermost 4 ft on each side was tilted down with 30° anhedral to allow the rest of the wing to have zero anhedral and thus maintain longitudinal stability. The whole of the level part of the trailing edge was occupied by large flaps blown with hot, high-pressure engine air. This can perhaps be regarded as a *quid pro quo* for VG, because flap blowing, a technique for preventing flow separation at very large flap angles and thereby greatly increasing maximum lift from a given size of wing, was pioneered by a US Navy team led by John D. Attinello from 1949. In Britain it was first used on the Supermarine 525 of 1954. In TSR.2 a very advanced form of flap blowing was combined with immense engine thrust to achieve the desired field performance.

Obviously an aircraft of this calibre must be designed around pretty well developed engines. Britain has always been good at aircraft engines, and TSR.2 actually had a choice. Bristol had long been working on supersonic reheat-equipped developments of the Olympus two-spool turbojet, and if the Gloster G.50 fighter had not been cancelled in 1956 these would have been available off the shelf. Rolls tried hard to knock out their rivals with an absolutely unbeatable reheat development of the Conway or Medway, the RB.142R, but the Minister of Supply gently commented that the winner of the engine contract would have to merge with someone. Offhand I cannot think of a more irrelevant criterion in buying defence hardware, but the merger talks by Rolls-Royce never got to first base—at Derby it seemed like a suggestion that the Church of England should enter into blissful union with the nearest fish-and-chip shop. This disqualified all the very attractive RB-numbers and left Bristol Aero-Engines Ltd and Armstrong Siddeley Motors proclaiming undying love for each other and for the Olympus. It was, as is so often the case, the right choice but for ridiculous reasons. Two Bristol Siddeley Olympus 320 (22R) turbojets, derivatives of the well-proven engines of the Vulcan B.2, each provided 19600 lb dry or 30610 lb with full afterburning and water injection, with a rating of 33000 lb having been cleared in bench trials. For mission radii below about 250 miles the resulting thrust–weight ratio was unity, a very rare thing indeed in any aircraft and unprecedented in a sophisticated bomber. It was sheer brutal acceleration that gave the TSR.2 its remarkable field length of under 3000 ft under practically all conditions. Take-off ground roll in ISA at sea level varied from 2400 ft at maximum weight of 95900 lb down to 1600 ft at the 80000 lb typical of all except the longest-ranged missions. This was at least as good as anything achieved by the VG F-111, and it was a truly amazing accomplishment with a very heavy aircraft lifted by a small, fixed-planform wing of thin, supersonic profile.

TSR.2 thus rested heavily on its engines, and if Bristol had not begun the two-spool Olympus in 1948 TSR.2 would have been as handicapped without it as would today's Concorde. Of course these two very powerful engines, giving almost twice the installed thrust of an F-111A, meant TSR.2 had to have lots of fuel. Fortunately Britain had, rather late, at last learned how to make good integral tankage. English Electric had been one of the UK leaders, learning with the original P.1 that what you have to do is to make a good fuel tank and then make it behave as a wing (in other words, the fluid problems transcend the aerodynamic ones, although aeroelasticity affects both). In fact, although the TSR.2 wing was full of fuel, it was so small it provided little over one-quarter of the total fuel load, which was almost three times that of a Lancaster. All the rest was in big integral tanks in the front and rear fuselage. On the port side of the nose was a nicely engineered retractable FR probe, a rare thing in the country where probes were invented. Jettison pipes were at the kink of the wing.

Structurally the aircraft was clean and conventional, with most of it in extrusions and machined planks of L.65 aluminium alloy and with RR.58 structure in the rear fuselage where the engines made it hot. Previously RR.58, a creation of High Duty Alloys Ltd, had been used mainly for pistons; thanks to TSR.2, BAC knew just how to use it for most of the airframe of Concorde, so that the French (who have renamed the alloy AU2GN) will tell you they invented it. The Concorde flies about as fast as TSR.2—say, Mach 2·05 in ISA—but has to soak at peak temperature for longer periods and has a design life of over 40000 hours. In contrast the life target of TSR.2 was only 100 hours at peak temperature, but for a combat machine this represents a lot of hard work. There was little high-strength steel, apart from the super vacuum-melted alloy of the landing gears, and virtually no structural titanium, in sharp contrast to the F-111 where a few steel parts came structurally unstuck.

Power systems were not startling, although the hydraulics used Silcodyne H (DP.47) at 4000 lb/sq in and the 400-cycle a.c. electrics relied for airborne emergency on a windmilling engine, the APU being used on the ground only. Much more unconventional were the flying controls, comprising an all-moving slab fin and left and right tailplanes each with geared 'elevators' operative when the wing flaps were lowered. Use of slab tailplanes drew upon Lightning experience, but a quite new feature was that TSR.2 was controlled in roll by differential tailplane movement—one up, the other down—non-linearly related to speed and altitude and with the limits of travel opened out as the flaps were lowered. The tail reminded one of the Vigilante, but the British designers were bold enough to do the obvious thing and dispense with spoilers or ailerons, control surfaces which have caused untold trouble since the start of the jet age and which I am never sorry to see thrown away. In turn this freed the wing for the vital blown flaps. The autopilot, autostabilization and integration with mission circuitry for such duties as toss bombing or terrain clearance were novel only in that everything was very up to date, comprehensive and quite unlike anything previously done in Britain. Parts were triplicated and even quadruplicated. I believe it was the first flight-control system designed to take every input the terrain-following or weapon delivery could give it.

Undoubtedly incorporating the most crucial and clever bits of the whole aircraft, and responsible for much of the R&D cost, the nav/attack system represented the very latest state-of-the-art and quite unlike the simple hardware carried by the Canberra and other aircraft still used for TSR.2 roles. The nose was a very special radome supposed to resist a Mach 1·1 birdstrike yet offer near-zero distortion to the beam from the FLR (forward-looking radar), which was packaged in a pressurized compartment along with the computer circuits for terrain-following and weapon delivery. Under the floor of the rear cockpit were the two SLR (side-looking radar) aerials, each about 7ft 6in long for X-band wavelengths, which formed part of the basic navigation fit. Behind them came the big air-conditioned equipment bay filled with scores of modular-rack circuits a generation later than anything flying with the RAF, around which were to be found oblique and centreline cameras and the radar altimeter aerials. Aft again, under the forward tank, was the inertial platform, sitting on the doppler aerial. And in the long weapons bay could be clipped a strategic reconnaissance pack including three big cameras, a 15 ft Q-band SLR, an optical Linescan and other options. Hardly any of this equipment was in RAF use in 1959, but the Air Staff knew very clearly what it could do, closely watched its progress through the Royal Radar Establishment and other labs in Britain and the USA and was spurred on by the obvious pace of avionic development in the Soviet Union. To anyone with the remotest understanding of the wide range of duties TSR.2 was to fulfil, through every possible hostile and climatic environment, such systems were as necessary as the wing and engines. But, as I shall later explain, critics of the programme chose to ignore this—perhaps because they were unlikely to be posted as aircrew to a TSR.2 squadron. The growing army of 'knockers' closed their minds and angrily shouted that Britain must 'stop building aircraft that merely thrill the technicians at the taxpayer's expense'. I asked one critic 'Would you be happier if we gutted TSR.2 of its systems, so that—even though it could not do its job—it would cost less?' The reply, by an intelligent journalist, was 'Yes, I would.'

In designing the weapons bay Vickers and English Electric were able to assume nuclear weapons far smaller than the monsters expected when the V-bomber specifications were written, and this was not because TSR.2 was supposed to carry only low-yield tactical bombs. If it had been designed for a 10000-ft runway TSR.2 could have been made to carry a large bomb load, but in fact the extraordinarily small h.e. load of two triplets of thousand-pounders was all that was asked for (although four more could be carried on wing pylons). Range could be extended by fitting under-wing, bomb bay and ventral tanks, although obviously with all these in place it was impossible to carry anything else. The aircraft had plenty of ground clearance and could have been persuaded to carry all sorts of stores, but I never heard of any consideration being given to guns or to anything for the air-to-air role. Initial climb at gross weight exceeded 35000 ft/min, but weight/fuel problems made TSR.2 unattractive as a potential fighter.

Before returning to the story I will list the main suppliers who worked so hard to create this weapon system: BSEL, engines; EMI, reconnaissance pack and SLR; Decca Radar, doppler; Ferranti, inertial navigator and terrain-following radar; Elliott, autopilot, digital computer and head-up display; Smiths, pilot displays and analog/digital converter; Marconi, HF; Redifon, crash recorder; STC, radar altimeter; Plessey, VHF/UHF and power generation; Dowty-Rotol, hydraulic CSD and accessory drives; Rotax, main alternators; Lucas, fuel system and variable intake controls; Martin-Baker, guess what?; Hobson, powered flying controls; Dunlop and Goodyear, wheels, tyres and brakes; Godfrey, air-conditioning; and GPS, simulator. I have left out about 500 others. It takes a big team to create a big system and, whereas in the United States money is saved by going faster, in Britain there used to be a powerful wish to try to 'save money' by going slower. I seriously wonder whether, had the Treasury been told TSR.2 was being developed by two men in a backyard, they would have breathed a great sigh of relief?

The development contract for TSR.2 was placed on 7 October 1960, at a cost of £90 million. This date and contractual figure, of course, were kept secret from the public and not disclosed until a Commons question of January 1969. Defence Minister Harold Watkinson said there would be 'fewer than 20' aircraft for development; actually the original contract bought nine, plus production jigging and tooling, but the number was later increased to 20. Watkinson waxed almost lyrical about the aircraft. It would give Britain 'an amazing number of options' (like the original concept of the weapon system, which was invariably misunderstood in Britain, the notion of options now joined the list of American terms picked up by British leaders who wanted to seem 'with it') and it would 'even give a theatre commander immediate TV pictures of the battle, in all weathers.' Then he stunned listeners by proclaiming TSR.2 could 'carry an air-launched ballistic missile'. Douglas hastily said 'not Skybolt', and I am still wondering which ALBM the Minister had in mind.

For more than a year TSR.2 was allowed to grow in peace. The knockers seemed to have forgotten about it, and by 1962 drawings were being issued to the shops despite continual tinkering with the specification. On 23 February 1962 the Olympus 22R flight prototype engine begain air tests under Vulcan XA894, mounted in a ventral pod with very unrepresentative twin intake ducts. Before long there were severe structural and control problems with the reheat (afterburner)—and worse was to come.

In September the new Minister of Aviation, Julian Amery, visited Weybridge and said 'TSR.2 is unquestionably the most important new aircraft in production for the RAF'; and maybe there are some today who would agree that nine aircraft constitutes production. In February 1963 new Air Minister Hugh Fraser finally put the record straight: 'TSR.2 will operate in the strategic role, both before and after the introduction of Polaris submarines.' This made the Trenchardist Air Staff feel very much better; and by this time Aubrey Jones was no longer Minister of Supply, so he didn't mind being contradicted. But down-under the Australian Minister for Air, David Fairbairn, expressed impatience with the long and trying campaign to get him to buy the British product. 'The RAAF cannot wait for TSR.2', he announced, 'it must replace its Canberras within two years.' So he said future attention would be directed to hardware that could be bought almost off the shelf, naming the Vigilante, Phantom and Mirage IVA; he also said he would discuss chartering or leasing V-bombers.

On 31 July 1963 the Minister of Defence, who this month was Peter Thorneycroft, announced 'production orders . . . will probably be placed towards the end of this year.' And on August 30, having raised the number of aircraft on order from nine to 20, he added, 'In addition to orders already placed for aircraft for development and for introductory flying by the RAF, BAC are now authorized to acquire long-dated [what used to be called long lead-time] materials to enable production for squadron service to begin.' By this time negotiations with the Australians had reached a critical stage, helped along by the flat declaration by the British Labour Party that, if they were returned at the next general election, the TSR.2 would be cancelled. The Ministry of Aviation was told to do all it could to make the programme look firm, in the advance of signing the production contract. In September Hugh Fraser hurried to Canberra to discuss the use of the Weapons Research Establishment at Woomera for TSR.2 supersonic trials. While there, he said an RAAF order 'would be of great value to the RAF'. To my amazement he also said he did not think such an order 'would affect unit production costs all that much'. If he literally meant 'costs' in terms of materials and man-hours he was right, but an RAAF order would have made a difference of about 20 per cent to the price charged to the customer. I can only conclude Fraser knew the game was lost, and was trying to put a bold face to the world by claiming it didn't matter. He had gone to Canberra empowered to offer 25 aircraft for a price of £65 million, with deliveries made concurrently with those to the RAF and with the loan (on unstated terms) of V-bombers until the TSR.2s were ready. This would, in retrospect, have been an excellent deal that would have been of great benefit to both nations. But it was killed by the British Labour Party's urgent campaign to convince the Australians that TSR.2 would be cancelled as soon as they were returned to power. RAAF officers and senior Australian officials have told me how effective this campaign was. One of them said 'By the time Fraser got here we knew we simply dare not rely on TSR.2 ever happening.' So on 24 October 1963 Fairbairn signed for 24 F-111Cs at US$90,749,040, saying 'It may be that the Canberras will see us through'. A full ten years later the Aussies were just getting these aircraft, having paid three times the contract price.

Unprecedented delay and cost-escalation were not at all what was expected of the F-111. But in October 1963 Denis Healey, Labour spokesman on Defence, was like a puppy with two tails. At one stroke his party's efforts had ensured that TSR.2 would be more expensive, making it easier to cancel, and the glittering F-111 cheaper, making it easier to buy as a replacement. His party then stepped up its campaign on the home front, doing all it could to convince the British public that TSR.2 was useless, and a thoroughly bad buy. The motivation stemmed from a hatred of the planemakers (but only British ones), a hatred of nuclear weapons (especially British ones) and the correct judgement that Labour could use the high costs of TSR.2 to its own massive advantage in its coming election campaign. I am certain that not one member of the Labour Shadow Cabinet ever considered the possibility that, whereas TSR.2 would give a staggeringly good performance in its flight trials, the American aircraft would become the centre of an almighty storm based on technical shortcomings, cost-escalation and supposed contractual intrigue. Some of them almost foamed at the mouth when, on 21 October 1963, the MoA said it was 'negotiating for a full production contract for an initial batch of 30 TSR.2s for squadron service' and—most unusually so far in advance of first flight—released for publication two photographs of the first aircraft in the works at Weybridge. To Labour politicians the thing portrayed was the arch-enemy, a costly symbol of British Imperialism, a nuclear weapon for use against defenceless peoples and, above all, the ultimate expensive product of a featherbedded industry that had for years milked the gullible public and government and caused untold millions to be poured down the drain in wasted projects. They appeared not to notice that the industry had merely built exactly what successive governments had told it to, and that the waste had been due to consistently inept political management. Many were the violent speeches that were made about what the Labour government would do to the wicked planemakers as soon as it was elected. Healey himself proclaimed 'TSR.2 is becoming the biggest scandal in British politics since the South Sea Island [*sic*] Bubble.' Clearly, it was 'outlook, stormy.'

A few days after the photographs were released I visited Weybridge. That very morning Mr Healey thundered that the programme was going to cost £1000 million, and that 'each aircraft is going to cost £20 million.' In reply the government adhered to its estimated total programme cost of £400 million, including all production aircraft, which it said was 'unchanged for three years' (news to me, because they had never previously announced this figure). BAC's Sir Geoffrey Tuttle was furious with everyone, pointing out to me that at that time the total amount of the corporation's signed contracts came to only £50 million, and he vehemently disagreed, thumping the table, when I suggested this would not pay for the R&D alone. Other BAC management saw big trouble ahead and regarded the general election due in 1964 rather like a death-sentence. It was at these discussions that I gained confirmation of my long-held impression that it was to mollify the Treasury that Mr Jones had described TSR.2 as a cheap little limited-war device for use on the battlefield, when in reality it had always been planned to offer Mr Watkinson's 'amazing number of options'. Labour were mistaken when they insisted TSR.2 had been 'hurriedly altered to take over the strategic role when Skybolt was cancelled.' Apart from the vexed question of price, the government could have demolished the opposition attack, but all Mr Amery could manage was to mumble about the 'defeatist forces which drove the Australians to look for support elsewhere.' But at least, in another statement, he claimed the supposed unit price of £20 million was 'an exaggeration by about a factor of ten.'

TSR.2 was perhaps the original crunch project in which the most advanced and complicated technology had to be justified and explained to a noisy crowd of angry and hostile people who knew little about it and didn't want to know any more. To the man in the street Mr Amery's pacifying £2 million a copy merely seemed a lot of money. To the man with a dangerous little learning it seemed the planemakers were taking everyone for a ride (again), because TSR.2 was 'a small twin-engined machine' yet £2 million would have bought almost five of the big Valiant V-bombers. It was extremely difficult to try to tell people where the costs came from. Britain has a long history of never telling anybody anything in any governmental matter if it can be avoided, and especially in keeping quiet about defence or high-technology programmes involving really big money. All sorts of increasingly unsatisfactory reasons have been put forward for this policy, which has led to disaster upon disaster. In the case of TSR.2 I could see this massive and vitally important programme falling to pieces because secrecy was opening the door for rumour and counter-rumour, for wild claims which might or might not be true, and above all for a public image of the whole project which simply stank. It was all harrowing in the extreme for the 40000 or so dedicated citizens who laboured 90 hours a week to make the thing, to schedule and to budget, and who knew the score and had to keep their mouths shut.

There were at least 27 major lines of development which had to be done if Britain was to keep making clever aerial weapons and which had to be charged to TSR.2 because this was the only contractual outlet for the work. In the US all these things had been managed as part of the onward march of aerospace technology on a broad front, and they were written off against the F-105, B-58, Vigilante, B-70 and many other programmes and used for the common good. With TSR.2 it was usually impossible to pull suitable developed hardware off the shelf. Even the Olympus engine had to be very largely redesigned and restressed for flight conditions unlike anything met in a Vulcan, as a result of the 1956 cancellation of the Gloster G.50 twin-Olympus all-weather interceptor. Time and again hardware items for TSR.2 had to be developed from scratch which would have existed but for the cancellation of some earlier programme. I have often tried to discover how the British government takes such factors into consideration in taking its big procurement decisions, but the system (up to 1971 at least) was rudimentary in comparison with the highly refined techniques used by DoD in Washington. British defence procurement has frequently seemed too strongly programme-orientated and insufficiently capability-orientated, and TSR.2 is a particularly glaring example of it.

Throughout the early 1960s I watched scores of teams from Kent to Scotland trying desperately to create TSR.2 systems and techniques that ought to have existed in Britain but didn't. Time after time the industry had to labour to put right government mistakes or ineptitude. To take one example, the digital computer shows the quality of British defence procurement in the previous decade. By 1952 it was clear that future advanced aircraft, both military and civil, were going to need to carry an on-board computer to handle their information-processing needs. An obvious case concerns the interceptor, where no pilot could navigate, fly the aircraft, track his quarry and manage his weapons at the real-time pace of supersonic combat. By 1953 three companies in the US were working on airborne digital computers, Hughes probably being front-runner but being gradually overhauled by NAA Autonetics as a result of their early plunge into silicon planar microcircuitry and their work on inertial navigation for X-10, Navaho and Vigilante. In 1956 the Ministry of Supply seemed to notice the flood of unclassified reports on airborne digital systems, and thought it would be nice to do something in Britain. So it funded an in-house programme which soon produced Dexan (digital experimental airborne navigator) which served for several years as a research tool. The first British airborne-computer programme, the Auto-Attack system for the Lightning, ran very successfully indeed, so it was promptly cancelled. When TSR.2, the ideal 'clean sheet of paper' application for a British system, came along, the Ministry ponderously decided such a device could not be produced by British industry within the aircraft timescale (having chosen a timescale ahead of that of the actual programme). So in 1960 Elliott Flight Automation were given an order to make the Vigilante's Verdan computer under licence, even though this was not wholly suitable for TSR.2 and needed various changes. In 1962 the Treasury was horrified at the cost of the American computer and called for the contract to be 'reviewed'. The MoA again said British industry could not produce a British computer, even though it had never been asked, despite the fact that such equipment could be seen to be needed by all future advanced combat and transport aircraft. The only good part of the story is that what today is Marconi-Elliott Avionic Systems was finally allowed to turn the Verdan computer into the 920M series computer for the Nimrod, and has since sold digital equipment for the Jaguar, Concorde, Lynx, C-5A and Corsair as a result. My point in relating all this is that the early procurement management was myopic in the extreme, and it was the great tradition of secrecy that allowed it to happen.

British procurement quality was run close by British defence statesmanship. In December 1963, when NATO was buzzing with Mr McNamara's proposal for a 'multi-lateral mixed-manned nuclear force' of surface vessels armed with Polaris missiles, Minister of Defence Thorneycroft went to a NATO Ministerial Meeting in Paris and calmly proposed a NATO mixed-manned force equipped with TSR.2. His colleagues round the table had no prior briefing and merely probed to see how detailed the presentation would be. It was soon clear it was just a vague idea, backed up by no considered thought, no detailed documentation and no numerical data whatever. It was said that Mr Thorneycroft 'seemed to be thinking aloud'. Maybe his proposal was no more undesirable than Mr McNamara's, but the US SecDef backed his up by about a ton of paper which at least ensured that it was thoroughly considered.

In February 1964 Air Minister Hugh Fraser said 'A weapon being developed for the TSR.2 will be applicable to the V-bombers.' This turned out to be Martel, which was not applicable to the V-bombers. By this time Labour spokesmen were wanting to know why the first TSR.2 had not flown, and at least two were suggesting it would never fly at all, trying to give the impression it contained an incurable fault. The original idea had been to fly XR219 at Wisley; this machine was actually taken by road to Boscombe, and finally wound up based at Warton. From the start it came under the charge of Wg Cdr R. P. Beamont (Bee), flight-test director and veteran of many programmes from the Typhoon to the Lightning. As week followed week BAC became increasingly embarrassed, and must have wished the MoA had not issued the pictures of a seemingly finished aircraft so many months before. It seems odd that responsible politicians often choose to reap a short-term gain, in this case by planting in the public mind in October 1963 the belief that the first TSR.2 was about to fly, at the expense of paying bitterly for it later on. Again perhaps the real culprit was the tradition of secrecy, compounded with an equally well established British tradition of never having a meaningful schedule anyway. BAC would have been no better off if the first-flight date had been published along with the pictures, because they missed it by six months.

TSR.2 was one of Britain's few major pre-1965 aircraft programmes that was well managed at the industrial level. How did it come to be so late? The first answer is undoubtedly that it suffered greatly from the attentions of the biggest army of government officials that ever gave its undivided attention to a single project. It would be nice to find something constructive that this horde accomplished, but all I can think of at the moment is a long, long list of wrong decisions, changed decisions (still wrong) and failure to take any decision at all. But even without their help the TSR.2 would not have been on time. Bristol Siddeley suffered terribly with the new 22R engine. On 3 December 1963, while the big new Olympus was being run up under the Vulcan test-bed on the ground at

Filton, the LP shaft and turbine disc burst. The resulting conflagration destroyed not only the heavily instrumented Vulcan but also (and I'm afraid I find this very funny) an enthusiastic fire tender which rushed too close to the scene. A month later a second engine blew up on the bed at Patchway. At least two more, one a prototype flight engine, blew up by the summer. It took months to confirm that the cause was a 'bell-ringing' singing of the LP shaft, its diameter oscillating at high frequency, caused by the impingement frequency of the cooling air at over 97% LP speed. Such a shaft failure could cause disintegration of the engine interior and pose a containment problem by bursting the casing. In TSR.2 the engines were surrounded by fuel, so the only answer seemed to be not to exceed 97% rpm until modified engines could be fitted. In turn, this caused engine-out problems with landing gear extended. The Farnborough show, the first for two years, came and went with the wheels still firmly on the ground. And on 9 September something happened that I still find hard to believe: the fuselage of the second aircraft was severely damaged when the truck that had brought it from Weybridge *overturned as it was manoeuvring into the hangar at Boscombe.*

But by this time Bee was at last racing up and down the runway in white-painted XR219, and he and navigator (in this context more of a systems manager) Don Bowen finally lifted it off on the golden Sunday afternoon of 27 September 1964. Bee kept the gear down in a modest local flight, but knew from the start that the air vehicle portion of the great weapon system with which he had lived for so long was even better than he had hoped. On return he said 'I thoroughly enjoyed the flight; this looks like being a real winner.' The engines stayed in one piece and it was an amazingly snag-free flight, so the man in the street was puzzled when XR219 stayed on the ground for the next three months. In fact it was symptomatic of the fact that TSR.2 was a complicated modern aircraft, and BAC was determined to proceed in a thorough and cautious manner. In contrast General Dynamics, Fort Worth, began 1963 with the F-111 17 months behind TSR.2 and ended 1964 seemingly (and I think this word is important) ahead of the British aircraft in almost all parts of the programme.

Bee knew how good TSR.2 was, but Denis Healey knew better. Four days before the first flight he told his constituents 'TSR.2 will only drop ordinary high explosive on tanks and bridges . . . new anti-aircraft weapons will be able to shoot it down by the time it is in service, so at £16 million an aircraft it is going to make all Mr Amery's other blunders look like chickenfeed.' This was in a rousing election speech, and maybe one ought not to expect sense on such occasions, but Mr Amery seemed rather piqued. He called a news conference to set the record straight. He heatedly proclaimed that 'Nothing like £250 million has been spent' (nobody had said it had—yet), and to one questioner who reminded him he had given an eventual programme total of £400 million in the Commons he retorted 'I can't remember . . . but whatever I said stands.' How could he recall such details at election time?

The result of the election was a Labour government. Mr Wilson became Prime Minister proclaiming that he was going to thrust the nation into the age of 'white-hot technological revolution', while at the same time doing his utmost to stamp out the aircraft industry where the revolution had its spearhead. Sir George Edwards was not at all surprised to see in each day's paper that the new government had no love for 'this inherited monster' which had 'already gone on long enough.' Daily he waited for news of cancellation. Imagine his feelings when the axe fell not on the hated TSR.2 but on Concorde. Wryly he said 'We just didn't see this one coming.' (Ultimately, after Aviation Minister Roy Jenkins had shown his skill in handling a tricky situation, and the French had politely said they would take Britain to the International Court at The Hague, the government explained they never really meant to cancel Concorde at all but just take a good look at it.) So TSR.2 still lived, and Bee was airborne again on the last day of the year.

By this time TSR.2 had supplanted the Spitfire as the one military aircraft known to everyone in Britain. And everyone felt passionately that it ought to be cancelled—or ought not to, as the case may be. The British love prolonged arguments, and arguments can thrive in conditions of secrecy, when heat can replace light. Early in 1965 *Flight International* risked being sent to The Tower by publishing a figure of 'about £190 million for R&D and nine pre-production aircraft. . . . As far as can be ascertained, a further £50 million for subcontractors and suppliers and tooling for 30 production aircraft.' Meanwhile government voices daily shouted that the eventual bill would run to £1000 million. It was interesting to see the way a low rate of spending was called for as an advantage, in the good old Treasury way, whereas R. G. Worcester put his finger closer to the truth when he pointed out '£250 million over six years is far too low a rate of spending on our biggest-ever programme.' Dick Worcester, who in the previous decade had been a courageous phenomenon in daring to criticise British aviation, was coming into the limelight as 'the aviation adviser to the Labour government.' In fact he found this accolade a hard row to hoe, and said he was merely a bit friendly with George Wigg, the Paymaster-General; but Fleet Street liked to present this free-lance writer and consultant as the menacing power behind the throne where aerospace was concerned, and certainly Mr Wigg was involved in the machinery of cancellation and visited BAC as hatchet man. In any case, despite the formation of BAC and Bristol Siddeley, I doubt if the UK industry could have managed a higher rate of expenditure than it achieved on TSR.2. What bothered me was that the British public, who were paying for TSR.2, were told it was going to cost £50 million, or £120 million, or £200 million, or £190+50 million, or £250 million, or £400 million or £1000 million, and denied the slightest help in discovering which figure might be somewhere near the truth.

One wondered if either the Conservative government or the new Labour one had any idea itself. In an off-the-record discussion, Healey, now Defence Minister, said the 'first detailed cost estimates' that he had been able to discover were dated October 1960; they comprised £90 million for R&D, and 158 production machines at £1·5 million. He poured scorn on the figures, saying they were not worth the paper they were written on; and he highlighted the in-service date of 'the end of 1965' and said 'now it's 1968.' He struck me as competent and well-briefed, but he had to toe the party line and make nice angry speeches. Within a day or two of our meeting, on 8 January 1965, he appeared in the papers saying 'It is not the duty of the defence forces to act as a wet nurse to the overgrown and mentally retarded children in our economy.' He later assured the Commons this was 'not directed at the aircraft industry', without saying who it was directed at. One remembered the tradition of British law that the meaning of a statement depends on what 'the man on the Clapham bus' thinks it means. In any case the Minister said his utterance was 'not intended for publication.'

By this time the climate was so hot BAC formally requested a 'meeting with the government', and the following week we saw the unusual spectacle of mass meetings of worried workers fearful of what their own Labour administration was doing. These meetings embraced not only BAC but also Hawker Siddeley at Kingston and Coventry whose 1154 and 681 were equally threatened. BAC Weybridge went even better with a protest march 10000 strong from Waterloo to Westminster with banners flying, which was probably the first and last time the so-called working class demonstrated in favour of an expensive nuclear weapon system. In fact most of the chaps who crossed Waterloo Bridge that day were more concerned at the technical and industrial significance of TSR.2, and I think this counted in their minds at least as much as merely keeping their job; the question of national defence hardly came into it. On Rediffusion's TV programme 'This Week' on January 14 Mary Goldring of *The Economist* took a brief moment off from knocking the Concorde to take a sideswipe at TSR.2, claiming 'Britain has no need of such a sophisticated aircraft while we have Polaris.' She did not explain how Polaris was to find point targets in the jungle or carry out multi-sensor reconnaissance after a strike. The whole programme performed a series of quite remarkable gymnastics in blending an amalgam of fact (sparse), rumour (plenty) and nonsense (abundant) to demonstrate to the British public that, whereas the nation had no need of TSR.2, it had a great need of the American F-111.

On 2 February Prime Minister Wilson, while not terminating TSR.2 as expected, did give a lot of figures which had never before been disclosed from such a source of authority (although not all his listeners remembered that when a Prime Minister wants to prove something he can pluck from behind the veil of secrecy any figure he likes to support his case). 'The original estimate for R&D', he revealed, 'was £90 million. It has now risen to the region of £300 million, and the most authoritative estimate I can get today for research, development and production is £750 million which, on an order for 150, would cost £5 million per aircraft or 25 times the cost of the Canberra it is designed to replace. . . . The aircraft flew for the first time in October [*sic*], over a year behind schedule [*sic*]. It has flown a number of times since at slow speeds and, of course, has not begun to be tested as a complete weapon system. Even at its present stage many technical adjustments are having to be made every week. . . . It is far too early to say whether, operationally, it will succeed or not.' In the ensuing debate Mr Wilson contrived to prove the aircraft wholly cost/ineffective by pointing out that each of them 'costs as much as a pre-war battleship'—amazingly, he made no mention of schools and hospitals—and that its continuance was costing the taxpayer £4 million a month. Clearly he judged that there were still a few 'don't knows' who needed to be won over, and the emotionally charged atmosphere was better for their conversion than cool reasoning. His comments were chosen to make the man in the street think TSR.2 a bad aircraft. The suggestions were so overt and damning that BAC undoubtedly would have had a case in court (why not, they had little to lose?), because it is what the listener thinks that matters, not the words uttered. In fact the F-111 had also flown only at slow speeds, had not been tested as a weapon system and needed technical adjustments each week (whopping great adjustments, which went on for seven years until 1971). But the Prime Minister made the British public think these things were evidence of an incompetently conceived white elephant that ought not to continue.

It was blindingly obvious the Labour government was eager to get rid of TSR.2 and buy the F-111 (TFX) instead. On pure cost grounds the idea appeared to make sense. The American aircraft was supposed to perform so many wonders that it was to be the standard fighter and attack bomber of the US Air Force and US Navy, and its enormous scale of production was going to bring down the unit price to a tantalisingly low level. Moreover, as the aircraft was American, the whole thing was obviously credible. It would not do to suggest that it might encounter problems, or that the prices quoted might be based on totally unfounded assumptions. To Mr Wilson it represented the perfect alternative, and it seemed a good idea to laud its qualities to the skies while pouring scorn on the British product. Later in February 1965 he said 'To replace TSR.2 with TFX would certainly save at least £250 million of public money.' Sir Arthur Vere Harvey, MP said 'It would pay the Americans to *give* the TFX to us; we would forever after be in the clutches of the American aircraft industry.' Liberal MP Eric Lubbock merely questioned the PM's maths, and said he could not 'find a saving greater than £164 million.' I do not think he was being sarcastic; I think he actually believed that in the British environment it was possible to work out a precise, meaningful figure where hundreds of millions of pounds of taxpayers' money was involved. If he did, the next few weeks must have put him right.

On 22 February Bee and navigator Peter Moneypenny took off from Boscombe for the 14th time, with persistent undercarriage snags overcome, and brought the aircraft home to Warton, flying at supersonic speed through bumpy air. The accompanying Lightning chase plane reported 'severe turbulence' and found the trip singularly unpleasant, but XR219 was 'steady as a rock.' Bee said TSR.2 was 'in a class of its own.' On 10 March he was to deliver the Barnwell Memorial Lecture to the Royal Aeronautical Society, but the Ministry of Aviation instructed him to cancel it because it would be most inconvenient if the TSR.2 pilot said he had a good aeroplane (in fairness to the brilliant minds in Whitehall I must record that they did let him deliver the lecture in September 1966, when TSR.2 was history). On March 27, with the forbidden lecture still in his desk, Bee completed the first phase of the flight-test programme. His reports, which were tersely factual and in no way coloured by the crisis just beyond his door, read almost unbelievably well. Indeed the completion of Phase I in 23 flights speaks for itself. Bee wrote "It can be said with certainty that the TSR.2 is a sound and satisfactory flying machine with superior qualities of stability and control to the predicted, or better than predicted, values; and there is now good reason to suggest that a high success rate may be achieved in the remainder of the CA programme' (CA = Controller, Aircraft, MoA).

He knew in his heart it wasn't likely to be permitted. How could it in a country where the Prime Minister, having been reminded of the Avro 730 (which was as much like TSR.2 as chalk is like cheese), proclaimed that the previous government were a bunch of fools because 'having cancelled a bomber on the ground that it would not be in service until 1967 they then spent hundreds of millions of pounds on one that would not be ready until 1968'? The inevitable end came on 6 April. In the course of the Budget Speech, tucked quietly away with an extra sixpence on cigarettes and four shillings on whisky, Chancellor James Callaghan announced the immediate cancellation of the TSR.2 programme. The decision was said to have been taken at a 'late night Cabinet meeting on the 2nd', although Dickie Worcester wrote in *The Times* (26 June 1965) that it was 'taken four months before the General Election.'

At once the Defence Ministry issued a long statement in startlingly blunt and almost ungrammatical terms: 'It was decided TSR.2 is too expensive and has got to be stopped. The planned programme would have cost around £750 million. An order for 150 aircraft would have meant each one would have cost £5 million . . . an order for 100 aircraft would have meant each would have cost over £6 million of which nearly £5 million still remains to be spent. . . . In order to ensure that our services will have appropriate aircraft in sufficient numbers Her Majesty's government have secured from the United States Government an option on the F-111A aircraft at a price per aircraft which even on a full-scale programme would represent less than half the estimated total TSR.2 research, development and production cost. . . . After taking full account of all future charges and payments on both aircraft it is now estimated that a full programme based on the F-111 would be £300 million less than the corresponding TSR.2 programme. The nature of the option is such that HMG has until the end of this year to decide to take it. Any initial order would be for a very small number for training purposes. It would not be necessary for HMG to place a follow-up order until April 1967. . . .'

Denis Healey held a press conference, backed up by Roy Jenkins, Minister of Aviation. They were probably the two best, smoothest, most competent men in Mr Wilson's administration, and they were each capable of demolishing critics who were in any case conspicuously absent. I ventured to ask why it was necessary to denigrate TSR.2, instead of just terminating its development on grounds of cost; Healey sharply pointed out that he had never denigrated the aircraft 'which was undoubtedly a splendid achievement.' For a moment I thought he was going to do a heartfelt piece on behalf of those who had laboured to make it, but he merely added 'You must understand feelings have run high on this project, and some of my colleagues have expressed those feelings.' Certainly he and Jenkins were 'the terrible twins' where the industry was concerned, for they had curtly stopped the three chief British military aircraft development programmes and replaced each of them with an American product. It was a time without parallel, yet nobody at the press conference could think of anything effective to ask. The Labour administration's sour propaganda eroded any support there might have been for the aircraft industry, and most of the men from the mass media not only filed stories effectively saying 'good riddance to TSR.2' but believed such a viewpoint themselves. So the press conference was a tame one. Nobody was present from BAC or BSEL. Nobody asked why the cost figures took no account of the fact that, in a British programme, the money was partly recovered by the government in taxes, and all stayed in Britain, whereas in buying a foreign product it all went away. Nobody even asked about industrial or technological consequences. Healey merely said 'We must see if TSR.2's strike role can be carried out by sea- or land-based Buccaneers or Phantoms. . . . On a certain extreme hypothesis about long-term commitments it might even be possible to reshape our defences in such a way as to dispense with this type of aircraft altogether. . . . I am not sure that the F-111 will be able to use our carriers. . . . The first aircraft will be delivered in about 1968, about the same time as TSR.2 would have been delivered.'

Lest it be thought that I attended that conference feeling that I was witnessing a tragedy, I had already formed the view that termination of the programme was the lesser of two evils. It would be inconceivable for an industrial contractor to continue to produce government hardware which, for whatever reason, was regarded almost with loathing by the government. The costs involved were very large by comparison with any previous British programme, and it was plausible for a new government to tell everyone this was due to bad management and in particular to poor financial control. Because of the fact that everything was 'secret' it was impossible to see how far the costs were TSR.2 costs, how far they were paying for supporting technology that the nation lacked, and how far they were creating a basis of know-how that (presumably) the nation was going to have to acquire anyway. It was this knowledge that upon TSR.2 fell the burden of equipping the technical spearhead of British industry for the next decade that made it difficult to judge costs which seemed to me high, and to most Britons probably seemed outrageous. Had TSR.2 been an American programme the matter would have been investigated in detailed cross-examinations in public. But as it was British all we had were wild charges and counter-charges, all useless for any analytical purpose and made by men who were technically illiterate and mainly concerned to score some political party advantage.

Soon after cancellation Roy Jenkins announced that 'The total TSR.2 write-off amounts to about £120 million . . . to which must be added cancellation charges nearer to £70 million than £140 million.' This seemed a circuitous way of describing the cancellation charges, which a cynic would have expected, on this basis, to come out at about £104 million. In October 1965, however, the total bill was put at £120 + 75 million, which tallied very well with Jenkins' figure, so it was a bit of a shock when in January 1969 J. P. W. Mallalieu told the Commons the total was actually £125 + 53 million, or only £178 million in all. To show where secrecy gets you, the government announced in 1969 that, '£126 million had been spent up to the time of cancellation', while the MoD told me in 1972 the 'total cost of the programme was £192 million.' It all depends what you include. At least it is fair to say the total write-off was something short of £200 million, and probably half this bought hardware or knowledge that subsequently proved to be of great value.

According to Healey 'The total liability which the airframe and engine firms would accept was £11½ million, only 2% of the target price.' Thus simple arithmetic suggests the target price for manufacture of 158 aircraft was £575 million. Jenkins added 'At this target price there would have been no profit, and for a limited stage beyond it they would have shared losses, up to a maximum of £9 million for BAC and £2½ million for BSE.' This target price, which was proposed by BAC on 27 January 1965, was coupled with a formula for sharing profits and/or losses up to the maximum penalties quoted for non-compliance with specification or schedule. BAC pointed out that 'This proposal was made as it was not practical for us to accept liabilities without limit on a project in which so many factors were outside the control of the corporation.' Jenkins 'didn't blame BAC' for its inability to quote a fixed price. At the time I thought this remarkable, especially as US prime contractors did not then share this inability. Today, however, even the best American firms have gone so sadly adrift with their costings in major defence programmes that one must regard TSR.2 as perhaps the first of the big, difficult projects in which accurate costs simply could not be calculated in advance. It is the central problem in determining the schedule and budget for big aerospace programmes that no human being is clever enough to know in advance what troubles will be met nor how long it will take to find solutions. In TSR.2 there were many hundreds of such problems, ranging from the engine LP mainshaft down to bonding problems with microscopic integrated circuits. As *Flight International*'s Roger Bacon would say, life is easier making mauve shirts.

This difficulty in trying to cost the unknown is an old, old story. What worried me much more was the high price BAC apparently quoted for merely making the aircraft: £575 million for 158 aircraft is £3,640,000 a copy, with hints that it might be more, on what was a substantial production run. The Labour government clouded its superficially reasonable financial case for stopping TSR.2 by unfortunate and irrelevant overtones of violent antipathy towards the planemakers in general and TSR.2 in particular, when in reality TSR.2 was an excellent weapon system that had been financially estimated with the usual gross optimism. Perhaps the crux of the matter was that the Wilson government was so emotionally against TSR.2 that it did not want to examine any compromise solution, any way of broadening the market or cutting costs, or any positive answer at all.

At the World Gliding Championships in May 1965, at which my wife was an official, Jenkins assured me privately that the sole reason for cancellation was cost. He agreed 'there was never any reason to doubt that the aircraft would fully meet the requirement', but claimed that over the four years 1969–72 the programme was expected to cost £740 million, on top of the R&D costs for 1960–68. He told me this figure openly, yet despite its magnitude and the fact that it was new information, I could find no record of it being debated in Parliament as it would have been on Capitol Hill. Later Jenkins said that the 'price of the Mk 1 F-111 is 20% less than the price at which we did all our comparative calculations with the TSR.2. . . . On a full purchase we should save at least £300 million after making allowances for the TSR.2 cancellation charges and the lower running costs of the F-111.' Thus began a continuing argument about supposed 'savings' which sometimes took into account costs incurred during operational service, as did Jenkins' £300 million, and sometimes did not, as when Mr Healey, in a broad review of defence economies, put the 'total saving' on all three axed aircraft programmes (TSR.2, P.1154 and HS.681) at a mere £110 million. For the record, in the Plowden *Report on the Aircraft Industry* of December 1965 the cost of TSR.2 was given as £5·5 million each on a run of 110 aircraft (the reader was left to guess if this included R&D costs) and the cost of the F-111 as 'hardly one half of this.' Imagine such vagueness in a report for the US Congress! In any case it was wildly incorrect, as the F-111 chapter shows.

So TSR.2 was killed, and, to make sure BAC did not by mistake start the assembly line rolling, as early as April 8 their staff had to begin the arduous task of ripping the production jigs out of the Weybridge concrete floor (throughout the *Daily Mail*'s front-page story they were called 'gigs'). Many of the men who had to perform this harrowing task had already done it once, after the V.1000 military transport was cancelled shortly before first flight in 1955. In 1968 John Stonehouse, Minister of State for Technology (who that week was the chap looking after aviation), said that £53000 had been recovered in TSR.2 tooling scrap value, so the public only lost £11,947,000 on this account. As for the aircraft themselves, Jenkins said he 'would be very glad to get some value out of the £120 million spent' (yet another contradictory figure). One aircraft had flown, ten more were almost complete and there were major assemblies for some 20 others. Preston was in full swing delivering rear fuselages in the final coat of white anti-flash paint, while the rest of the aircraft came from Weybridge, Hurn and Itchen (Southampton) in green primer. On

22 April the MoA announced 'three aircraft will be kept flying', and on 4 June it said they wouldn't. There was a mild storm in Parliament, Opposition members suddenly waking up and pointing out the advantages of, for example, 150 heavily instrumented hours at a fixed contract price of £2 million. But by August the MoA had decided to scrap almost everything. Ollie Heath of BAC considers that, 'whatever the rights and wrongs of cancelling the main programme leading to operational service, the rejection of the limited flight-test programme (at a cost estimated by the Ministry themselves as £3 million) was unforgivable.' Sir Ian Orr-Ewing suggested 'at least the third prototype' should have been kept flying to prove the reconnaissance, navigation and attack systems; he thought that the urgent decision to destroy everything, and the jigs and tools, 'suggests that there is somewhere in government circles a pathological hate against this superb new British aircraft.' I wondered where he had been all this time.

XR219 had flown 24 missions, totalling 13 hr 9 min, all very successful and yielding more than the planned amount of data. Three pilots and three navigators had flown. Bee had always been aware of the conflict between the two philosophies underlying TSR.2. On the one hand it had to be a superb flying machine capable of safely surviving systems-failure even at supersonic speed at low level. On the other there was a wide belief that it was 'a form of military computer, with holes provided for a crew to sit and monitor the progress of the device.' That the dichotomy was successfully resolved was partly due to the fact that the aircraft was simply wonderful. Had it got into service I think pilots would have been tempted to read the morning paper during supersonic terrain-following. Bee rated it 'potentially one of the most effective military aircraft of all time.'

Bee, who writes as well as he flies, published his view of the tale in *Phoenix into Ashes* (William Kimber). Another book that reached the public is *The Murder of TSR.2* (Macdonald) by Stephen Hastings. He relates how he and other Conservative MPs had invited Bee to Westminster. 'The test pilot made no complaint. He told us simply, directly and factually, as is his way, about what had been achieved and now destroyed. He left several of my colleagues and myself stunned with the magnitude of the tragedy, with a sense of the utter and massive waste of human devotion and effort. We wandered to the smoking room in a mood of impotent indignation.' My old friend Bob Blackburn pointed out that the crux of the matter was that these same men had, during the crucial period of the project's life, been totally unaware of the issues involved. Right up to the final cancellation secrecy had been maintained, whereas on the very day the axe fell all the leading British air correspondents were wandering freely round the F-111 plant at Fort Worth, whither they had been conveniently invited by General Dynamics. 'TSR.2', wrote Blackburn, in *Flight International*, 'was never a fact in the national sense. It was an image, shadowy and distorted. Secrecy is the ideal climate for intrigue and mismanagement.' And Sir Dermot Boyle of BAC said 'The less people seemed to know about TSR.2, the more they talked about it.'

Sir Dermot agreed with Lord Portal, then BAC's chairman, and with A/Cdre Bell of the Electronic Engineering Association, who both came to the conclusion that to run so complicated a weapon system under a Weapon System contract had been a mistake. The WS style had been almost universal in the United States since 1954, and I may tell of the good it did there in other volumes dealing with fighters. But for BAC, which in the lifetime of TSR.2 was still to a large degree English Electric and Vickers, to bear responsibility for the whole system caused many devoted engineers almost to crack up (some did). The MoA thought hard before issuing a WS-type contract, and it seemed to me absolutely right. But British industry did not appear to me to have enough of the right species of programme manager; and, unlike the US industry, it had to do its work in the worst political and financial environment that could be imagined.

The actual rise in estimated R&D costs gives the measure of the supposed 'cost escalation' on the TSR.2 programme, which is not untypical of the British aviation scene. As listed in *Civil Appropriation Accounts* for January 1966 the original R&D estimate, covering work up to full release for all roles in 1966, was put in December 1959 at £80–£90 million; in March 1962, the total up to CA release in 1967 was £137 million; in January 1963, to CA release in 1968, it was £175–£200 million; in January 1964 it was £240–260 million; and in January 1965 the estimate for R&D and production was put by the MoA at £604 million and by BAC at £670 million initially, later frenziedly trimmed to a target price of £650 million (which was still at variance with the £575 million manufacturing cost calculated from Mr Healey's figures). The Olympus 22R began life in July 1959 as the usual slight modification of a proven engine, with an R&D budget of £8 million; such a lowly figure rather let the side down, and it climbed to £15 million in January 1962, to £20 million in January 1963, to £30 million in September 1963 and to £32·5 million in March 1964. Auditor-General Sir Edmund Compton observed that cost control had been hindered by the 'inadequacy and inaccuracy of the information made available to the MoA'. The MoA blandly said the rising costs were due not to their failure to control them, but to 'under-estimation of the scale and technical difficulty of the problems involved . . . due to the technical uncertainty inherent in all advanced development work' (a gramophone record Sir Edmund had heard before, but which happens to be true). BAC said nothing at the time, but in September 1967 Dr

A. Hall, VG chief project engineer, recalled 'Only 17% of TSR.2 costs were in house [i.e. at BAC]. The MoA was responsible for monitoring the project. There was a lack of controlling action. We were watching the thermometer rise, but nobody was opening the windows.'

During 1965–66 people at the Ministry of Defence continued to work out ever more impressive sums to show how terrible it would have been had TSR.2 been allowed to go on. In March 1966 Mr Healey asserted that 'TSR.2 would have cost £1200 million.' Later one discovered this was a total programme cost over ten years. It was quite a figure, but he could do even better. In May 1967 he came up with a 15-year cost of £1700 million. Only later did it transpire that, to arrive at this total, he added in the cost of designing, developing, manufacturing and operating for 15 years a non-existent naval aircraft to replace the Buccaneer, as well as spares and support costs that I think he would now agree to have been unlikely, to put it mildly. He also 'updated' the TSR.2 costs to 1967 values 'to allow for inflation,' presumably because this made the figure larger. When a Cabinet minister could produce such so-called 'costs' from behind the security curtain I began to think even Washington not such a bad place.

Despite all the insinuations by Harold Wilson of technical failure, I think nine people out of ten today who know the programme would ascribe its termination to one ground only: cost. At the time the rising cost figures were reaching levels that seemed astronomic, evidence of poor financial control and many times greater than the estimates. But from my desk in 1974 it is obvious that the point where the gross error occurred was in the estimates. Britain has a long heritage of stupidly optimistic aerospace estimates, and it is here that the programme should have been examined in the greatest detail. The costs themselves, which seemed so exorbitant, were rather lower than those for recent US programmes for smaller aircraft able to draw much more heavily upon off-the-shelf systems and equipment. Unfortunately the only yardsticks Britons had with which to compare TSR.2 costs were those for programmes approximately a decade earlier. If only Britain had been able to view the whole TSR.2 programme in proper perspective it would either have been successfully completed or else never begun. But at the time nobody could say what the cost would be, or what it ought to be.

Taking the longest possible view, could TSR.2 (or whatever the programme may have been called) have been successful? There is plenty of evidence that *any* major programme for the RAF begun in 1957 would have been almost bound to fail, no matter how well it was conceived or executed. The British nation was too confused by slick aircraft/missile arguments, too incapable of judging cost levels and too vulnerable to tantalising US products for there to be much chance of success. The possibility of planning TSR.2 from the start as a bilateral UK/US or Anglo-French project was close to zero. In fact TSR.2 and the F-111 could well have been the same aircraft, but such a possibility was squashed by the facts that such an idea would have been quite alien to Britain and the United States, and in any case would have been thwarted by the blighted American concept of 'commonality'. So TSR.2 had to be a purely national programme. It still could have won, had there not been an F-111 (and a total absence of people able to view the F-111 objectively), plus a vague belief that the RAF might not need an aircraft in this class at all, plus a dramatic change in government in an election in which this very programme was presented to the public as the biggest possible scandal of modern times. There is no reason at all why the TSR.2 should have been judged a scandal, but the British public were not in a position to judge.

For the record, there were at the time of cancellation 49 aircraft on the line plus XR219 on the tarmac. These comprised the remaining eight development aircraft (all of them surprisingly close to the final standard), eleven pre-production machines and the first 30 for squadron service. XR219 was eventually trucked from Warton to the gunnery range at Shoeburyness in the hope that someone might use it as a target. XR220, about to fly at Boscombe, was in the summer of 1967 trucked to RAF Henlow; we may one day be permitted to see it at the RAF Museum. XR221 and 223 were sent straight to Shoeburyness. XR224 to 227, which were structurally almost complete, were smartly cut up by oxy-acetylene torches, with fuel areas carefully chopped open by axes beforehand. XR222, still incomplete, was sent to what is now the Cranfield Institute of Technology—'the most expensive exhibit we've got' said Wg Cdr McClure—where students have henceforth been able to learn about hardware and perhaps about politics.

How does one conclude such a many-faceted story, that shows, despite the pervasive blanket of secrecy—or perhaps because of it—how pathetically the British managed this vitally important programme? At the Fighting Vehicles Research and Development Establishment in September 1966, before military staffs from all over the world, a special display was put on of TSR.3, Britain's new and highly secret weapon. An ice-cream barrow appeared, manned by a crew of two, and bristling with machine guns. Boldly it rolled down the slope into the deep wading channel, where it vanished completely into the muddy water. After a few seconds, with a thousand pairs of eyes riveted on the water, a large balloon floated to the surface bearing the word HELP. I am told Soviet officers worried for days over the significance of this. Perhaps they thought the British mad. If so, I'm not disposed to argue.

Hawker Siddeley
HARRIER

IN 1955 I looked out of a thundering Valetta transport at the greatest and most densely packed group of airfields in the post-1945 world. The NATO countries, having decided that their World War 2 bases were inadequate and in the wrong places, had spent something in excess of £300 million to build up what military staffs burdened with the name 'infrastructure'. To support an air war in depth the Fifteen Nations had decided upon a BOP—basic operating platform—comprising a strip of thick concrete measuring 80 m by 2½ kilometres (262 × 8,200 feet), leading to a concrete apron and a tall control tower filled with US electronics. This BOP then went into mass-production. As the gleaming white strips passed the Valetta every minute or two, as we cruised down the frontiers between Federal Germany, the Benelux countries and France, I was writing a story about the vital role they would fill in providing a solid foundation for NATO's airpower.

It never occurred to me that what I was writing might soon turn out to be an outmoded way of thinking. But a renowned French aircraft designer, Michel Wibault, did wonder if NATO's runways might be a mistake. Even in retirement he couldn't stop drawing on the backs of envelopes, and early in 1956 he showed up at the French Air Ministry with a g-a. drawing of a ground-attack fighter he called the Gyroptère. Near its centre of gravity was a Bristol Orion turboprop, connected via a series of bevel boxes to four large centrifugal compressors, two on each side. Each compressor was encased in a rotatable scroll. When the four scrolls were in one position the compressors blew four air jets straight downwards, and the Gyroptère lifted off the ground on pure engine thrust. To transition to forward flight the four scrolls were rotated in unison to make the four air jets blow straight backwards. But Wibault's countrymen were sceptical. The Gyroptère seemed a complicated, clumsy and extremely limited proposition compared with the splendid supersonic machines that were already blasting off the more than 100 new concrete strips each 2½ kilometres long. Wibault's suggestion that the strips might prove vulnerable, and that something that didn't need them might prove worth having, was contrary to NATO policy. The French suggested that Wibault should try and get some dollars from the Mutual Weapons Development Program, because MWDP was a nice fat American milch cow that supported everything on the Allied (ie, anti-Soviet) side. MWDP were at once interested. They suggested that, as Wibault's idea was based on the Orion, and Bristol Aero-Engines was already very *persona grata* at NATO because of the Orpheus, he should put the idea to that company.

When Stanley Hooker at Bristol saw Wibault's scheme he was immediately tickled by its originality, and he also at once saw the importance of the long-term possibilities. Rolls-Royce, then his deadly rival, was very busy with jet lift schemes involving large numbers of purpose-built lift engines. Wibault had suggested a new jet VTOL (vertical take-off and landing) aircraft needing only one engine. But Hooker was not enamoured at the arrangement Wibault had chosen. In a matter of weeks his staff at Patchway had drawn the BE.52 in which an Orpheus turbojet was arranged to blow straight aft in the usual way and also drive a fan, comprising the first two (or three) stages of Olympus LP blading, discharging through vectoring side nozzles. Hooker then took the idea to Hawker's Sir Sydney Camm. Together their teams quickly devised an improved scheme in which the engine discharged through four nozzles, two cold ones behind the fan and two hot ones further aft, the four jets being disposed around the c.g. in such a way that they could lift the aircraft without imparting any pitching or rolling moment. The engine had a completely new fan, with two stages of transonic blades, with no guide vanes ahead of the first rotating stage (then a radical idea). To minimise gyroscopic effects the LP and HP shafts were to spin in opposite directions. Bristol called the engine the BE.53 (much later it was called Pegasus, although a few of Fedden's classic poppet-valve engines of the same name were still in use). Hawker's team designated their partner-study the P.1127.

From the start, in June 1957, the P.1127 was planned as a potential combat aircraft, with structural strength and space provisions for operational equipment and weapons. But it was amazingly small. The stumpy delta wing was under 24 feet in span and the gross weight not much over 10000 lb. It looked odd mainly because the wing had to be above the engine, to allow the four jets to blast downwards. What was not apparent was that there were reaction control jets at the nose, tail and wing tips, fed with LP fan air through enormous ducts, to control the aircraft at airspeeds too low for conventional surfaces to be effective. It had a high-mounted horizontal tail of curiously traditional shape, with elevators cut out to allow for rudder movement, and a most unusual landing gear consisting of twin wheels just aft of the c.g. and two main gears further forward which retracted outwards and upwards through 180° to lie immediately behind the large intake ducts. Later, in 1958, the design changed greatly, with a better-profiled body, more conventional wing and tail, and a tandem bicycle landing gear. Both the BE.53 and the P.1127 epitomized British inventive genius, besides offering an entirely practical escape from 2½ kilometres of undefendable concrete. But when Camm sought some support to carry the P.1127 from paper to hardware the 1957 White Paper on Defence was only five months old. This document stated that fighters or bombers were simply not wanted, even if they were covered with anti-gravity paint.

So Hawker and Bristol went to MWDP in Paris. It is unkind to call that agency a milch cow, because its officials were extremely skilled at evaluating proposals and most certainly did not dole out money as a matter of course. They were only too well aware of the curious belief of the British that the RAF would be unlikely to require any more manned fighters or bombers—that is the exact way it was put in the White Paper—and so were in no way influenced by the fact that the brilliant scheme for a single-engined jet VTOL combat aircraft had failed to evoke the slightest interest in Whitehall. After much discussion with people wearing many air force uniforms, it was decided that MWDP would provide 75 per cent of the funds for a small batch of BE.53 engines and that a draft specification would be written for a jet-V/STOL (vertical or short take-off and landing) replacement for the Fiat G91 close-support/reconnaissance aircraft. The aircraft was to attain Mach 0·92, and to meet the various stipulated numbers would have come out at a weight of about 11000 lb. This tallied very well with the P.1127, but Hawker's way ahead was anything but clear. For one thing, the British government continued to express supreme disinterest, so that Bristol had to find the remaining 25 per cent of the engine money themselves. Hawker had no support at all, and had lately spent over £1 million of their own money on the P.1121 which had likewise been damned in ministerial eyes because it had a man in it and competed with TSR.2. And a further element of gross uncertainty was contributed by the fact that the air staffs of the Fifteen Nations had no sooner written their V/STOL requirement than they began to argue whether or not they ought to ask for something much cleverer still, with supersonic performance. The fact that in the early 1950s the maximum speed of combat aircraft had increased by an average of rather more than 100 mph per year had tended to make generals, politicians, engineers and practically everybody else take it for granted that subsonic aircraft were obsolete. For VTOL the installed thrust obviously has to exceed the gross weight, and thus should suffice for highly supersonic performance in forward flight. This all seemed obvious. It seemed obvious to me, and in 1944 I had a famous maths tutor who said

'If ever I see the word "obvious" in one of your proofs it will be marked wrong'.

Camm knew all about Mach 2, and in May 1958 he watched the last hardware for the P.1121 (which would have exceeded Mach 2) being cleared away from the plant at Kingston, six months after the Hawker board had decided they would put the project into mothballs. Hooker had told him the BE.53 was sized to give an eventual thrust of 15000 lb, with possibly slightly more much later. Both of them would have liked more, but time, existing hardware and certainly money made a bigger engine out of the question. A 15000 lb engine was just big enough for a VTO demonstrator capable of doing a marginally useful job. On the other hand the four rather low-velocity jets were not at all well suited to supersonic propulsion, and a supersonic airframe would have eaten severely into the available weight. Camm soon realised the P.1127 had to be a high-subsonic machine, and that even then he was going to have to save every possible ounce of weight. He could, it is true, have planned a Mach 2+ design to a much later timescale, and coming after the P.1121 such a project would have seemed a major step forward instead of a step backwards. That he chose Mach 0·95, and secured immediate acceptance of the idea from the Hawker board, shows that in May 1958 there were a few people in Britain with remarkable breadth of vision. Admittedly most people at Kingston probably regarded the P.1127 as the only thing that could be done at that time to get vectored-thrust VTO into the air—something that would give way to a 'proper' operational machine (which then meant Mach 2) as soon as the Government could be persuaded of the error of its extraordinary posture on manned aircraft. However this may be, the vital fact was that in May 1958 Hawker Aircraft Ltd authorised a company-funded programme to construct and fly a high-subsonic research aeroplane, capable of being developed as a ground-attack fighter, around Hooker's BE.53 engine. It was one of the most significant decisions in the history of aviation.

I was fortunate enough to be briefed by Camm himself from time to time, and I shall never forget the hunched-up writhing of his shoulders as he scornfully quoted the little men in Whitehall who were either unable to see that the P.1127 might be important or were afraid to admit as much. He had deliberately planned the P.1127 to be small, simple and likely to develop fairly quickly, and he had explained to the MoS that 'V/STOL is going to bring many new problems and many new possibilities, and the P.1127 represents the best hope of exploring both the problems and the possibilities in the shortest time'. Yet one eminent expert had told him the MoS 'could not possibly have any interest in such a small and limited proposal'. Rolls-Royce had by this time begun to sketch pictures of

Mach 2+ fighters with a dozen or more lift jets, and these were far more exciting; and they would make use of the experimental SC.1 which was funded and built. Yet by the beginning of 1959 the fact that the P.1127 and BE.53 were both actually being constructed, and promised a brilliantly simple answer to a problem that could no longer be ignored (how to be independent of airfields), had begun to penetrate the almost closed minds of the officials. Though they dared not admit that any interest attached to the P.1127 as a potential combat aircraft, they finally decided that their careers would not be too much at risk if they drafted an experimental requirement (ER.204D) around Camm's design, and in December 1959 this enabled the MoS to provide financial cover for the two flight prototypes which the Hawker board had authorized.

Today it is getting on for 20 years from the time when the belief that manned combat aircraft were a dying species was beginning to permeate the echelons of government. Many observers are taking the line that the 1957 White Paper was only a piece of paper after all, and could not really have had all that much of an effect. So I will harp a little longer on the environment into which the P.1127 was born. Duncan Sandys, who as Minister of Defence had to put his name to the document, was very far from being a myopic fool with a great bee in his bonnet, neither was he the mere tool of a government bent on saving money at all costs. The view that the RAF would be unlikely to require any new types of manned fighter or bomber was the distillation of opinion of the best experts in the RAF, reinforced by the considered opinion of the best experts in the MoS. Sandys, as minister, saw no reason to disagree with all these experts, though before drafting the White Paper he examined his closest advisers in some depth to make quite certain that the rather fundamental change in policy was sound. Once drafted, the policy was the policy, and it could hardly be subjected to a sudden and seemingly capricious about-face. Thus it was that when in the winter of 1957–58 Camm and his men went to the ministry, and told them they had abandoned the P.1121 but wanted support for the P.1127, nobody could view the proposal objectively. When I later talked to the most senior civil servant concerned with aircraft procurement he assured me that 'not one man-hour' had been devoted to assessment of the operational potential of a P.1127-type aircraft. From the start it had been self-evident that the only possible way of supporting the programme was on a basis of pure research, and Camm's decision to design the P.1127 to a 3000 hr structure life at an ultimate load factor of 12, and to make provision for internal and external payloads, actually counted against it!

There were just two faint glimmers of light. One was the interest of the newly formed NASA in the United States, which immediately saw that the Hooker/Camm formula offered very great promise indeed and was in many respects superior to any of the multitude of V/STOL schemes that NASA (and its predecessor NACA) had investigated. One of the best NASA vehicles was the Bell X-14, with two vectored Viper turbojets; Hawker c.t.p. Bill Bedford flew this shortly before starting flight development of the P.1127. In 1959 NASA gladly undertook to build a transonic tunnel model of the P.1127 and also a large free-flight model for hovering and transition research, and to test both fully. The resulting reports from Langley Research Center in 1960 were encouraging in the extreme, and cheered up the depressed engineers at Kingston. The other ray of hope was that in April 1959 the Air Ministry had written a draft operational requirement, OR.345, around an 'ultimate' P.1127 with 18500 lb thrust. This was not done with any view to buying any such aircraft, but simply because there was in the RAF a strong and growing feeling that a close-support aircraft that did not need 2½ km of concrete might prove useful—especially if, as seemed blindingly obvious to anyone bold enough to think about it, none of the other aircraft could get into the air. Hindsight is probably a rather inferior kind of wisdom, but from the perspective of 1974 it is enough to make anyone weep great salty tears to look back to the P.1127 taking shape in the jigs at Kingston, the BE.53 running on the bench at Patchway, and OR.345 lying on various vital desks, all before 1959 was out, and to realise what could have been done and when.

What actually was done was all done by the wicked planemakers, who just kept adding two and two, finding the answer kept coming to four and deciding that the official policy must be wrong. The BE.53 ran in August 1959, and behaved very well. The prototype flight engine was rated at 11000 lb, and it seemed desirable to start off flight trials in the tethered hovering mode. Unfortunately Camm's team found great difficulty in keeping the total mass of XP831, the first prototype, even to 10999 lb. For all I know they may have mused on the possibility of getting someone much smaller than Bill Bedford to sit in the cockpit (though I very much doubt it!). But the margin between thrust and weight was close. When Bedford began hovering trials on 21 October 1960 I asked Camm if he had waited for the cooler weather and was taken seriously. The thrust-limited fuel was just enough for two minutes of hovering. On 19 November 1960 the tethers came off and Bedford hovered free. This brought a new problem: the ground intercom had to be unplugged, which meant XP831 had to carry a radio weighing lots of ounces. But of course my facetious comments refer to a transient state of affairs, and Hooker soon cleared another 1000 lb of thrust. XP831's next task was to fly as a conventional (CTOL) aeroplane, and this it did at the RAE Bedford on 13 March 1961. By this time it had been improved in several respects, notably in having a more powerful reaction control system. Before much metal was cut the wise decision had been taken not to use LP air but to control the aircraft in the hovering mode with reaction jets fed by HP air. Even though this is at 350°C, needing Nimonic pipes and reaction valves, its density is so high the ducting is much smaller and lighter. But early hovering showed more control power was needed. For example, the tremendous intake momentum drag overcame the combined effect of the yaw reaction valves and the natural weathercocking of the fin and rotated the aircraft tail-on to any wind.

Late in 1960 the MoS screwed up courage to fund four development aircraft, and became rather cross when I tried to find out if these might be regarded as not necessarily pure research machines ('Of *course* they could be useful for some future operational type, but the RAF has no requirement for such an aircraft . . .'), and also picked up Bristol Siddeley's tab of 25 per cent on the engine. In 1961, as XP831 steadily closed the unexplored gap between the 1g stall and the hover, the Federal German government sent a mission to London which sewed up an agreement with the MoS for future bilateral joint development and management of the P.1127 and its engine. There is no doubt the Top Neddies in Whitehall viewed the scene as the Saunders-Roe 177 all over again; the P.1127 seemed to be something Britain didn't want but which might be 'sold to the Germans'. Still nobody appeared to appreciate the massive importance of the tiny, underpowered aircraft—perhaps because nobody appreciated how fast Hooker's men could give it more power. And of course it was damned from the start not only by not being a missile but in being subsonic. My dear chap, it was almost an insult! Sir William Dickson, Chief of the Air Staff, said at a private luncheon 'I hope you aren't one of those people who actually expect us to *buy* the P.1127?'

One of the things that coloured his judgement was that at the beginning of 1961 Hooker and Camm had come up with the supersonic P.1150. This would have had an improved engine with plenum-chamber burning (PCB) in which fuel is injected and burned in the fan air to increase the velocity and energy of the flow through the front nozzles. The PCB engine would have given about 22000 lb thrust. Its nozzles were streamlined in the lee of the supersonic intakes, the fuselage would have been longer and thus had a supersonic fineness ratio, and the design Mach number would have been 2·1. Nor was this all. The allied staffs whom I earlier left arguing at SHAPE over their proposed V/STOL close-support fighter had finally reached agreement in March 1961. They issued NBMR-3 (NATO Basic Military Requirement) which was a brief document setting forth the characteristics of what seemed a desirable piece of equipment. NBMR-3 did not actually ask for VTOL, but the requirement to 'use a 200 metre unpaved strip at maximum overload weight' meant a T/W ratio greater than unity combined with jet lift. Speed was to be Mach 1·5+ at altitude and Mach 0·92+ at sea level, both figures having been agreed the previous autumn. And a bomb load of 2205 lb (the metric people having beaten the US suggestion of one short ton) was to be carried over a low-level (lo-lo-lo) radius of 250 nautical miles. Originally the date for operational clearance was to be '1965'. In August 1961 the final NBMR-3 draft called for bidders to quote for the first squadron of 12 aircraft to be operational in 1966. The final requirement also introduced a very important refinement to the field capability: NBMR-3 aircraft had to clear a 15 m (49 ft) screen in a distance of 150 m (492 ft) from brakes-release. (To accompany this aircraft, and feed it with supplies when operating away from established bases, there was a parallel competition for NBMR-4, a V/STOL transport.)

These two documents had aircraft engineers on both sides of the Atlantic scurrying around like ants. In retrospect it was all slightly unreal. Although both 'requirements' were bold and challenging yet not impossible demands, and were potentially capable of promoting a quantum jump in the state of the battlefield art, they were not really requirements at all. No government or military force had said it would buy anything. There was just a vague supposition that, after a frantic and exciting competition among the West's planemakers, the winning design would become the subject of a vast multinational manufacturing programme and would go into service with practically everyone. Nobody liked to go into this too closely, because the G91 had demonstrated that in the real world it just doesn't work like that. But to a score of engineering staffs, all eager to explore a new area (and especially to people in Britain, where aircraft was a rude word), it was manna from Heaven.

The resulting submissions, which had to be in by the last day of 1961, were of enormous technical interest. I would love to dwell on their various merits and faults, and some actually flew, but this tale will be quite long enough without them. The one that concerns this story is the Hawker P.1154, which originally was a direct outgrowth of the P.1150 but powered by a new engine. The Hooker and Camm teams explored every way of stretching the P.1150, but just could not quite meet the full requirement. After casting a jaundiced eye over the P.1152 with a PCB BS.53 engine and two added lift jets, the P.1154 emerged as a 'clean sheet of paper' design with the BS.100 engine, the first completely new major engine proposal by the Bristol Siddeley firm (formed, as related in the TSR.2 chapter, in 1960) and having a mass airflow almost 60 per cent greater than that of the BS.53 and thus starting life at 33000 lb. During the second half of 1961 Camm's men put in much more effort on the 1154 than they did on the 1127, which began to be regarded not as a bird in the hand but as a probably limited programme that might not get beyond the six flight vehicles then ordered. Nevertheless its very existence generated intense interest.

XP836, the second P.1127, flew in July 1961 and helped close the gap which was finally eliminated on 20 September after 2½ busy weeks at Dunsfold. Thenceforth the P.1127 could rise vertically, accelerate forwards to high speeds and then slow down and hover again. Some of the low-speed flying was done with rubber inflatable intake lips, which could be puffed up to a large radius of curvature at low speeds and let down to give a fairly sharp lip at high speeds. In the event this idea proved operationally impracticable, and a compromise fixed metal lip was adopted for the Kestrels, the next stage of development. A setback came on 14 December 1961 when XP836 lost one of its glass-fibre front nozzles. Bedford pointed it straight at RNAS Yeovilton and tried to land there, but found that as soon as he lowered the flaps and reduced speed the aircraft rolled uncontrollably. He ejected at low altitude. By the time he got back to Dunsfold—he stopped off on the way (not with parachute under his arm) to attend the RAE apprentice prize-giving—the decision had been taken to make all the nozzles of sheet metal.

In the same month the US government, after some months of quiet talking in the Pentagon, proposed to the British government that the P.1127 should be the subject of a joint British/American/German programme to evaluate V/STOL under operational conditions, and that some more should be built under tripartite funding to form a 'three-nation squadron'. The Americans had for a long time felt that their own prolific and sometimes expensive V/STOL research programmes were not even showing promise of later yielding anything that could be used in combat, and the strikingly effective P.1127 programme did. Quite apart from the fact that the P.1127 seemed to be a good thing to have a part of, the Americans had become slightly edgy at the prospect of it becoming an Anglo-German programme. As no less a person than Gen. John P. McConnell (later USAF Chief of Staff) put it to me, 'We reckoned an all-British P.1127 would die a natural death—it would just wither away in that environment—but with the Germans in, the picture looked different'. The upshot was an announcement on 20 February 1962 of a Tripartite UK/US/FRG programme to explore a useful list of operating techniques, training methods, logistic supply and similar topics. The work would be done by a specially formed Tripartite Evaluation Squadron (TES) of aircrew and ground personnel from the RAF, Luftwaffe and the US Air Force, Navy and Army. Its equipment comprised the final P.1127 prototype XP984, mentioned later, plus nine aircraft to a later standard called Kestrel FGA.1, the designation signifying 'Fighter, Ground Attack'. The nine Kestrels were all bought by the MoS on a British vote, but the running costs of the squadron were split equally between the three nations (the original American idea had been an 18-aircraft squadron, six per country). Each country was to have the option of buying its three Kestrels at the end of the programme.

The TES formed at RAF West Raynham, Norfolk, on 15 October 1964 under the command of Wg Cdr D. McL. Scrimgeour, RAF, a little behind schedule. The Kestrels were ordered as XS688–696 by the lately formed MoA on 21 May 1962, and the first flew on 7 March 1964. It is of the first importance to realise that Camm's team was now busy with several quite different types of P.1127-derived aircraft. There were six (five if XP984 is judged to be a Kestrel) P.1127s, with weights in the range of 11000–14000 lb and thrusts in the range 10500–13700 lb. There were nine or ten Kestrels, with a largely new airframe (in particular, with a totally new swept wing), a fair amount of military equipment, weights in the range 14500–17000 lb and engine thrust of 15200 lb. From these later stemmed six 'P.1127 RAF' pre-production aircraft of a third completely new design, the Harrier, with weights and thrust in the 20000 lb class. There was the much bigger and highly supersonic P.1154 for NATO, which later split into the P.1154 RAF, with weight and thrust in the 25000–35000 lb range, and the largely redesigned P.1154 for the Royal Navy with maximum weight in the 40000 lb class. It would be confusing to tell the story of 1962–65 in strict chronological order because no two consecutive sentences would deal with the same aircraft. A better answer is to deal with one programme at a time.

The original P.1127s continued very valuable flight development in 1962–65, mainly based at Dunsfold, Surrey, though on 8 February 1963 Bill Bedford flew the first prototype out to the carrier *Ark Royal* in the Channel and completed a seemingly perfect series of demonstrations. It is significant that when he did this, at the invitation of a very interested Royal Navy, he had never piloted any aircraft on to any ship before. He and colleagues Hugh Merewether and Duncan Simpson had since December 1961 been reaching supersonic speeds in shallow dives, and by mid-1962 the aircraft had been cleared to Mach 1·2 (a figure many times exceeded, even by the P.1127, and which was the subsequent design dive speed of the Harrier). A lot of flying had been done at night, and altogether surprisingly little trouble had been encountered, apart from two maddening accidents. On 30 October 1962 the engine of the very new third aircraft suffered a compressor-blade/casing rub whilst pulling a tight turn, and eventually caught fire. Merewether, emulating Neville Duke in a prototype Hunter ten years earlier, dumped XP972 very hard on the grass at Tangmere. Hardly anybody watched this unpremeditated arrival, but at the Paris Salon on 16 June 1963 Bedford graunched the original prototype in front of a crowd of about 110,000. He was hovering, only a score or so of feet up, when the four nozzles swivelled round to point to the rear. The aircraft pitched nose-down and slumped on to the Le Bourget grass hard enough to be judged a crash. The P.1127 was not damaged beyond repair (today you can see it in the RAF Museum), and indestructible Bedford climbed out fuming. Though never proved, the culprit was probably a speck of foreign matter which jammed the pressure-reducing valve in the bleed-air supply to the nozzle motor. In the absence of restraining motor torque, the nozzles, locked in synchronism, freely pivoted round to the rear under the slight torque imparted by the jets. This was at once fixed so that it could not happen again, but few pilots could have been as embarrassed. As always, the French were trying to be one-up on the perfidious British. Only a few minutes before, the announcer had broadcast that the P.1127 was 'une développement d'une création Française', even though by this time not one nut or bolt owed anything to Wibault. Rivalry was especially intense between the P.1127 and Dassault's jet-lift Balzac. Without wishing to be horrid to Dassault it is a matter of historical fact that the Balzac, which on that day looked so smugly at its rival's misfortune, achieved the distinction of killing two pilots in two quite separate crashes.

The last three P.1127s each introduced visible modifications to improve stability, handling and other aerodynamic factors. XP976 had an interim wing with kinked leading edge; XP980 had an enlarged tailplane with sharp anhedral and (with modified XP972) introduced streamwise 'Küchemann' wing-tips; and XP984 introduced the new swept wing of the Kestrel. In fact 984 also had the 15200 lb Pegasus 5, as well as the Kestrel's extra fuselage bays spliced in above the front nozzles and below the rear nozzles to lengthen the body and, in effect, move the wing to the rear. With a sharper kink in the hot nozzle ducts to bring the rear nozzles forwards, the repositioned wing perfected the relationship between the four engine nozzles, the c.p. of the wing—which moved aft with the Kestrel's sweep—and the c.g. of the laden aircraft. The P.1127/Kestrel/Harrier story is full of important engineering changes which could be overlooked by the casual observer who might think today's Harrier just the P.1127 with more thrust. Sweeping the wing added area at the rear and improved trim with drop tanks on the wing pylons, though in this condition longitudinal stability was still only passable. The streamwise tips reduced induced drag. Later the Harrier extended the tips still further, to give additional rearwards area and improve behaviour with loads on the four pylons of that aircraft. The swept wing of the Kestrel had a much thicker root which totally altered the 'sit' of the aircraft, the straight top line being replaced by a pronounced hump-back. Other changes introduced with the Kestrel included more efficient all-metal intakes and a nose terminating in a forward-oblique camera instead of a long pitot probe.

So far the programme had not yielded big numbers of aircraft, but it had meant a massive engineering effort by a lot of companies. Usually there is keen competition to decide who shall supply an item, but when somebody has won that is generally the end of the fight. In the case of the P.1127 Camm and his team never doubted that the aerodynamic control surfaces ought to be powered. The fortunate powered-control contractor on the Hunter had been Fairey; the unfortunate one on the P.1121 had been Dowty-Rotol. Showing the wisdom of Solomon, Camm split the P.1127 between them. Fairey obtained clearance first and flew on XP831; Dowty then flew on 836 (lost near Yeovilton through no fault of theirs). When the four funded development aircraft came along, the battle continued: Fairey controlled 1 and 2 and Dowty-Rotol 3 and 4. When the nine Kestrels were planned, Sir George Dowty told Camm his group had lost roughly £250,000 on the P.1121 and the Kestrel could help get a bit of it back, so Dowty-Rotol equipped all the Kestrels. At the eleventh hour, for rather poor reasons of 'cost and timescale', the Ministry decided to omit autostabilization, although I am sure any Harrier pilot today would say hovering in turbulent air is hard work without it. Autostabilization had been provided for in the Dowty (and Fairey) units, but the ports had to be blanked off in the Kestrels. Then along came the P.1154; Fairey won this but were denied any benefit from it by cancellation, as later described. To equip the Harrier the whole thing went back into the melting-pot, and Fairey won 'on engineering and cost grounds'—which was rather nice because it was their turn, wasn't it?

By 1962 the massive engineering effort and seemingly open-ended future for the P.1154 had made this project much more interesting to the British government than the little P.1127/Kestrel, and in January 1962 the OR.345 requirement was cancelled. As if in self-explanatory reasoning, the former Minister of Defence, Harold Watkinson, confided in 1964 that 'the requirement was really written around the P.1127, which was a subsonic aircraft.' But in the United States the Army had come to view the P.1127 as an aircraft of uncommon interest. It seemed to reconcile almost all the previously incompatible factors such as V/STOL performance, high flight speed, ability to carry weapons and operational equipment, ability to hover or at least loiter at very low speed and gross weight not much above the limit (strictly, then 12500 lb) for Army fixed-wing machines. The Army began to wonder, almost out loud, whether or not it might be able to buy such an aircraft and steal a large march on the rival Air Force. Northrop kept its ear close to the ground and eventually decided it might be able to wangle the political problems and build an Americanized P.1127 under licence. In January 1962 Hawker and Northrop announced a collaborative deal whereby the two firms would share information in the V/STOL strike field (I'm not sure what information Northrop had to offer, but this was reflected in the financial clauses) and Northrop would make the P.1127 under licence in the event of an American order. On 1 May 1962 US SecDef McNamara said the US was contributing 'in the order of $30 to 35 million towards the development of the aircraft and its engine', and in July Fred Drinkwater and Jack Reeder from NASA Ames Laboratory evaluated a P.1127 at Dunsfold.

On 9 February 1963 the Italians signed an agreement for a full exchange of technical information and an option on a manufacturing licence. I was most interested to see the way the Italians had kept out of the exciting P.1154 programme, yet wanted to be in on the P.1127. This seemed to be swimming against the tide, and it may be that they were beginning to judge the whole NBMR-3 scheme unrealistic, and wanted to share in the single programme that seemed close to a usable end-product. In May 1963 it was announced (apparently from the Pentagon) that the three nations engaged in the TES had put 'about £37 million' into the Kestrel and that this would 'cover the whole of the development and cost of evaluation.' But the programme seemed to be going off slightly at half-cock. I cannot quite share the view of *Flight International*, which wrote in July 1963 'It is lamentable that the RAF did not long ago ask for 50 or so of the straightforward P.1127, so that by now some practical experience and potential export sales might have been achieved.' The P.1127, like any VTOL aircraft, was crucially dependent upon engine power, and I doubt that much would really have been gained by trying to put 50 of the 'straightforward P.1127' (whatever that means) into operational service. What worried me far more was that the TES, an obviously sensible idea, was going to have an aeroplane nothing like as useful as it might. When he became Minister of Defence, Denis Healey said (18 February 1965) that a Pegasus rated at 18000 lb had been 'already offered but refused for the nine tripartite aircraft'. In my opinion, sticking at 15200 lb crippled the value of the Kestrel. In particular, the TES never carried weapons!

The Kestrel, half-cock though it may have been, did at least achieve full CA Release in December 1964. This was the first time any jet-lift machine of any kind had been granted full release for service use, and as far as I can recall there were no limitations; certainly there were no speed restrictions, and night flying was included. The TES began operating on 1 April 1965 (birthday of the RAF), and—provided one worked on a cold day, or got airborne around 5.30 a.m.—everyone had a good time. Kestrels roared up and down from every sort of dispersed temporary base imaginable, and when the syllabus was completed, 11 months later, there had been 938 take-offs and about 600 hours flown. A very great deal had been learned, and shared, but I was vaguely apprehensive that the end of this evaluation might be the end of the road.

The Kestrel was incapable of doing a military job, without the addition of more power and equipment, and I wondered whether those 11 months might be used as the excuse for quietly letting the whole thing fade away. One aircraft had been written off, and Germany declined its option to buy its three aircraft, so two Kestrels stayed in Britain (one at BLEU and the other being rebuilt at Brough with the 18000 lb Pegasus 6 and Harrier intake) and six were shipped to the United States, which had agreed to buy the German aircraft at the same 'used' price as that written into the original agreement. In the US these machines flew very busily for some months, from Edwards, Pax River, Point Mugu and two assault ships, USS *Raleigh* and *La Salle* of 13900 short tons each, with 200 × 84 foot decks, as well as from the carrier *Independence*. A lot of good work was done, the aircraft being designated Hawker Siddeley XV-6A, and much fundamental research was accomplished by two of the six which were passed on to NASA. Yet this again was a slightly half-cock exercise. The American journal *Aviation Week*, which doesn't exactly support foreign industry, commented that the XV-6As had been 'imported into this country, since when everybody has been trying to decide what to do with them.' In 1973 I tried to find out what had happened to all the XV-6A trials reports and the answer seems to be 'they were lost in the files.'

So at this point I will break off from the XV-6As being played with over blue oceans and hot deserts, and return to the big conference room at Richmond Road, Kingston, Surrey, whence on 17 November 1961 representatives trooped in not only from Hawker Siddeley, the hosts, but also from Breguet (France), Avions Fairey (Belgium), Focke-Wulf (Federal Germany), Fokker (Netherlands), Republic (USA) and Sabca (Belgium). There had rarely been such a gathering of the clans of industry, especially as each was working flat out on a supersonic jet V/STOL to meet the NBMR-3 specification and wanted to beat everyone else. Before the day was out there had been a massive shaking of hands and an agreement signed which said: the seven firms will form a consortium; each can submit any design it wishes; the NBMR-3 winner will become design leader and prime contractor; and subsequent R&D and production will be shared among all seven in relation to their abilities and national orders. It was an obvious thing to do, to try and avoid a repetition of the silly G91 impasse. The meeting was at Hawker's initiative, and Camm certainly felt that, if there was any sense or justice in this world, the P.1154 would win. So the other six partners stood to gain from collaboration rather than lose, and no longer had any reason to feel 'I'll play ball as long as our entry wins'.

NBMR-3 was the biggest international design competition there has ever been, of any kind. All bids were in in January 1962. There was such a wealth of clever vectoring nozzles, batteries of lift jets and high-lift or swinging wings that the NATO evaluation staffs in Paris must soon have suffered mental indigestion, and possibly began to take refuge in the easier question 'Who can we most assuredly rely upon to turn this clever proposal into hardware, within the timescale and price quoted?' Even this was no real help because it was soon obvious that the crunch was going to be between the P.1154 and the Mirage IIIv. Hawker could point to the P.1127 already flying, and to unrivalled simplicity in the basic scheme. Dassault could point to the existing Mirage III, a Mach 2 aircraft, to the flight trials of the Balzac and to the supposedly superior efficiency of a 'composite' V/STOL (with lift and thrust provided by separate engines each tailored to its own task) over a vectored-thrust single-engined design which (so the argument went) was burdened in cruising flight by an oversize engine that had to be throttled down so far that its specific fuel consumption was poor. Quite apart from this, everyone could see that Breguet, which had then not been taken over by Dassault, would find itself in a difficult position if the P.1154 were to win. It was Dassault that had thumbed its nose at the G91, and in 1962 Dassault and De Gaulle seemed to have some very adequate noses ready for the P.1154. What to do? The answer was simple. In April 1962 the assessment team announced that the P.1154 was the 'technical first choice'. At the same time they announced that the Mirage IIIv was of 'equal merit', because of the factors I have already listed. In other words, although the P.1154 was first, the IIIv was certainly not second.

This virtually guaranteed the collapse of the whole house of cards, because it gave everyone a perfect reason for not adopting either aircraft. Most NATO air forces were terribly interested in these new machines that could rise vertically from a boggy field, fly at Mach 2 and carry practically every tactical offensive or defensive weapon. They just couldn't wait to see how everyone else got on with the job of operating them, so that they could then take a considered decision on what they ought to do themselves. By this time the Whitehall scene was not quite as bleak as it had been, and with TSR.2 going full steam ahead it no longer seemed contrary to the laws of nature to buy yet another manned military aeroplane. The P.1154 promised to be an uncommonly fine-looking weapon system. In its nose it had a radar that Ferranti promised would serve in both the air-to-air and ground attack roles, having both a conical scan and ranging mode and a terrain-following mode. In the single-seat cockpit was to be not only a head-up display, by the new breakaway outfit called Specto, but a controller for a lightweight inertial navigation system, a moving-map display, and an advanced weapon control subsystem with an integrated pilot's panel. The powerful BS.100/9 engine would be coupled with an on-board gas-turbine starter giving complete independence of ground power supplies when running in the APU mode. It would carry 30 mm Aden gun pods, 8000 lb of stores manually winched under the thin but tough wings, and have an airframe design life of 3000 hours in battlefield conditions.

It is not to be wondered at that the British government, regarding the P.1154 as a fine horse to back and a potential sales winner not only among the Fifteen Bickering Nations but also in many other countries, should urge the RAF and RN pretty smartly to come up with some draft Operational Requirements of their own so that the project could actually get started. They chose the name Harrier (the original Hawker Harrier was a Jupiter-engined bomber of 1927), to be announced after the first flight. In May 1962, when both ORs were in, the MWDP kindly put up the money (again), this time for a Pegasus rig for PCB trials, aimed squarely at the P.1154. In the following month I received word on 'the grapevine' that a full development contract for the P.1154 (something Hawker had never had on the P.1127 or Kestrel) was about to be signed. And on 18th July 1962 Air Minister Julian Amery announced 'We are proceeding with the first stages of development of the Hawker P.1154 as a Hunter and possibly a Sea Vixen replacement, and are backing the aircraft in NATO.' From the start the admirals had been rather doubtful, because their primary consideration was the air-superiority role, they wanted a 2-hr loiter endurance on station, they wanted to carry a navigator and lots of powerful radar and guided weapons, and also wanted at least one more engine. Apart from this, the 1154 suited them very well.

Obviously Britain's politicians were bent on taking the most publicised leaf out of McNamara's book in attempting a major exercise in commonality. In 1962 this seemed a good idea, and the TFX (see F-111 chapter) sounded marvellous. The contrasting missions of the air force and navy were virtually identical in both countries, and some people thought the only reason the TFX was not a vectored-thrust V/STOL was because the US did not possess the technology. One of the most senior British technical civil servants, a man who utterly scorned the P.1127/Kestrel, suggested 'The P.1154 is in my view the first time since the heyday of Frank Whittle that we have been on the brink of revolutionising military aviation.' Indeed the 1154 seemed to be such powerful competition that it began to be 'knocked' by rivals all over the world, the greatest compliment that can be paid to a programme. I was delighted to read a brochure issued (confidentially, of course, but taking care nobody failed to see it) by Dassault in June 1962. Dassault had managed to bring in Sud-Aviation and Boeing to back up the Mirage IIIv for NATO, and then scored a major win by getting Freddie Page's team at the BAC Military Aircraft Division at Warton to promote special versions for the RAF and Royal Navy in head-on competition with Hawker. This brochure began by assuming that the P.1154 would be bought for the RAF and Royal Navy; each successive page then traced through the predicted train of events that would follow, each of them (on the surface) disconcertingly plausible and convincing; the final page showed the 1966 SBAC show and the mass take-off of the first Mirage IIIv squadron built by BAC. I asked Camm if he had seen it and he said 'Yes . . . if I lived in any other country I'd laugh at it'. What neither of us then would have believed was that in 1969 BAC's chairman, Sir George Edwards, would say 'In the P.1154 Britain was technically and nationally way out in front.'

At the SBAC show dinner in 1962 Amery, now Minister of Aviation, rose to Dassault's bait and proclaimed (with regard to vectored thrust versus composite jet lift) 'Having developed both systems in this country we have come to the firm conclusion that the P.1154 represents the better solution to the NBMR-3 requirement. Whether separate lift engines or vectored thrust represents the best solution for heavier aircraft, such as transports, is another question not yet resolved.' The second comment was highly relevant because, following upon the successful British entries in the NBMR-4 competition (which in the event died natural deaths, as did the NBMR-3 proposals), the British government had decided to fund a V/STOL transport appreciably bigger than the NBMR-4 designs to support the P.1154 in its operations away from bases. This was considered a vital necessity, because it would be ridiculous to have P.1154s dispersed in remote hiding places yet unable to operate because fuel and stores could not reach them. So OR.351 was raised, and eventually Hawker Siddeley's lately formed Avro Whitworth (later Whitworth Gloster) division received a contract for the AW.681, a tremendously impressive vehicle in the C-130 class but powered by four R-R Medway turbofans with switch-in deflectors for highly STOL performance, and with the option of extra lift pods for VTOL. It would have carried a 40000 lb load (or 100 troops) 1500 miles at 500 knots with a take-off run of 1700 feet of earth. If I ever write a book about transports the 681 will make a fine chapter, especially as the US Air Force is now getting round to exactly the same kind of thing with the AMST (Advanced Medium STOL Transport).

Amery went on to claim that, in the field of jet V/STOL, Britain had 'a very long lead over the rest of the world.' He must have been fully aware of Dassault's feverish haste with the IIIv, yet he went out of his way to say, of the P.1154, 'we shall take a considerable time to complete the project study'. In view of the completion of the P.1150 project study early in 1961, and the three large volumes sent to NATO at the beginning of 1962 spelling out the P.1154 in the utmost detail, I began to feel this was foot-dragging for foot-dragging's sake. It was Amery himself who had caused the only major delay to the nationally funded P.1154 programme by insisting on trying to do a common aircraft for the RAF and RN. I am certain he and his advisers were mesmerised by the TFX/F-111, and the subsequent story was a startlingly close parallel with that US programme. 'Commonality' was at first bent and twisted, and was finally thrown out of the window. It was the Navy who suffered most, because their requirement demanded very large internal fuel capacity, notwithstanding the extra length due to the tandem-seat cockpit; the g-a drawing of the P.1154RN more or less gelled late in 1962, with a length of more than 60 feet, a gross weight of 40000 lb and catapult-compatible main landing gears retracting into 'Tupolev-type' pods projecting behind the wings.

By the autumn of 1962 the P.1154RN was being schemed with twin Rolls-Royce RB.168 (Spey) engines. These were arranged side-by-side, with several novel features. Fan air was discharged through a volute leading to a single nozzle on the outboard side, equipped with a rotating cascade deflector. The volutes incorporated PCB, almost a *sine qua non* for supersonic flight. The hot pipes at the rear were even stranger: they had to cross over, so that the left engine discharged through the right rear nozzle and vice versa. This was necessary to allow for the engine-out case. With the hot pipes crossed, loss of one engine in the hovering mode merely made the aircraft sink, whereas with two nozzles blasting on the same side of the very broad box-like fuselage the aircraft would have rolled out of control (though it would have been better off than some composite or multi-engined aircraft with lift applied much further out from the centreline).

The first major submission of the twin-Spey P.1154RN was made in December 1962. Although commonality had (predictably) sunk to a low ebb, the aircraft was very interesting indeed and seemed to me to meet practically every one of the Navy's demands. The 7500 lb-weight engine package was a bit of a box of tricks, and there were clearly going to be engine-change problems (I could not see why each engine could not be pulled out sideways). Rolls-Royce claimed the whole package to be priced lower than the BS.100/9. Dry rating of each RB.168 was 13000 lb, but the installation was based on the use of PCB, and with this operative the gross lift was 38000 lb, compared with a nominal 30000 lb for the BS.100. On the other hand the discharge through four curved ducts and VTO-tailored nozzles degraded the high-altitude performance, the calculated thrust at Mach 2 at the tropopause being 26000 lb compared with 42000 lb for two straight-through Speys with full reheat. The Navy further grumbled that the use of two engines did not give 'twin-engine safety' in the normal sense. Certainly one could fly back to the carrier on one, but the P.1154RN would have a high wing loading and was quite unable to make a conventional landing without engine lift. With one engine out the minimum airspeed on recovery would have exceeded 140 knots, which at P.1154RN weights would have pulled the wires out; with neither engine operative the speed exceeded 170 knots. These speeds are for an aircraft with no weapon load and minimal fuel. Indeed it seemed inescapable that with the twin-Spey package the loss of a single engine inevitably meant a high-speed ditching a mile ahead of the carrier, and smart work by the plane-guard chopper.

Rolls naturally made a great thing of the fact that their scheme used 'a proven engine' (discounting all the peripherals), which Bristol Siddeley countered by pointing out that 'a vast amount of work' would be needed by either installation. As the BS.100 had to be funded for the RAF anyway it was obvious what the MoA thought, and late in March 1963 they chose the BS.100 for both P.1154 versions and actually announced the fact publicly—adding that 'Rolls-Royce will assist Bristol Siddeley'. Doc Hooker told me the two companies held their first meeting on 27 March. He said, off the record, that the chosen BS.100 incorporated a number of components, including some stages of discs and blading, common to the Olympus 22R for TSR.2. Maximum thrust was to be about 35000 lb, 'suitable for an aircraft in the 30000 lb class.' Clearly the admirals were going to have to down-grade their requirement slightly. I also learned that in the first quarter of 1963 Bristol Siddeley had spent over £250,000 on company liability on manufacture and testing of steel and titanium BS.100 and PCB parts as a calculated risk to meet the P.1154 schedule. I began to sense a feeling in industry that the utter failure of the two customer services to agree was hurting the programme, perhaps lethally. Camm said that everything the company suggested was being turned down 'either by the Air Force or by the Navy, and sometimes by both.' At the 1963 Paris Salon wind of this had reached the waspish continentals; a Dassault man said, in a pitying tone of voice, 'The P.1154 could have been a real winner; but what have you accomplished in the past 18 months? Pah! Nothing!' This was not true. During those 18 months the Navy had had a lot of discussions about American Phantoms with Spey engines.

On 30 July 1963 the Minister of Defence, Peter Thorneycroft, gave a briefing on the RN carrier force, saying that *Ark Royal* and *Victorious* would serve 'at least to the end of the 70s', and that *Eagle* and *Hermes* 'can be extended into the 80s'; and the new CVA-01 (the first time I had found the proud RN copying American ship-class designations) of well over 50000 tons would probably see the century out. Someone asked him why such big ships were needed to carry V/STOL aircraft. Instead of pointing out that they would also have to carry CTOL types, Thorneycroft answered 'You can get twice as many into a 50000-ton ship as you can into a 30000-ton ship, for a price about 25 per cent more . . . and the P.1154 is as big as a Sea Vixen anyway.' He then made the startling and very welcome announcement, almost as if he had just thought of it as a casual extra comment, that 'agreement has been reached between the RAF and Royal Navy on a common aircraft, based on the P.1154.' I at once made enquiries of the Naval Air Warfare staff, who came down like a ton of bricks with a very different story. They had obviously been under great pressure to fall into line, and they confidentially let their hair down with their insistence that they needed a navigator (in view of pilot work-load . . . moving carrier, in a different place in the limitless ocean . . . radio silence . . .) and totally different weapon fits (air-to-air mode . . . scanner dish size . . . on-board missile system equipment . . .) and much more fuel than the RAF (the best we're offered is a CAP of 1·7 hours; even the Vixen can do 2·5 . . .). CAP, the combat air patrol, always seemed to call for more fuel than could be provided. I did not then know that the scorned 1·7 hours of the P.1154RN was better than the figure for the Spey-Phantom (and much better still than the endurance of the US Phantom) operated with restricted fuel from the small RN carriers.

In September 1963 Hawker Siddeley received authority to cut metal on the RAF aircraft, which of course had always been one man and one engine and could (I thought) have gone ahead much more than a year earlier. The next thing I saw was that the London newspapers were reporting that the project would be cancelled 'and possibly re-orientated on a long-term basis for the 1970s.' The *Daily Telegraph* announced that Lord Louis Mountbatten, Chief of the Defence Staff, wanted the Phantom for the Royal Navy and that the Treasury had been asked to sanction 60 at a price of £45 million. On 21 November, while Hawker announced that 'no notice of termination has been conveyed to us', and also commented that they wished that holding contracts were not funded on 'such an impossibly short-term basis', Thorneycroft admitted publicly that the programme had 'run into difficulties.' The project study aimed at meeting the combined demands of the RAF and RN, 'with all the implications,' was 'under consideration by the Weapons Development Committee.' To help along the ulcers in the harassed design teams, a twin-RB.168 aircraft for the Navy was again urgently being studied a few days afterwards, while before the new year dawned Thorneycroft had bowed to pressure from the Treasury and demanded a brochure for a single design that would form the 'best compromise' in meeting the needs of both services. A child could see that this would not only be instantly rejected by the Navy, which had earlier rejected custom-built RN versions, but would also go far towards alienating the RAF. I began to wonder what this exercise in total 'commonality' was actually meant to accomplish.

Predictably, the sailors just replied that they wanted the Phantom; indeed they minuted the opinion that 'no other aircraft available offers any hope of meeting the minimum requirement.' So in February 1964 they were allowed to open negotiations in Washington and St Louis, and after an amazing amount of technical bother they finally got a working Spey-Phantom in January 1969. Meanwhile on 27 February 1964 Thorneycroft announced 'The P.1154 has been ordered into full development for the RAF as a ground-attack aircraft capable of someday light interceptor role [*sic*]. . . . It would be a magnificent achievement if we could get a common aircraft in this role for the RAF and Royal Navy—a really genuine effort was made to get this aircraft—our joint judgement was that it was too near the margin . . .' He added 'We should make the simplest and most robust P.1154 we can.' Camm nearly went through the roof when he heard this, because Hawker aircraft are not unnecessarily complicated and weak; he said it could be done in solid cast iron if that would get the programme moving.

After two years of frustrating argument the 1154 actually did begin to move ahead, and by August 1964 Air Staff Requirement 356 had wrapped up every detail except some vital points on the nav/attack system, and the first aircraft was taking shape in the jigs. The definitive BS.100 ran at Patchway on 30 October 1964, P. F. Green (chief engineer, aero) saying 'beautiful first run.' But by this time a Labour government had been elected, and it came into office determined to do away with British military aircraft. This was not because it believed in the 1957 doctrine but because the Labour politicians had worked up a passionate hatred of British planemakers, who—they declared—were draining the public of hundreds of millions of pounds in building complicated and expensive aeroplanes that could be replaced by 'cheaper' types already in production in the United States. On 21–22 November 1964 Prime Minister Wilson had the service chiefs come to Chequers for a 'defence reappraisal' which was intended to see what British programmes could be replaced by US ones and which could simply be done away with. After four months in which the tension in the air could almost be seen, the P.1154 and its partner WG.681 (ex-AW.681) were curtly terminated on 2 February 1965, just as Keith Thompson of the *Daily Express* had forecast on 17 December 1963.

In explanation Mr Wilson, after emphasizing the 'wobble' in the programme caused by the Navy, said that the idea that the P.1154 should replace the Hunter was 'not a practical proposition. It is not so much the question of cost . . . the problem here is that on these present estimated requirements, and on the latest realistic estimate of the remaining life of Hunter aircraft, the P.1154 will not be in service in time to serve as a Hunter replacement. In these circumstances, and on defence grounds alone—quite apart from the cost argument—it will be necessary to extend the late government's purchasing programme for Phantoms and to use this aircraft as a partial replacement for the Hunter . . . we are urgently examining the possibility of manufacturing, or at any rate of assembling, them. . . .' Seen from almost a decade later it is even more obvious than it seemed at the time that Mr Wilson's administration, having decided to replace the P.1154 with the American Phantom, then had to look round for a reason. Most of his public were unable to question the statement that the Hunters simply wouldn't last out until the P.1154 was ready. He must have had some funny expert advisers. Almost every one of these Hunters has been rebuilt by Hawker Siddeley for a long period of combat service with nine overseas air forces. These Hunters are now very busy indeed from Chile to Singapore, where Mr Wilson can see them at least up to 1980. (As I write, one squadron is being extremely aggressive over Beirut.)

At a subsequent press conference I asked Roy Jenkins, Aviation Minister, whether Mr Wilson knew that the Hunters were not really falling apart, and could be rebuilt for at least a further 15-year period of use. He replied 'The Prime Minister only gave one of the reasons for cancelling the P.1154. There are many others. It would have been excessively expensive . . . geared only to British requirements . . . shown no serious prospect of improving our export picture . . . not in service until 1970–71.' In March 1966 Defence Minister Denis Healey amended the latter figure to '1972, and it could well have been later'; and he said 'the estimates have almost doubled in under three years.' Quite obviously it was a case of 'Don't tell us the facts, we've made up our mind.' At an average unit cost of $15 million I suppose you could say the F-111 was 'excessively expensive', because that is four times the unit cost of a P.1154; and if you were the contracts manager at Kingston with a piece of paper with '1969' written on it, you couldn't really hold your own press conference and say Mr Healey had made a mistake; and I suppose you could say lots of other combat aircraft were designed just to meet one nation's needs; and if you cancel it, then it certainly won't help the export picture (and wasn't the P.1154 supposed to be bought by practically all the NATO nations?).

A small row developed on the sidelines when Hawker Siddeley said it calculated the cancellation would cause 14000 redundancies during the year. Roy Jenkins smartly 'corrected' this estimate to 7700 and George Brown issued a strong rebuttal, in the course of which he said 'the government has made it absolutely plain that it will arrange for any manpower, any resources, any factories which are released, to be used for other work.' At this the Hawker Siddeley chairman, Sir Arnold Hall—a man with whom I am not prepared to take issue on any matter of fact—calmly repeated that the figure of 14000 was based on a detailed survey of the Hawker Siddeley workload over the coming year and was perfectly correct. At which a group of Labour MPs promptly tabled a Commons motion 'That this House is of the opinion that aircraft firms which threaten mass dismissals unjustified by the circumstances shall be considered to have failed the nation and to be suitable subjects for public ownership.'

In those days this notion of the British planemakers having 'failed the nation' was a cherished one in the Labour heart. The hatred of the planemakers was a psychological phenomenon of deep and lasting interest. I have discussed it with many Labour politicians—who today, on the whole, would much rather forget it because the damage this hatred did is now indisputable—and some of them are candid enough to agree with me that to a considerable degree the whole thing was deliberately contrived for political ends. Anyone in politics will tell you that it helps enormously if you can have a few baddies whom you can tear to shreds in election speeches and generally blame for everything from the economic situation to the weather. In 1964 an obvious target was the aircraft industry. In reality this industry consisted of patriotic and dedicated engineers desperately trying to build the hardware that had been ordered by an impossible financial and political environment. Perhaps 'impossible' is not the best word, but the inability of the customer to specify what it wanted, to adhere to the specification, to monitor the programme and to manage everything in a competent way so that the production article was delivered on schedule and at an agreed price, did make success impossible. As a result the planemakers had a hard row to hoe. It was simplicity itself for the Labour politicians to hold them up to the public as the villains, or fools, who were wasting outrageous sums of money in their fumbling attempts to build useless aircraft that nobody really wanted. As the public were not very expert in this field it was simple to claim that these British aircraft were not very good, and that they should be done away with. In fact, for a major programme of any kind to be cancelled in midstream ought to be a wholly exceptional and very rare event, but the new Labour administration in 1964–65 made it seem a natural and inevitable thing. For years, at every Labour conference, there had been a call for this wicked industry to be nationalized. Obviously it was easier to do this if you first took away its work.

What worried me more than these dark ideological threats was that the government had knocked away its existing programme before it had signed anything on a new one. It had no idea how many Phantoms it would need, what their standard of build would be, or what they would cost. It had deliberately stripped itself of every shred of bargaining power and then proposed to go to the US government (who in turn would talk to McDonnell Douglas) with a long list of Phantom change orders, every one of them unpriced. Mr Wilson had no idea what the RAF Phantom programme would cost when he announced that the switch from the P.1154 would 'save at least £300 million over the next ten years.' Nobody else knew either, so they couldn't say he was wrong. In the event, the estimates of time and cost for developing the Spey-Phantom could hardly have been more inaccurate, but that is another story. The total write-off on the P.1154 and BS.100 amounted to a remarkably low £25 million; it wasn't really an expensive programme, and if it had not been abandoned it would have been a world-wide success.

On 21 July 1965 Denis Healey assured the Commons that the Phantom —which, by the way, was designed in 1955–57—would 'give the RAF a supersonic aircraft of the nature it requires four years earlier than under the former government's programme.' I can only comment here that the RAF were scheduled to receive the P.1154 in 1968–69, and the first RAF Phantom unit was formed in 1969. What Mr Healey did not comment upon was that we were right back to 2½ kilometres of concrete from which we had spent ten years trying to escape.

In fact, when Mr Wilson announced the termination of the P.1154 he rather surprised everyone by saying 'We believe that there is an urgent need for an operational version of the P.1127. . . . As soon as it can be negotiated, a contract will be placed for a limited development programme so that the RAF can have, by the time they need it, an aircraft which will in fact be the first in the field, with vertical take-off for close support of our land forces. . . . We are also going into the question of further R&D into this to see whether it can be boosted into something much more substantial.' Obviously the 'P.1127' was still regarded as not quite adequate. In fact as soon as he heard Mr Wilson's proposal the former Air Minister, Hugh Fraser, got to his feet and helpfully proclaimed that the P.1127 'from a military point of view is a toy, unable to carry any weapons, unable to have a great range and unable to fly above sonic speed.' It was in the same month that a British university debated the motion 'That this house considers this nation to have a death-wish'. The motion was carried.

Even Dobbie (Sir Roy Dobson, HS director) seemed anything but elated. He moodily said 'Thorneycroft came down to Dunsfold 2½ years ago. . . . I thought there would be an order for a wing of P.1127s so that the services could get used to VTO. Absolutely nothing happened.' Even now there was no order, but merely a promise of further development. In effect what happened was that the Men from the Ministry (which this week was called Mintech) called at Kingston and said 'You mustn't build the P.1154 (and, by the way, we hate British aircraft). But you can take some of the nav/attack system out of the P.1154 and see how it fits in the P.1127, with an uprated engine. We then might buy it for the RAF.'

Camm, John Fozard, Ralph Hooper (who had drawn the original g-a. of the P.1127 in 1957) and their project team lost no time trying to establish a standard of build for the 'P.1127 RAF'. On 19 February 1965 Hawker received a contract for six development aircraft, XV276–281. Settling the specification was impossible until it was known what they would carry. The MoD in turn were uncertain just how to draft the Operational Requirement and in the end re-issued OR.356, the final document for the P.1154, with most of the numbers down-graded to match the expected abilities of the P.1127 RAF. And these abilities rested squarely on engine thrust. Despite (indeed, to some extent because of) their great effort on the BS.100, Bristol Siddeley had never stopped developing the Pegasus, and told Camm that 19000 lb—without PCB—would be forthcoming during 1966. It was this, more than any other single fact, that made the P.1127 RAF a viable 'replacement' for the P.1154.

It would have been convenient if the P.1127 RAF could have used the same airframe as the Kestrel. Perhaps surprisingly, by the late spring of 1965 it was clear that it would have to differ as much from the Kestrel as the latter did from the original P.1127, and in fact 95 per cent of the drawings were new. Not only were many parts changed in shape but much of the airframe was of newer concept in materials and manufacturing methods. I began to try to compile a list of parts of structure which were obviously altered, but gave up when I failed to find anything that stayed the same! Even items that superficially look the same, such as the landing gear, were actually totally different in capability. And another factor that does not show too much is that the P.1127 RAF was designed from the start to fit into a modern and highly professional Air Force environment that could lay down specific requirements for reliability and maintainability and knew how aircraft should be engineered to perform well under the most adverse field conditions. In this case, sustained operations might have to be mounted from a base that was nothing more than a sod field, a small wood and a few tents. This affected—say Hawker—'almost every engineering feature in the design.' In retrospect, I wish it could have been designated P.1155, or some higher number, because it was a completely new design. Making people—such as Hugh Fraser—think it was just an old P.1127 was surely bad psychology.

By the summer of 1965 a standard of build had been generally agreed upon. Almost every item of the P.1154 nav/attack system had been incorporated except for the radar. There was room for this in a re-profiled P.1127 nose but it was a very clever set that would cost a great deal, and it was the least-developed of all the 1154 avionics—indeed, Ferranti had not even received the main development contract. But Ferranti still made a massive contribution with the complete FE.541 navigation and weapon-aiming system, comprising inertial platform, nav display and computer, nav control, weapon-aiming computer, ballistics box, hand controller, present-position computer and power unit. The ballistics box, a new item to me in 1965, is an electronic module into which 'ballistic plugs' can be inserted for gunfire and for selected types of air-launched store, to fit the dynamic characteristics of the system to the armament carried on any given mission. Backing up this comprehensive system was to be an improved HUD by Specto, which was then still an *enfant terrible* but later was gobbled up by the respectable Smiths empire; and Smiths themselves supplied the air-data computer. By 1973 the first Harrier with a Ferranti LRMTS (laser ranger and marked-target seeker) was also doing so well that I expect most RAF Harriers will grow blunt noses.

Whereas the Kestrel had had a single hard point under each wing, and never carried weapons in service, the P.1127 RAF was planned with four wing stations and three under the fuselage. At first, for any practical range, it was doubtful that all would be loaded; but it was obviously sensible to build them in from the start. To quote some figures, the empty equipped weight of the aircraft was found to be about 12000 lb and the VTO gross weight about 16000 lb, so this left only about 4000 lb for fuel, guns, bombs and other stores (later the VTO gross rose encouragingly). Much bigger loads of fuel and armament could be carried using additional wing lift in the STO or 'rolling take-off' mode, and a 4000 lb weapon load was fixed as the limit at entry to service (which was planned for 1969). No provision was made for internal armament, but one of the options was a pair of 30 mm Aden gun pods on the left and right fuselage hard points. An FR probe was to be provided as a bolt-on option for ferrying, together with extra bolt-on wing tips.

Although I doubt that lack of a production order made much difference, many people professed surprise that the Defence Review (White Paper) of February 1966 merely reaffirmed that a production order would be placed. In the Commons debate the following month Sir John Eden asked 'Why is the Pegasus still being supported by month-to-month development contracts? Is this "full speed ahead" on an important programme?' (Answer: a massive silence.) At Hanover in May 1966 Bill Bedford had nothing to fly but the low-powered Kestrel prototype. Despite this he put on a flying demonstration that was nothing less than breathtaking. It was the first of many impressive shows with much more powerful Pegasus engines, and it had seasoned air attachés and Luftwaffe generals in almost non-stop applause—not the polite kind but the really excited sort. On 31 August 1966 he flew a much refined machine: XV276, the first pre-production P.1127 RAF. He got it airborne in the late evening after a round-the-clock hustle, and thus just made the scheduled date. Aerodynamically this machine was almost identical to the proposed production aircraft, but few of the operational mission systems were yet fitted.

By this time Hawker had received an ITP on long-lead items for production aircraft, and at last it was clear that failure to agree on contract terms was not going to become a reason for delay. At Hanover the rumour had been that the P.1127 RAF buy would, initially at least, comprise 60 aircraft plus sixteen two-seat conversion trainers with combat capability. Over in California, on 30 November 1966, Northrop's zeal to push the P.1127 was at last rewarded by a $330,000 contract from the US Air Force to provide 13 months of support to a flight-test programme with Kestrels at Edwards and elsewhere. It was in the course of this programme, using the old 15200 lb engine on a hot day, that the world record time to 10000 feet was several times broken. The DoD stated that, as a matter of policy, it would not provide backing for an officially observed record with 'a foreign airplane'. To everyone's regret Hawker at home were simply too busy to set a record themselves. Finally S/Ldr T. L. Lecky-Thompson did it on 5 January 1971 in a standard service machine, reaching 9000 m (29527 ft) in 1 min 44·7 sec and 12000 m (39370 ft) in 2 min 22·7 sec.

Early in 1967 the P.1127 RAF was at last named: Harrier, the name originally chosen for the P.1154. And the initial buy was fixed at 60 Harrier GR.1s (GR signifying 'ground attack, reconnaissance') and 10 Harrier T.2s with dual control. Later these orders were increased, first to 77 + 12 and then (in 1973) to 93 + 15.

July 1967 was an interesting month on two counts. One event was Israel's amazing 'six-day war', in which the vulnerability of airfields was dramatically driven home for all to see. Bob Rodwell returned from that campaign convinced that the black boxes of the forthcoming Harrier were a waste of time. Bob is a forceful advocate, and I can still hear him arguing that the Israelis had needed no nav/attack systems at all to find and clobber practically every hostile aircraft within 500 miles. As he cannot answer back as I write, I think he was applying the lessons of a brilliant campaign to different circumstances. The RAF cannot count on superb VMC weather, terrain where a 40-gallon drum stands out like a sore thumb, camouflage confined to a few crude decoys, and ECM that were almost non-existent. The sort of warfare the RAF might conceivably get involved in is utterly different, in which the chap up at the sharp end needs all the help he can get. The other July 1967 event was an eye-opening air display by the Soviet Union at Domodedovo at which, among other jet-lift aircraft, appeared an odd Yakovlev machine (NATO code name 'Free-hand') which, though not necessarily proving very much, did have the useful effect of making vectored-thrust more respectable (because there are many people who lack the courage of their own national convictions but instantly appreciate the same thing when it is done by others).

In August Duncan Simpson flew the sixth development aircraft to Rome, landing vertically, and after refuelling went on to complete tropical trials at the NATO base at Sigonella, Sicily. The Italian naval interest, that I commented upon much earlier has never flagged. In October 1967 Hugh Merewether flew another development Harrier out to the Med. and completed very successful trials from the helicopter platform of the anchored cruiser *Andrea Doria*, which measures just 98 × 56 feet. I was assured that Harriers could operate from platforms 'very considerably smaller'. But it was the HMS *Blake* trial, of August 1969, more than any of the many other occasions when Harriers have gone to sea, that really made the world's navies look at this aircraft very keenly—especially after the Egyptians used a Soviet cruise-type missile to sink the Israeli destroyer *Eilat*. The *Blake* was moving, and rolling in winds up to 40 knots.

The first production Harrier GR.1, XV738, was flown by Simpson on 28 December 1967. Early in 1968 the press were invited down to Dunsfold to see (and hear!) the six development Harriers and the unpainted first production machine, performing at a distance of about 20 yards. It was stated that the entire nav/attack system was in full flight development, that various loads up to thousand-pounders had been dropped or launched, that successful dry contacts had been made with all three refuelling points on Victors up to 40000 ft, that 50000 ft had been exceeded, and that Pegasus thrust would soon increase from 19200 lb to 20500 lb and then to 21500 lb, making a big increase in possible loads for VTO or STO missions. Bob Lickley, HSA chief military executive, quoted prices 'in the band £750,000 to £1 million, depending on quantity and equipment.' One of the unexpected items of equipment was a neat recce pod, carried on the centreline, mounting one vertical and four oblique optical cameras.

At the 1968 SBAC show there was a mild flurry at the Hawker Siddeley chalet when three officers of the US Marine Corps walked in the door and said 'We're interested in the Harrier. We'd like to evaluate it . . . Could we please study the Pilot's Notes?' The Marine Corps buys its aircraft through the Navy, and has sometimes tended to be fobbed off with Dad's old boots. Yet the Marines have a history of aviation pioneering. In 1947 they worked out just how helicopters could be used to best effect in an amphibious landing, and by 1951 the principle of 'vertical envelopment' had been brought to a fine art. By 1960 they were trying to do something similar in the jet age, but found the only answer the SATS airfield (Short Airfield for Tactical Support). They were becoming tired of filling Liberty Ships with aluminium planking, gas-turbine catapults, arrester wires and other gear and then using about 1000 men for three weeks to bolt it all together. Hawker seemed to have some sort of combat airplane that didn't need an airfield at all. Behind all this was the fact that even the most senior Marine is a 'Grunt'—a tough, mud-covered infantryman—who has to fight for the best equipment and yet has less political power than the bigger services when it comes to votes and appropriations.

It was the master-mind of General G. McCutcheon that, early in 1968, rediscovered the Harrier—which, as the XV-6A, had been flying in the US since early 1965—and schemed the grand design of the Marines becoming an all-V/STOL force by 1980. Thus it was that, in September 1968, Brig-Gen Johnson, USMC, and two test pilots, Col Tom Miller and Lt-Col Bud Baker, came knocking on the door of the chalet at Farnborough. Soon Miller was airborne, and he and Baker returned to Washington full of enthusiasm. At Christmas 1968 the Corps publicly announced its interest, and stated it had received DoD approval for an initial buy of 12 aircraft, subject to budget funding. In January 1969 the Defense Budget emerged without funds for the British aircraft, which had been slashed in the final Pentagon cuts to keep within the White House ceiling on expenditure. This seemed to kill the Marines' hopes of buying 'about 100'. And a second blow was that in the same month Maj Charles R. Rosberg was killed flying a Harrier at Dunsfold.

This was the first fatal accident in the entire programme. What went largely unnoticed at the time was that Rosberg was an officer in the US Air Force, which had decided the Harrier merited an evaluation. Their report was almost lyrical, and in no way coloured by the death of one of their evaluators (which need not have happened). Yet a further event in January 1969 was the Preliminary Evaluation of the US Navy, whose pilots and engineers from Pax River explored what the aircraft could do at Dunsfold and Boscombe and departed deeply impressed, even though most of the new VIFF manoeuvres described later had not been invented.

Operations with the Harrier began (again on the RAF's birthday) on 1 April 1969 when a GR.1 was taken on charge by the Harrier Conversion Unit at Dunsfold. Soon the HCU moved to Wittering and American accents were heard at the Huntingdonshire base as Maj Jacob E. Iles USMC completed the course and started teaching others. In London a full US liaison team and Harrier Project Office was set up at Mintech. During the rest of 1969 the RAF and USMC accomplished much. The biggest headlines were gained in May 1969 in the Transatlantic Air Race, when two RAF Harriers flew from the centre of London to the centre of New York and back. The pad-to-pad distance was 3490 miles, from Somers Town coal yard, next to St Pancras Station, to the Bristol Basin, Manhattan (which 25 years earlier had been filled with rubble from buildings blitzed in 1940 in Bristol, home of the Pegasus). The times were 5 hr 57 min westbound, the fastest recorded in that direction by any entrant, and 5 hr 31 min eastbound. Late in the year the RAF's No. 1 (F) squadron (motto *In Omnibus Princeps:* Always First) became fully operational. It soon gained immense operational experience in dropping things, shooting at things and, above all, in dispersed-site exercises.

Meanwhile in Washington the Marines finally got Congress to sanction their first buy of AV-8A Harriers, which at first were almost identical to the GR.1 apart from having a different IFF, some wiring put in to mate with Sidewinder air-to-air missiles, an altimeter and HUD reading inches of mercury instead of millibars, and sundry other minor mods that showed by their triviality how adequate the original aircraft had been. Indeed Gen Homer S. Hill, DCOS (Air) of the USMC, when grilled by Congress on his disquieting insistence on a foreign product, described the Harrier as 'very clean; by comparison to other aircraft that we've examined over the years, the aircraft had very few discrepancies and corrective measures were already under way.' It was on this occasion that Hill quietly answered 'Yes, sir' to a succession of questions from Senators who simply refused to believe it, like the yokel who went to the zoo and saw a giraffe. Hill had said 'An aircraft which is deployed and based as simply as a helicopter but which packs the punch of conventional attack aircraft is going to have a far-reaching effect on military aviation.'

The initial buy was 12 aircraft built in Britain. But there are logistic, emotional and, to some degree, financial reasons for making military hardware at home, and in mid-1969 McDonnell Douglas took out a manufacturing licence. By this time the Marines had fixed their total AV-8A force at 114 aircraft, and the US firm expected to tool up to make the AV-8A for the Marines and any other US customer. The plan was to start delivering in 1971, using a high proportion of British-made hardware, and to reach 100 per cent US content by 1975. In the event it didn't work out this way. Despite all sorts of confused pressures in Congress, from people who either didn't like a 'foreign product' or else wanted it if it was home-built, the extra costs involved in US tooling for small-batch production made such a choice unattractive. Three subsequent buys of 18, 30 and a further 30 took the 1972 total to 90. Then the Fiscal 1973, and supposedly last, procurement, was expected to be for 24, to reach the planned force level of 114. In fact the Marines devoted this budget to 12 AV-8As ($58·2 million, including ground equipment and spares) and 8 TAV-8A trainers ($53·6 million), making the total 102 single-seaters and 8 two-seaters. This equips four squadrons, plus a training unit with a mix of AVs and TAVs. McDonnell Douglas provides some service support for the Hawker product, just as Hawker Siddeley does for the McDonnell Douglas Phantom in British service, but hardware is made in Britain.

Marine Corps operations began in earnest in 1971. The testing organization for new hardware trying to enter the inventory of the US Navy or Marine Corps is the Board of Inspection and Survey. The AV-8A waltzed through its BIS trials at Pax River in February–March 1971. The first squadron, VMA-513, formed at Beaufort, S Carolina, in April 1971, and the following winter took part in a major exercise at China Lake, Calif, and at sea aboard USS *Guam*. In March 1972 a sortie-rate validation test was held under the name Battle Cry, and this is worth a brief report. The plan was to disperse six aircraft to various unprepared sites for ten hectic days, to fly four sorties per aircraft per day except for a randomly chosen 'surge day' when each AV-8A had to fly six sorties. This is a stern task, because in such a test a sortie means a properly planned combat mission, with the accurate delivery of up to 4000 lb of live ordnance, not just a few seconds with daylight under the wheels. In the event the average sortie rate was higher than that planned for the 'surge day', and on the surge day itself the planned 36 sorties were flown plus a further 25! There was no engine unserviceability and no problems due to FOD (foreign-object damage) or jet blast on the rough ground. Altogether 384 missions were flown from all kinds of austere places, the whole thing being done just as it would in real warfare, with scrupulous security and camouflage, and front-line supply and communication systems. This proved the intriguing concept of 'ground loiter': an AV-8A can be at instant readiness, yards from its target, with the wheels on the ground!

Bogue Field, the geographical HQ for Battle Cry, was the centre for sustained military airpower as rough, tough and effective as any in history. The Marines needed something like this if only to show outsiders that what they had bought was diametrically opposite to 'a toy, unable to carry any weapons . . .' From the points of view of range, speed and load the Harrier in its initial form is very similar to a late-model A-4 Skyhawk. It is also about the same size. On the other hand it has massive differences, notably in having an engine of twice the power, which can push on the airframe in different directions. One little-publicised result is that the Harrier can attack at high-subsonic speed with the engine throttled back to 75 per cent power. Trials in the US with an AV-8A in formation with an A-4M, A-6A, A-7A, A-7E and F-4J, all gave the uncanny result of obvious black dots boring in at a steady 405 mph, propelled by visible or even sooty trails, to be joined at close range by a very tiny dot that had previously been unnoticed. The Harrier has earned a reputation as 'The Invisible Fighter'. Even at close range it is often impossible to see the wings, so you cannot predict which way it is turning until it has done it. More than this, it can turn in ways no combat aircraft ever did before, as I will describe in a moment.

When the RAF bought the Harrier they bought a 'ground attack and recce' aircraft. They have learned to use it well in these roles. Many eminent people have reported the RAF experience, notably the ACAS (Ops), Air Vice-Marshal R. L. Wade, in the 2nd Camm Lecture in 1973, although the British tradition of secrecy prohibits open discussion of all the vital numbers involved such as maintenance man-hours per flight hour, defect rates, and just how many aircraft have crashed, and how many losses have been due to reasons other than birdstrikes. Big fan engines at low level swallow lots of birds. A Commons question did prise out the fact that in a nine-month period in 1972 there were 12 severe RAF birdstrikes, and that Harriers were being retro-fitted with a manual fuel control system to facilitate relights after bird-ingestion. Fortunately as the AV-8A is used by the United States we do have complete figures available from that side. Indeed I can tell the British public that they have paid 80 per cent of the aggregate R&D cost of £256 million (the US paid 13 per cent and the Germans 7 per cent), because Congress asked Admiral Gaddis, USN, to tell them. Her Majesty's Commons can ask people such questions until they are blue in the face and get no answer other than 'It is not policy to tell you—unless it suits some party-political purpose'.

In contrast to the RAF, the Marines bought the AV-8A as a 'fighter' in the vague portmanteau-type meaning that this word has come to have. Indeed, to get it, they had to give up two squadrons of Phantoms. So they have been more enterprising than the RAF in finding out just what the Harrier can do. (The RAF will not like this, and certainly life is more difficult for them. In Germany their flight operations are so ridiculously constricted they often cannot go higher than 3000 feet, and can only just about fly beyond the perimeter fence.) One of the first things the Marines asked was how far they could do VIFF (Vectoring in Forward Flight), an intriguing blend of variable brute force, aerodynamic science and a new sort of pilot art that was first explored by NASA at Langley with a Kestrel. When the AV-8A was first delivered it was, like the RAF machine, subject to limitations on engine thrust and nozzle angle as flight speed was increased, so that at 300 knots (345 mph) IAS the limit was 80 per cent power at 45° nozzle angle. Today Hawker Siddeley has cleared the use of any angle at 80 per cent fan rpm up to 500 knots IAS—so the US press reports (such things are secret in Britain).

This makes today's Harrier a fantastic thing, especially if you are an enemy fighter pilot trying to shoot it down. Thanks to the Marines' vital interest in how the AV-8A can stand up in aerial combat over an enemy beachhead or battlefield, the Harrier has been wrung out against every fighter in sight in the United States. I believe one aircraft almost contrived to stay with it; this was an obsolete FJ-4 Fury with uprated Sapphire engine and stripped down to light weight. Everything else was completely foxed. In fact I am told 'those Phantom jocks are the most amazed guys in the Western Hemisphere.' Any experienced fighter pilot gets to know what his target is doing or is about to do, and can sense things in advance. How does he feel when the target suddenly shoots past him apparently going backwards? Or when, having slowed in a tighter and tighter turn at slower and slower speed, until the Phantom is just about to stall, the target, without changing its attitude, suddenly jumps a few hundred feet vertically? There are countless tricks involving all sorts of manoeuvres in the vertical and horizontal planes that the Harrier can pull that can suddenly put it on the tail of the fighter that was about to shoot it down. I am told you can deliberately let your adversary get closer and closer, with his missiles about to be launched or guns about to fire; then, having judged the exact moment, you just flick round a few square corners or 'impossible' loops or split-S turns and proceed to clobber the poor chap in any way you choose. One Marine squadron programmed the AV-8A and a certain excellent Warsaw Pact fighter on their computer and were interested to discover what would happen if they should meet 'for real'. According to the Marines 'It would spoil their whole day.' I might add that you do not need to shoot down the enemy. There are many Harrier manoeuvres guaranteed to put a conventional aircraft straight into the surface of the Earth if he is fool enough to try to follow through.

All this leads one to the obvious question 'What about a true fighter Harrier, with a bigger wing, raised all-round-vision canopy and special air-to-air radar and weapons?' The answer is clearly, 'Well, what about it?' In 1940 Miles Aircraft flew a fighter, made of non-strategic wood, faster and more manoeuvrable than the Hurricane, with more ammunition for its eight guns and much greater endurance on patrol, just 65 days after getting permission to proceed. Today it would take 65 weeks to get a policy decision on what to do. After all, the Harrier was not supposed to be an air-superiority fighter, and it is most inconvenient when people put forward new ideas. So maybe I had better take refuge in the fact that Hawker and Rolls-Royce have McDonnell Douglas and Mr Pratt on the same side (Pratt & Whitney are collaborating in further development of the Pegasus). In May 1972 a demonstrator engine incorporating some features of the 25000 lb Pegasus 15 easily exceeded its design rating within five hours of first running. This is just what the doctor ordered, and hopefully this engine can be put into production before too many more years have gone by.

This engine is a natural for another Harrier, or Super Harrier, derivative which is intended to operate over the most distant oceans. The thinking behind such an aircraft stems from a fundamental series of problems concerning today's giant carriers. Traditionally the carrier has been the way a major nation maintains a 'presence' in a disputed or troubled part of the world (unless it happens to be Tibet). The Labour decision to eliminate British carriers as a symbol of expensive Imperialist power may well have been the right decision for the wrong reasons. The trouble with the giant carrier is that it is a giant. When the *Big E* steams over the horizon you can almost feel the menace, even if you happen to be on the same side. It almost invites someone to have a bash at it. There is no civil population to cause complications, and the most ham-fisted sprog pilot in the latest upstart air force could hardly fail to hit it. More than this, giant carriers cost enormous sums to build and operate, and it is becoming difficult to find crews to man them. In the past two years even the most dyed-in-the-wool Big Ship Admiral has been forced to see the sense in making use of V/STOL aircraft operating from smaller vessels. That one needs a 'presence' is not in question. The presence is needed not only near scenes of riot and revolution but to keep open the world's shipping lanes, which took nine of every ten tons sent to Vietnam, and by 1985 will carry two-thirds of America's strategic trade.

The US Navy's answer is the Sea Control Ship, a low-key carrier without either catapults or wires, carrying an assortment of weapons to defend the surrounding region against enemy aircraft or ships (and, one hopes, against enemy missiles—why not?). A high-performance V/STOL aircraft would be an obvious item for inclusion, and the only big question is how far it ought to strike enemy ships as well as enemy aircraft. Rockwell International is working on a very interesting contender, the XFV-12A, tailored to fulfil Sea Control requirements and to fly as a conventional aircraft (cheaply assembled using modified bits of other aircraft) in April 1974. In October 1974 the definitive XFV-12A was scheduled to fly with very advanced and complex lift systems installed. Against this is almost certain to be pitted the Advanced Harrier, jointly proposed by the two British and two US airframe and engine partners, which could offer a simpler solution much sooner. The only completely new feature of this US Navy aircraft would be a supercritical wing, giving increased lift and possibly containing more fuel. This is one of those situations where somebody has to make a considered judgement on what rival proposals will actually cost in terms of money, time and technical risk.

In Britain there is only one horse in the race, and even this may never see the starting gate go up. The Sea Harrier would be matched to the Through-Deck Cruiser, which would serve not only as a flat-top but also as a command ship and so would be somewhat bigger than the US Sea Control Ship. Obviously a Sea Harrier would have maximum commonality with the RAF Harrier of today, but I cannot see any time-wasting 'crunch situation' being allowed to develop on this account. One P.1154 lesson is more than enough, and there is no reason to doubt that the Sea Harrier (or, as it is called in Whitehall, the Maritime Harrier) will learn as much as possible from the P.1154 without falling into the earlier programme's problems of incompatibility. The airframe is likely to be a minimal modification, though if the Pegasus 15 is funded this will undoubtedly be used because of the range/payload benefit. In the nose will be a radar, and late in May 1973 Ferranti were awarded a study contract for 'a new intercept, search and strike radar' for the Sea Harrier. This multi-role mission is a very difficult one, and I know some experts who say that ideally it needs two radars, one optimised for aerial combat and the other for surface attack. The new Ferranti radar incorporates lightweight techniques proved with the Seaspray radar of the Lynx helicopter. It will owe less to the radar of the P.1154, and very little to the radar of TSR.2. Cancellation of the TSR.2, it will be remembered, triggered the wail that henceforth Britain would be out of the combat-aircraft radar business. My own view is that Britain is indeed likely to be out of this business if development is not accelerated on phased-array sets with LSI (large-scale integration) microcircuits, with multi-target track-while-scan, such as are already in production in the United States for the latest generation of fighters.

Hopefully the build-standard for the Sea Harrier will have been agreed by the time this book is published. I would be surprised if all were to be two-seaters; there is a continuing debate on the need for a navigator at sea, and in the Foreword I suggest that even one man on board may soon be judged too many. But if ever a tactical aeroplane did need men on board the Sea Harrier is it, because this is a very demanding spectrum of missions. Obviously the weapon options must include air-to-air missiles, as well as surface-attack missiles such as Harpoon, Exocet or Martel (flown from a Harrier in February 1973 but not used by RAF Harriers at present). There is no doubt in my mind the Sea Harrier could prove of enormous value, but the small number involved does raise problems of cost and credibility. Fortunately several other countries could use just such an aircraft, and I shall be surprised if there are not quite a lot of ship-based Harriers by 1980. Too bad that, as I write, everyone is so eager to impress upon me that no decisions have yet been taken.

In 1974, when I proof-read this book, progress almost seemed to be in reverse. Britain has a Labour government eager to chop defence expenditure below a level that is already frighteningly inadequate, while in the United States the immense enthusiasm for the Harrier is tempered by an official party-line that it is foreign and must therefore always be regarded as a sort of limited interim prototype that people can play with while home industry produces the real thing. But just under the surface is the knowledge that the Harrier is almost exactly right as the basis for tomorrow's multi-role V/STOL. Early in 1974 VMF-513 embarked on the helicopter carrier *Guam* (simulating a Sea Control Ship) and demonstrated the amazing speed with which Harriers can lay sonobuoy barriers in a completely new role: ASW (anti-submarine warfare). This is despite the fact the carrier has to watch the Harrier's IFF transmission on radar and guide it to the right places. The view of the Navy is 'Already the AV-8A can get sonobuoys out faster than anything else. The whole thing just cries out for development into a proper system.' This proper system would be the AV-16 Advanced Harrier mentioned earlier. It deserves the most rapid funding possible. Maybe the British government could see if the Russians would like to take over the UK part of the programme?

It was as late as 1969 that development went ahead on a tandem-seat Harrier, and it proved a surprisingly tricky job to arrive at the best shape and size for the new fin and rudder. There are many other changes, and though the two-seat versions are mainly used for pilot-conversion they have full weapon capability. The two-seaters could derive even greater benefit from the Pegasus 15 engine, because of their increased airframe weight and the need to carry ballast when flown solo. In 1971 one additional two-seater was slipped into the production line, assembed from parts freely supplied by Hawker, Rolls and their suppliers, on an embodiment-loan basis. The result was the most attractive Harrier yet, bearing civil registration G-VTOL. It has been seen in various 'civil' and 'military' paint schemes and enables Hawker to give demonstrations, to let potential customers evaluate the aircraft for themselves, and also to run necessary trials programmes in a way that would be out of the question if they did not own the aircraft. Lots of interesting people have flown G-VTOL and I hope lots more will.

This tale has turned out surprisingly long. I have not even mentioned the saga of how the Swiss decided they wanted to replace the old Venom, wrote a specification for a CTOL that could take two tons to Moscow, correctly decided in 1972 the best answer to this spec. was the Corsair and never asked themselves whether the spec. was right in the first place.* Neither have I mentioned the endless series of questions everyone who does not know the Harrier always wants to ask. To anybody who believes it must be terribly 'inefficient', or has to pay some great 'penalty' because of its big engine for V/STOL, or who simply thinks there must be some other hidden snag, I can only say that Hawker Siddeley have written all this down in a book called 'The Harrier—Military Misconceptions'. Far from being a mere sales puff this is a highly numerical document which incidentally provides a basis for the re-education of military staff officers all over the world.

Until the Harrier, these officers sat secure in a Maginot Line atmosphere. They knew just where their comfortable, centrally heated airfields were. They knew just how their aircraft would operate, and they considered themselves top-notch professionals. They had been to Staff College and learned all about it. I suppose nobody can blame them if they try to pick holes in the new sort of aircraft that overturns all their beliefs and experience. Yet really an air force on the move, operating from any convenient hiding place, is as old as air power itself. It was done many times in both World Wars. What makes it seem revolutionary today is that other modern military aircraft need long, smooth runways, and there are some problems in carrying these around and hiding them with the mobile air force.

**They didn't in the end buy the Corsair at all. They bought* 60 *of the Hunters that Mr Wilson said were unable to last until the P.*1154 *was ready. And they have been to Dunsfold to evaluate—guess what?*

Collaboration

SEPECAT JAGUAR

GOOD aircraft, especially supersonic ones, can scarcely happen by chance. They must be the end-product of a long series of clear and correct decisions. So it is odd that the Jaguar, built to meet conflicting needs of two mutually suspicious nations, and redesigned by one of those nations rather against the will of the other to meet an extraordinary training requirement that was subsequently forgotten, should emerge as one of my favourite aeroplanes of modern times. The two nations, of course, are Britain and France; and the French would say the perfidious British turned the nice cheap French strike-trainer into a complicated and expensive one, suddenly decided they had made it too complicated and expensive, switched nearly all their trainers to single-seat attack aircraft, and decided to buy a cheaper strike-trainer of their own. This is literally true; but it omits the fact that out of the cheap and very limited French project has come a versatile tactical combat machine, available in several versions, that has capabilities out of all proportion to its size. Any ex-Lancaster chap will be interested to hear that the Jaguar, with a span ten feet less than a Spitfire, can take off from a UK base and clobber a point target in Berlin, in solid clag, with *ten thousand pounds* of h.e.

The more one studies the Jaguar, the more one can delight in its good engineering design, clever packaging and excellent fitness for operational service in adverse environments. Indeed it is hard to find much to criticize about today's hardware at all. The more incredible it is, therefore, to recall the Gilbertian way it all started. The French wanted a simple close-support aircraft that could fly at about Mach 0·9 and get out of short grass fields. The British wanted a trainer, but they wanted it to fly at almost twice the speed of sound and to carry a comprehensive nav/attack system. One instinctively felt there was something wrong and that the specifications had become mixed up. And, after a year or two of bilateral stirring of the melting pot, the ingredients were rearranged. The Jaguar is highly supersonic, has a comprehensive nav-attack system and is used mainly as a very effective weapon, not as a trainer. And the two nations involved have thought again and started trainer programmes—not in collaboration—at Mach 0·85–0·9.

Traditionally, Britain likes to keep everything secret. This is almost wholly bad, and in the context of international co-operative programmes one of its effects is that it gives the impression that the project stemmed entirely from Britain's partner(s). There are many Frenchmen who think the Concorde was based solely upon the Sud Super Caravelle, because a model of this proposal was exhibited and models of the Bristol 198 and 223 were not. In the case of the Jaguar the design was basically French, for political reasons, but the British secrecy hid the fact that an even greater amount of project study had been done in Britain. It began at BAC Preston in 1963 when, following low-priority R&D on variable-sweep (see AFVG-MRCA, p. 129), studies were put in hand for various configurations of the P.45 supersonic strike-trainer. In that year the Air Staff Target 362 was prepared for a trainer to replace the Gnat and Hunter in 1974. The Air Staff had noted that the 1957 White Paper had said nothing about trainers, and thought that, as it would probably get past the Treasury, they might as well make it a rather impressive one (they thought this would help export sales and also produce an aircraft capable of filling a front-line role). AST.362 called for two engines and a sustained Mach of about 1·7. BAC's P.45 took shape in 1963 as a non-VG tandem two-seater, less draggy than side-by-side and more like a 'real' combat aircraft with two reheat RB.172s or Vipers of about 6000 lb thrust each or a single Spey. But BAC were not allowed to reveal it, so posterity could think Britain came to the Jaguar conference table empty-handed.

In fact it is my personal belief that, had the two nations not come together at all, France would today have a trainer and close-support aircraft unnecessarily big and costly for the training role yet too light and underpowered as an operational attack machine, while Britain would have an aircraft strictly comparable to the Jaguar as it is today. How the timing and costs would compare with those of the joint effort would be a most interesting exercise, but unfortunately one that could never be more than an opinion.

Since 1960 the French Air Staff had been considering a light tactical trainer for the Armée de l'Air and possibly for the Aéronavale also. For five years before that, the French had been unable to take their minds off light fighters with two baby engines, and they even wasted a lot of money funding four competing engines before NATO decided a single Orpheus was better. Still insisting on two baby engines, the French officials and industry continued their studies even after the hated Fiat G91 was entering service with non-French NATO forces. By January 1964 they had drawn up their definitive requirement, called ECAT (Ecole de Combat et Appui Tactique). It specified a simple, subsonic, robust and state-of-the-art aircraft, for use at low and medium altitudes, that could be developed swiftly and at modest cost. It was largely the brainchild of General Martin, the Chief of Staff of the Armée de l'Air. Like his colleagues he was fed up with the Mirage IIIv and its interminable and expensive problems. ECAT was a swing of the pendulum away from costly supersonic and V/STOL complexity towards cheap agricultural hardware that might be of more practical use (something very similar was happening in the Pentagon with the Co-In and AX programme). The French wanted the ECAT quickly, if possible by 1967, to start replacing the SMB.2, F-84F and F-100, and at a later date to replace the T-33 trainer. During the first quarter of 1964 competitive design studies were submitted by Breguet, Dassault, Nord, Potez and Sud, all based on two small American turbojets of the GE J85 or P&W J60 type, despite GE's intense probing to see whether they could sell their new GE-1/J01, one of the first of their 'building-block' family of engines.

By March 1964 the British, at least, had begun to think of a joint programme. Undoubtedly a commanding part was played by the British wish to make de Gaulle's 'non' to the UK's Common Market application change to a warm 'oui'. Gp Capt Lee Malins (who much later helped sell the *Queen Mary*) played a central role in the informal discussions to see how far AST.362 and ECAT could be screwed together. The two documents spelt out such different requirements I consider the man who thought of a merger must have been either unusually dim or unusually far-sighted. Malins himself reflected British Air Staff thinking when he said 'Of course it has to be supersonic; if it wasn't, we might as well buy more Hunters.' In contrast the philosophy of the Armée de l'Air, as put to me, was 'We will count the number of parts in each submission and buy the one with the fewest.' By April 1964 it had got up to government level, and Thorneycroft and Messmer were talking about possible co-operation on a broad front. The initiative came from Thorneycroft. It set the stage for a typical bit of horse-trading in which it was decided, with the scantiest of reference to the RAF and Armée de l'Air, that there should be two consecutive joint programmes. The 'simple strike-trainer' would be French-led and based on the ECAT specification. In return Britain would lead on a second programme—surely the most ill-founded project in aviation's recent history?—which would be a challenging variable-geometry project. This proposal, which for want of a better name became known as the AFVG (Anglo-French variable-geometry) as described on p.129, was at first regarded by the French chiefly as a strike aircraft and by the British as a fighter. The preceding ECAT was also regarded by the French as a strike aircraft rather than as a trainer, yet on 27 April 1964 the British Minister of Aviation said he was discussing with France 'a joint programme for a tactical aircraft concentrated mainly on the training role.' I would not like to insist that this is a contradiction in terms, but it serves to underline the conflict and perhaps even confusion regarding the purpose of this first-ever exercise in collaboration between Britain and France on a military aircraft. Indeed it was the first collaborative *design* in the history of combat aircraft.

On the whole the British Air Staff were delighted at the idea of a joint programme, provided the aircraft was nothing like what the French had in mind. I was told 'ECAT doesn't meet our requirement by a mile.' The P.45, of course, did; but it would not help Britain get into Europe. What happened to this is unique in aviation history. It was, to quote Ollie Heath of BAC Military Aircraft Division, 'split into two', one half being used to help redesign the French ECAT winner that would serve as the basis for the first joint programme, and the other half providing the starting point for the AFVG. To see how wide was the gap between AST.362 and ECAT in July 1964, the installed thrust of the French aircraft was half that of the British. But by this time it was evident that the RAF really did want a much larger flight envelope and comprehensive avionics. This tended to split the French into those who clung to the vision of simplicity and cheapness and those who agreed with the British supersonic complexity. Obviously, if there was going to be a joint programme the foundation ought to be a joint requirement, and in October 1964 the two air staffs began a useful series of joint discussions out of which emerged, in April 1965, a joint requirement. It was very close to the original British specification, which the Armée de l'Air had come to agree with surprisingly wholeheartedly. But this did not mean the end of all argument.

By the end of 1964 it was clear the joint requirement was going to need the 'British' level of installed thrust, and, as the four obvious engine firms had been left in no doubt the engine would have to be a collaborative programme, two engine consortia were created almost overnight with no fuss at all. Bristol Siddeley (BSEL) had the BS.116, but agreed to hop into bed with SNECMA and make a joint submission based on that company's M45 Mars which had already been planned around various existing parts including a scaled Olympus HP spool. Rolls teamed up with Turboméca, bringing together the RB.172 (preferred engine of the BAC P.45) and the Turmolet, each of about 4400 lb dry thrust. Unlike the rival M45 consortium, which went all-French, the link between Bordes and Derby hit on the novel solution of a neat reheat turbofan incorporating the front of the T.260 Turmolet and the middle and rear of the RB.172-45R, with some bits actually of joint design and all produced to metric drawings. Engines take longer than aircraft but nothing more was done until there was a firm aircraft programme. And the way the programme took shape showed that the British negotiators had, for obvious reasons, been told to agree with almost anything the French wanted. This in turn meant the French could decide whichever ECAT design they wanted and could then tell Britain this was the basis of the programme.

In January 1965 a rather piqued spokesman for Dassault told me 'It's Breguet; but we're after bigger fish.' He confidentially told me of the swing-wing Mirage G, which he thought might kill the AFVG and find wide sales after 1970. The choice of the Br 121 was not unexpected; more pedestrian than the rival design it stemmed directly from the Taon family of NATO light fighters (which the French always insisted actually won in 1957, not the G91) and in any case Breguet needed the work. It was a trim high-wing machine, in the original proposal propelled by two J85 turbojets without reheat to Mach 0·95 or by reheat J85-5s to Mach 1·1, and capable of carrying a weapon load of 1300 lb. On 2 February 1965 the new British Prime Minister, Harold Wilson, said 'Britain will join in studies with the French for a light strike/trainer aircraft' (which is what they had been doing for a year), and it was soon clear there was mild confusion in Whitehall. Nice collaborative programmes for Anglo-French tactical strike and trainer aircraft were beginning to proliferate. I asked Aviation Minister Roy Jenkins 'Does the strike-trainer employ variable geometry?' and received an equally clear answer: 'Er, I think the Prime Minister said it did.' This response, most untypical of the man, was right; Mr Wilson had explicitly said the new project would be 'using the variable-sweep concept.' It was, of course, the second joint proposal, the AFVG, that had this feature; but the previous (Macmillan) government had a vague idea the strike-trainer should have it as well, as I shall relate.

By this time Bristol Siddeley had planned much of their future, both military and civil, around proposed derivatives of the M45, so it was a blow when on 18 February the French Air Ministry leaked out that the engine for the Br 121 would be the 'RB.172/T.260', the amalgam of the RB.172 and Turmolet which was soon to be called the Adour (thus maintaining the Rolls 'river' names while making it appear to be an all-French engine). In April the series of joint air staff meetings bore fruit in the bilateral common requirement. This cleared the way to the formal start of the joint programme.

On 17 May 1965 came the milestone everyone had been waiting for: the Defence and Aviation Ministers of the two countries signed the Memorandum of Understanding that set both the new programmes on a firm legal footing. The MoA described the less-ambitious of the two aircraft, still unnamed apart from being based on the ECAT Br 121, as 'a supersonic fixed-wing aircraft which we shall use both in the Air Force and Navy [*sic*] as an advanced trainer to replace the Hunter and Gnat and which the French will use both as a trainer and in the light strike role . . .'. It was added that safeguards 'will enable either government to withdraw for reasons of national importance.' It may be recalled that this was six months after the Labour government had, unnecessarily ineptly, tried to pull out of the Concorde programme and been thwarted by the absence of a break clause; so they insisted on a break clause, and the French cordially agreed, provided that the financial penalties were astronomic. I think they had begun to appreciate that, no matter how much the strength and experience of the British industry might exceed that of their own, the supine posture of the British government—Conservative or Labour—would ensure that France would be the dominant partner. It took more than five years for this feeling to die a natural death, and even today many Frenchmen feel they have every right to criticize Britain for having the temerity to make any British aircraft. Had Britain been able to maintain, at the negotiating level, an image of competent professionalism and detached objectivity, the negotiations would have been quicker and smoother. The only problem would have been French mistrust of the British caused by the fact that, at that time, the British aerospace industry was more than twice as large as the French. But the British government, at the very highest level, adopted two quite unnecessary policies that put their negotiators in an almost impossible position. One was to make it clear that the French must never be offended, so that in most differences of opinion the British simply gave way. The other was to state publicly that Britain would 'never again produce any advanced civil or military aircraft' alone. Coming at a time when Gaullist France was striving to hoist itself to a position of commanding grandeur, and in no field more ardently than aerospace, the British attitude evoked a natural response of arrogance and scorn. It practically invited the French to be rude and difficult just to see if there was any point at which the worm would turn.

Fortunately the Memorandum of Understanding had named the four main industrial partners as Breguet, BAC, Turboméca and Rolls-Royce, and the managements of all four believed in friendly collaboration rather than arrogant nationalism. What had they to lose? Instead of the whole of a little programme they looked like having half of one at least twice as big—or so the notion went. Executives of BAC and Breguet met late in May 1965 in an atmosphere of harmony. The programme seemed to be getting off to an encouraging start. The general feeling was that this was going to be a nice little aircraft that would not cause the slightest trouble to anyone, either technically or because of cost. Someone asked Roy Jenkins what it would do that the Northrop F-5 was not doing already—which seemed a fair question—and the Aviation Minister replied 'I don't think ECAT is going to mark a great advance in aeronautical knowledge. . . . But we think it will be a useful plane and one for which we both have a demand.' This seemed a fair answer; what Mr Jenkins didn't know (because the sums had apparently not been worked out) was that this little aircraft was going to do very many things that no F-5 will ever do. Defence Minister Denis Healey said Britain was committed only to 'an initial expenditure of £20 million on this and the VG aircraft covered by the same memorandum.' Rolls took Memorandum of Understanding to mean memorable understatement and announced that the cost of developing the Adour would be 'about £4 million' (and they didn't mean just their share either!). The following week the French government stated that their share of the prototype cost would be £9·4 million, and that the unit price in production should be £450,000. Having just lived through TSR.2 I wondered why people were so eager to make such announcements.

Broadly, this was the background to one of the most politically contrived aircraft it is possible to imagine. Its basis was a French design proposal planned to meet the ECAT requirement, a document which had by May 1965 been completely changed. The numerous engineering solutions and test results already achieved with the P.45 programme could not be used except to modify the Br 121. The two airframe contractors and two engine contractors were not the result of competitive tendering but were teamed up after being nominated by their respective governments after 'old boy' discussions behind locked doors. It all sounds terrible, yet it led to the programme that I think most people would pick as the one best demonstrating that a collaborative project can deliver the goods.

In my view many of the supposed advantages of a collaborative project are specious. One of the greatest is that it doubles (or trebles) the size of the market; yet no collaborative aircraft has come anywhere near getting worldwide sales on the scale of the best national products. Why should it? Another is that each nation bears a smaller R&D burden; one can never prove anything here but, to put it mildly, there is room for argument. There are several other claimed advantages which I believe to be doubtful if not discredited. But there is one advantage so huge and definite it makes up for all the deficiencies in the others. It is that each participant makes a firm commitment at the start. In this case the Memorandum of Understanding launched the project with a promise of 300 aircraft. The French opted for 75 single-seat strike aircraft and 75 trainers while the RAF chose 150 trainers. To the British Treasury such a commitment must have generated near-apoplexy, because it had long been a national tradition to procure military aircraft in tiny dribs and drabs so that the manufacturer could never plan further ahead than next week.

A firm commitment is an absolute godsend, and from 17 May 1965 the programme never looked back. And, despite the confused background to this programme, the Joint Requirement, which was virtually the same as the British Air Staff Requirement, was a good one. This, plus the firm commitment, combined to yield a fine success story. But at first things were still a bit shaky at Westminster. The Tory Defence spokesman, Christopher Soames, could have enquired why it was necessary to take the Br 121 and try to turn it into something like the P.45 instead of taking the P.45 itself or an optimised joint design. Instead he merely asked why the agreement had taken so long 'because it was virtually complete last October.' Mr Healey replied that the previous government had 'wanted the strike-trainer itself to have variable geometry; this would not have met the urgent French timescale and would have made it quite impossible to reach agreement with the French.' There is no doubt the Macmillan government had been as mesmerised as the Wilson one by the F-111, and had concluded there was nothing about military aircraft that swing-wings and 'commonality' could not solve. Yet in this case (as in most others) neither panacea made sense. After the most detailed parametric analysis of possible AST.362 submissions BAC had thrown out VG for this class of aircraft in 1963. In the event the wing was a very good compromise which somehow contrives to be small enough for lo penetration, and big enough for training.

Lord Shackleton, Minister for the RAF, said 'The French want the aircraft by 1970 and will take the first production run; we hope to be taking delivery of the strike-trainer in 1973 or 1974.' By the summer of 1965 the joint programme had been under discussion 18 months and still did not have a name. It is a reflection on the Whitehall mentality that, while Britain's leaders did not in the least mind basing this very important project on a French design that then had to be completely redesigned, they objected very strongly to the aircraft being known by its French designation. They insisted that a sort of mid-Channel name should be found. At last, with the blessing of the Coventry car company, the name Jaguar was chosen—and it sounds totally different in French. The name was disclosed at the 1965 Paris air show. (The French got their own back when they named the joint company set up to manage the programme, as noted later.)

At this time there were still urgent arguments, although these did not hold up the work in the design offices. There was a widespread feeling among the French that they ought to go ahead quickly with the Br 121 for their own use and that later the British could turn this into their sophisticated Jaguar to meet the RAF's later timescale. This seemed to me rather like two programmes, but fortunately, after some tough sessions, the Jaguar emerged during the summer of 1965 as a single basic design. All versions were to exceed Mach 1·6, all were to carry an external load of up to 10000 lb (a bit of a change from 1300) and all were to meet the Joint Requirement even down to the 2600-mile RAF ferry range which the French at first insisted had no relevance to them at all. (Indeed the previous year the British negotiators were reduced to trying to get the French to accept large drop tanks or bolt-on wing tips.) It was obvious from the start there could only be one type of engine and not too much time was wasted wondering whether the British Jaguar might have an afterburner and the French aircraft not. This was fortunate because the British were still thinking primarily of a trainer and the French of a tactical strike machine.

I do not have room to go into the great jungle of conflicting mission parameters that entered into this programme, but a lot are obvious. For example, trainers have to have good mission endurance, long life, reliability and the sort of trouble-free engineering called for by any aircraft that might make 25 flights a day. Tactical aircraft need a small highly loaded wing for mild gust response, high-lift systems for STOL, good acceleration and manoeuvrability, good carrying capacity and, in this case, lots of fuel. Great attention also had to be paid to easy maintenance and the attainment of a strong airframe with a long fatigue life. Some of these qualities would have been built into the Br 121 had this gone ahead as a national programme, but I cannot over-emphasize the crucial importance of the massive engineering effort applied to turning the 121 into the Jaguar. Most of this work was done at Preston in the summer of 1965. Not too much showed on the outside. Even walking round the aircraft it would be hard to tell it is made of machined panels instead of the bonded honeycomb that Breguet wanted (and which they used on the Taon). The aircraft was made longer and sharper-looking, fully area ruled, with a bigger but thinner wing (t/c ratio 5 to 5·5 per cent instead of 6·5 per cent), taller and thinner vertical tail and much bigger and thinner slab tailplane. Far more of the new engineering was hidden. Ivan Yates, the project manager at Preston, said 'There's a lot of BAC refinement in it. . . . Hundreds if not thousands of parts have been redesigned, and many completely changed, but the aircraft looks much the same.' The design was frozen in November 1965. This was a performance that can only be called marvellous.

All this work was done in the advance of any contract, except for the engine and some major new systems for the British aircraft, but the declaration of intent to buy 300 aircraft was comforting, because *two* governments had said it. During 1965 further inter-governmental discussion led to a plan for an Anglo-French committee of officials to manage the programme, and this was formed in 1966 with the rather uninspired title of Anglo-French Management Committee. For the airframe it was agreed that contracts would be let by the French DTCA to a joint company formed by Breguet and BAC, registered in Paris, called for by the original Memo. This took some time to create and finally set up shop in May 1966 as SEPECAT, or preferably Sepecat, for Société Européenne de Production de l' Avion ECAT (Avion ought to make it Sepaecat; and why ECAT rather than Jaguar?). These French company names have to include the ownership, usually as anonyme, National or Française but in this case as European (so others might come in). For the engine Mintech was to issue the contracts to a corresponding joint firm, registered in London on 22 June 1966, which despite the collapse of the original R-R is still called Rolls-Royce Turboméca Ltd.

By mid-1966 metal was being cut. According to the Memo the programme is split 50-50 by value. Broadly BAC do the wing, rear fuselage and tail, and Breguet the fuselage back to the engine bay. On the engine, Turboméca make the compressors, casing and external pipework (and, to keep the 50-50 split, subcontract the reheat jet-pipe to SNECMA, with major contributions by Dowty Fuel Systems) and Rolls make the rest. Adours for the Jaguar programme are assembled alternately at Derby and at the Turboméca plant at Tarnos, near the Breguet Jaguar works at Biarritz. Jaguars are assembled at both Toulouse-Colomiers and Preston, the duplication of tooling for assembly being a small item. Systems and equipment contracts have been broadly 50-50, and there is practically no US hardware involved as there would be for a civil aircraft.

Almost the entire airframe is high-strength light alloy, the wing box being a single, remarkably small unit with a machined upper and lower skin from centreline to tip. There are a few titanium parts around the engine bays. Some structures, notably flaps, control surfaces and big doors, are filled with bonded aluminium honeycomb. Fairey (French partner, SAMM) make the powered flying control units, which are outstandingly neat and advanced in design, driving slab tailplanes, a small rudder, and two-piece spoilers (for roll) on each outer wing. The wing has full-span flaps of the double-slotted type running on titanium rails. The dog-tooth leading edge has powerful slats over the extended outer portion, driven by hydraulic motors in the fuselage and cleared for use in combat under the control of buttons on the throttle levers. This high-lift wing is very much to my liking. Another good feature is the neat and tough landing gear, with main legs by Messier and nose gear by Dowty, and with Dunlop wheels and anti-skid brakes. Twin low-pressure main tyres are used for rough-field operation, although the naval Jaguar had single high-pressure tyres to save weight.

It was only to be expected that there would be different types of Jaguar.

At first it was thought there would be three, a French and a British two-seater, and a French single-seater. But by the end of 1966 there were: the French E (école) two-seat trainer, A (appui) single-seat tactical aircraft and M (marin) single-seat carrier-based strike aircraft; and the British B (British) two-seat trainer and S (strike) single-seat tactical aircraft. The M and the S were announced on 16 January 1967 when Defence Ministers Messmer and Healey put their signatures to an amendment to the Memo which raised the numbers to 200 aircraft each. France chose to add to her original 75 A and 75 E a further ten E plus 40 M; Britain's 150 B trainers were cut by 40, leaving 110, and the 40 were added to the extra 50 to make a viable strike force of 90 of the new S model. The following month, on 9 February, four more flight prototypes were placed under formal contract, plus a fatigue airframe, to make the total prototype series E-01 and 02, A-03 and 04, M-05, S-06 and 07, B-08, and a static and a fatigue airframe. In February 1967 the estimate for R&D was put by Sepecat at 'over £50 million', including the eight prototypes and two test airframes. It did not say how much over.

In October 1966 there was a mild rumpus in the French Assemblée Nationale when a Gaullist deputy moved a motion that the 1967 vote for the programme of NF255 million (about £18 million) should be postponed for a year. This would have been about the silliest thing anyone could have done to the Jaguar, but it came at a time when the French leaders were distinctly cool to the British and were doing their best to muck about with joint projects. Only a week later the AFVG (p. 136) was in desperate trouble because the French said they couldn't afford it, and Mr Healey was reported by *The Financial Times* as being 'prepared . . . to sacrifice the Jaguar' to keep France from pulling out of the VG. And two weeks later poor René Bloch, the young director of international affairs in the French Ministry of the Armed Forces, was sacked after de Gaulle had studied the dossiers on Anglo-French aircraft programmes and decided they 'safeguarded British interests more than French ones' (how very strange that British officials had formed precisely the opposite view). The Gaullist *Paris Presse* said Bloch's departure did not mean 'the total renunciation' of aircraft co-operation with Britain, but merely 'putting an end to certain onerous contradictions.' Bloch suffered simply because aerospace is an emotional field where everyone—especially the French—wants his national posture to be dominant.

In May 1967 I went to the Paris air show wondering if I would assist at Jaguar's funeral. Instead I heard Messmer, standing in front of a fine new exhibition model of it, say he thought France alone would need 300 Jaguars eventually, and that he thought Britain would also. The new Sepecat literature emphasized how different the Jaguar would be from the half-baked proposal of 1965 (when the pressman couldn't see that it would improve on the F-5), by proclaiming it would cost about the same as an F-5 but would carry the same load for 100 per cent more range at 14 per cent more speed and with 33 per cent shorter field length. For the same range it would carry 100 per cent more weapon load. It was here that the military world realized that this small aircraft was going to be worth noticing. I went to talk to the Armée de l'Air, to confirm it had their unstinted support. At a time when the AFVG fiasco was souring the whole relationship between the two nations (it collapsed later the same month) the senior officers to whom I spoke were unanimous in emphasizing the importance of Jaguar. They had never regarded AFVG as a firm programme at all, and did not appear concerned at its imminent demise, but 'Jaguar . . . nothing must be allowed to interfere with this programme. It remains an absolute need. We need it very urgently to replace the out of date Mystère 4A, SMB.2, Vautour, the F-100, F-84F, the T-33. . . . Only now can we relax and feel sure it will not come to grief.'

Breguet, however, was in no position to relax. While the Jaguar was going swimmingly, the 60-year-old firm was facing the most dramatic change in its history (it had escaped the disastrous nationalization of 1936). In 1956 Sylvain Floirat, head of the Aigle Azur airline and a giant contractor to the French forces, wished to extract a personal fortune from Indo-China (where much of it was made). The French government got the money out for him and then quietly told him where he would invest it: in Breguet. He agreed, for ten years. He practically owned the firm, and he also ran it as board chairman with great success. But when the ten years were up he said to de Gaulle 'I want out.' After examining its small range of options the French government chose to pass control to Dassault, which in the early days of Jaguar had done its best to rock the boat, and still smarted at losing out in the ECAT competition. The news was announced on 9 January 1967. I was in Paris in June 1967 when the merger took effect. I met General Gallois of Dassault and, feeling extremely angry at the collapse of the AFVG programme, opened a friendly chat by asking 'Well, are you going to foul up the Jaguar now?' He was affability itself. 'It is natural that the British should feel hurt at the difficulties with the AFVG. It was never a soundly conceived project. The Jaguar is. Monsieur Vallières will be appointed by Dassault to head a new Breguet board of management. We hope the two companies will enter into close collaboration at the planning and research level, but I see no reason to interfere in Sepecat or the Jaguar programme.' He was right; the Jaguar programme continued just as happily with very sharp, very French Dassault running Breguet. The old firm has never lost its identity and retains considerable freedom of action.

A week or two later everyone was agog with the possibility of Federal Germany either coming into the programme or at least placing a substantial order to replace the G91 as a tactical reconnaissance and strike aircraft for the Luftwaffe and Kriegsmarine. But a month later the Bonn government announced it would keep the Fiats until 1975, and instead of Jaguar they were going to spend huge sums on the RF-4E Phantom. On 9 January 1968 Messmer and Healey again met to sign the production agreement for 400 Jaguars that had been agreed a year before (I was getting a bit lost trying to decide exactly what the documents were that were cropping up; the January 1967 one had been a mere amendment and not the production agreement, although I failed to see the difference). Somebody leaked that the 'production cost', which I took to mean unit price, would be 'not greatly above £0·5 million, this suggested the programme was quite unnatural in having shown practically no escalation in the five crucial formative years. A month later *Aviation Week* reported that the Germans had rejected Jaguar as a contender in the NKF (Neuenkampfflugzeug) competition because its price was $3·5 million (ie, £1·5 million) and still rising. It never was an NKF contender, and on the matter of price BAC promptly said they had 'no knowledge of the grounds for this claim.' This seemed a weak statement, but they were expressly told by the British MoA not to disclose Jaguar prices. There was nothing funny or shameful about the price; it was just that in Britain such things have to be kept secret so that the press can get it wrong and rumour-mongers spread scurrilous stories, as in this case. In fact the price quoted to Bonn as a G91 replacement was close to £700,000 complete with about £100,000 worth of operational equipment including comprehensive reconnaissance gear. The Phantom was chosen instead almost solely because the bill for more than £265 million (for 175) could be offset against the immense financial burden of the US forces in Germany.

On 17 April 1968 the first Jaguar, E-01, was rolled out for ground tests at Vélizy-Villacoublay, the Breguet HQ and prototype factory near Paris. Finished in glossy green and grey camouflage the two-seater looked even better than I had hoped. For the first time it was possible to appreciate the modern proportions of the Jaguar. The wing is less than 28 feet in span but so high off the ground that a shortish man could not reach up and touch it. The body is 54 feet long, but the shortish man can open up about half the exterior surface (which is covered in access doors) without a ladder. Everything, including underwing stores, is splendidly easy to get at, and the interior engineering is a delight. But a ladder is needed to gain the cockpit. First man to climb the ladder and light the Adours was Bernard Witt, Breguet chief test pilot. Between April 17 and the end of the month he carried out numerous ground tests, in the course of which taxying speeds up to 100 knots were reached. The first flight date of 15 June looked easy, even though the aircraft had to be dismantled and trucked some 600 miles to Istres, but it was not to be. French social disorder stemming from a left-wing alliance between 'students' and 'workers', that didn't quite know what it was trying to do but did it with enormous gusto, caused a gradual breakdown in urban society. By 13 May it was practically a state of revolution—a unique revolution, with the objective not the bloody overthrow of the government but merely a noisy and prolonged letting-off of steam. Industry gave up. Breguet fared better than Sud-Aviation where managements were locked in and hangar doors were welded together, but the Jaguar programme in France came to a full stop. Of the 35 BAC engineers with Breguet, 20 returned to Lancashire hot-pot and the rest had a holiday at Villacoublay.

As the summer wore on, the French picked up the pieces and by July all was again swinging. But E-01 did not get into the air at Istres until 8 September. E-01, a French tandem-seat trainer, at once demonstrated that the design was basically right. Within five hours it had flown at supersonic speed, and during October 1968 Witt and BAC's Jimmy Dell were flying it up to three times a day with encouraging reliability. Its mission was aerodynamics and handling, flutter and general system behaviour. Most of the problems were minor, although the spoiler lateral controls needed some weeks of development. E-02, assigned to engine and flight performance, and later to flutter, flew on 11 February 1969 (not 22 February as widely reported). The first single-seat attack Jaguar, A-03, flew supersonically on its first flight on 29 March 1969; it was assigned to nav-attack system development. A-04, assigned to stores carriage and weapon firing, flew on 27 May 1969. With the static-test airframe this completed the first prototype programme. The day after A-04 flew, the Sepecat partners issued a release stating the programme was 'firmly following the timescale envisaged. . . .' This was obviously one of those amusing cases where the schedule is altered in exact step with the programme. The 'timescale envisaged' had called for E-02, A-03 and A-04 all to fly in 1968, and for deliveries to the Armée de l'Air 'at the end of 1970 or early in 1971.' While the early years of Jaguar went fast, the programme slipped from 1967 onwards, and in 1972 was running about 18 months late. At least it is a change to find a very clear reason for at least part of the delay: prolonged strikes at both Breguet and BAC.

BAC Military Aircraft Division, one of the best sources of combat aircraft in the world, got the first RAF single-seater, S-06, into the air on 12 October 1969. It was assigned to British avionics and weapons and in-flight refuelling. Next came the single-seat carrier-based M-05, flown at the Jaguar flight-test centre at Istres on 14 November, and naturally assigned to French naval systems and carrier qualification. S-07, detailed to clear the British nav-attack system, flew on 12 June 1970. B-08, the first RAF two-seater, assigned to the two-seat cockpit and nav-attack system, flew very late on 30 August 1971. It was assembled largely from production parts, being officially classed as the sole 'pre-production' Jaguar. With the fatigue airframe this completed the R&D buy. It is important to note that, whereas since 1955 the UK had always bought a development batch of a new military aircraft built in production jigs, the Jaguar programme has followed the French policy of hurrying handbuilt prototypes into the air and testing them before making the costly production tooling. The French method obviously scores if the design is sadly awry and massive airframe changes have to be made. In the case of the Jaguar my view is that the British method would have been quicker and cheaper in the long term.

Most of every Jaguar is identical. All have similar engines and major aircraft systems, and apart from the forward fuselage the airframes are generally to a common set of drawings. The tandem-seat nose is 35·4 inches longer than the single-seater, increasing the overall length from 51 to 54 feet. Among the last decisions to be taken regarding the standard of build were to adopt the taller fin first flown on S-06, the plain pitot (as distinct from wedge) intakes which showed improved efficiency in most flight regimes when tested on A-03 in 1970, and the perforated pattern of airbrakes. Avionics, however, differ markedly. The French E model has vhf/uhf, VOR/ILS, Tacan, a CSF sight, twin-gyro platform, air-data computer (added in 1968) and a traditional cockpit with a spherical attitude/heading indicator. The A adds a doppler, weapon-aiming and navigation computer, panoramic camera, and—to prove it can be done outside the United States—a singularly neat folding FR probe, which worked well on development aircraft and was then left off the first 14 production machines! The M further added a laser ranging unit and has an airframe beefed up for carrier operation. The RAF Jaguars are more advanced (and more expensive), with hf/uhf, vhf/uhf, IFF, VOR/ILS, Tacan, Elliott inertial platform, digital integrated nav and weapon computer, air-data computer, advanced Sperry compass system, radio altimeter, and a very new cockpit with Specto (now Smiths) head-up display, horizontal situation indicator and Elliott projected map display. The S version has the FR probe, panoramic camera and a Ferranti YAG liquid cooled laser ranger and marked-target seeker in a distinctive 'chisel nose'. The RAF machines and the M version have the Martin-Baker Mk 9 rocket seat, cleared for use from zero to 600 knots and zero to 50000 feet; the Mk 4 seat of the A and E Jaguars is not cleared below 90 knots, which could cost a man's life in a forced landing or ditching.

All versions can pull a sustained 8·6 g with 10000 lb weapon load at Mach 0·8. Design ultimate factor is 12, and the design life 3000 hours (6000 for trainer versions) making reasonable assumptions for loads and gusts. The design MTBF is 20 hours, expressed as 'a 95 per cent likelihood of completing a one-hour mission', and the MMH/FH maintenance target is 10·5 (one document said 10·3). If this is reached it will be almost unbelievably good; preliminary figures are running closer to 15, but compared with earlier, less complicated, aircraft this is marvellous. Of course with modern aircraft the true maintenance burden is masked. If something malfunctions it can be smartly whipped out and a perfect one plugged in, and the time this takes hardly shows in the figure calculated at the end of the month for MMH/FH. Nobody adds in the hundreds of man-hours that may be devoted to making the faulty item work again in some remote workshop or even in the maker's plant.

It is still too early to get a useful idea of what the MMH/FH figure may turn out to be, but the aircraft was expected to start service life at about 14, a superb figure, and get even better. The figure written into the contract was 10·3. Certainly the flight test programme, when this has involved use of full combat equipment, has called for a much higher maintenance burden than this. On the other hand, there have been few really big problems. Possibly the worst have centred round the engine. The Adour first ran in May 1967 and was planned to be compact, simple, self-contained, light and robust, and to reach a TBO of 1000 hours at an early date. It was matched to the Jaguar with an integral reheat system, and both this and the basic engine initially gave rise to several problems. A shortfall in thrust and high specific fuel consumption took over two years to rectify, in a series of painstaking improvements, and in 1969 Admiral Jacques Thabaud of the Aéronavale acidly proclaimed that the engine was simply 'not up to specification'. He went on to claim that his service had always preferred the American Corsair, anyway, 'at about half the price'. As the sterling equivalents of the prices at that time were £920,000 for the Jaguar M and £1·05 million for the original Corsair, I thought he was exaggerating. Doubtless he was cross because M-05 had been bent in a very heavy single-engine landing by a pilot who was caught out, on the back of the drag curve, by the way the Adour responded to increased power demand. Thrust increased up to full throttle dry; further movement into the reheat region gave no added urge at all until about 30 per cent afterburner had been selected, when the reheat system would smartly ignite. To improve the situation Rolls-Turboméca introduced part-throttle reheat (PTR) which gives a smooth modulation in thrust from flight-idling to maximum reheat. Perhaps one day this type of response will be taken for granted; heaven knows it has taken long enough to achieve, although it was becoming a feature of US aircraft 20 years ago.

Today I think the Adour is feeling much better. Rolls claim that all production engines delivered have met the original guarantee of 4400 lb dry and 6600 lb with reheat, and in fact since 1971 the average thrust on the bench has been 5000 lb/7500 lb. The engine is conservatively rated, and could give another 25 per cent thrust without more than trivial redesign or changed blade material, and I expect before long to see a Jaguar with even shorter field length or over-wing pylons. As it has a by-pass ratio of unity the Adour could also have a reheat boost of at least 75 per cent, compared with the current level of 50 per cent. Increased thrust ideally ought to be paralleled by increased stopping power, and heavier Jaguars could well have thrust reversers, structural-carbon brakes or a bigger Irving drag chute. All Jaguars have an arrester hook, that of the M being stronger.

So far the only catastrophe in the programme seems to have been the result of finger trouble. On 26 March 1970 a fire warning (thinks: it was probably a false alarm) suddenly lit in E-01. The French pilot, flying from Istres, shut down the engine and worked the suppression system. He should then have been able to make a nice tidy approach and landing but, possibly having memories of the single-engined arrival of M-05, decided to throw the aircraft at the ground from a gross overshoot position. What appears to have happened is that he shut down the remaining engine, stuffed the nose down, found he had no control over the aircraft and hastily ejected, fortunately landing safely not too near the resulting conflagration. Shutting down both engines and failing to select emergency hydraulic power almost immediately caused the flying controls to lock solid. This is the sort of thing that ought not to be able to happen; stand-by hydraulic power, from bottles, a ram-air turbine, windmilling engines or an electrically driven pump, ought to cut in without pilot action (since writing this I have learned that an electric pump with automatic cut-in is being fitted to all Jaguars).

From the operational viewpoint the Jaguar seems to me close to the best that can be achieved with current technology with one man in the cockpit. The one big omission is a large forward radar, and apart from the fact that there is not much room for one I doubt that a single pilot could make proper use of it. So the Jaguar will not be able, by itself, to find targets of opportunity at night or in bad weather, although it ought to be able to operate in these conditions. All present versions have guns, the basic armament being two Aden (UK) or DEFA (Fr) 30 mm cannon with 150 rounds each in the single-seaters; in the two-seater the sharper nose has pushed some of the avionics into the bay formerly occupied by the right-hand gun. Jaguar A number 12 switched to the improved DEFA

553, with long-life barrel and feed from either side, and the fuselage shroud was changed in shape. No pilot experienced in modern warfare is likely to argue against the inclusion of guns, although one could spend hours discussing the type of gun. The big and heavy 30 mm pack quite a punch but have rather low muzzle velocity and rate of fire; on the other hand the newer US guns would consume their tankful of ammunition in about one second; but that one second may be the only chance you get, and so the argument goes on. Suffice to point out that the present Jaguar guns are not much better than the German MG-213 of 1944 and in Britain at least there is no replacement in sight, so we had better stay friendly with wherever the next gun comes from (probably the German Mauser company, who made the MG-213).

Jaguar's main duty is to tote ordnance. There is a centreline pylon and two inner wing pylons, each rated at 2400 lb, and two outer wing pylons cleared to 1000 lb; in addition provision is made for Sidewinders or similar light air-to-air missiles on the wing tips. Gross weapon load can in theory slightly exceed 10000 lb, which is two-thirds of the equipped empty weight and a commendable figure for an advanced supersonic aircraft. With this load the radius of action on internal fuel only is 360 miles in the all-low profile or about 510 miles in the hi-lo-hi mission, again good figures. Maximum Mach numbers are about 1·1 on the deck (840 mph), clean, and 1·6 at altitude (1055 mph). Minimum landing speed is as low as 115 mph although about 125–130 is more likely in practice. The design ground roll on grass with tactical load was to be 500 m for both take-off and landing; typical measured figures are 1900 ft (580 m) on take-off and 1550 ft (475 m) on landing. Sustained operations from grass are possible with maximum ordnance load. With such an all-round performance, plus convincing arguments in favour of twin engines, plus a wide range of cockpit and equipment options, the compact Jaguar is extremely hard to 'knock', as its competitors have found. Put another way, it is easy to beat the Jaguar at one particular mission, but almost impossible to beat it all-round, especially when costs are included.

Costs for the Jaguar ought to be one of its strongest points, but in fact the industrial strife and delays have added to galloping inflation in Britain and France to cause a massive rise in programme cost and force an increase in unit price of some 100 per cent since the go-ahead in 1965. The French, who have never quite got over the vague belief that the British made the cheap Jaguar expensive, have often sniped at the programme. Admiral Thabaud's outburst was followed early in 1972 by a formal request from the Aéronavale to drop the Jaguar M and buy instead the A-4 Skyhawk at about £600,000 a copy. This was disallowed, and the Aéronavale's Etendards are now to be replaced by a new version of the Etendard! It seems odd to me that this should be preferred to an enormously more capable aircraft which is some 10 years newer in concept and, on any sums I can do, apparently more cost/effective. I have never seen any quantified evidence that the French Navy would not be able safely to use the much more effective Jaguar M, nor any similar evidence to demonstrate the superiority of the Super Etendard. It also seems odd that the Corsair (p. 234), which according to Thabaud was originally everyone's first choice, should have suddenly gone out of favour.

The winter of 1971–72 was marked by a 'let's be horrid to the Jaguar' campaign in France. Indeed the French tried to do all they could to knock any Anglo-French aviation programme that appeared to contain any British influence, pouring especial scorn on Rolls engines (the Adour, Concorde-Olympus and Lynx-BS.360). In November the Assemblée Nationale's finance committee suddenly reported that the unit cost of the Jaguar had escalated to almost £2 million. Soon afterwards Gen. Gallois, who in this context appeared to work for Dassault but not for Breguet, made the remarkable assertion that the Jaguar was 'proof that international aircraft projects are not only more costly but produce hybrid designs satisfying only the countries building them and useless for export elsewhere.' I greatly like and respect Pierre Gallois, and have no brief whatever for collaborative programmes, but as a basis for heated argument this statement is hard to beat. The implication cannot be that national programmes, such as the Mirage, are even worse because they meet the needs of only one nation. Would the gallant general prefer all the possible overseas purchasers to come into the programme at its inception and produce a global joint specification? Doubtless Dassault had its own reasons at that time for wishing to unsell its own product, but the £2 million cost was seemingly put forward either in ignorance or as the result of a miscalculation. The price tag on most Jaguars is still close to £1 million. The British journal *Flight International* tried to work out how the French came to double it, and decided they might just manage it by adding in all sorts of R&D costs, inflation, service operating costs, 50 per cent for spares and the French 23½ per cent value-added tax. It was all very difficult, and no wonder the *Sunday Times*, which I suppose likes to get its stories right, printed the headline JAGUAR COSTS INCREASE BY £500 MILLION. In Washington one can simply ask questions and be told the answers, but in Europe the black curtain of secrecy enables big programmes either to wreak havoc with the public purse without anyone knowing, or else, as in this case, to be damned by totally misleading stories which cannot be corrected because it is not policy to disclose the truth. It was enough to make me feel the French, at least, did not deserve the Jaguar.

Fortunately the Jaguar was by this time about to reach the service users, who are gradually improving the bad public image created by the politicians and mass media. Many E-series aircraft have come off the line at the assembly plant at Toulouse-Colomiers, from whence the first production aircraft emerged in June 1971. In 1972 the first squadron formed at Saint Dizier, in eastern France, with a primary role which involves the AN.52 tactical nuclear weapon. Early in 1973 the Armée de l'Air Chief of Staff, Gen Claude Grigaut, flew a Jaguar at the CEAM and then said some very nice things. He called it 'a straightforward aircraft of great reliability'. He said it handled 'extremely well' and that it complied exactly with the French OR. He even compared it with the Mirage III, saying 'It has additional characteristics in respect of low-speed handling and landing approach. . . . Fuel capacity is greater and it can fly longer in supersonic flight. It has new-generation equipment such as an autopilot coupled with ILS, automatic defect testing and so on . . .' By the time this book appears we shall know if the Aéronavale want any of their M Jaguars; if they do not, there is little doubt the Armée de l'Air will be only too happy to buy them as A models.

Turning to the British scene, all the chaps who were on strike at BAC have long since returned to shipping (by ship) the relevant hardware to support the programme. No more Jaguars were assembled at Preston until late 1972 when the S programme picked up. In 1970 the British performed a massive rethink and, whereas they had started out with nothing but trainer Jaguars and then switched in 1967 to a mix of 110 trainers and 90 single-seaters, they finally decided on a complete about-face and opted for 35 trainers and 165 single-seat S models, enough for nine squadrons and the most powerful element in all Britain's forces assigned to NATO. The remaining trainers are not trainers at all in the original sense but simply to help conversion to the S-model Jaguar. I cannot think of a parallel case where a nation has ordered a big fleet of aircraft for one mission and then bought the same fleet of aircraft tailored to a totally different mission. It has often happened that aircraft roles have been changed because their performance fell short of the original mission, and it is even more common for aircraft bought for one duty to find their actual employment very different, but the Jaguar is the outstanding case of an aircraft whose purpose was utterly changed by the customer before delivery. More than ever does one feel the original RAF Air Staff Target was too much of a compromise. Fortunately the Air Staff thought the same way, and at last the needs of AST.362 to replace the Gnat and Hunter will be met by the Hawker P.1182 from 1976, which means those hard-worked trainers must stay at work at least a further two years.

By mid-1973 RAF Jaguars were coming off the line at Warton. The first (S4) was delivered on 30 May 1973 to the OCU at Lossiemouth, the former RN station mentioned in the Buccaneer story. (It was originally planned to be at Brawdy, another ex-RN base in rugged Wales.) CA Release was planned for July 1973, and the first RAF squadrons Nos 6 and 54, were activated in the spring of 1974 at Coningsby. In service the S becomes the Jaguar GR.1, backing up the Harrier and releasing Phantom FGR.2s for interception duties in place of early Lightnings. The B-model trainer becomes the Jaguar T.2. Both will delight their pilots and will initiate them to a new world, familiar to up-to-date combat aircrew, which revolves around such acronyms as the IP, the HUD, the HSI, the PLF on the WAMS, and maybe using NAVWASS for a TGT OPP. These are the things that make the Jaguar useful.

Nobody would pretend Jaguar is the world's best air-superiority fighter; it has about half the thrust needed. Neither would many people disagree that its effectiveness in the attack mission might be increased by cutting its speed to Mach 0·9 and giving it a bigger wing, carrying a 20000 lb load of stores, and lots more protection against ground fire. But for an air force that just wants to buy one modern combat aeroplane the Jaguar is quite hard to beat, and it looks certain to be a smashing export success. It is the first product of a totally collaborative programme, with the possible exception of the Transall transport. In the long term one of its major contributions will be to show that people can put narrow nationalistic feelings behind them, even in a field where such feelings can be very strong indeed.

The RAF adopted the Hawker Siddeley Buccaneer 16 years after the specification was written and ten years after it first flew, yet it is still an extremely effective weapon. These four S.2 aircraft come from 15 Sqn at Laarbruch, Germany

One of the abiding pilot impressions of the BAC TSR.2 is that, even at light weights around 55,000 lb, it rode as steady as a rock at all speeds and under all flight conditions. Here XR219 is seen with partial flap, leaving the characteristic double tip vortex

There is no technical reason why the Hawker Siddeley P.1154RN, with twin integrated Spey engines, could not have become a successful supersonic strike-fighter for the Fleet Air Arm. The observer would have served as navigator and radar intercept officer.

Never previously illustrated publicly, the AFVG would have been superior in cost-effectiveness to the F-111 but a pale shadow of what has been achieved with MRCA. The author, who drew this sketch, is glad the programme was terminated, mistaken as it may have seemed at the time

Undoubtedly the best buy for an air force that merely wants a fully developed cost-effective attack aircraft, the SEPECAT Jaguar has been handicapped by an ill-conceived belief that it is important to fly at vast speeds and heights and shoot down the enemy while he is in the air. This Jaguar GR.1 of the RAF is carrying tanks and retarded bombs

The incessant sniping at the Panavia MRCA by the French and Americans serves to underline the fact that this aircraft is in a class of its own, combining outstanding performance in a wide spectrum of roles (surpassing anything that can be accomplished by any other aircraft) with first cost approximately half that of any competitor. Its capabilities are

The F-111 is a fine long-range attack aircraft, which brought a quantum jump in all-weather strike capability. Pity its early years were marred not only by desperate technical problems but also by almost unbelievable political storms triggered off by the concept of commonality and the supposed mistaken choice of prime contractor

Recovery of an A-7A carrying one tank and one Buddy store. Results in Vietnam exceeded the most optimistic hopes of the Navy and Marine Corps and confirmed the decision of the US Air Force to buy this subsonic bomber in large numbers.

316

This McDonnell Douglas A-4C, being recovered at high weight with two tanks and a Buddy refuelling store, emphasizes the workhorse-like capability of one of the cleverest little aircraft ever built. This example was made four years after the original planned shut-down of the production line and about 14 years before the actual planned shut-down (unless they order some more!)

Serene in the 20,000 foot level, this Grumman A-6A Intruder of Navy attack squadron VA-65 usually operates with its overloaded wings flexing in the rough air at 200 feet. This aircraft showed that black boxes are more important than supersonic speed

Fairchild Republic A-10A parked at Edwards with all 11 pylons loaded and the GAU-8A gun fitted. Not far short of some twin-jet transports in size, the A-10A believes in giving and surviving hard knocks

AFVG

TO this strange title could be added others, such as ACA, FCA, MRA-75, NKF, AVS, CAMRA, UKVG, VGCA and US/FRG. Behind each set of initials once lay a ton or two of paper and sometimes computer tapes, test hardware and endless worries and hopes. Since 1960 the development and production of competitive combat aircraft in a competitive timescale and for a competitive cost has been realised to be a task no nation can do easily and most cannot do at all. These sets of acronyms are testimony to the difficulties that big and powerful nations, both alone and collaborating in groups, have encountered in trying to do their own thing in this field. Linking these initials together forms a story without parallel. Practically the only thread that ties it all together is BAC's team at Warton, Lancashire, and even they had no part in some of the studies and at times went almost out of the picture. There were times when the difficulties seemed likely to triumph, and the mountains of studies become a way of life in themselves. This was deeply frustrating, because the end-product was meant to be the thunder of squadrons taking the air. Today, however, hardware has at last taken shape, and thunder can be heard. Similar hardware will probably be on the assembly lines of three nations for the next 20 years (p. 149).

But although Europeans have at last woven a strong and visible fabric, the threads from which it was originally made were diffuse and hidden from the public. They began at different places and times. Perhaps the earliest beginning of all was when Dr Barnes Wallis at Weybridge in 1944 began to ponder on the possibility of making improved aircraft that were polymorphic (able to change their shape) and in particular to sweep their wings and wiggle them in all directions to match the aircraft to every flight regime and pilot command without the need for a tail or any control surfaces. When English Electric Aviation began project studies to meet the GOR.339 (TSR.2, p. 38) they took a hard look at the ideas and patents emanating from Weybridge (which was then an entirely separate company, Vickers-Armstrongs) because variable wing sweep seemed a possible way of meeting the difficult requirement. Although TSR.2 finally gelled as a fixed-wing aircraft, the teams at Warton and Weybridge never lost interest in variable sweep and, after their union within BAC in 1960, they gradually eliminated the basic unknowns and by 1963 had total confidence in their ability to do a VG aeroplane. B. O. 'Ollie' Heath of BAC, today the corporation's MRCA director, has acknowledged his team's debt to the early work at Weybridge, while emphasizing the greater problems of fitting VG wings on a safe-life basis to a slim, dense, compact supersonic combat aircraft quite unlike the large airliners, with fail-safe wings, that were Wallis's main concern.

In 1963, when TSR.2 had moved out of the project stage, the project staff at Warton schemed a private-venture study for a military VG aircraft, the P.45. Powered by two RB.172 turbofans with reheat, or a single reheat Spey, this was planned as a supersonic light attack aircraft and trainer which, in the course of time, was expected to develop into air-superiority and strike versions with fuller avionics. Compared with the F-111, then in flight-test, the P.45 was considerably smaller and differed in ways that were more important than they looked. Whereas the F-111 was Wallis technology leavened with expediencies injected by NASA, the P.45 stemmed from later development. Its wing pivots would have been close to, or even within, the body. The horizontal tail was placed much lower than the wing. The engines were fed from long ducts with intakes ahead of the wing. And the stores pylons were not on the swinging wings but on the fuselage.

It is significant that these decisions had been taken the previous year before the original winning TFX configuration had been published. The P.45 brochure was issued to the MoA and Air Staff in May 1964. The political environment was not auspicious, because TSR.2 costs were considered very worrying and the F-111 was already being viewed as an obvious possible alternative. When the Labour government was elected in October 1964 one of its first aerospace tasks was to devise a viable strategy that could meet the nation's defence and industrial needs after cancellation of TSR.2, and it endorsed the concept of two separate collaborative programmes with France. The first was for the AST.362/ECAT fixed-wing aircraft that became the Jaguar (p. 108), with France leading on the airframe and the UK on the engine. The second, and much later in timing, was for a VG aircraft to meet a long-term British need for an air-superiority fighter and a French need for a superior strike aircraft. This second project was conceived rather hastily and, in my opinion, after superficial assessment of the situation, but it appeared to be necessary to give some long-term stability to a national aerospace scene that lay in tatters. It was to have a British-led airframe and French-led engine.

Prime Minister Wilson announced the programme on 2 February 1965, saying Britain intended 'to enter into discussions with France, and possibly other European countries, about a jet strike-trainer using the variable-geometry concept.' Calling it a strike-trainer was just a muddle, as related in the Jaguar story. The British were interested in using it to replace RAF Lightnings and all Fleet Air Arm fighters in 1974–76, and saw an eventual need for more than 200. The French wanted the aircraft to replace Mirage IIIEs, and possibly the Aéronavale Crusaders, in 1972–75. The programme was formally launched by a Memorandum of Understanding of 17 May 1965 to which the British and French Ministers of Defence and Aerospace (respectively Messrs Healey, Messmer, Jenkins and Jacquet) put their signatures. In addition to launching the Jaguar this provided for each partner 'to examine a variable-geometry aircraft for the middle and late 1970s and thereafter . . . and to examine such an aircraft in relation to the projected operational needs, to formulate technical specifications and make preliminary industrial studies with the full intention of entering upon a joint programme in due course.'

Although BAC Warton had been chosen as the British airframe contractor on the strike/trainer, they were again chosen for this second project in view of their long experience at Mach 2, their unique VG expertise and the loss of TSR.2 on 6 April 1965. The French contractor was to be Dassault (known throughout the programme in Britain as AMD, for Avions Marcel Dassault), who had since 1960 been conducting a VG study programme and in 1964 had begun the engineering design of the Mirage G series with VG. Even without official help from NASA it was by this time easy to see the basic arrangement of that organization's successful swing-wing, but Dassault did not copy all the errors made by General Dynamics in laying out the F-111. It has long been as rigid a policy as Dassault can make it always to build on what they know from flight experience. Accordingly, they adhered to the arrangement of the original Mirage and, in particular, of the Mirage F series. So they gave the Mirage G long inlet ducts starting well ahead of the wing and a tailplane mounted much lower than the wing. As a result, to quote a Dassault test pilot, 'It was a technical success which astonished even ourselves.' Dassault planned the G as a multi-role aircraft optimised for tactical strike, and they made it considerably larger than most earlier Mirages. In its original form the engine was the big SNECMA TF306 reheat turbofan derived from the American TF30. The proposed TF306E had a sea-level rating of 15000 kg (33070 lb) thrust.

This Mirage G was very close indeed in role, size and performance to the collaborative aircraft on which Dassault were to work with Britain. Even before the Memorandum was signed on 17 May Dassault knew what was coming and discussed with the French government the proposal that they should develop two aircraft for identical roles yet possibly totally different in design. Superficially this looked a bad way of allocating national resources. They were told that, officially, France could not fund the Mirage G as a full-scale programme and that the joint programme with Britain had been agreed. Knowing the French I have no doubt in my own mind that Dassault were confidentially told at the highest level that the game had not yet been played out, and that it might be a good idea for Dassault to continue work as fast as they could on their own swing-wing Mirage. Anyway, this they certainly did. From the first meeting with BAC late in May—top engineers got together in August—Dassault were completely frank about the Mirage G. I think any outside observer would have thought that, as Dassault had been chosen as the French airframe contractor in what looked like being the biggest military-aircraft programme in Europe, it might be a good idea to participate in this programme at full strength and drop the Mirage G. It is interesting that Dassault did not do this, yet Dassault is no fool and he seldom plays mere hunches. From the start he backed hardline nationalism and his own team against what he judged to be an ill-conceived exercise.

Had the project found any other partner for Britain but France it would probably have been brought to a successful conclusion. But although the Dassault engineers worked very well with their British partners, and there was never any suggestion of an abrasive relationship (except in the press), Dassault himself, and many other top Frenchmen including de Gaulle, never wanted the programme to succeed and were concerned merely to play Britain along to the maximum advantage to France. To the men at the difficult interfacial stratum, such as Dassault's top engineers Henri Deplante and especially Jean Cabrière, the situation was certainly unusual and variously tragic and funny. Their own Mirage G must often have seemed to them a breath of welcome reality compared with the parallel VG project that they probably suspected was unlikely to come off.

Throughout the project's two-year life it was a ghostly shadow. The public never knew its proper shape or wing span, perhaps because it never settled down in a final form. It never even had a proper designation, but was laconically called the Anglo-French Variable-Geometry aircraft, shortened to AFVG in Britain and GVFA in France. It goes without saying that everything had to be prepared in both languages.

To an outside observer the engine seemed to be much firmer. It had a proper designation, M45G, and it could be read about in advertisements and brochures. The job was not put out to tender but simply given to the losers in the Jaguar programme: SNECMA and Bristol Siddeley. SNECMA had originally offered civil and military versions of the M45 Mars two-spool turbojet in 1963, saying they hoped it would form the basis of European collaboration 'especially with German constructors.' The link with Bristol Siddeley dated from the strike-trainer submission of 1964 with the M45A and B, the latter having reheat. For the AFVG the two firms did the obvious thing and stuck a fan on the front and an enlarged supersonic afterburner and nozzle on the back. The resulting M45G had an LP spool (derived from the SNECMA TS12 engine) comprising a three-stage fan and two-stage compressor, and a seven-stage HP compressor scaled down from the Olympus 320 of the TSR.2. The HP turbine was Olympus-derived, and the two-stage LP turbine came from the SNECMA M33 and TF106. Downstream there was reheat in both hot and cold flows, giving a maximum thrust of 12230 lb with some potential for growth. Engine weight was 1755 lb, a good figure. The M45G was by far the most important of a family of engines launched by an agreement between the two firms on 26 February 1965. But in fact it was anything but a firm design, and Bristol Siddeley, who never complained at having the supposed junior position, never knew how far they could bring pressure to bear in getting SNECMA to take correct design choices matched to the missions.

A week after the Memorandum of 17 May 1965 it was stated that the two airframe companies would receive separately funded feasibility studies and would submit the airframe specification (one specification, not two) in one year. SNECMA stated that their share of the engine R&D would be £10·7 million. From the outset the chief architect of AFVG, Roy Jenkins, had taken it for granted that Britain would lead on the airframe, in return for the French-led Jaguar. In practice this is not an important consideration, provided some formula is available to start the work and keep it moving; but it matters tremendously to politicians and to almost everyone in the two nations outside the programme. This rather basic question was not settled at the start, although the French always knew what the British expected. Momentarily thinking more of Concorde than of his leader's 'white-hot technological revolution', Reginald Paget MP asked about the provisions for withdrawal, to be told by Mr Healey 'Until 1 June 1967 either side can withdraw without notice, but it could be required to complete its work on the engine within agreed financial limits.' Lord Shackleton, Minister for the RAF, showed the precision of the programme-timing by announcing 'We hope it will come in in the second half of the 1970s.'

At the 1965 Paris air show, where I had an interesting talk with a Dassault representative who apparently thought the Mirage IIIG *was* the AFVG ('but the British version may differ slightly from this model'), I was amused to discover the RAF were calling the project 'ECAT 2', although they did agree it had nothing to do with training, while a friend from the MoA confided 'We are going to insist on design leadership, provided the French negotiators agree.' On 21 July Mr Healey, having been asked what the AFVG was for, replied 'The Buccaneer, the Lightning and the Phantom will all start to be withdrawn from service in the middle and late 1970s. The VG machine is likely to be a suitable replacement for some if not all of them. . . . Its weapons have still be be decided.' To an outside observer the image of the project was that it was completely half-baked. It was no comfort to discover that, whereas originally the British had regarded the aircraft primarily as a fighter and the French regarded it as a strike aircraft, the roles were fast becoming reversed. I managed to speak to Mr Healey himself about the problem of commonality. With the F-111 etched in my mind I wondered if, as both sides seemed unable to make up their mind what the aircraft was for, perhaps they might be persuaded to agree a common specification. He was fairly bristling with diplomatic tact, and fell over backwards to emphasize how improper it would be for him to dictate to the French how they should specify their own version. If this mentality had prevailed with Concorde we should today have two versions (at least); as it was, Sud and BAC were practically locked in a room and told not to come out until they had a common SST design. Of course it really takes months, not a few hours, but the point I am making is that it has to be a compromise, with each side prepared to yield something. But from August 1965 it was blindingly obvious that with the AFVG we were going to go through all the nausea of radar dish sizes, weapons fits, avionics fits and flight performance. I did not then know how splendidly the basic aircraft design would adapt itself to conflicting requirements; but neither did the perverse customers.

When I spoke to Mr Healey another pressman asked him about the 'US/FRG', the still uncertain concoction that later in the year gelled as a VG, jet-lift V/STOL fighter involving EWR-Süd in Munich, Fairchild-Hiller Republic at Farmingdale and with Rolls/Allison lift engines. The Defence Minister replied 'Very obviously there is a potential competition between the proposed German-American aircraft and the AFVG. I would hope that there would be room for both if they came into existence at about the same time.' Inwardly he must have felt less sanguine. Federal Germany and the United States were the two biggest markets for combat aircraft in the world outside the Soviet Union, and—to me at least—the participation of the US in the rival programme lent it a perhaps unwarranted air of credibility. Rightly or wrongly, I considered the AFVG a programme based largely on political needs, stemming from Britain's wish to enter the Common Market. The vague belief of the British government that at least 1000 would be sold seemed to me unlikely to be realized without sales to Germany or the US and preferably to both. In any case the whole RAF procurement situation was in the melting pot. Obviously the 'Air Marshals' (as the newspapers called the people who took the decisions, at least half of them civilians) were almost to a man mesmerised by the F-111 (p. 170), but no decision to buy had been taken. They were being urged by BAC to look at the Spey-Mirage (see companion 'Bombers' volume) and by Hawker Siddeley to consider the Buccaneer 2** (p. 33). The British government had a hard time trying to walk a tight-rope which simultaneously gave the RAF a modern aeroplane, gave the UK industry some work, pleased the French, and seemed sensible to the public. It was not helped by the fact that the same government had not only destroyed all the main British programmes but had deliberately made the industry the target of insults.

The French, terribly sensitive to what they considered an unnatural special relationship between Britain and the USA, took the view that Britain could either collaborate with Europe or buy the F-111, but not do both. Jean-Marie Riche, editor of *Air et Cosmos*, thought it worth writing to the London *Times* that 'an F-111A order is very likely to endanger Anglo-French co-operation to the vanishing point.' I even got an extremely senior MoA official to admit 'obviously, as you say, lots of Phantoms and F-111s would diminish the need for the AFVG.' In fact it was clear he wasn't quite sure why we were buying the AFVG at all, except that it was very important to the government. Aware that his house of cards was looking shaky, Roy Jenkins claimed, on 13 December 1965, 'the improved Buccaneer or Mirage are more of a barrier to the AFVG than the slightly earlier purchase of the F-111. The VG plane is required by the French in 1974 and, on current thinking, by us in 1975. . . . We attach the greatest possible importance to the variable-geometry project, which we are determined to protect.' At which the French Air Attaché commented 'Your Minister of Aviation has almost managed to convince the House of Commons that the F-111 is good for collaboration with my country. As a politician he will go far.' What the gallant colonel did not say was that two months earlier, in October, his government had awarded Dassault a contract for a prototype of the Mirage G.

October was a significant month for the AFVG project in a second way. BAC and Dassault arrived at a common datum aircraft and submitted the brochure to the two governments in that month. As it was secret at the time I have sketched this original AFVG showing its appreciable increase in size compared with the original P.45, in the way envisaged when the P.45 was schemed. Fortunately there was never any lengthy consideration of side-by-side seating, but the side view does not reveal the very fat, wide nose needed to accommodate the big radar aerial for the French (previously British) fighter mission. The aircraft had a small fixed 'glove' at the root of the wing (to please Dassault), tailerons, a small rudder and three stores pylons on the fuselage. To the team at Warton—and, indeed, to Dassault's project staff at St Cloud which saw eye to eye with their partners on most of the essentials—this was a wholly sound design. Already its inherent flexibility was astonishing. Much later Ollie Heath wrote 'The aeroplane rode up and down all these various changes of requirement and still the same characteristic aeroplane emerged; we feel that we are also catering for the requirements which have yet to emerge.' But, apart from the fact the whole thing was based on shifting sand, the two customers were really asking it to do rather a lot. In February 1966 the question was asked 'How can it replace the 45-ton F-111 and still operate from French escort carriers at a gross weight of 36000 lb?' Such details did not appear to worry Mr Healey. On 22 February in his *Defence Review* he stated the AFVG would have 'the ability to obtain early warning of an enemy's intentions through reconnaissance and to strike at his offensive forces from a distance. . . . By the mid-1970s we intend that the Anglo-French variable-geometry aircraft should begin to take over this and other roles. Both operationally and industrially this aircraft is the core of our long-term aircraft programme.' This last sentence was to be long remembered.

In June 1966 SNECMA ran the M45F, a turbofan demonstrator engine, on the bed at Melun-Villaroche. On the 22nd of that month Mr Healey emphasized how well the programme was going, and to a Conservative questioner who asked 'surely there is not even an operational requirement?' he replied 'This is totally untrue . . . we now agree with the French on the operational requirement and on the time-scale.' This was smart work, because just two weeks earlier the Air Correspondent of the *Daily Telegraph* had reported 'It now seems that Britain and France will agree that their differences in requirements are such as to make collaboration impossible.' The moral here is that in some other countries, such as the United States, the press is told exactly what is happening and so have no reason to make incorrect guesses. At the end of July Mr Healey, accompanied by the new Aviation Minister Fred Mulley, reviewed progress in Paris with M Messmer; afterwards the French issued a brief press statement saying they had 'no intention of abandoning the programme.' I talked with an engineer from McDonnell, who had found it much easier to pick holes in the AFVG project than to interest Britain in his swing-wing Spey-Phantom S. The Phantom S had been proposed to Britain even before the cancellation of TSR.2 in April 1965, and throughout the St Louis firm considered their carefully engineered study a natural follow-on to the fixed-wing Phantoms of the RAF and RN. They had come to accept that they could not unsell the F-111, which British officials regarded as somehow endowed with supernatural properties, but by mid-1966 McDonnell were able to try a come-back because of the US Navy's very serious interest in the Phantom S as a possible replacement for the defunct F-111B. They wrapped up a nice-looking set of proposals and put them on the desk of the Minister of Aviation before the July meeting in Paris. Among the claims were that the Phantom S was 'superior on every count' to the AFVG in the strike mission which was the prime British requirement, and that it 'could be 80 per cent British' and in service as early as 1971. I doubt that this proposal was even mentioned in Paris. Instead the two Defence Ministers agreed that each would have his own version of AFVG (this was how the operational requirement had been 'agreed') and that they would meet again in October.

Of course the basic airframe was meant to be the same for both aircraft, but agreeing the precise standard of build was a task that never was accomplished. The basic design, which had been mutually agreed very early in the summer of 1965, was thrown back into the melting pot when Dassault decided to 'reneg' on the joint configuration. One of the bones of contention was exactly where the wing pivots should be, and it is interesting to recall that right at the very end of the programme, at the 1967 Paris air show, the only publicly displayed AFVG model was constructed from signed drawings showing an in-between pivot position that showed no bias to either partner. But this is a relative triviality. Probably more important was the fact that the instructions to the two airframe firms were always separate and sometimes not quite the same. And they never went deep enough for the real co-operation such as BAC have enjoyed with Jaguar and MRCA, but contented themselves with requests for g-a. drawings, weights, performance, programme dates and, on one or two occasions, costs.

Inside the programme costs never seemed to loom large, or give rise to any crisis; outside, it was a different story. To the mass-media the letters AFVG meant instant controversy, and probably some new worry over cost-escalation. Certainly on the British side the autumn of 1966 was spent studying several simpler sorts of AFVG, many of them even single-engined, in an attempt to get the price down. In August Sir George Edwards had predicted the project 'could hit turbulence', and chucking out one engine seemed a fair-sized gust to me. The numbers associated with the single-engined AFVG were in my view simply not viable, and the general consensus of opinion was that the degradation was out of all proportion to the financial saving. No notion of costs had then been disclosed, but unofficial estimates suggested an R&D bill of £200 million. On 1 October the Air Correspondent of the *Daily Telegraph* revealed that the MoA had 'not accepted' BAC's cost estimates but had added 'a considerable percentage' (much later said to be 50 per cent) for contingencies. He viewed the AFVG as 'A doubtful starter' and went on to suggest that Britain would have to buy the American-German rival which would be the subject of 'a £3000 million joint scheme' involving several American aircraft companies led by Boeing. In fact the only US airframe partner remained Fairchild. And, far from being the subject of a '£3000 million scheme', the AVS (Advanced Vertical Strike) design study was the subject of deep disenchantment in both Bonn and Washington. Its project-definition phase was due to run until October 1967, and a year before that it was pretty clear that this particular proposal was not going to lead to production and probably not to hardware at all. In the long-term this was crucial for the Warton VG team, and the prediction of the London newspaper was the reverse of what actually happened.

Four days later Michael Donne of *The Financial Times* showed his capacity for investigative journalism with the first feature article on the project. He reported 'The two manufacturers believe they could build it for just under £1 million a time, after spending some £85 million on research and development. For procurement of 300 aircraft, or 150 each for Britain and France, costing around £300 million, the total cost would thus be in the region of £400 million or £200 million for each country. This figure is not accepted by the Governments, which feel that . . . the proper price per aircraft seems likely to be around £1·75 million. . . .' Predictably, costs were the nub of the difficulties, and on 25 October M Messmer showed how fraught the coming talks would be by describing the project as 'extremely expensive'. He went on (in the Assemblée Nationale) 'If for this reason we should postpone the project we would supply the Armée de l'Air with another type of powerful strike aircraft based on less advanced techniques.' On 3 November Lord Shackleton said 'This is a worthwhile project with excellent prospects and with a great deal of agreement at a technical level on the operational requirements.' Within thirty seconds he added 'It is true that the British and French operational requirements are different technically. . . .'

Ths supposedly crucial talks took place in London on 7 November 1966, spurred on by a pile of telegrams from the Action Committee for European Aerospace—a shop-floor group of British workers who were afraid their industry might fold up entirely—urging the ministers to reach agreement. Chapman Pincher, of the *Daily Express* suggested Britain was offering to split the bill 'something like 60-40' to please the French, but all the subsequent communiqué said was that no decision had been taken, and that M Messmer had gone away to look at the French bank-balance 'so as to obtain a decision in time for a further meeting . . .

before the end of the year.' On 28 November the indefatigable *Telegraph* air correspondent torpedoed this coming meeting by pointing out that de Gaulle had just dismissed 'M René Block' (Bloch, actually, as mentioned in the Jaguar chapter), described as 'the Frenchman responsible for joint projects', and concluded that 'new friction between the two countries makes cancellation certain of the £200 million project. . . .' Exactly a month later his headline on the same aircraft ran 'AIR INDUSTRY EXPECTS £425M RAF ORDER.' On 13 December the *Daily Mail* headline proclaimed 'FRENCH PULL OUT OF SWING WING PROJECT', while on 13 January that of the *Express* ran 'FRANCE READY TO COME IN ON THE VG.' I got the impression the situation was confused.

On 30 November 1966 Fred Mulley told the Commons that Britain was 'very well advanced with contingency planning'. I think what he meant was that he was still being got at by General Dynamics to buy more F-111s, by Hawker Siddeley to buy GLARE (yet another new Buccaneer) and by McDonnell on the Phantom S, that the Germans had no faith in the AFVG at all, and that he was practically being told to clinch a giant helicopter deal with the French just to keep them in the programme. It was interesting to see how M Messmer unfortunately was unable to settle his budgetary problems by the agreed meeting date in mid-December, and was granted a postponement (while the big helicopter deal was thrashed out). At Christmas came a surprising new turn of events. Unknown to the public General de Gaulle himself said he would accept the aircraft provided it could 'surpass the Phantom'. Throughout the programme the French had thrown the Phantom in Britain's face and regarded it as a danger to AFVG. Now, because of the Phantom, the AFVG had to be given a higher flight performance.

Everything gelled early in the new year. On 16 January 1967 the long-awaited go-ahead was announced by the two ministers in Paris. Mr Healey announced massive orders for French helicopters and said it would be 'a tonic for our aircraft industry' (he meant the British one, in case there was any doubt). A 'senior executive of a British engine firm' told the indefatigable man from the *Telegraph* 'I cannot accept Mr Healey's assurances that the helicopter deal is not connected with the Anglo-French negotiations for a swing-wing plane. The deal is too one-sided to be otherwise.' In fact I think everyone knew the deal was just another instance of a good ploy by the French. The deal was not overtly in any way connected with AFVG; it just happened to be conceived at a crucial time in that project's life. As for AFVG, this continued on its uncertain way. *The Times* said R&D would be 'about £200 million, to be shared . . .' while *Flight International* put it at 'about £400 million total'. The weekly said 'Among the concessions made by the British side is believed to be agreement to accept a higher proportion of both R&D costs and production deliveries.' According to *The Financial Times* the partners were 'each expected to take an equal number of aircraft and to share cost, work and export sales on a strictly 50-50 basis.' The programme was described as 'The Anglo-French £1,700 million project' (*Telegraph*, 17 January), '£650 m. pact on VG project' (*Financial Times*, 17 January) and 'the £850 million Anglo-French project' (*Telegraph*, 19 January). It just shows where official secrecy gets you.

Curiously, while the public was fed only speculation on these vital issues, lots of things were said officially that need not have been. I am sure Mr Healey regrets proclaiming that the 16 January 1967 agreement provided 'an assured future to the industries of both our countries.' Likewise John Stonehouse, who had gone to Paris after having been Minister of Aviation for ten days, did not really have to say 'As far as we are concerned the main agreement has been reached and we are very satisfied with it.' I wonder if they really did dismiss the idea of the whole thing coming unstuck?

It was soon clear that Britain had indeed agreed to bear an unfair share of the costs, in Healey's words 'to free funds for the many pressing demands made on French finances.' Moreover, although the French had originally wanted the aircraft first, as noted earlier, Britain was now to take more of the first batches, and also to take a bigger total: 'about ten squadrons', or 175 aircraft, compared with 125 for France including 30 naval versions for the carriers *Foch* and *Clémenceau*. A meeting would be held in March 1967 to 'complete the technical specification' (again ?) and 'take the necessary decision to implement the programme' (again ?). In the meantime 'we shall be consulting possible purchasers in the next few weeks to see whether any adjustments to these specifications will attract a larger market' which apparently had not been done before. The deadline for bending the specification to suit third parties was April 1, but as at this date the specification for the British and French aircraft had still not been agreed (!) it was put off for a further month. Most important of all the January decisions was that the programme was expected to move from study into prototype construction on 1 January 1968, and that the deadline for withdrawal from the programme without notice, and without penalty, was to be extended from 1 June 1967 by no less than 18 months, to 1 January 1969. In Healey's words 'The French and ourselves believe it is a great mistake to commit ourselves to a programme of this size without the right to review it at any stage later on.'

I tried to find out what 'study' was going to occupy everyone's time between agreeing the specification, presumably on 1 May 1967, and deciding whether to cut metal in 1968, but all I was told in reply was that the 18-month extension in the withdrawal period did not 'imply any slippage in the programme'. This did not answer my question, nor the implied rebuke of the defence correspondent of *The Times* who recorded 'three months ago the British Government was confident that work on a prototype could start by March 1967.' When I look back at what is on public record the whole programme seems to have been run by muddled fools. In reality the industrial partnership was good—they were experienced, brilliant people working well together—but not a glimmer of this ever leaked out to the public.

Mr Healey's patient steering of the AFVG through stormy seas and uncharted hazards did not make him especially popular in Britain. Although newspapers said his saving of the project was 'a personal triumph' he had to defend it from all sides. On 14 February 1967 he faced a barrage of questions from the Labour Party Defence Committee (was it not a reversal of our policy of building no more combat aircraft; why were so many needed, plus all the Phantoms and F-111s; who else would buy it; why was it going to replace V-bombers when this was the task of Polaris; was he not over-optimistic about the whole thing?), most of which had already been answered and some were even a matter of public record. His colleague Tam Dalyell sniped at the programme continually, and once suggested 'It is the first major and disagreeable duty of the Minister of Technology . . . to have rough, tough and unpleasant scenes with the Minister of Defence to get him to drop the AFVG and break the vicious circle whereby we have to build ever more sophisticated aircraft.' It was to Dalyell that Healey said he did not regard the Mirage IIIG as 'a serious competitor.' Dick Worcester, who previously had been thought a friend by most Labour politicians, calculated the AFVG unit price on a run of 300 would be £1·8 million. And Conservative MP Enoch Powell put his finger on a pretty significant debating point when he asked in what circumstances Britain would need a 1500-mile radius in the strike role East of Suez in the later 1970s—'such an operation as that implies an involvement of this country in vast operations in all three elements of a character such as the party opposite has entirely forsworn.' At this Healey came very clean indeed and retorted 'Without this programme there would be no design work for the British aircraft industry after Concorde, and without that design work there would be no future for the industry, not merely in Britain but in Europe.' This seemed a remarkable statement, because the RAF did have a real need for something like the AFVG after 1975. It also showed a remarkable change in heart from the time 18 months earlier when Labour had assumed office vowing vengeance on the wicked planemakers for building costly warplanes.

There is no doubt the record shows the Wilson administration, which started off swinging hatchets at every British aircraft it saw—and Concorde, until stopped by the French—was by 1967 very much better informed on aerospace matters and deeply concerned that it should not, by its actions, hand over Europe to the United States as a helpless captive market in this colossal military and civil field. AFVG was to a considerable degree contrived to help Europe preserve some independence, yet the leaders of France refused to believe this. In a feature entitled 'The Swing-Wing Fantasy' the business editor of *The Observer* (London) quoted one of these leaders as saying 'The AFVG agreement is just politics. The General will pull out. It is a most monstrous arrangement to make the innocent French taxpayer subsidize the British aircraft industry.' Many Frenchmen even today think this a fair reflection on the programme. The French are most difficult partners who instinctively distrust their opposite numbers and love to pretend that, were it not for these partners, the whole thing would be simpler, better and cheaper. In fact in this case the British requirement stayed more or less the same while the French chopped and changed and sometimes seemed deliberately to be trying to add to the costs. Throughout the first quarter of 1967 a separate study was undertaken to cost the modifications necessary to meet the new French interceptor requirement, voiced the previous Christmas by de Gaulle, calling for a greater combat ceiling and an increase in dash Mach number from 2·2 to 2·4. On 12 April 1967 Healey reported that the increase in costs would be very great; he added that, in any case, the cost of the RAF strike version 'can be contained within' the higher cost of the French interceptor version. I would still be interested to hear how in this programme the French were being made to subsidize the British, especially after Britain agreed to pay more than its fair share of the costs.

Despite the facts that the proposed British buy was now bigger and the French buy smaller, and that the French led every other major project in sight, Dassault strongly fought the suggestion that they should not be undisputed leaders on the AFVG programme. Although the French never gave way, on 28 February 1967 Mr Stonehouse announced that 'The Ministry of Technology will be the executive agency on the airframe, letting contracts to a joint BAC/Dassault company registered in the UK, while the French government will let the engine contract to a joint SNECMA/Bristol Siddeley company registered in France.' He assured the Commons 'There is no doubt in our minds that this agreement is going through . . . we have had that assurance from the French.' He revealed that preliminary studies were near completion, that the 'detailed project-definition stage' was due to begin in April (the previous stage, begun in May 1965, was 'feasibility', in which the contractors helped the governments decide what they wanted and could afford) and would last about six months, and that full development, including the manufacture of prototypes, would start 'early in 1968'. A little later he did admit the programme had been 'slower to get under way than we at first anticipated.' On 1 March 1967, when the four main contractors were due to report on their management plans, a formidable Anglo-French delegation (led by Air Marshal Sir Reginald Empson and Brig-Gen Claude Grigaut) tried to sell AFVG to Federal Germany, represented mainly by General Johannes Steinhoff. The papers all thought the Luftwaffe chief's choice was Phantom or AFVG, depending on whether it replaced the F-104G sooner or later; in fact it bought the Phantom to help offset the massive costs of the US forces in the Federal Republic, running at £330 million a year.

Had the Germans come in there is a faint chance the French might not have withdrawn. Their buy would have been well over 200 aircraft, making a big difference to the unit price. By March 1967 the R&D estimate had reached £240 million, which on an Anglo-French run of 300 raised the unit price with amortized R&D from £2·1 million to £2·3 million. Had AFVG been just AVG (a British programme) its eventual market might have been in no way smaller, it would have got off the ground much quicker and the R&D bill would certainly have been much less. It was Roy Mason, Minister of Defence (Equipment), who pointed out that 'most of the design elements' and avionics for the RAF strike version had already been almost fully developed for TSR.2, funded by the British taxpayer. Yet for the AFVG the two airframe contractors had to provide for two almost totally different avionic and weapon installations, with primary capability for strike and interception and secondary capability in the alternative mission. BAC alone had to price out 12 different 'fits' from the cheapest permitted for safe daylight operation to the most expensive that 'did everything' (to quote Dr J. V. Hughes, BAC manager of VG avionics). Their final recommendation for the RAF version came very near the RAF requirement at a price the government thought it could afford.

As 1967 progressed it was clear the French were going to do as little as possible with the programme until after their national elections early in April. In these M Messmer lost his seat, but despite this was retained in office as Minister of the Armed Forces. On 17 April he came to London to confer with Healey, and in the subsequent communiqué it was said that both nations intended to continue the project 'within the cost ceilings laid down earlier this year.' At the time I think nobody close to the programme could have thought this anything other than window-dressing, although why the people who find the money should be thus deceived escapes me. Not only had the costs undoubtedly risen—although in a Commons reply on 12 April Healey refused to confirm any cost figure on the grounds that 'precise figures cannot be given until the project study has been completed'—but Dassault's dislike of the programme became more overt. So sure were they of their own expertise, especially with the Mirage G that was fast approaching completion, that they simply refused to admit that BAC led on the airframe. In April Sir George Edwards, who ought never to have been worried in this way, went to have a summit talk with Marcel Dassault himself and found that, although the meeting was certainly not frigid, his French counterpart was simply determined to be bloody-minded. This did not get into the papers, but on 2 May Dassault's adviser on military affairs, General Pierre M. Gallois, told the London *Times* in very straight terms of his total disenchantment with the whole idea of Anglo-French programmes and with this one in particular. The newspaper seemed surprised. It then got on the phone to BAC, who had by this time ceased to present a party-line of happy unity and were only too glad to tell someone that the blame for increased costs 'lay entirely with the French who had dithered for months and then produced a lot of technical innovations.'

What these costs were began to be disclosed in the Defence Debate at Westminster on 1 May, when Healey said he had allowed up to £150 million in R&D on the British vote for the period 1965–80. He agreed he had previously 'given support' to a figure between £100 million and £125 million (I don't know where; as noted above, he had just refused to confirm or deny a pure guess of £100 million). Anyway, on the next day Lord Shackleton said there had been 'no change'; the Defence Minister had given a figure for 15 years, not ten, and had 'taken account of possible improvements in the aircraft after the ten-year period had expired.' This was odd, because Healey had explicitly told his colleague Tam Dalyell the R&D bill would 'probably be considerably more than the estimate.' He also claimed that, over a 15-year period, the TSR.2 'would have cost £700 million more than the adopted programme' of F-111s and AFVGs. The editor of *Flight International* conducted a wordy battle in print with the Defence Minister over this, feeling certain that the figure could not be justified. Apart from extracting the information that the two supposedly equivalent totals were £1000 million and £1700 million he merely reinforced the lesson that, in a land where the public is told nothing, and gets nowhere by asking, ministers can trot out any figure they like and hide behind security when challenged. Of course, not all the public are mere sheep. The British aircraft industry had kept its mouth shut, almost to a man, while subjected to turbulence the like of which had never before been experienced by any group of manufacturers in the world.

But in May 1967 Frank H. Robertson, chief of preliminary design at Short & Harland, had the nerve to suggest that the claim the AFVG would be cheaper than TSR.2 was 'unadulterated bunkum.' He elaborated on this: 'The very high cost of TSR.2 was almost entirely due to its extremely complicated environmental and weapon systems; the airframe was relatively simple. If the swing-wing fighter does not have similar systems it won't be any use, and the airframe is bound to be more expensive.' I have no doubt his directors told him to shut up and not rock the boat. In any case I think he was on very shaky ground, because TSR.2 had paid for most of the 'extremely complicated . . . systems' and had an airframe as costly as that of AFVG.

On 8 May 1967 Healey and Messmer met again, and two days later the first formal meeting at ministerial level with the Germans took place between Messmer and the Federal Defence Minister Gerhard Schroeder. The Bonn government's main considerations were to make the right choice of successor to the G91 and F-104G, give massive work (design as well as manufacture) to their anxious industry, and pay the crushing dollar costs of US forces in Germany. While AFVG filled the political air on both sides of the Channel, the US/FRG had become quite a firm project study as the AVS (Advanced Vertical Strike) aircraft, still a partnership between EWR-Süd at Munich and the former Republic team at Farmingdale. The project had its genesis in the defunct NBMR-3 NATO competition for a V/STOL jet-lift fighter in 1960. The cleverest of all the NBMR–3 submissions was the D-24 Allianz (Alliance) proposed jointly by Fokker and Republic, with swing-wings and vectored-thrust jet lift. Republic kept the work going because it was demonstrably better than the rather wasteful German jet-VTOL machines that were actually funded as experimental hardware, notably the VJ 101C, the Mach 2·4 VJ 101D (never completed) and the Fw 1261 which later became the VFW-Fiat (Fiat then dropped out) VAK-191. By 1966 their work with Herr Bölkow's engineers at Munich had produced a brochure which for sheer technical interest has rarely been equalled. Apart from swing-wings it featured two pairs of Rolls-Royce/Allison XJ99 lift jets, which swung out from the sides of the fuselage behind the cockpit, and deflectors on the two GE main propulsion engines. The funding was in the ratio Germany 2, US 1, and although the Germans gained much experience from their intimate association with US programme control and management techniques—which may perhaps have misled them subsequently—they were increasingly daunted by the cost. On 27 April 1967 *Flight International* said the R&D for the AVS would be £145 million over six years, but this was the sum for the project-definition phase and airframe engineering alone, and covered neither systems nor engines. By the beginning of 1967 the Bonn government had begun to fund studies into a simpler VG aircraft called the NKF (Neuenkampfflugzeug). From 1966 onwards the Germans looked increasingly seriously at the possibility of collaboration with Britain, but AFVG, and their own project with the Americans, were barriers rather than a means to this end. An eminent Luftwaffe staff officer told me his government 'had reservations' about participation in this programme; he refused to be drawn further, but it is not hard to see what some of the snags were.

One of them continued to be the Mirage G, the prototype of which was rolled out at Melun-Villaroche on 27 May 1967, with flight scheduled in July. During the Paris air show Dassault coolly threw a big press conference and demonstrated the G's swing wings on the ground, carefully refraining from describing the aircraft as an operational weapon but inviting guests to draw their own conclusions. Dassault's visible proof of VG accomplishment was impressive; the only thing that degraded his credibility was his claim he could develop an operational version for a total R&D cost of 'US $90 million, compared with $700 million for the AFVG.' I believe de Gaulle had waited for this event before informing Messmer that the latter was to find reasons for pulling out of the AFVG programme. On 1 June Healey told Sir Ian Orr-Ewing that '£500 million covers the cost of R&D, development [presumably different from the D of R&D], production, support equipment, spares and operation until 1980'. The land seemed to be full of officials all trying to hammer some semblance of viability in costs and timing into a programme that had suddenly gone sour (again). On the 11th Messmer told the Assemblée Nationale Military Affairs Committee that 'no money could be spared' for the programme under the 1968 and 1969 budgets, the two years remaining of the Fifth Plan (*Loi Programme*). He also made it clear—just in case Britain meekly acquiesced to a two-year postponement—that it was very doubtful France could find much money for the AFVG in the Sixth Plan of 1970–75. Just to add fuel to the fire, Dassault was said to be demanding a production order for the fixed-wing Mirage F1, a scaled-down version of the big F2 which had flown on 12 June 1966. This 'F' family arose from the realization that, though a tailless delta seemed right in the melting-pot of 1954–55, a conventional configuration was much more efficient. Dassault built the F1 prototype very quickly as a private-venture for the air-superiority role. It was partly a 'belt and braces' hedge against failure of the bigger and more difficult G, and, though primarily a fighter, Deplante and Cabrière calculated it would be at least as good as the AFVG in short-range attack missions. The first F1 broke up in the air on 18 May 1967, killing René Bigand, but by this time the F1's great potential was obvious. Dassault, playing his cards boldly as always, told de Gaulle himself he would agree to take over Breguet (see the Jaguar chapter) only if the F1 was bought for the Armée de l'Air. At first the latter said no, chiefly because there was no money, but in his statement on 11 June Messmer implied that a favourable F1 decision had been reached, and linked this fact with the absence of funds for the AFVG. The F1 contract was not signed until more than two years later, but it killed the AFVG in June 1967.

On 21 June *The Times* diplomatic correspondent reported Messmer had sent Healey a message making it clear it was 'extremely unlikely the AFVG would ever be built.' On the same day, Healey was cross-examined in the Commons on the story; he replied that he had 'received no communication from the French government', but also said he was 'in continuous contact' with Messmer. He angrily insisted he was 'not responsible for the reports in the press', and it appeared not to occur to him that he should have been. On 26 June he said he had received a letter from Messmer; he even went so far as to add there was no reason to believe the project was not 'in accordance with the desires and interests of the French government.' I think he must have known the French were inventing new reasons for getting out about once every hour. The amazing six-day war in the Middle East had put Israel's Mirages in headlines around the world. Dassault's queue of customers seemed to be growing daily. And de Gaulle used Harold Wilson's speech about 'freedom of passage in the Gulf of Aqaba' to demonstrate the total disparity of strategy and missions between France and the UK. He even produced a report showing 'fantastic' spiralling in AFVG cost, and evidence of technical disputes on how the project should be split between Dassault and BAC. He didn't really have to do all this; it was quite enough to tell Messmer to say there was no money. To a Briton the most unlikely reason of all was unearthed by the good old *Daily Telegraph*: it was that the French were worried Britain might want to drop the project!!

Healey met Messmer on the afternoon of 29 June 1967, the day on which a big feature in *The Financial Times* examined four possible courses open to Britain after collapse of the AFVG and still missed the right one. On 30 June *The Times* defence correspondent reported—under the incredible headline 'Reprieve for the Swing-wing'—that 'Of the £11 million allocated . . . between £3 million and £5 million has been spent. The programme is more than 18 months behind schedule . . .' (the figure for actual spend was possibly correct if the engine is included). The following day a public-relations man in Messmer's ministry announced 'We are not aware of any reason which could cause the government to abandon the programme. To say that the project has been dropped by France is a statement without any basis.' I'm sure that chap could get a job anywhere, especially as on 29 June his minister had formally told

Healey that France was withdrawing for budgetary reasons. He did, of course offer all sorts of assurances on all the other collaborative programmes, and he even opened the door to future ones (the last bit ought to have been checked first with de Gaulle, who had expressed the view that Britain's East of Suez pretensions alone were sufficient grounds for making partnership schemes impossible). Healey broke the news to the Commons on 5 July. After the two years of nausea and Alice in Wonderland nonsense I suddenly felt very sorry for him.

I felt sorry because Healey is not an old-fashioned politician who likes nothing better than streams of angry rhetoric from both sides. He did not enjoy saying 'Her Majesty's Government have received this decision with great regret. It raises a number of fundamental issues—(Opposition cheers and cries of "Resign") . . . I think that when he has reflected, the Hon. Member . . . will regret the words he has used—(Opposition cries of dissent) —and attempting to drag some petty party advantage—(cries of "Oh")— —out of what is a very serious matter not only for Britain but for Europe as a whole. I have been repeatedly, and I think rightly, urged by the Opposition to try to make a success of Anglo-French co-operation in aircraft. If I have failed that is not my fault—(renewed cries of "Oh").' Perhaps I am merely displaying my political naiveté in being surprised at the way the thing was played by the Wilson administration. I could have expected Wilson himself to make a very strong statement on the whole programme. It need not have been more than a few hundred words but it could have spelt out in clear terms the contrast between Britain, which regarded AFVG as important and tried to make a success of it, and France, which regarded the whole thing as a political football.

So lightly did the French regard the programme that they invented difficulties when it suited them, let these melt into thin air when they had extracted what they wanted from their partner, and then invented fresh difficulties when they had squeezed the deal dry and saw no purpose in staying in. Outwardly the French conduct seemed at the time to be disgraceful. The British must have been aware (I certainly was) that throughout France the name AFVG had been portrayed as a giant confidence trick played by the British on the unsuspecting French, as a result of which hardworking French taxpayers were being made to pay for a wickedly complicated creation of the British aircraft industry. This notion was utter nonsense, but at no time did the British government say so, nor did it explain in terms that a child could understand that AFVG was meant to be needed by both partners equally, bought by both equally, designed and made by both equally, and paid for by both equally (sorry, I forgot: Britain was paying more than her share). Instead, when France got out I personally know several ordinary French folk whose attitude was pure relief, while in Westminster Wilson left poor Healey in the role of Aunt Sally, even though he had done more than any other man to make the project a success.

Perhaps the Prime Minister's silence reflected his own view of the programme as a politically inspired one. If one had to find a single adjective to describe his administration it would surely be his own favourite word, 'pragmatic'. The AFVG was a means to an end, and that end was perhaps not primarily concerned with the RAF's order of battle. Two days after the bombshell he went to Farnborough to open an immense Concorde test building, and said 'The announcement this week of the French decision . . . to withdraw from the AFVG—which is, of course, only one of the joint projects under way—underlines the limitations and difficulties of co-operation in the present circumstances of an economically divided Europe. It is the belief that it will bring advantages, not only in economic terms but also from closer political identity with our fellow West Europeans, that has inspired us in the application we have made to join the European Economic Communities.' (In opposition, of course, he has been violently opposed to the British entry; as I said, he is a pragmatic man.)

Future historians may discover why, when on 30 November 1966 his administration was 'very well advanced with contingency planning', the ultimate French knock-out, which was telegraphed in unmistakable terms, should have caught it with its pants down. Healey, seeing it coming and putting five minutes aside to think about it, could have taken the helicopter agreement home one evening and tried to see how that might also go sour. Instead he told the Commons he was deeply concerned that this agreement 'will involve advantage . . . to the UK . . . which is totally commensurate with that derived by France' and said 'We shall be studying the matter further later in the year.' And instead of being able to announce major progress with an aircraft to meet the known requirements of Britain and likely European partners he could only announce 'We are ordering a project study by British firms on a VG aircraft to a modified specification.' The only reasonable conclusion is that he really did not think the programme would collapse, or that he considered the correct attitude for the nation was one of injured innocence and dazed surprise.

In the summer a Commons written answer gave the 'cost of the programme' as £2·5 million, showing how the French avoided entering the expensive phase. On 18 September 1967 Messmer told the Assemblée Defence Committee the Mirage G would lead to 'an operational aircraft for the Armée de l'Air in 1975', which was precisely what Healey had assured MPs on 5 July would not happen (in fact it will not, but nobody knew this in 1967). On 26 July *The Financial Times* reported Lord Shackleton as claiming 'No impetus has been lost on the swing-wing project', despite the fact that the previous day the irrepressible *Telegraph* air correspondent had reported 'Britain Abandons European Swing-Wing Plane Plans.' To anyone disinterested in the programme the AFVG story is a cause for sarcasm, wry amusement and occasionally disbelief that people could be so amazingly silly. But to Britons, and I earnestly hope to Frenchmen also, it is a dreadful lesson in what happens if you launch a controversial project, involving huge sums of money, and then pursue a policy of silence so that the public is fed a continual diet of speculation.

My own jaundiced view of the programme is self-evident. This may seem unfair to the dedicated officials, design and project engineers, air force staffs and others who laboured against all the headwinds to make AFVG a success. I certainly do not mean to criticise their endeavours, but the environment in which they worked. Inside the programme almost everyone got on with the job. The obvious wish of the British designers to make it a success largely overcame the initially scornful view of the French, who not only never forgot that the British government had said it would never again do its own combat aircraft but were absolutely incredulous that it announced this policy at a time when it had the P.45 airframe, the RB.153 engine and the TSR.2 avionics laying around waiting to be put together. Can one really blame them for taunting their British colleagues with 'Why should you work with us? You will just buy more Phantoms in the end.'

To the people inside the AFVG programme it was nothing like as bad as it looked to those outside. Apart from private ventures, every other combat aircraft in my lifetime seemed to begin with a requirement by the user(s), and then, after keen competition, decide on the builder and the programme. This one seemed to begin with the programme and the builders; and the users' need seemed so ill-defined that the two partners switched over their requirements in mid-stream. In fact the requirements were perfectly valid. What defeated the officials were their detailed implementation; such things as Dassault's personal pride, the glory of Gaullist France, and British humility in order to get into the Common Market, probably played a much smaller part in the outcome than they seemed to do at the time.

AFVG lasted just 27 months. For me it only brought one spark of brightness and this came after its death. In the Commons debate on aviation on 13 July 1967 Healey was, predictably, taunted for having called the programme the 'core' of Britain's long-term programme. He replied that he had looked the word up in his dictionary and found it meant 'the central part, normally to be cut out.'

MRCA

PARADOXICALLY, as soon as the link with France was severed, the British VG programme recovered a sense of purpose and progress. The 'project study with British firms' interested the technical press because of the plural participation; indeed 'Interavia' explicitly reported it involved 'both BAC and HSA'. In fact the recipients were BAC Warton and Rolls-Royce (which had taken over Bristol Siddeley in October 1966). On about 22 July 1967 both firms were awarded six-month contracts to examine an AFVG optimised for the strike role. Heath and his team, under the Preston Division (now Military Aircraft Division) managing director Freddie Page, knew the slight change in role would scarcely alter the shape of the aircraft, but having only one set of avionics made things much easier. The only big bother was something which, though it had never made headlines, had been the main technical problem all along. From the outset the engine had been a source of worry because engines need a longer timescale than aircraft and it had been difficult to agree on the right level of propulsion technology to balance performance against technical risk. French withdrawal put this debate back in square one, because the M45G was not continued by the engine partners. Perhaps SNECMA made a mistake here. Had they gone on funding the engine Bristol Siddeley would have done also, and it could have found an outlet in both the British VG aircraft and in the twin-engined version of the Mirage G which was already on the Dassault drawing board in 1967. Instead SNECMA elected to develop their 'Super Atar' M53.

As it was, BAC looked keenly at two all-British proposals, the BS.143 and 145, and finally settled on the RB.153 reheat turbofan developed jointly by Rolls and MAN-Turbomotoren and actually running since November 1963. In fact one RB.153 was running at Munich with a 90° deflecting nozzle which handled the whole efflux of engine and after-burner, to support GE's proposed propulsion engine for the AVS. Although Healey caused some alarm by announcing V/STOL was 'being considered for the UKVG aircraft' both Britain and Germany had by the summer of 1967 decided to rely solely on STOL without the V. A team from Warton went to Munich as early as 10 July, before the AFVG dust had settled (a typical example, the French would say, of British perfidy). They found intense interest among their colleagues at Messerschmitt-Bölkow in BAC replacing Fairchild in the AVS programme which was pretty obviously not going to be supported by the US beyond the definition phase in October 1967. They also told BAC of the parallel NKF. This was a 'gut reaction' project, by which I mean that it satisfied the emotional wish of the powerful German industry to do its own thing while reflecting disenchantment with the complicated AVS. NKF was a simple—and probably a very optimistic—VG replacement for the F-104G, with one engine, one seat and no jet lift. It seemed irreconcilable with the bigger twin-engined design at Warton. Moreover, as John Stonehouse had been told the previous February, the Germans expected to buy the biggest number of aircraft and so expected design leadership. It was largely because they knew Dassault would never concede this that the German industry was disinterested in the AFVG programme. BAC, they thought, might be less unyielding. In reply the British engineers pointed out that this was a matter for their governments to decide, but that it was an emotive thing that had little real meaning; it could be overcome if there was a real will to co-operate. BAC had had more influence on the Jaguar than had Breguet, although constitutionally 'leadership' in that programme was vested in France. What was much more important was that the Luftwaffe requirement was even closer to the British one than the French one had been. It was not an air-superiority mission but a close air support role, similar to the RAF strike mission but with less need for range and more need for STOL. When one ignored the emotional trivialities, the prospects for collaboration looked good.

John Stonehouse struck similar sparks from the Italians in Rome on 13 July, and a week later Defence Ministers Healey and Schroeder began formal negotiations. In August Air Vice-Marshal W. D. Hodgkinson, ACAS (OR), and Handel Davies (then Deputy Controller of Aircraft, R&D, at Mintech and now BAC technical director), spent two days talking specifications in Bonn. At Warton work went ahead fast, involving not only tunnel models but also a full-scale wing sweep rig. BAC had eliminated the fixed 'gloves' at the wing roots which reduced the maximum lift coefficient but which Dassault had wanted because the IIIG had them. By the late autumn they knew they had all the elements for a first-class design, that would suffer from none of the F-111's structural and aerodynamic problems. They wrote the UKVG into a brochure and delivered it on 30 November 1967. This very significant document was probably the chief technical foundation for subsequent work, even though the UKVG was an East of Suez aircraft with long range and drop tanks. On 6 December a team from the Bundestag came to London while the NKF went ahead in place of the dying AVS. By this time the Germans had conducted their own negotiations with everyone in sight, and some had begun to feel the best course for them would be to launch an international project based on the NKF with as many partners as possible. The question of design leadership still vexed the British. BAC's view was that it ought not to matter, but that if the inexperienced German engineers were going to be leaders in more than just name the result could conceivably be disastrous. The deep wish of the Germans for design experience was understandable, but it seemed illogical for them to gain this experience in the role of masters rather than as partners. To which the Germans retorted they were the natural choice, as their requirement was 'at least double the size of any other possible participant.' This turned out to be untrue.

By the end of 1967 it was clear that the hope that Britain could just find other partners to replace France was a pious one. The main users of the F-104G—Germany, Italy, Belgium and the Netherlands—had got into a huddle with Projekt Hornet to find the most cost/effective replacement to do the same F-104 job after 1975. By mid-January 1968 their requirements had crystallised as the MRA-75 (Multi-Role Aircraft for 1975), envisaged as a small VG single-seater with STOL performance and probably a single engine, based squarely on the German NKF. The remaining big user of the F-104, Canada, was then independently working on a parallel CAMRA (Canadian MRA) project. Britain, unlike all these other NATO countries, had a very flexible and highly refined VG design and the capability of producing an engine for it. But in the winter of 1967-68 the British government was in the throes of a drastic policy revision which finally accepted that there was no viable role for Britain outside Europe (not as a routine peacetime commitment anyway), and BAC was asked to reshape the UKVG into the ACA (Advanced Combat Aircraft) for a new and generally shorter-range spectrum of missions. In the long term this clearly made the UK requirement even more compatible with the European ones, and some of the ACA gross weights were lighter than some of the NKF. When the MRA-75 partners first met, in Germany in February 1968, Canada sent an observer but Britain did not even bother to do that. In March 1968 the Under-Secretary for the RAF, Merlyn Rees, just about hit rock bottom with the opinion 'The whole question is very difficult. What is clear is that there is no new type of aircraft which can be developed for the RAF to offset the withdrawal of the Canberra in the strike role, which must take place in 1969 and 1970. . . . We need to remember that we are part of an alliance, and that our

American allies have a capability for long-range strike and reconnaissance. . . .' This was, of course, precisely what TSR.2 was for, and by March 1968 this would have been in squadron service.

Back in September 1967 Freddie Page had grumbled about the consequences of lack of guts in Whitehall: 'If people can't screw up their courage to prime the beginning of the VG project . . . valuable business will be lost . . . and the equipment of our forces will be at the mercy of other countries.' At government level the British seemed to have made a few mistakes. In 1957 the nation had doubted that anyone would want combat aircraft at all. In 1959 it had started to build a very considerable combat aircraft and stopped it after six acrimonious years. In 1965 it had said it did, after all, need new combat aircraft but would never again make any without foreign partners. It had launched out, cap-in-hand, on a collaborative project with France and seen the French walk away from it. In 1967 Britain had the best VG design team on Earth, an excellent design, a superb engine and accessory industry, a desperately waiting air force and no particular lack of funds, yet seemed quite unable to go ahead and do anything. I suppose the barrier was the statement that the British would not make any more of their own advanced aircraft?

Germany, shouting that it was the biggest market, played a central role in the negotiations of 1967–68. BAC, guided by what they had been able to find out about NKF, CAMRA and MRA-75, had studied an FCA (Future Combat Aircraft) matched to the German requirement but also having great potential as an interceptor to meet the needs of Italy and the Low Countries. Its two BS.143 engines would have been based on the LP spool of the RB.193 used in the V/STOL VAK-191 and an HP spool scaled from the Olympus 320 and thus similar to the M45. R&D cost was put at £148 million, compared with an estimate of £230 million for AFVG, although whether the startling disparity was due to the costs of collaboration remained unexplained. Stonehouse said in March 1968, the month the study was completed, that his talks with the Germans were going well 'but the stage has not yet been reached where design material has had to be exchanged.' What he could not then disclose was the massive change in British defence thinking; whereas a typical hi-lo-lo-hi radius for the AFVG had been 1150 miles, the ACA figures were much less than half as great on similar profiles. Early in 1968 BAC were sent off yet again with a ten-month, £0·5 million study while the RAF thought again and again on what they might have to do in a European context. Meanwhile, a package proposal involving almost immediate production of the Jaguar, as a trainer as well as a strike aircraft, to replace the G91, followed by a joint VG programme, to replace the F-104G, was rejected by Bonn early in 1968. The Germans did not want to be hurried into the vital F-104G replacement, and never lost sight of their wish to lead a giant consortium. The Jaguar appealed to the Luftwaffe, and almost certainly was the right technical choice, but the Phantom was a known quantity and its purchase could help offset the costs of US troops in Germany. And a third consideration was that Northrop claimed to be able to meet all of the German requirements with a single aircraft costing about half as much as an FCA and not much more than half as heavy. This was a bold claim—which the Germans decided not to test—but it did have the effect of dismissing the Jaguar/UKVG and also finishing off the AVS.

The idea of making a single new aircraft replace both the G91 and F-104, and serve as a close-support aircraft, strike/recce machine and air-superiority fighter with the Luftwaffe and Kriegsmarine, was fascinating and attractive. In the long term this was the turning point of the whole story, because while the NKF or MRA-75 could not do this, the slightly bigger BAC aircraft could. Gradually the Germans came to feel they ought to lean up against the patient and experienced British, provided they could have a share of the design and manufacture commensurate with their supposed big market.

After parametric studies in January–June 1968 involving both single and twin-engine versions, the propulsion scene was given a major shake-up in May of that year by the emergence of the RB.199. For three years Rolls-Royce had been hard at work on very advanced turbofans for subsonic civil airliners—latterly the RB.211—characterised by having three concentric shafts all turning at different speeds. Far from making the engine more complicated, the three-shaft arrangement enables a very high pressure-ratio to be gained by a simple and short engine that offers unique gains in performance, economy, handling and costs. These arguments, even the cost part, are not one whit invalidated by what happened to Rolls in February 1971. Studies showed a three-shaft arrangement to be equally applicable to a reheat engine for supersonic combat aircraft. A new engine was the last thing BAC expected, although they had assumed it in some studies with Rolls and Mintech. It was the ideal way of meeting the emergency requirement with a small, comparatively cheap aircraft. Moreover, whereas the AFVG had simply nominated the engine supplier, it was clear any future project was going to call for a more professional approach with competitive bidding. Rolls may have known as much. In any event, if they had not produced the RB.199 when they did, I think they would have failed to win the eventual propulsion contract. More than this, the 199 plays a crucial part in the qualities of today's MRCA, and is instrumental in making it far better all-round than the AFVG would have been.

BAC delivered the all-British ACA submission on 31 May 1968. By this time discussions at the government and industrial levels had at least suggested that a multi-national programme was desirable and theoretically possible. I was told that the Canadians, Dutch and Germans were quite near to joining with the UK on what had just become called the MRCA (Multi-Role Combat Aircraft). The long, long search for a good European programme at last seemed to be nearing a happy ending, for the very good reason that people were getting together who genuinely wanted a part of it. On 25 July 1968 a Memorandum of Understanding was signed by Belgium, Canada, Germany, Italy, the Netherlands and the UK expressing mutual interest in an MRCA-type aircraft and a desire to study the situation jointly. Four of the countries—Canada, Germany, the Netherlands and the UK—undertook nationally funded feasibility studies. In August 1968 BAC, Canadair and Messerschmitt-Bölkow submitted their proposals against the Operational Equipment Objective (OEO) cooked up by the participating air staffs. The OEO called for the mostest of everything: it was a sort of summation of all the individual maxima in fuel, defensive weapons, offensive weapons, avionics, armour, crew, field length, manoeuvrability and everything else. BAC demonstrated that the MRCA's weight and cost were determined quite directly by what was demanded of it. The two key parameters were mission radius and SEP (SEP, specific excess power, is a measure of the margin by which thrust exceeds drag and thus of the ability of the aircraft to manoeuvre, climb or accelerate). Throughout 1968 the more experienced engineers talked to their possible partners in other companies and with the officials who talked at government level to try to arrive at a reasonable set of requirements. In a Royal Aeronautical Society lecture Ollie Heath recorded that 'each nation was putting in a bit as a bargaining point'; and, to show in a lighter vein how people think up stringent requirements, he mentioned the case where the aircraft had to land in hot-day conditions, to give minimum reverse thrust, on a runway so slippery it was obviously covered with ice.

I do not know whether there is an optimum number of participants for a collaborative programme, but, like the Little Nigger Boys, the countries in the MRCA programme dropped from six to three. Belgium was never a strong participant and dropped out at the end of 1968, partly because building the Mirage 5 was going to keep its small industry busy (but only in the short term). In October 1968 Canada pulled out. The reason given was money, but in fact it was due to the deep re-thinking on the place of armaments in the human world called for by the very liberal 'mod' regime of Pierre Trudeau. This reshaped all Canada's armed forces into one force and then started to go back to first principles in trying to decide how man ought to arm himself (if at all). Faced with a sort of sanitized peace-keeping role, the Canadian Armed Forces said 'We haven't the faintest idea if we shall need MRCA, and it's not worth paying half a million dollars a year in fares to Europe in order to take part.' It certainly did not imply criticism of the aircraft or programme; they might even come back in, in the fullness of time. Third to wave goodbye was the Netherlands, in July 1969. In this case the reason was that the design did not meet their requirements, but there is much more to it than this.

The Dutch role in MRCA was a curiously ambivalent one. At the technical level they were deeply interested. Their prime need was for an air-superiority fighter, a role their NF-5 can scarcely meet today and certainly will not meet in the 1980s, and they were not much interested in STOL performance or the various air-to-ground missions. They spent a great many man-hours examining the way the design variables interplay while looking for long radius of action and maximum performance in air combat at all levels, and finally wrote in requirements for SEP and manoeuvre that were almost as severe as the Canadian ones. This had a major effect on the aircraft, for it demanded more engine thrust and a bigger wing, and then in turn additional fuel to maintain the specified combat radius. It was largely because of the Dutch that the aircraft was made slightly larger and more expensive, yet it was this aircraft growth that made them go off grumbling that it would be too expensive. In fact a very big factor causing them to pull out was that they knew they would never be more than a minor partner, with little chance of controlling the project, yet they would have to pay quite a big cheque each month. But this is what collaboration is all about. And in case I have left the impression the Dutch harmed the aircraft by cranking in a severe interceptor mission, I think they improved it.

Even without the Dutch experience it was plain by the autumn of 1968 that a middle course would have to be steered between excessive demand and excessive cost. By this time the programme was being run by a Joint Working Group (JWG) of nationally appointed officials and a JIC (Joint Industrial Company) formed from representatives of the likely manufacturers, BAC, MBB and Fiat. It is probably true that the more participants there are in a programme, the greater will be the demands made on the aircraft; with enough of them somebody is sure to want Mach 4, or an air/sea rescue version. In November 1968 the JIC told the JWG they must moderate their requirements, partly by lopping off the extremes in the way that Procrustes was supposed to lop off the extremities of his guests to make them fit his spare bed, and partly in 'the small print' details. The JWG went further and in the vital Statement of Work of 19 December 1968 proposed a comprehensive but perfectly reasonable set of requirements that the experienced members of the JIC thought would lead to a potent but cost/effective aircraft which also met absolute cost limits.

By Christmas two big advances had been made. The JWG had been told a complete and economic solution was possible to the full requirements, and a plan had been devised to overcome the German demand for overall control. The Germans, Italians and Dutch based their thinking on F-104G operations in daylight with one man, and it was proposed to centre engineering surveillance of single-seat MRCA operations at Munich. The British, and also the Kriegsmarine (German Navy), were more interested in long-range interdiction/strike in all weathers, with a crew of two, and it was proposed to locate the corresponding lead of the two-seat MRCA at Warton. Commonality between the two variants was shown to be very high indeed; far more important differences were going to be demanded by the changes in 'avionic fit' to meet the contrasting national missions.

Detailed technical work on MRCA got going in January 1969. In February teams from Messerschmitt-Bölkow (MBB, Messerschmitt-Bölkow-Blohm from May 1969), Fokker/VFW and Fiat spent several weeks at Warton, and everyone then went to Munich. On 14 March the Baseline Configuration brochure emerged, a detailed project study which met all the requirements, pleased all the participants and was commonly agreed to form the basis for the MRCA up to Minister level. It was based on two RB.199 engines because these were the only standard available. Never backward, GE furnished data on the GE1/10 in March 1969, incorporated as an Annex to the brochure on 19 March, while Rolls countered with an improved RB.199 incorporated as a second Annex on 28 March. Pratt & Whitney were, as usual, handicapped by US security but made sure the JIC knew about the JTF16, TF30 developments and the programme which later became the JTF22. All these engines were aimed at a twin, but MBB continued to demand work on possible single-engined versions until persuaded otherwise by the unanimous preference of all the customers. BAC and Messerschmitt also spent much time in 1967–68 studying a fixed-wing (non-VG) MRCA mainly to confirm the advantages of variable sweep. The fixed-wing aircraft would have had a much broader wing and an even bigger tailplane, and a wing big enough to meet the STOL take-off case would have given an impossibly rough ride in the lo attack mission. This is not the place to argue the technical parameters involved, but many of the MRCA missions—the Dutch interception, the lo penetration and the STOL close-support—are difficult or impossible to meet with a fixed wing. Perhaps alone of the national requirements, the RAF interdiction mission from a good runway could have been met by a fixed-wing aircraft rather like a grown-up Jaguar, but this would have been much less flexible, uncompetitive in the fighter role, and incapable of being stretched to meet future needs.

In the July 1968 Memo it was decreed that the industrial programme would be run by international companies along the lines of those created for Jaguar. By 1968 some Europeans knew quite a lot about how a complicated programme ought to be run (for example, they knew in great detail, from the F-104G and Phantom, how the Americans do it) and they also knew the special needs and possible pitfalls of a collaborative programme. The result is that MRCA is a very closely integrated and professionally organized endeavour. The three main partner nations, Britain, Germany and Italy, appoint officials to NAMMO, the NATO MRCA Management Organization which is the ultimate customer. It has a board of directors and its own Management Agency (NAMMA) in Munich serving as the link with the contractor. The contractor comprises three international companies. For the airframe, Panavia Aircraft GmbH was registered in Munich on 26 March 1969, occupying the same big office building as NAMMA. Initially its shareholding was: BAC and Messerschmitt-Bölkow (now MBB), one-third each; Fiat and Fokker-VFW, one-sixth each. After the Dutch departure, some changed buying patterns and some industrial mergers, the company settled down as: BAC and MBB, 42½ per cent each; Aeritalia 15 per cent. For the engine, Turbo-Union Ltd was registered in Bristol on 30 September 1969, with offices in Munich and Turin, and with shareholding divided between Rolls-Royce (1971) and MTU each holding 40 per cent and Fiat holding 20 per cent. For the avionic systems Avionica Systems Engineering GmbH was registered in Munich on 26 September 1969 with one-third of the shares each allotted to EASAMS (UK), ESG (Germany) and SIA (Italy); later this was judged an unworkable scheme and Avionica was dissolved.

The work split on the airframe was originally: MBB, centre fuselage, including wing bridge and pivots; BAC, two-seat nose and rear fuselage; VFW, single-seat nose; Fokker, tail surfaces; and Fiat, wings. Since VFW-Fokker left the programme BAC are doing all noses and tails. The engine, the RB.199-34R, was chosen on 5 September 1969 after a keen competition against Pratt & Whitney begun on 14 July. Since then the engine has gone ahead satisfactorily, the first run having taken place at Bristol in September 1971 and with further prototype engines having run at MTU and Fiat. A Vulcan, previously used to fly the Concorde nacelle, began flying with a simulated half MRCA fuselage on 19 April 1973. Thrust of the RB.199-34R remains restricted, but is unofficially said to be 8500 lb dry and 14500 lb with full reheat. The most worrying thing about the engine is that escalation in wages, material prices and other costs have in three years caused the R&D bill to leap from £80 million to £180 million. Pretty obviously, Europe's future aircraft must be developed in a great hurry, before they escalate away out of reach.

MRCA has become metal within two years of the first joint document, even though there has been slippage since 1969. The study phase slipped from March 1969 a further month, so that the project definition phase did not begin until 1 May. This phase was costed at £12·5 million and was complete on schedule by the end of 1969, but the officials wanted ample time to think and the contract for the next stage, the development phase, was not signed until 22 July 1970. Possibly the main change in the definition phase was the adoption by all partners of the two-seat version called the 'Panavia 200'. Another decision was a cut in the German buy, from about 700 to '420 at the most' (since cut further, 'for budgetary and management reasons' said General Gunther Rall, Luftwaffe CoS, to 322). This did not indicate any disenchantment in Bonn, and the once very strongly supported NKF project had been allowed to die well before mid-1969, thus eliminating any fall-back project. What it did indicate is that the Germans, having calculated they needed 420 (or 322) aircraft, at first said they wanted 700 in order to get the lion's share of the international programme. More significant was the decision of the German government to standardize on the tandem-seat aircraft chosen by the British and preferred from the start by the Kriegsmarine. The decision was reached at a meeting on 24 March 1970 between Healey and his new opposite number Herr Schmidt. On that date they considered project definition 'essentially completed' and decided that, on the basis of the outcome of that phase, the two-seater alone would be continued, resulting in 'the contraction of development resources and a reduction of development costs. . . . The inherent technical risk which is in every development programme is correspondingly reduced. In addition to this the two-seater version has considerable advantages from the point of view of in-flight safety. . . . The Italian partner has been informed of this intention. . . .'

Unlike the Jaguar the two-seat version of MRCA had been associated with a very comprehensive avionic fit, and the resulting heavier nose required wing sweep settings a degree or two further forward for balance. A further difference is that the German and Italian aircraft were to have no fuel in the wings while the RAF were to use the whole of each wing as an integral tank. Although commonality between the single- and two-seat noses was good, there are very real cost advantages in standardizing the airframe. Reading between the lines, however, it is obvious that in the spring of 1970 the Italians were only half in the programme. When the development phase was launched on 22 July of that year the Memo was signed by Britain and Germany only. The Italians were in trouble over money, over the fact that they were a junior partner and over the dropping of the single-seater, originally called the Panavia 100. But gradually the sense of the whole project was inescapable, and they announced their intention of continuing as a full participant on 1 October 1970. On that date the Defence Minister, Sig M. Tamassi, said 'By continuing . . . we shall get the benefit not only for our airframe, engines, avionics and systems manufacturers, but also for a much wider field ranging from scientific research to highly specialized industries such as precision engineering and super-alloy metallurgy.' This, again, is what collaboration is all about.

Continuation of Italian participation held the total buy, as far as the three original customers are concerned, to 800–900: 385 for Britain, up to 320–420 for Germany and up to 100 for Italy. The number of prototypes, originally to have been 13, was cut to seven and then raised to nine: four assembled at Warton, three at Munich and two at Turin. The estimated R&D programme cost, originally £410 million, was cut to £320 million by standardization of the airframe, although I have no doubt it must rise again as a result of the spiralling of wages in all three countries. Unit price on a run of 900 has been quoted as £1·7 million at May 1970 level. This is too good to be true, although the latest information I possess is that the price to new customers in 1974 could still be under £3 million. This compares with more than £5 million for an F-111F or an F-15, neither of which is as well suited to so wide a spectrum of roles. The nearest rival is the F-14 Tomcat, which is slightly less versatile and costs £7 million a copy (if you buy a standard F-14A). To me the most important thing about MRCA, considered simply as a piece of military hardware, is that the initials MR in its name have a real meaning. Its primary roles are close-support, interdiction strike, naval and beachhead support, and reconnaissance. I will talk about air-to-air a little later.

The basic aircraft is rather smaller than AFVG and completely different in detail design, and though it is a Warton thoroughbred MBB and Fiat (Aeritalia) have made major contributions to the airframe. At least three-quarters is aluminium alloy, though the wing box is titanium and the pivot bearings are of Teflon. The wings, which are now to be full of fuel in all versions, are so well equipped with high-lift devices they would not disgrace Boeing (which is the highest praise I can bestow). The RB.199 engine, with high pressure-ratio, medium by-pass ratio, large reheat boost and outstanding response to pilot command, can fairly be described as the first engine of the jet age to give wholly good flexibility at all combat speeds and altitudes. I am bold enough to predict that its installational problems will be mild compared with those of the F-111. As in all the Warton VG studies the engines breathe through long inlet ducts with prominent wedge intakes which leave a flat dorsal surface mating perfectly with the wings. The latter are essentially pivoted to a rectangular box to which are attached a long nose and a stubby rear end carrying very large swept vertical and horizontal all-moving tail surfaces.

Gross weight will be 40000–45000 lb, depending on role. With a self-start APU the aircraft can scramble in two minutes without ground aids and take off (clean) from 1500 feet of Autobahn. For quick stopping there are thrust reversers and large belly speed brakes, and there certainly ought to be a hook. Under the fuselage, inlet ducts and wings can be hung what Gero Madelung, Panavia managing director, calls 'a tremendous spectrum of stores'. Apart from nuclear and conventional bombs the MRCA will carry various cluster bombs, especially the Jumbo Streuwaffen, and such guided weapons as Martel and Kormoran for surface attack, and the Sparrow, Viper and SRAAM (Tail Dog) for air-to-air use. In the lower part of the nose will be the excellent new 27 mm gun that is putting the German Mauser company back in the air-combat business. Mauser had a big emotional wish to do this gun, because in 1945 they were roughly a decade ahead of everyone else in the world in aircraft guns. Today GE and Philco-Ford will take some beating (see A-10A) but the new European gun ought to have a big future. At least in its first form it uses cased ammunition, and its flight development is being done with Lightnings.

Elsewhere three Buccaneers are busy flight-testing some of the major elements of the avionics. MRCA is worth very little without its avionic systems, because it must fly challenging missions in any weather and often against well-defended targets. Collaborative programmes begin with everyone wanting to 'lead' on the airframe, and when this has been sorted out everyone wants to pick the plums among the systems. Horsetrading on the airframe is usually straightforward, but avionic collaboration never is. In the case of MRCA the situation was almost wholly determined by the UK and Germany. Nobody disputed that Britain was streets ahead in avionic capability and experience, but the situation was strongly coloured by the supposed bigger buy of the Germans, by the existing Luftwaffe operational techniques, and by the need to keep the price down.

As the day of the crunch decision in 1971 approached, the RAF looked on rather wistfully, because they could see that the political and cost factors were going to outweigh the technical and operational advantages of the system on which they had spent several years in very detailed planning. Whatever one may think of the Trenchard-inspired Air Staff, it is my belief that the RAF offensive-avionics planned for the MRCA have never yet been equalled elsewhere for a surface-attack aircraft intended to strike a target of known location in a single blind pass. There were to be three systems, used consecutively. The aircraft would motor to its target on X-band terrain-following radar; a few miles short of the target the crew would switch to a Q (Ku) -band radar; and when in line-of-sight range they would switch to a laser. The Q-band, from 26·5 to 40 kilomegahertz, would pick out targets smaller than vehicles with good definition. The final sensor, the laser, would be optically combined with a TV system to give perfect ranging and alignment, so that, in partnership with the obvious inertial sensor, weapons could be released with supreme accuracy. The system was proposed jointly by Ferranti and Elliott. This three-tier system was opposed by two American radars. One was an extremely advanced design by Autonetics based on first-generation electronic scanning. This scanned only in one plane, had other limitations and undoubtedly would have posed an almost insuperable data-processing problem; but it was the forerunner of new technology, and so appealed to the Germans very strongly. Few would disagree that before long a radar that uses a mechanically-aimed dish will be a museum-piece, and the Germans wanted to be in on the ground floor with electronic scanning. The other candidate was a straightforward set by Texas Instruments (TI) derived from the TFR of the F-111.

In view of the hard line taken on costs, the outcome was predictable. The TI set, even though packaged differently from the F-111 radar, was dramatically cheaper than any other answer. Moreover, there were very strong operational reasons why the Luftwaffe wanted to use just a plain X-band radar (though this would lead me into classified areas). So the choice was the TI radar, though it will have to guide the MRCA at 'lo' heights less than half the 500 feet that is commonly set on the F-111. Precisely what will fill the nose of the MRCA is still classified. The RAF are resigned to the fact that their fully optimised scheme will not now happen (not until after 1980, anyway), but there remain the basic problems that the nose is not very big, that all the users of MRCA would like the radar(s) to do simultaneous ground-mapping (with side-to-side scanning) and terrain-following (with vertical scanning), and that the only immediate answers seem to be to make the aerial and scanner move faster (impossible) or use a single radar (impossible data-handling problem) or reduce the data rate by flying higher (and get shot down). There are all sorts of other solutions such as using forward-facing parts of the airframe for a big-aperture SLAR (side-looking aircraft radar), but to get any performance from a SLAR facing forward the MRCA would have to be a quite different shape—for example, the lo attack would have to be made with the wings at near-zero sweep. Suffice to say the problem is solved, and MRCA will work quite well at levels around 200 feet or even less, and the RAF has been told not to mind that the radar fit does not meet their specification. At least they will have a laser, a rather heavy Eltro (Hughes-licence) gas-cooled YAG device which can be extended for use below the nose;

unfortunately it does not appear likely to use common optics with a TV set for blind aiming and ranging as the RAF had wished.

It was not unexpected that Ferranti won the inertial navigation system, as well as the big 'combined display' which dominates the rear cockpit. The centre display can show radar pictures superimposed on a projection of a moving map (presumably a topographic map, but I can see no reason why it should not also include a stored film of radar map). On each side is the TV tabular display, by Elliott, on which can be presented vertical or horizontal situation displays, Martel-TV guidance, and any of a wide range of alphanumeric data concerning such things as navigation, fuel management or weapon states, the navigation information being called up from the computer. Such tabular displays will become common in combat aircraft, especially two-seaters, but when the term was new and unfamiliar it was mis-read by someone at Westminster as 'tabulator', and when Ian Gilmour, Minister of State for Defence, announced the contract decision on 19 November 1971 he called the displays 'TV tabulators'. This had me fooled, because I had never heard of such a thing. What is more serious is that the announcement was picked up by every major newspaper, aerospace periodical and even the august 'Jane's' and it will be years before people stop getting it wrong.

During the past two years I have been fortunate enough to talk with scores of companies who are responsible for major bits of MRCA. Among them I can list Dowty (landing gear), Lucas Aerospace (many extremely advanced pieces of machinery all over the aircraft and especially round the engines), Fairey (powered flying controls), Litef (the European subsidiary of Litton who make the 24k 16-bit computer), Smiths (head-up display) and Decca (doppler radar). There is a fair sprinkling of British names here, and certainly the UK has no cause to complain at the general industrial distribution of work. Yet there seems to be an enduring belief in the popular press that collaboration is all right provided one gets a lot more out of it than one's partners. All three of the MRCA partners have contrived heated arguments in their news-media to persuade their readers, listeners and viewers that MRCA is unfair to them. Mass media normally concentrate on issues that can be treated grossly superficially—such as AFVG—and ignore anything that their public might think technical. I recall one Fleet Street editor telling me 'Most people don't even know what an avionic is.' Yet now and then one of them would think he smelt in MRCA some sort of juicy scandal.

Read what the London *Times* printed on 29 September 1971, from the pen of Kenneth Warren, who as MP for Hastings is not very directly concerned with the MRCA programme: 'The Germans and Italians together are committed to supplying $57\frac{1}{2}$ per cent of the capacity required.

In the equipment area they cannot produce even half of this from their existing resources. So, mostly after buying expensive licences from the United States, they are going to build new factories, recruit new workers and train them, while here in Britain our skilled, unemployed men and machines are forced to stand idle and watch. The Memorandum of Understanding says that tenders can be accepted from non-participating countries if they show substantial price and technical advantages. . . . Briefings are said to have been given by the US Government to American salesmen to tell them how to win MRCA orders. The German Embassy in Washington, I have been told, is the best source in the world of the MRCA equipment specifications. The rules of MRCA contract awards—that the lowest bidder usually gets the job—sound fine until one appreciates five vital things. First, the Americans have a reputation for bidding low to wipe out rivals and then escalating the costs. . . .' Warren's four other points were equally valid, in that they were part-truths.

For a decade Britain has led the crusade for collaborative aerospace programmes. Intelligent people are now complaining that the result is skilled men on the dole in Britain while unskilled labour is trained to work in newly built factories in the lands of Britain's aerospace partners (or are they rivals?). In the field of avionics Britain has for 30 years been the only country able to offer across-the-board competition to the United States, and win. But if the British refuse to build their own aircraft and instead enter into collaborative deals with others, I think that means they must abide by collaborative rules. If the British want to break out of restrictive collaborative agreements the answer is obvious.

I could even throw in at this point the basic question underlying all expensive and difficult endeavours. Everybody wants to do everything himself, but all nations do not have the same skills, facilities or money. It could be that, on grounds of sheer cost, Western Europe should buy all its military aircraft from the Soviet Union. It could be that, on grounds of gaining independence and building up home industries, every tiny emergent nation on Earth ought to be part of a collaborative combat-aircraft programme. Most people would think reason lies somewhere in between, and MRCA avionics is just one of many areas where the right decision is pragmatic compromise. It may be that Western Europe has for ever lost its ability to produce an attack radar (though I doubt it). If so, this is better than losing the ability to produce attack aircraft.

As I write, the avionics for the RAF, Luftwaffe, Regia Aeronautica and Kriegsmarine still have a few i's to be dotted and t's to be crossed, but the basic idea is that each service will buy a few (definitely a few!) 'national increments'. There will probably be differences in operating frequencies, dish and aerial sizes, computer programs, weapons interfaces and even in some details of the airframe and systems. But each partner is going to tailor his final detailed MRCA standard around a common reference aircraft, instead of devising a nationally tailored 'avionic suit' matched to his own primary mission. Obviously there are fundamental problems. Britain's main interest is long-range interdiction, the Luftwaffe's is close support, the Regia Aeronautica's is aerial combat and the Kriegsmarine have yet a fourth different slant. MRCA is a fair compromise in trying to reconcile these irreconcilables, and the same goes for its avionics. The best attack radar has a wavelength shorter than X-band, but the perfect air-superiority radar does not. Their scanning needs to be done in quite different ways, and the 'fighter' needs to use CW doppler (monopulse) emission with a 'look-down' capability and background clutter suppression to see enemy aircraft scooting along at tree-top level. It also needs to track-while-scan with multiple targets, and this imposes a distinctive computer program and high workload. This work-load may be too much for one man, the F-15 Eagle notwithstanding, yet from other viewpoints the air-superiority machine definitely wants to be a single-seater. At an even more fundamental level, an MRCA 'fighter' would need much more thrust, much less weight and possibly a fixed-geometry wing.

I am sounding off in these terms not to criticize the MRCA of today, which is undoubtedly—in my view—the best multi-role combat aircraft ever designed in this world. I am emphasizing the problems to show the impossibility of making it best at each contrasting job, and perhaps to prepare the reader for variations on the basic theme in the course of this decade. One obvious variation, to my way of thinking, is an MRCA optimised more in the aerial combat role. Britain's Lightning, Germany's F-104G and even the relatively new Italian F-104S all have very sharp limitations which will become acute after 1975. Panavia, having built up one of the finest military-aircraft teams in the West, is looking at this situation keenly. It is hardly a secret any longer that Panavia has been exploring the market for a small air-superiority fighter with a single RB.199, but there are many other possibilities.

Metal was cut on the first nine MRCA prototypes, six pre-series aircraft and various static and fatigue specimens in November 1970, and a BAC pilot will fly aircraft 01 at Manching (Munich) well before the time this book appears late in 1974. Hopefully by this time the aircraft will have a proper designation or name. The programme has slipped, and costs have risen; but the slippage and cost-escalation are about par for the course, and the programme shows up very well indeed in comparison with all its possible and projected rivals. The vast spread of subcontracts are mostly on a basis of 'fixed price but allowing for inflation'; this sounds self-contradictory, but I am unable to come up with a better formula. This gives me new hope that Europe need not necessarily be inferior to the United States in programme management. The main development contract was signed on 11 August 1972, and the R&D budget of £558 million to the end of 1973 is unlikely to be exceeded. The predicted buy of up to 905 aircraft, with some 3000 engines, is expected to cost around £2900 million. This may prove a sanguine hope, because European nations, especially Britain, are finding it a hard struggle to try to control inflation. It is instructive to see how assiduously American and French rivals of MRCA are using such matters to try to make this great venture appear uncertain, likely to prove exorbitantly costly and likely to fold up at any moment. (I have just read a confidential sales brochure for a proposed US air-superiority fighter which is a particularly flagrant example of this.) By the time I proof-read this book, in 1974, Britain had elected a Labour administration which for years has eyed MRCA greedily as a lovely big programme that (if the Germans and Italians agree) could be axed forthwith, saving a useful sum. There is a strong feeling in this new government that 'expensive' MRCA could be replaced by a 'cheap' American aircraft. It's as if the clock had been put back ten years. This time there is a difference that none of the American aircraft come near to meeting the MRCA specification, and they are more expensive (or on paper). Perhaps we just ought to settle for European air forces equipped with American brochures?

When Americans become really aggressive in knocking a rival product you can be sure that the product is good, and that they can see it is going to hurt them. AFVG—has been one of the longest stories in this book, and it is a matter of supreme satisfaction for me that this MRCA story of political mismanagement has been patiently transmuted by European aircraft engineers into a product that worries the Americans very much. The existence of Panavia as a viable and immensely competent outfit linking three big European countries worries them very much more. After all, it just could prevent an American monopoly in the big-league of Western military aviation until well into the next century. But at present the MRCA is still slightly vulnerable. It is vulnerable to the enormous dollar burden of US military forces on the Germans. It is vulnerable to the Italian feeling of dissatisfaction that it costs a lot of money, is not quite tailored to their needs and is managed mainly by their partners. It is vulnerable to all kinds of timidity, stupidity and myopia among people who have not yet learned how big and powerful Western Europe is (it outstrips the United States on almost every count except in share of the world aviation market). But if MRCA survives until 1975 it will survive beyond the year 2000 and its many users will judge it the most universally useful and versatile combat aircraft since the Mosquito and Ju 88.

United States

General Dynamics F-111

MOST readers of this book will not be personally familiar with this big swing-wing 'fighter', but they will undoubtedly know of it. Unless they have been living on a desert island they will know that for at least ten years from 1962 the 'One-Eleven'* was the subject of a political storm beside which almost every other controversy seems brief and insignificant. In financial terms the F-111 was planned to be the biggest aircraft programme, and possibly the biggest programme of any kind, in all history. It was partly because of this that the circumstances surrounding the contract-award were investigated by Congress. In turn, this made the F-111 a subject of intense public interest. Although the probe completely failed to unearth any skulduggery, it tried for seven years to assassinate the characters of the civilian Secretaries in the Pentagon and finally published a remarkable report which put in all the bad things and left out all the good ones.

There are plenty of good things. The F-111 could hardly fail to be an aircraft of outstanding merit which, now the dust is settling, can take its rightful place as a landmark in military aviation. But there were also plenty of bad things. Never before had an aircraft suffered such escalation in weight, escalation in cost, drag so much worse than prediction, and a propulsion system that was not only down on performance but misbehaved so badly it was described in an official report as 'a hazard to safe flight'. When the One-Eleven finally got into service, and became admired by its very professional crews, it suffered catastrophic powered-control failures, catastrophic fractures of primary structure, and even failure of the crew-escape system. Deep trouble in drag, weight, thrust, systems and structure doesn't seem to leave much unaccounted for. On top of everything else, the programme was launched on the basis of a shining goal—'commonality' between versions of the aircraft intended to fulfil different roles for different services—that, after agonizing efforts, had to be given up as impossible to attain.

**This is how it is said, and often written, in the United States. But there is absolutely no connection with BAC's short-haul jetliner.*

Hindsight probably teaches us more from the One-Eleven than from any other aircraft in history. Some of the lessons are obvious. A less obvious one is that programmes of the very first magnitude can be greatly influenced by the vehemently expressed views of people who actually have only superficial knowledge, which is often worse than no knowledge at all. Another somewhat hidden lesson is that little purpose seems to be served by trying to convince the public that a technically difficult programme is the result of the plotting of knaves or the antics of imbeciles.

The great story of the F-111 will forever be a classic wherever politicians, generals, engineers and pilots forgather. It opens back in 1950, when the scalps that were being hunted were not those of scapegoats but of Communists, whom many Americans imagined were lurking behind every machine tool and filing cabinet. The planemakers as a group were investigated no more than anyone else, and although 'renegotiation' hearings meant they sometimes had to pay back to the government sums as high as $28 million, nobody bothered to hunt for scalps publicly even when major aircraft and engine programmes ground to a halt because the hardware could not be made to work. In any case, the machinery of defence procurement was constantly being improved. By 1952 the weapon system concept ensured that each new programme was treated as an integrated system instead of as a changeable collection of bits. By 1954 the Cook-Craigie plan had struck a compromise between the need to modify aircraft as the result of flight development and the need to get the production line rolling. By 1957 the procedures for studies, RFPs, competitive bidding and source-selection had been worked out to a fine art, with the very powerful spur of competition retained to the latest possible moment to sharpen the wits of the industrial contractors and give the armed forces the best product at the lowest price. Despite the almost runaway growth in system complexity, and an inexorable trend towards inflation, systems of assessment and evaluation had been devised to try to determine with much better accuracy what a major programme ought to cost, through the phases of RDT&E, production, and service usage. In the case of the largest and most important programmes bidders were investigated by 1959 in unprecedented depth, extending from the type of trash bin used for titanium swarf to the type of pencils used in the project office and the typography of the manuals, and key engineering staff had their family environment probed in merciless detail to ensure they had no emotional problems. The notions of 'response' and 'visibility' had been coined, and altogether the process of procurement tried to quantify and measure everything that could possibly influence the programme and the contractors' performance.

By 1959 there had been parallel major developments in the technology of military aircraft. For a decade an increasing proportion of the US Air Force and Navy funds had been devoted to guided missiles and since 1955 the missile budgets had been so large they had forced a corresponding reduction in the programmes for aircraft. But the technology of combat aircraft raced ahead, and, even though many wondered if fighters and bombers might not be rather passé, it was obvious that by combining the new advances it would be possible to make superior aircraft. Perhaps the biggest single advance was made by the Langley Laboratory of the new NASA, where in 1958–59 the variable-sweep wing was at least realized in a form that suffered from none of the fundamental faults that had for 15 years kept it from practical application. The Langley researchers had devised a way of making a wing that could spread out to a large span, with little or no sweep, for high lift at take-off and landing and low-speed loitering, yet which could fold back at a very sharp sweep angle for supersonic efficiency. The basic advance was to have a large wing-root section that did not move, carrying near the extremities of its leading edge the pivots for the swinging outer wings. The latter were made twisted and cambered from root to tip, and for maximum lift were fitted with powerful slats and flaps which could be extended in the minimum-sweep position to give a high lift-coefficient for STOL performance. In the supersonic position the twist and camber were nullified by the changed direction of the streamlines, but tunnel testing showed that the interaction between the wing and the tailplane immediately below and to the rear could be important in giving good manoeuvrability with adequate supersonic stability.

A second major advance had taken place in propulsion. Thanks partly to British work, the turbofan engine had emerged as the ideal blend of turbojet speed with turboprop economy, and with it had come continuing advances in cycle efficiency gained by higher compressor pressure-ratios and higher turbine gas temperatures, a major factor in the attainment of the latter being the British development of air-cooled turbine blades. Studies showed that the turbofan, in which the hot jet from the core engine is surrounded by a cooler jet from the fan in which no fuel has yet been burned, could be matched very well with an afterburner to give unprecedented thrust-augmentation for supersonic propulsion. There were many other significant advances. Titanium was becoming well understood, and in the 2000 mph A-11 being built secretly in Lockheed's Skunk Works it was being used for primary airframe structure. Thrust reversers were being widely used on British engines in varied types of installation to shorten the landing roll, especially on wet or icy runways. By no means least, the development of accessory systems, and particularly avionics, had run even faster than in the early 1950s, leading to the possibility of a quantum jump in installed power and 'packing density' to fit a combat aircraft for a great range of missions. At the same time the maintenance burden could be held down by the use of self-checking electronic systems and readily accessible modules which could be pulled out when faulty and replaced in a few minutes even by a crewman wearing fur mitts in the Arctic. An especially valuable development was the replacement of thermionic valves (vacuum tubes) by solid-state devices offering a million-fold reduction in size and power consumption (and thus in heat generation) and vastly better reliability in harsh environments.

There were also more radical advances, many of them again due to British work, in which jet engines were used to give lift as well as propulsion and thus enable even a supersonic fighter to rise vertically from any patch of level ground that could bear its weight. As an alternative there was the American Zell (zero-length launching) technique in which a large rocket motor could blast an otherwise conventional, and thus uncompromised, aircraft into the air with no ground run. All these new advances were keenly eyed by the US Air Force, and in particular by Tactical Air Command. TAC's commanding generals, Otto P. Weyland and his successor Frank Everest, had by 1959 become uneasily aware that existing attack aircraft were not very well matched to their duties. The best TAC fighter/bomber, the F-105 'Thud', had been planned in 1954 at a time when nobody stopped to question the availability of long paved runways. A study of F-105 operations in Europe showed a distressing incidence of overruns and barrier crashes on an 8000 foot base (Bitburg) and a complete absence of such trouble on a 10000 foot runway just six miles away. To Everest and his staff this seemed nonsensical. If there was a war, nobody could count on even 1000 feet of concrete being available.

By 1959 TAC had crystallized its requirements for a better tactical strike aircraft to replace the F-105, as well as earlier types such as the F-100. Its central demands were 'independence of concrete runways', the ability to carry a nuclear bomb at 'supersonic speed at tree-top height' under enemy radar screens and 'inter-continental ferry range without in-flight refueling.' There seemed to be three ways of tackling the design problem: to make a conventional 'short roll' aircraft (what later became known as STOL); to use jet lift; or to blast a conventional machine off by the Zell technique and use an as-yet unavailable arrester system for recovering the aircraft in rapid succession on a short bulldozed strip. All three ideas were studied in depth. Zell posed seemingly insoluble problems in cost and logistic supply (with expensive rocket motors weighing several tons), apart from the fact that nobody knew how the technique could be turned from a hair-raising stunt into a practical wartime method. Jet lift for VTOL appeared to degrade flight performance and make it more difficult to meet other requirements, especially that of long range.

Maj-Gen Bruce K. Holloway, then USAF Director of Operational Requirements, pointed out that short-roll take-off and landing posed fewer intractable problems and gave better gain in performance in relation to cost than any VTOL method; and there were other difficulties in deploying a VTOL aircraft: 'In order to disperse one or two flights at appreciable distances from each other we would require major changes in the supporting base structure. A fleet of VTOL supply aircraft would be required. A vastly increased communications net would also be necessary. Operational and maintenance needs would go up across the board, and the tactical advantages would be somewhat negated by the operational disadvantages. . . .' Holloway was too polite to agree with me that the RAF thus seemed to err in choosing the P.1154 and its supporting AW.681 V/STOL transport, but he said flatly 'Our own studies indicate VTOL trade-offs penalize the flight performance too severely.'

Had TAC not wanted a seemingly fantastic ferry range their new aircraft might well have been VTOL, very like the ultimate twin-Spey P.1154 (p. 86). But their wish for global mobility was based on bitter experience. Hear General Jim Hackler, one of TAC's most senior pilots, recall how on 15 July 1958 his unit at Myrtle Beach was given seven hours' notice to send a squadron of F-100s non-stop to Adana, Turkey, during the Lebanon crisis: 'As it turned out, the first refueling south of Newfoundland and the second one near the Azores were conducted at night under adverse conditions of turbulent air and heavy thunderstorms. Only four aircraft made the mission non-stop, as programmed, primarily due to air refueling difficulties. An ability to quickly show the flag or make a show of force may mean the difference between outbreak of hostilities or maintaining peace. . . .' But the 'intercontinental' demand made experienced engineers scratch their heads when TAC opened informal discussions with industry in the spring of 1959. The demand for supersonic penetration at low level implied wings of very small span and area, while intercontinental ferry demanded slender wings of the greatest possible span. Variable sweep was the obvious answer, but work by Baynes and Wallis in Britain, Messerschmitt in Germany and Bell and Grumman in America had merely demonstrated that attempts to realize this panacea in practice were fraught with difficulty. Indeed three eminent designers judged the TAC requirement beyond the current state of the art.

One can thus imagine the interest shown by Everest and his staff when tousled, ebullient John Stack, deputy director of the NASA Langley Lab, came to see them in 1959. Stack was a man with a great reputation; it was he who unblocked the world's wind tunnels and got them to work through the transonic regime, and the world of aviation suffered a loss when he recently died after a fall from a horse. In 1959 he staked his reputation on the two-pivot swing wing. The result was that on 14 June 1960 the Air Force issued Specific Operational Requirement 183 for a new aircraft with the weapon-system number of WS-324A. The SOR called it a 'tactical strike fighter' but the vital word 'strike' was omitted from the popular designation applied to the programme of Tactical Fighter Experimental, or TFX. The main numbers written into SOR-183 were a high-altitude dash Mach number of 2·5; a lo-lo-hi mission radius of 800 nautical miles (all subsonic except that the final 200 n.m. to the target had to be flown at Mach 1·2) while carrying an internal nuclear weapon, an unrefuelled ferry range of 3300 n.m., and the ability to use an unpaved bulldozed strip 3000 feet long. Thanks to Stack's team nobody any longer cared to assert that these demands could not be met. Unfortunately they were, taken together, so severe that they later made the F-111 seem a failure because its superlatively good performance still fell a long way short of the demand.

If TAC had not insisted on a low-level Mach number of 1·2, but instead chosen M 0·95 (which would have in no way harmed the ability of the aircraft to penetrate), millions of dollars would have been saved and the requirement would have been met with ease. If TAC had ignored the air superiority role and not asked for M 2·5 at altitude but instead decided they were buying a subsonic bomber, the cost/effectiveness would have been multiplied by a factor of at least three. If TAC had realized that the emphasis was swiftly moving from the nuclear mission to the carriage of a dozen tons or more of 'iron bombs' they would again have moved much closer to the equipment they really wanted. And if only, having done these things, they had smartly sent out the RFP to industry in 1960 there would probably have been lots of TFXs in service in 1964 and the programme would have been a resounding success.

To recap: hindsight shows the Air Force really wanted a bomber, able to find and strike ground targets with precision at night or in bad weather while carrying very heavy loads of bombs or air-to-surface missiles. It had to have very long ferry range and be able to use short rough strips. To combine these demands with the ability to penetrate at close to the speed of sound it needed a swing wing, and this feature, coupled with the installed thrust needed for the field performance, would automatically make it supersonic at altitude. But it was basically a subsonic bomber, and although this is less exciting than a Mach 2·5 fighter it happens to be what was wanted. Compared with the F-4, F-105 or any other types used to hit ground targets in Vietnam it would have done twenty times the job for not much greater cost. Unfortunately the Air Force called for supersonic performance at all heights, they called the aircraft a fighter, and they delayed launching the programme. In doing so they changed the course of

US military history for the worse, and roughly trebled the number of pages I must write.

This volume does not deal with fighters, if by fighters one means aircraft intended primarily to destroy enemy aircraft in the air; but the fighter mission was destined to become inextricably interwoven with the F-111 story. This arose from the wish of the US Navy in 1959 to fund a new Fleet Air Defense Fighter (FADF) to protect the fleet at sea. The Phantom, then called the F4H, was appreciated to be the best all-round combat aircraft the Navy had ever had, although just how good it was was perhaps not realized until it was bought in even bigger numbers by the Air Force. In 1959 the Navy had contracted with Douglas for the F6D-1 Missileer to meet a completely new FADF requirement. The F6D was basically a subsonic transport, with a cargo of avionics and missiles, rather than a fighter in the traditional sense. It had turbofan engines and long-span wings and could loiter for half a day while its pilot and observer sat side by side scanning rather special radar scopes. The whole burden of intercepting enemy aircraft was put on the F6D's missiles, which were the giant Eagles under development by Bendix. This highly supersonic, jagged-looking weapon could fly over 100 miles whilst homing on to a chosen aircraft in a tight formation. It looked sensible, but in December 1960 a lot of people who thought they were experts decided that a subsonic fighter was something quite outmoded—a supposition that took almost ten years to overcome. So, in one of his last acts before he handed over the reins to a new man, the Secretary of Defense, the Hon Thomas Gates, terminated the F6D programme.

His place at the head of the giant Pentagon machine was taken by one Robert S. McNamara, who came from the Ford Motor Company with a brilliant brain and very soon showed he was going to run the department in his own way. If he found anything that seemed questionable, however long it may have been that way, he tore it up unless he could be convinced there were good reasons behind it. He sought ruthless efficiency, and with the unheard-of team of 'whiz kids' he built up around him—equally brilliant young analysts, engineers, financial experts and lawyers who could run rings round hoary old chief designers or generals—he began to work 12 or more hours a day seven days a week to knock into a new streamlined efficiency a gigantic edifice that many thought could do with just such a shake-up.

Within a day or two he had soaked up the SOR-183 requirement and the quite different terms of the FADF intended to replace the F4H. Very soon his fertile mind hit on something so obvious that nobody had apparently thought of it: why not try for 'commonality'? In his own words, 'These two planes would have many common missions and require many similar operational capabilities. After consultation with my military and civilian advisers, and independent study, I became convinced that one tactical fighter could be developed that would meet both the Navy and Air Force requirements. Accordingly, I directed that the Air Force re-orient its program, with Navy participation, to achieve the goal of a common tactical fighter.' Had there been a second brilliant brain around able to view things with complete objectivity it might have realized that here were the seeds of a possible error of gigantic proportions. Several of the advisers whose opinion Mr McNamara sought were his own whiz kids, who did not wish to start off by disagreeing with what seemed to be a bright idea by their mentor. Their slide rules and computers cranked out a round figure of a billion dollars as the potential saving of having a common basic design. After this the die was cast. Nothing was going to deflect the Secretary from his great goal of commonality. Those who disagreed seemed to do so because they hadn't tried to solve the problems, or they were hidebound traditionalists, or gripped by ancient inter-service rivalries. It became difficult to judge the importance of seemingly trivial points of design when there were a billion dollars in the other scale pan.

Had I been involved, I should have sided with McNamara. I have long believed that detailed official specifications usually result in indifferent or even disastrous aircraft. Nearly all the great military aircraft of history owed little to particular 'requirements' but were simply designed as brilliant aircraft which in the fullness of time were made to do a diverse range of duties better than any of the single-purpose conceptions. I should have agreed with McNamara that it ought to be possible, with competitive bidding for the most costly military-aircraft programme in history, to extract from the world's most powerful aviation industry a design combining all the advances detailed earlier that would, with comparatively small modifications, meet the needs of both services, and the Marine Corps, and go down in history as one of the great aircraft of all time. Compromises would be needed; but every advanced aircraft is nothing but compromise from stem to stern. I thought the new notion of commonality plausible, even though one customer wanted a fighter and the other a subsonic bomber, and the saving of a billion dollars appeared a likely figure over the whole operational life of the aircraft.

It was on 14 February 1961, after three weeks in office, that Robert McNamara directed that all services should study development of a single TFX based on the tactical fighter requirement of the Air Force. It so happened that in May the Director of Defense Research and Engineering, Dr Harold S. Brown, reported that a study by his office had shown that the close air support part of the tactical mission could be undertaken by a smaller and simpler aircraft than TFX, a view that led in 1966 to purchase by the Air Force of the A-7 Corsair (p. 230). This impressed even more firmly in McNamara's mind that TFX was a fighter, not a bomber, and reinforced the notion of commonality in a way that would have been much more difficult had the SOR-183 aircraft become the TAX, with A signifying 'attack'. In general the Americans are good at identifying new concepts and giving them names, such as 'software' or 'critical-path technique'. It is ironic that by calling their new bomber a fighter the Air Force set the stage for a nightmare.

From the start the two services agreed that a common TFX design was feasible—provided that the other service gave up its critical mission requirements. The Navy was especially upset because the method proposed by the Secretary of arriving at the common design was not to pour the requirements into a melting pot but to take the Air Force TFX and bend it a little to come part of the way to accomplishing the Navy mission. Clearly the Air Force, as by far the chief customer in terms of numbers, was the dominant participant in the study stage. On 7 June 1961 McNamara personally directed the two services to prepare 'a single work statement' that would provide a common TFX design specification, but on 22 August the Secretary of the Air Force, Eugene M. Zuckert, and the Assistant Secretary of the Navy, Paul Fay, reported to McNamara that it was not 'technically feasible' to build a single TFX to fulfil the stated mission requirements of both services. This came after six months of intensive analysis by both services of a possible compromise TFX. The Air Force aircraft came out to a length of about 80 feet, seated pilot and navigator in tandem and had a gross weight of about 75000 lb. The Navy aircraft could not be longer than about 70 feet and ideally should not exceed 56 feet, seated the pilot and observer side-by-side, had to accommodate a large radar in the nose with a search scanner four feet across, should not weigh more than 50000 lb, and was matched to a set of weapons completely different from the Air Force version. The Navy assessed the 'overall effectiveness' of the compromise TFX in the carrier-based air-superiority mission as a mere 37 per cent.

Ten days after this flat statement of incompatibility from the Air Force and Navy, McNamara wrote a memorandum that officially not only launched the bi-service TFX but even told the services how to design the aircraft. I suspect the Secretary was becoming a trifle irritated at what seemed to be short-sighted and partisan refusal to give an inch or two here and a few per cent there in order to save a billion dollars. His memo of 1 September 1961 reads: 'My office has reviewed the most recent positions of the Air Force and the Navy with regard to joint development of a tactical fighter for both services. I believe that the development of a single aircraft of genuine tactical utility to both services in the projected time frame is technically feasible. . . . A single aircraft for both the Air Force tactical mission and the Navy fleet air defense mission will be undertaken. The Air Force shall proceed with the development of such an aircraft . . . The Air Force . . . version . . . shall be developed to meet as nearly as possible the minimum required performance as specified in SOR-183 . . . within the following constraints: 1, the mold line of the aircraft shall be configured so that a radar dish of 36 inches in diameter minimum size may be accommodated in the nose. 2, the maximum length . . shall not exceed 73 feet in the Air Force version. 3, the weight . . . in the Air Force version with full internal fuel and 2000 pounds of internal stores should be approximately 60000 lb. 4, the aircraft shall be capable of delivering a minimum of 10000 pounds of conventional ordnance. 5, the basic design provision for stores shall allow for the carrying of at least two 1000 pound air-to-air missiles internally or semi-submerged. 6, the basic structure . . . must be able to accommodate the loads associated with carrier operations. The Navy version . . . shall be capable of performing the fleet air defense mission, carrying six 1000 pound air-to-air missiles at a radius of 150 n.m. with 3·5 hours of loiter time. Takeoff gross weight for this mission shall not exceed 55000 pounds without the concurrence of the Navy . . . Changes to the Air Force tactical version . . . to achieve the Navy mission shall be held to a minimum.' This historic document envisaged the RFP going to industry by 1 October, and signing of the weapon system contract by 1 February 1962.

On 1 October 1961 the RFP did indeed go out, in the form of the 'TFX Work Statement' which was a detailed amplification of SOR-183 with added paragraphs to cover the Navy mission. Major firms in the industry knew very well what had been going on, and on 6 December proposals were submitted by Boeing, General Dynamics (GD), Lockheed, McDonnell, North American and Republic. Candidate engines were the Allison/Rolls-Royce AR.168, the GE MF295 and the P&W JTF10A-20. None of the submissions specified the AR.168 as first choice even though this development of the Spey (very much like the later TF41 of the A-7 Corsair) was, to quote the Department of Defense, 'generally superior to its rivals'. Doubtless the suggestion that it was a British engine weighed against it, and Allison did not quite have the pull of the other two firms in this vital contest where every hairsbreadth of advantage counted. The Air Force Evaluation Group at Wright-Patterson AFB, a sharp team of from 120 to 360 analysts (the strength varies with time), augmented for this occasion by staff from the Navy and NASA, spent six weeks sifting the six enormous piles of documents. None of the six submissions was judged acceptable, but the Evaluation Group recommended study contracts for Boeing-Wichita and GD-Fort Worth, whose submissions received highest marks. But the Systems Source Selection Board (SSSB), composed of user representatives from TAC, AF Systems Command, AF Logistics Command and the Navy BuWeps, recommended only Boeing. In view of the importance of the programme, this seems precipitate. Boeing scored top in operational capability and GD scored top in technical factors, but both (like the other four designs) were judged 'unacceptable' by the Navy without major redesign. Boeing's first choice of engine, the MF295, was found unacceptable. The SSSB, though it could not fail to choose Boeing in view of that submission's clear superiority in the areas that most interested them (such as flight performance, apart from speed, and weapon carriage), nevertheless noted that Boeing's method of stowing missiles was unsatisfactory, the radar required revision and further work was needed to substitute a crew-escape capsule for the two ejection seats.

It is interesting to note that Senator McClellan's report entitled 'TFX Contract Investigation' states that 'The SSSB on 19 January 1962 unanimously recommended that Boeing be awarded the development contract.' In contrast McNamara himself has testified that 'The SSSB proposed that a letter contract be issued to Boeing for the limited purpose of refining a design specification which would be acceptable to the Navy and the Air Force. The recommendation was concurred in by TAC, AFLC and the Navy. The AFSC, however, which would have the overall responsibility for development of the aircraft, recommended against the selection of Boeing. . . .' The Senate report is in error in claiming the SSSB recommended a full development contract; as to whether it was unanimous, I can report AFSC records show this command did indeed vote against Boeing on 19 January, so the sleuths of Senator McClellan's committee either failed to do their homework or else thought a unanimous vote for Boeing would bolster their case that the contract award was a scandal. The investigaton sought to prove that McNamara and the two service Secretaries flouted a united military front in buying from GD. To suggest that the source-selection may have been a close-run thing, or that anyone in uniform may not have opted for Boeing, was something McClellan's committee were reluctant to admit.

After this big open competition there were no fewer than three further rounds of closed competition between Wichita and Fort Worth (a closed competition admits of no flow of information between the bidders, such as might be carried by the customer to screw one bidder's performance-point or design feature out of the other). In February Boeing were given a paid study contract to switch to the JTF10 engine. The second proposals were received on 2 April 1962, and although both contractors were judged as having done an 'excellent job' in correcting notified deficiencies, the Navy was unable to accept either, on the grounds of carrier incompatibility and inadequate loiter time on station. By this time the Air Force, and to a rather lesser degree the Navy, were making it quite clear they expected the eventual source to be Boeing. Doubtless Zuckert, and the new Navy Secretary Fred Korth, likewise thought Boeing would be the choice when on 1 June they suggested to McNamara a third 'short round' evaluation giving the contractors (the McClellan report says 'contractor' in the singular) time to refine the design and correct remaining deficiencies. But to McNamara the belief that Boeing merely had to make a few trivial modifications to gain the full award seemed grossly unwarranted: 'It appeared to me not only that neither contractor was meeting Navy requirements, but also that my primary goal was not accepted or not understood by the contractors or the Source Selection Board. . . .' So on 29 June Mr Zuckert sent a memo to the SSSB chairman calling for yet a fourth round, stressing the disregarded aspect of commonality. According to the McClellan report everyone in sight voted unanimously for Boeing. The Senate probe found no shortage of crucial letters and other documents emphasizing Boeing's superiority. Yet the Secretary of Defense testified that 'The fourth evaluation report did not choose as between the contractors. When I reviewed the report I could see why. The question was a very close one.'

It is inconceivable that the Defense Secretary should have been unaware of the great weight of military opinion in favour of Boeing, yet the McClellan report goes to considerable length to suggest that McNamara, in concert with Secretaries Korth and Zuckert, had a few idle chats over breakfast, chucked a few straws in the wind, and then blandly announced on 24 November that the TFX contract had been awarded to General Dynamics. The report left out all McNamara's reasons, so I will put them in. According to McNamara, 'The report [of the fourth evaluation] evaluated General Dynamics as having a better structural design, a simpler fuel system, a slight edge in the flight control area and better proposed programs in the personnel subsystem and aerospace ground equipment areas. The GD design had an edge in supersonic dash capability and supersonic manoeuvrability at altitude. It has a low radar cross-section and an integrated penetration-aids system. For deceleration it uses dive brakes in the air and brakes on the ground. . . . The Boeing design has the edge in ferry capability, conventional weapon carriage, loiter capability and landing performance. It has the advantage in low-altitude manoeuvring capability. For deceleration it uses a thrust-reverser which offers an excellent performance but will require additional development effort. . . When I reviewed the fourth evaluation report I was immediately struck by the difference in approach adopted by the two contractors. The report found that GD proposed an airframe that has a very high degree of identical structure for the Navy and Air Force versions. On the other hand . . . in the two Boeing versions less than half of the structural components of the wing, fuselage and tail were the same. In fact the evaluation group concluded that Boeing is, in effect, proposing two different airplanes from a structures point of view. . . .' McNamara went on to discuss how worried he and his advisers had been over Boeing's proposed use of titanium primary structure, engine air inlets on top of the fuselage and thrust-reversers for use in flight.

On top of all other considerations were those of cost. There is no doubt McNamara was intensely concerned to buy the best system at lowest cost, and he laid down in his original memo of 1 September 1961 the fundamental importance of the chosen contractor's 'demonstrably credible understanding of cost.' On the face of things, Boeing offered to build the TFX (in their case, two TFXs) for less money. DoD were then introducing so-called 'fixed-price incentive contracts', and bidders were asked to propose on the basis of a fixed-price award for 22 RDT&E aircraft (five of them of the Navy version) and to estimate their production costs for a further 1704 aircraft (231 of them Navy versions). After the fourth round of bidding Boeing proposed $466·6 million for RDT&E and $4897·7 million for production, a total of $5364·3 million for the 1726-aircraft programme. GD bid $543·5 million for RDT&E and $4912 for the production run, a total of $5455·5 million. The Evaluation Group cost team then 'adjusted' these figures to a common detailed format, and added in various other items, and arrived at their own estimates of $5387·5 for Boeing and $5803 for GD. These were the figures put before McNamara. He went through the sums with a fine-tooth comb and, to his own satisfaction, unearthed 'additional evidence of unrealistic cost estimates in the Boeing proposal.' He detailed numerous cases of optimistic figures for Boeing's man-hours in RDT&E and production, and also in tooling costs. He discussed the likelihood of engineering change orders (modifications) occasioned by the contractor's failure to make things work first time, and gave many reasons why the more conservative GD submission appeared certain to result in lower total programme cost. He explicitly stated the importance of ensuring that 'a contractor, through ignorance or misunderstanding, has not imposed on himself a ceiling that could lead to serious degradation of the development.' Yet the McClellan report brashly claims that the Defense Secretary 'bought the second-best airplane at the higher price' and accepted the Boeing costs as if they were *faits accompli.* The implication appears to be that the US government must always give an award to the low bidder, no matter how ridiculous the bid may prove to be; and I'll leave the reader to judge how accurately one could at that time describe the GD submission as 'the second-best'. The Senate committee could have fulfilled a valuable public function by conducting a searching and impartial investigation; instead they merely tried to show that the Defense Secretary was a lunatic.

Senator McClellan's Permanent Subcommittee on Investigations, to give it its full title, was triggered off almost as soon as GD was named the winner on 24 November 1962. On December 5 it informed the two service Secretaries it was making a preliminary probe, and, as there were hundreds of people hurt by the choice, it was soon taking evidence by the cartload—practically all of it apparently damning. On 21 December, seeing that GD was due to receive the definitive 'letter contract' on that day, McClellan wrote to McNamara requesting a hold-up in signature until his subcommittee had had time to 'consider information now available to it. . . .' But nobody stayed the hand of the contracting officer at Wright-Patterson AFB. Five days later Deputy SecDef Roswell Gilpatric, an eminent member of the New York bar whom McClellan's committee tried to crucify through 'flagrant conflict of interest in the TFX award', replied that it was 'in the national interest for the program to proceed further without delay.' From this point McClellan was out for blood. Had he been able to view the scene objectively he might have considered that to hold up for an unspecified and possibly very long period the most important new weapon system in the non-Communist world, which was already starting ten months behind the Defense Secretary's schedule because of the unprecedented delay in having four rounds of competition, might indeed prove to be against 'the national interest.' But his report made the decision to go ahead seem positively wilful.

In retrospect the whole thing might have been played with a bit more finesse. McNamara had himself conceived the concept of a major multi-service weapon system, and brusquely banged together the heads of generals and admirals to get it. With his personal identification with TFX he had exceptional motivation for making the correct contract award, and the belief—which the Senate subcommittee tried to foster—that he chose capriciously is entirely false. Yet his actions laid himself and his closest Pentagon colleagues open to the vicious attack they received. For a Defense Secretary personally to order the development of a major weapon system that the two user services had said was technically impossible was unprecedented. For the contract award of this system to require four rounds of evaluation, taking almost the whole of one year, was unprecedented. For the final choice to be not the proposal enjoying the almost unanimous support of the user services was unprecedented. For this surprising choice to be seemingly taken as a result of one or two casual conversations, and supported by *no written document* except a five-page memo (written by Zuckert's department and signed by the three civilian

Secretaries on 21 November 1962) was unprecedented. McNamara must have known that the contract award would loose off a political storm—which just happened to be initiated by Senator Henry Jackson of the state of Washington, Boeing's headquarters. Had there been, in November 1962, one or more big round-table meetings between the three civilian Secretaries and the services, McNamara could have spelt out in detail his reasons and, not inconceivably, spiked the guns of the troublemakers before they got into action. He unquestionably had the personality and authority to accomplish this.

But there was no meeting and no consultation. In the memoirs of Phil G. Goulding, former Assistant SecDef for Public Affairs 'It never was of particular importance whether the public understood his [McNamara's] position' on the TFX. The result was that subsequent technical problems were grossly magnified and even distorted in the public mind. So great was the rumpus at the contract award that this was bound to happen. Once the mass media get the idea an aircraft is controversial it will make the front page if it blows a fuse. Unfortunately the TFX technical problems were enormous, and it is typical of the paradoxical behaviour of modern aircraft that the features expected to give trouble worked like a charm, and the features taken for granted caused terrible difficulties. And the superior 'cost realism' of GD, which had been one of the chief reasons for the corporation's choice, was forgotten as the size of the programme dwindled, inflation took its toll, new versions were introduced and the unit price rose to four times the estimate!

Although GD was now prime contractor, it had bid in partnership with Grumman, who undertook responsibility for all aft fuselages and landing gears, and to assemble and test the Navy fighter version. This version was henceforth called the F-111B, the Air Force machine being the F-111A. The rest of this story concentrates upon the latter, which began life compromised by having a restricted 73 ft 6 in length and side-by-side seating with no rearward view, and an internal weapon bay designed to carry a tactical nuclear weapon so that the subsequent massive load of conventional ordnance had to be slung outside. GD had contracted to fly the first F-111A in 25 months from November 1962, and the engineering and manufacturing programme moved furiously. Soon there were about 6200 companies in 46 states working on the aircraft. I was amused to see how piqued the McClellan committee was at the comment by Arthur Sylvester, Assistant SecDef for Public Affairs, on 8 March 1963, that 'You will hardly get a judicial rendering by a committee in which there are various Senators with state self-interest in where the contract goes. . . .' He was called before that august body and made to admit that he knew of no interest by the members for Arkansas, Maryland, New Hampshire,

Nebraska, N Carolina or S Dakota. Sylvester could have read off a list of the F-111 contracts in those states, except possibly S Dakota; instead he chose (or was told by McNamara) to apologise meekly. But although the job of building the aircraft moved fast, the fundamental question of what aircraft to build was still far from settled.

Never before had there been a production aircraft that could change its shape in flight in such a gross manner. It was going to need a lot of tunnel time; at first flight GD's F-106 Mach 2·3 interceptor had 2045 hours of tunnel testing, and their B-58 Mach 2 bomber 8280, but the figure for the F-111A was 20336. Today the F-111 total exceeds 44000 hours, which I believe to be a record for a single programme. At the start, things could hardly have been worse. Langley, who began tunnel testing under a subcontract on 21 January 1963, found 'major supersonic problems in the form of high drag, low maneuverability, low directional stability, and a serious transonic drag problem.' The NASA lab calculated that in some cases the power of manoeuvre was 'about half that specified in the contractor's proposal,' and it suggested alterations to wing-pivot location, rear-fuselage profiles and other items. From this point onwards the power of supersonic manoeuvre faded from the picture as the Air Force gradually remembered the F-111 was a bomber rather than a fighter. But the matter of transonic and supersonic drag was very serious. GD insisted that their guarantee of a 210 n.m. dash at Mach 1·2 (remember, the spec. said 200) would be met. Part of this assurance rested on tunnel tests by Cornell, but these results were discredited because, according to McClellan's report, 'the airplane model . . . was too large for the tunnel' (which might have been expected to give falsely high drag figures ?). The initial F-111A flight-test articles demonstrated a dash capability of 30 n.m., which appeared to be the biggest miss of the jet age. To me the demand for Mach 1·2 was mistaken in any case, and I doubt that there are many tactical situations where it is essential to fly more than the last 30 n.m. to the target at supersonic speed. GD pointed out that, taking the 800 n.m. outward mission as a whole, their shortfall with the first aircraft was 331 n.m., and that no less than 228 n.m. of this was attributable to 'the government-furnished engine and to other government-responsible changes.' The F-111A itself, they claimed, was 'only 18 per cent off the mark' [*sic*] and this could be recovered by adding two fuel tanks in the wings. In addition numerous small modifications were made to reduce drag, but aerodynamic performance remained one of the most serious controversial aspects of the F-111.

Another enemy of the designer is weight. Having suffered such crippling blows in the wind tunnel the Fort Worth engineers might have expected Lady Luck to make it up to them on this score, but instead she spat in their eyes. I can recall no other aircraft designed by experienced and dedicated people that suffered so severely on the score of weight. The original estimates, refined in four rounds of highly critical customer evaluation, might have been expected to come out accurate within a pound or two. To cut a long story short, the equipped empty weight escalated from the proposal figure of 36700 lb to over 42000 lb before first flight, and if you weigh an unloaded F-111A today I'd be surprised if it was much under 50000 lb! In the case of the F-111B the weight problem was so severe the Navy used this as a reason for scrubbing the whole project. The programme was terminated by Congress (the only time such a thing has happened) by refusal of the budget in July 1968, as I hope to describe in a later volume dealing with supersonic fighters. As the Navy fighter version then ceased to exist, the notion of commonality likewise evaporated, and with it the mythical billion dollars. But it is instructive to record that, while the F-111B was still alive, the succession of 'weight improvement programmes' (known as WIP, then SWIP for 'super', and finally CWIP-I, II and III for 'colossal') sharply decreased the structural commonality, the best guess being a reduction from the original 'near 80 per cent' to a final 29 per cent. This is despite the fact that all these programmes had to proceed within the ground rules calling for the preservation of commonality, which were never relaxed. Indeed some of the unwanted Navy requirements have spilled over even today to haunt the F-14 Tomcat which has succeeded the F-111B.

Troubles come in threes, and the third body-blow lurked unsuspected until the start of flight testing. As the engine came from Pratt & Whitney Aircraft (PWA) it was practically taken for granted that it would give little trouble. The TF30 reheat turbofan, which bore the company designation of JTF10A-20, was a typically conservative PWA design stemming from the original JTF10 planned for the stillborn four-engined DC-9 project of 1958. The only new bit was the afterburner and nozzle, and by the summer of 1964 the whole TF30-P-1 powerplant was running sweetly in the PWA Willgoos high-altitude lab up at Hartford. On 16 October 1964 Fort Worth rolled out F-111A number 63-9768, the first of the RDT&E batch (now increased to 18 of the A model, making a total of 23), knowing it was much too draggy and appreciably overweight but at least fitted with a fine pair of engines. The roll-out was 16 days early. On 21 December, still 10 days ahead of schedule, chief of flight-test Dick Johnson, with Val Prahl as observer, lifted the massive balloon tyres off the runway at Carswell AFB, Fort Worth, for the first time. The wings were locked at 26°, the maximum sweep angle permitting the use of flaps and slats, and Johnson cautiously explored the low-speed behaviour and found little wrong. On the second flight, on 6 January 1965, Johnson had an operable swing wing. He was personally determined to earn his harassed company a maximum bonus by demonstrating variable sweep 24 days ahead of schedule. After cautiously 'inching' the wings in small nibbles, in both directions, he smoothly folded the wings from 16° (fully forward) to 72·5° (fully aft, with the trailing edges aligned close to the slab tailplanes). The wing actuators, for which Jarry Hydraulics, of Montreal, would have been penalized $2500 for every pound of excess weight, took just 20 seconds to change the shape from subsonic to supersonic in a way no aircraft had done before. GD were cock-a-hoop, and banked a DoD bonus of $875,000. Johnson was less pleased. He had intended to gain a further bonus by matching the 72·5° setting with supersonic speed, not scheduled to be demonstrated until flight No 3. He had been thwarted by severe engine compressor stall.

Engine compressor stall is a phenomenon akin to the stall of an aircraft wing. The fan and compressor blades are essentially miniature wings, and turbulence or excessive angle of attack at any point can cause loss of purchase by the affected blade which immediately influences all other blades downstream, causing sudden and violent disruption in engine airflow. A common cause is an uneven flow of air entering the engine from the aircraft inlet duct, so any usable engine must be designed with a 'stall margin' adequate to ensure stall-free operation under every airflow condition that the engine could encounter in flight. Unfortunately stall margin is increased at the expense of engine performance, notably specific fuel consumption, and the PWA design had hewed too close to the stall line for the F-111 inlet system. It behoves the aircraft designer always to offer his engine the smoothest possible airflow, even if the engine is known to be tolerant to turbulence. In the case of the TF30 I think the answer should have been extreme caution until a prototype engine, well in advance of its flight clearance, had been run with a simulated F-111 intake subjected to adverse inlet flows. In Britain this would certainly have been insisted upon by Rolls-Royce's Hucknall establishment, but the United States has a curious history of regarding engines as mere chunks of GFE (see glossary) which are just sent to the airframe builder for him to bolt on. After the F-111 the disastrous tradition had gone for ever—I sincerely hope.

On 5 February 1965 flight testing the F-111 was suspended while GD investigated what it called 'erratic engine behavior', no doubt believing the fault lay wholly with Mr Pratt. In fact the problem involved the whole propulsion system, from inlet to nozzle, and it could later be seen that the world's first advanced afterburning turbofan and the world's first multimission, all-Mach, all-altitude intake system were likely to prove deeply troublesome partners when mated. PWA soon concocted a revised engine, the TF30-3, with a redesigned stator inlet and compressor spools with changed blade angles spinning at different speeds. A sixth-stage bleed was added to increase stall tolerance at high Mach numbers or in combat manoeuvres, and the -3 engine was also given a new afterburner fuel control system and a modified nozzle. Engines incorporating some of the -3 changes were rushed to Fort Worth and installed by mid-February. Johnson tried to make them stall, went into afterburner and succeeded beautifully!

Any GD engineers not trying to save weight or reduce drag were urgently put to work fixing vortex-generator vanes on the inlet spikes, and these helped at low speeds. For high Mach numbers various reprofiled intakes were studied. At first it was hoped that the modifications could be restricted to the splitter and ducts which divert the sluggish boundary-layer air close to the fuselage and dump it overboard. The F-111 intake is, of course, variable in shape; a HamStan hydromechanical system controls the axial position of the quarter-cone that creates the desired oblique shockwave at supersonic speeds. By 1966 the F-111A was cleared with the definitive Triple Plow I intake, the name denoting the three lips which plough off the boundary layer and dump it overboard through apertures above and below.

But this was by no means the end of the story. It was realized that the intake and inlet duct were only marginally large enough for the engine, and that the planned development of the TF30—which the excessive weight and drag of the F-111 had made doubly important—would demand an increase in the size of the duct. Accordingly GD developed the Triple Plow II inlet, with 14 extra square inches for the airflow, moved further out from the fuselage wall where it sucked in cleaner air. This bigger inlet did not become available until well into 1967, by which time most F-111 inlets were either flying or nearing completion. McClellan implied that the bigger intake was needed by every F-111, and castigated everyone for not taking 'a constructive decision to stop production' some time in 1965 or 1966 and go on again only when development had been completed on this enlarged inlet, the Mk II avionics and various other things, such as the structure around the wing pivots which later showed that it could break. He had the benefit of being wise after the event. GD and PWA assure me that the F-111A did not need the bigger inlet, which they say is required only to remove a Mach limitation to 2·2 (instead of 2·5) on the later, more powerful versions at altitudes above 60000 feet, where F-111s seldom go anyway (they mostly can't get there). Had it been fitted to the early F-111 versions the Air Force would have been able to re-fit these aircraft with more powerful engines that they could not afford to buy. In any case, I am not disposed to dispute that 'none of the shortcomings of the F-111A has compromised the basic mission' and that holding up production would have been 'extremely costly and unnecessary.' The F-111 inlet problem is a classic example of a situation in which people with an axe to grind could, and did, bend the facts to fit their case.

In any event the main route to eradicating the compressor-stall problem lay in the improvements to the engine, as noted earlier. These improvements could not be made overnight, and Johnson was allowed to continue flight development with the best engines available. On the ninth flight, on 5 March 1965, he managed to coax the first machine to a true Mach number of 1·2, despite repeated compressor stalls. On landing, locked wheel brakes stopped the aircraft impressively but blew both main tyres. It seemed an uphill struggle for reasons quite unconnected with the radical swing-wing. And GD's test pilots were unable to do anything about the basic lack of thrust. With full afterburner the engines of all F-111 models from the A to the E turn in a static thrust of 18500 or 19600 lb, which is less than the thrust of a reheat Spey. At an aircraft gross weight of approximately 110,000 lb this is just not enough for sparkling performance, and I have yet to meet an F-111 'Jock' who would dispute this. Today PWA has at last come through with a lot more power, but, as related later, this fine new engine went into only the last 82 aircraft.

Mr Pratt has also been in difficulties with the price. In 1962, on the basis of a single specification and a quantity buy of more than 2000 engines, a planning estimate was provided to the USAF in 1962 dollars for the two engines for a production Air Force F-111 amounting to $540,000. But the 2000 engines planned at that time were never ordered; instead the Air Force bought small lots of several types. Engine models for the Air Force went from the TF30-P-1 to the P-3 in 1966, the P-7 and P-9 in 1969 and the P-100 in 1970. Navy models went from the P-1 to the P-12 in 1968 and then to cancellation. Thus, with all these changes and for a much smaller quantity of engines, the price for a pair of powerplants was established at $1,346,000 in 1965 and at $1,420,000 in 1968. PWA do not dispute my belief that the price has risen since then. Poor GD have been lambasted from coast to coast for F-111 cost escalation, but airframe costs have risen only moderately and on occasion have actually fallen. Through all of this the engine supplier, whose price has gone up by roughly a factor of three, has managed to lie low while the tumult raged round him.

As I have now mentioned the chief difficulties that hit F-111 development at the very start, this is the place to record that British engineers predicted they would occur. In 1959 the Chief Scientist of the US Air Force in the Eisenhower administration, Courtland S. Perkins, visited the Vickers/English Electric teams working on TSR.2 and brought back to the

United States useful data on the British requirement and the way it was being met. In turn this sharpened BAC's interest in the TFX, and when the Warton design team saw the GD submission they were surprised at its shape. B. O. Heath thought it worth while writing a critique in which he stated: the wing pivots are not quite in the right place; the tailplane is at the wrong level; base drag will be excessive; there is too much body length ahead of the engine inlets, causing a thick boundary layer to form; and there is insufficient length between the inlet faces and the engines, so that distorted airflow could cause compressor stall. It does not need much imagination to guess how Heath's prediction of trouble was regarded by the British government, which was determined to buy the F-111 and had just thrown out Heath's own design. 'Sour grapes' sums it up.

To return to the chequered progress of the programme, one of its most curious episodes opened on Saturday 25 August 1966. At 9 am there gathered in the Pentagon a bevy of the top executives of the prime airframe and engine contractors who were told how to run their business by none other than McNamara himself. The Defense Secretary had decided to take over direct personal control of the programme, and to hold weekly management meetings 'until either the meetings were doing no good or the problems were solved'. This was just one more thing that was unprecedented. Before the end of the year somebody in the office of General A. L. Esposito, the F-111 Project Officer in the Pentagon (who was never invited to the meetings), had coined a name for this continuing exercise that was keeping everyone busy producing management documents at the end of each week; it was 'Project Icarus', after the son of Daedalus whose waxy wings, softened by the Sun's heat, suffered gross variable geometry causing him to drop like a stone. Frank Davis, president of GD Fort Worth, was equally sarcastic; he is on record as complaining 'I don't have time left between the meetings to solve the problems.' In the long term the chief end-product of Icarus was a massive file of ammunition later picked up by journalists and used against everyone from McNamara downwards.

Like all big programmes the F-111 RDT&E is difficult to assess from the cost viewpoint. The slick answer is that the 1962 bid for 22 aircraft was \$478·9 million and the definitive letter contract of 22 May 1964 was \$476·9 million, but this is rather meaningless. The notion of a fixed-price contract is fine, but, as witnesses testified before the McClellan committee, 'you have to have a fixed item, a fixed schedule and fixed quantities. Here you didn't have that.' So even the RDT&E 'fixed-price' contract escalated to over \$1000 million; for example, the flight-test programme itself, put at \$43·8 million in 1964, exceeded \$175 million by the end of 1969. And there is no point in comparing the two figures because the later one includes all the new versions that in 1964 did not exist. The engineering changes during RDT&E numbered many hundreds, and certainly were not complete by the 18th F-111A, last of the RDT&E batch, which emerged in December 1966. Drag was improved by chopping off the previously 'streamlined' fairings around and between the jet nozzles, fooling the air into thinking the fineness ratio was better than ever. Superior flexible seals were devised to fair the gap into which the wing trailing edge is housed at maximum sweep. Lift was improved, to a $C_L$max of more than 3·0, by extending the slats right in to the fixed centre section and improving the flaps. Severe buffet from the big speed brake was cured by simply restricting it to 50° extension; pilots instead chose to slow down by putting the wing in minimum sweep. The swing-wing itself, says Dick Johnson, 'gave least trouble of all. . . . The one thing we argued about endlessly was which way to move the handle.' Colleague A. S. 'Doc' Witchell, assistant programme director and ex-B-58 pilot, thought 'most people visualize the shape of the wing and feel the control should operate in the same sense.' So, after trying both ways, on every production 111 the trombone pistol-grip is pulled back for supersonic dash.

Early in the programme other countries were taking an interest in this apparent marvel, and Australia and then Britain placed orders; but I will defer these parts of the story until the end, because they would otherwise keep breaking the continuity. I mention them now because the first production negotiations, completed on 28 May 1966, involved 24 Australian F-111Cs and 50 British F-111Ks, as well as 331 of the basic F-111A and 24 Navy B models. Costs were being screwed down well, as far as contracts were concerned, because while GD had estimated $1889 million for 431 aircraft in 1965, the 1966 settlement for this number was $1653 million and the letter contract for 493 aircraft signed on 10 May 1967 was in the amount of $1,822,238,561 (including $16,885,440-worth of tech manuals!) despite the fact there were now the above four models to be developed, and the FB-111 for SAC, discussed later. This represented only $3·7 million per aircraft, excluding engines, avionics and ground equipment, close to the 1962 bid of $3·4 million.

Category I (contractor) testing at Fort Worth was a bigger job than anticipated but generally enjoyable and safe. No aircraft was lost until 19 January 1967, when F-111A No 9, undergoing Cat. II (AFSC) testing at Edwards, was unbelievably brought in to land at 50° sweep, with no slats or flaps. One is reminded of the days when retractable landing gears were novel, and people persistently forgot, but how could it be that this interesting and important new aircraft was not being watched from the tower through binoculars? There was, of course, a check on wing-position in the handling notes. Johnson considers landing even at full sweep feasible on a good runway—'It would be much like a B-58 circuit', with touchdown at about 175 knots—but this unintended arrival, short of the runway, was fatal.

The F-111 actually made favourable headlines when on 22 May 1967 two flew the N Atlantic non-stop without external tanks and without in-flight refuelling. Taking off from Loring AFB, Maine, one flew to Lakenheath, England, and the other landed at the Paris air show, after 5 h 54 min, with 2 h 30 min fuel remaining. The Paris pilot was Lt-Col (then Maj) Tom Wheeler, undoubtedly the most experienced 111 Jock there is, because he flew every Air Force aircraft that left the GD plant when he was chief of flight-test and acceptance there. We'll meet him again later.

One of the great days for the Air Force was 17 July 1967. The first of the impressive green and ochre birds to be put to work was on that day flown to Nellis AFB, near Las Vegas, by Col Ivan H. Dethman, commander of Detachment 1, 4481st Tac Ftr Sqn. Category III (user) tests could now begin. Every man at Nellis—even the rivals on the gape-mouthed F-100 squadrons—longed for the One-Eleven and wanted to disprove the lousy press it had had ever since *Barron's National Business and Financial Weekly* had started the knocking process on 15 August 1966. Frankly, most of the men in uniform didn't know if they could do this. Since the days of the 'TFX wonder plane' five years earlier the programme had taken terrible blows. Even Dr John S. Foster Jr, the urbane and impartial Director of Defense Research and Engineering, had been forced to testify that the F-111A had not met the SOR-183 figures for range, altitude, rate of climb or manoeuvrability. But Dethman, who had got some hours in, made it clear he would stub out his cigar on anyone who again called the big bird 'a lemon'. He bulldozed into an intensive-trials programme called Harvest Reaper intended to work the F-111s either to death or to glory. Although the first five aircraft were all different, in flight envelope, systems and maintenance tasks, they flew 304·1 hours in September 1967, an unprecedented 60·8 hours each compared with the requirement of 30. The figure for October was 59·7 hours each. In that month Dethman collected the 31st F-111A, officially the first production-configuration with P-3 engine, GE APQ-113 attack radar and other changes (but really they still differed in small ways until No. 42), and flew it on autopilot 1000 feet above the ground the entire 1047 miles to Nellis. This was one of the first long overland flights using the vital APQ-110 terrain-following radar (TFR), which has two small dishes almost lost under the giant GE attack radar. Texas Instruments made it both feed the GE flight controls and check its own behaviour. If it senses an error it automatically commands a 2g pull-up, away from the ground, and tells the pilot smartly to wake up.

Those first few weeks at Nellis confirmed beyond doubt that even the first A models were very far from being lemons. Once pilots had overcome their unease at sitting in a left-hand seat, where they had a limited view to the right and none to the rear, all the crews found the F-111 marvellous, and the ground crews loved the thoughtfully laid out hardware. The F-111 contract was the first ever to specify numerical requirements for maintainability. Among other things it called for not more than 35 MMH/FH (Nellis soon demonstrated a minimum of 19 and an average of 30), start to taxi within five minutes of an alert (demonstrated three), require no more than 15 minutes for identifying any fault (done), remain on continuous alert for five days (easy) and be ready to go 75 per cent of the time (done). Almost every maintainable item can be reached from ground level, more than half the acres of aluminium honeycomb skin is made up of 323 access panels, all but 15 of them of the interchangeable kind, and altogether it is not surprising that the F-111 maintainability was used as a model for later DoD procurement specifications. At last the supposed sick bird was winning friends and influencing people in the right way.

Let's walk around one of these curious, ungainly birds at Nellis in 1967 and see just what the Air Force have bought. First impression depends on whether you remember what sort of bird it is. If you remember it is a long-range bomber the reaction will be 'How small, how neat, how fighter-like!' But if you expect to see a fighter the immediate reaction is 'How can anyone tangle with Migs in a great hulking brute like that!' The answer is that you hope you will not tangle with Migs. If you have to, at least you can choose the best sweep angle, pull smooth manoeuvres (with a self-adaptive command augmentation system to give the same response at any aircraft height, weight or speed) and try and blast the enemy with a 20 mm Gatling. But the aircraft is built to drop bombs, and a typical load is four pylons each loaded with two triplets of 500-pounders, which, at a true weight of about 600 lb each, comes to 14400 lb. With this load you can just about work up to 500 knots. With a small external load, on the pylons which swivel on the swing-wings to keep the stores aligned with the airflow, you can exceed Mach 1. Take-off run is 4000 feet at maximum gross of an admitted 91500 lb (real limits generally exceed 100,000, and the Aussie aircraft can fly at 110,000 lb). Ferry range is better than McClellan's claimed 2750 miles, around 3500 being reasonable. In the 800 n.m. radius strike mission (clean) the lo-dash portion can reach 110 miles.

Altogether, thanks to coaxing a lot more lift from the wing and putting 12·5 per cent more fuel inside the airframe (to a total exceeding 32000 lb) the F-111A recovered much of its missing performance. Tom Wheeler would be happy to crook one finger round the stick and roll the big aircraft on its differential tailplanes at Mach 2 at 180° per second—and then stand on the brakes on landing and stop in 1300 ft. Gradually the pilots, who are perhaps as well qualified to pass judgement on an aircraft as people who have never seen it, spread the missionary word around. Perhaps the best thing of all was found to be the feeling of immense confidence engendered by the comfortable cockpit, reliable systems and enough endurance to ride serenely past a succession of circumstances that would previously have meant crises, ejections or ditchings.

The enthusiasm of the pilots crystallized the decision of the Joint Chiefs of Staff to send a detachment of six aircraft from the 428th TFS to Vietnam in a combat evaluation called Combat Lancer before even Cat I testing (let alone II and III) had been completed. It was on 17 March 1968 that Col Dethman landed at Takhli AFB, Thailand, after some splendid work by the Litton inertial navigation system which set him down at Guam with an error of less than six miles after an uncorrected 3000 miles from Hickam (Hawaii). By 19 November the Lancer force had flown 55 missions 'for real', almost all using TFR at night or in bad weather and putting down heavy loads of 750 lb bombs with precision at least as good as other bombers could achieve by day. But, although the aircraft behaved very well and, according to Maj Bob Autrey, the Lancer maintenance chief, were 'always ready to go . . . and so easy to maintain we were able to use younger, less experienced men . . .', the force suffered the worst luck imaginable. The reason for Combat Lancer was to silence critics by 'demonstrating outstanding combat capability'. On 28 March, 30 March and 27 April aircraft failed to return from lone combat missions in adverse conditions, and the survivors were withdrawn. The immediate reaction at home was that half the force had been shot down in the first month, but—while it is almost impossible to erase such a belief once it has formed in the public mind—the Air Force was later to cast more light on the business. One of the crews ejected in their capsule. Their evidence, and examination of the wreckage, eventually showed what had happened, after the discovery of a lump of tank sealant in the tailplane power unit had put everyone on the wrong track. A vital welded joint on the rod of the control valve of the power unit of the left tailplane had failed in fatigue. This had allowed the hydraulic power unit to slam the stick back into the pilot's stomach, while simultaneously driving the left tailplane fully down, causing a violent roll and pitch-up. It seemed likely the other two crews had not accomplished the amazing feat of surviving such circumstances in low-level TFR flight. The possibility that they had been shot down was remote. The ECM systems of the Lancer force recorded 'no prolonged tracking . . . by enemy radars' at any time they were on operations, and it was found that 'no F-111A received hits from small-arms fire, anti-aircraft weapons or SAMs. . . .' And the clincher came on 8 May when, before the true cause had been identified in Vietnam, a Nellis F-111 went violently out of control, the crew surviving. This accident was positively attributed to the weld failure. Had not this one component failed in fatigue at least twice and probably four times the already good accident record of the One-Eleven would have been phenomenal.

At the same time, more aircraft might have been lost had not GD discovered additional cracks in ground fatigue testing. The swing wings are secured by 8½-inch-diameter pins of Ladish D6AC steel which fit into upper and lower bearings at the extremities of the wing carry-through box (WCTB). The WCTB is a massive bridge, also of D6AC steel (a conservative material which earned good marks at the bid-evaluation stage), which forms the structural heart of the aircraft. The WCTB is held together mainly with large precision-fitted bolts. The technology of such bolts has for 20 years involved scrupulous avoidance of sharp changes in section, scratches or anything else that might induce fatigue, yet fatigue is just what GD discovered, in the form of cracks around the bolt holes, late in 1968. At once all aircraft were restricted to 3·5 g until GD had fitted 3 × 8-inch reinforcing gussets along the lower corners of the WCTB. Although laborious rather than difficult, the modification added some 500 lb in weight to each box and cost several million dollars, of which GD paid part. But they still weren't out of the wood. Frank Davis bravely said 'The cracks happened just where we wanted them to—on the ground . . . With the 'fix' we expect the F-111s to meet their full service life.' Engineers at GD and in the Air Force worked day and night, getting ulcers (again) to try to erase the bad public image which guaranteed front-page treatment for the slightest item of bad news. Imagine how they felt when, on 22 December 1969, the left wing came clean off a Nellis aircraft pulling out from a low-level attack. The wing and WCTB were to the latest standard, and the speed, load factor and gross weight were well within limits. To make the cross harder to bear, the immediate vicious roll defeated the crew's efforts to escape.

A frantic probe that went on through the Christmas vacation suddenly discovered a strange flaw in the lower plate of the wing pivot fitting (the hinge on the swinging wing). It was in the form of a crater, about an inch across and extending almost the full 0·246 inch depth of the D6AC steel. The part was studied by GD and Air Force laboratories and it was eventuall decided it could only have formed during the forging and cooling of the plate. The part must have been inspected at least three times, and various theories were put forward to explain why ultrasonic and magnetic-particle testing failed to discover it—a fact which any structural engineer will consider deeply disquieting. All 223 aircraft then built were grounded, and after the Scientific Advisory Board had studied 'all aspects of the materials, structures and aerodynamics' of the F-111, the unprecedented decision was taken to undertake detailed non-destructive inspection and proof testing of *every airframe*. This was done not to unearth similar flaws, for such an eventuality was thought (rightly) to be remote, but because the F-111 simply had to be protected against any fresh disasters, and spending many additional millions of dollars preventing further structural failure seemed a good investment. By mid-1971 more than 250 TAC and 70 SAC aircraft had been tested to + 7·33 and −2·4 g at 56° sweep at −40°F, the refrigeration greatly adding to the cost but imposing a more severe condition. No wing-pivot flaw was found. On the other hand, a test at Fort Worth broke the left tailplane pivot shaft of an F-111E, while an F-111A tested at Sacramento suffered complete failure of the lower plate of the WCTB at not much over half the 7·33 g load, so two possible crashes happened on the ground.

These successive problems with the most crucial primary structure were the chief reasons for delay in the delivery of the F-111 to Australia. In 1963 Britain had hoped to sell the RAAF the TSR.2 (p. 50) but this, being British and uncertain, was eclipsed by the scintillating American TFX. On 24 October 1963 the DoD announced an Australian decision to buy 24 F-111s. These finally gelled as the F-111C, similar to the basic A model but with the long-span bolt-on wing tips of the Navy B fighter and a stronger landing gear with bigger tyres and brakes, such as were later adopted for the F-111K and FB-111 described shortly. The contract was signed in 1964 at $A112 million ($90,749,040). Prime Minister Menzies said 'No government could spend money on anything else'. Defence Minister Athol Townley angrily brushed aside suggestions that, with an open-ended contract, the price might escalate, by explaining 'There is far more chance it will be reduced because our figure is based on the present production run.' Until delivery in 1967 the US offered to lend B-47 bombers, but this was declined. The RAAF decided that in 1970 they would return six of their fleet to Fort Worth to be turned into RF-111Cs with a special reconnaissance pallet. Plans went ahead eagerly at RAAF Amberley (Brisbane) for the assimilation of by far the most advanced aircraft anywhere in the southern hemisphere. By February 1964 Air Minister David Fairbairn was having to deny that development problems would cause any delay in delivery, but today this batch of 24 aircraft have the doubtful distinction of being the only aircraft I have had to mention in every one of the past eleven volumes of *Brassey's Annual: the Armed Forces Yearbook*.

The first C model flew in July 1968; in September 1968 it was accepted by the Aussie government and then returned to the US Air Force. With the other 23 it was put into storage, with the fuselage at Carswell AFB, the wings at Fort Worth and the avionics in a constant-temperature hangar, to await the outcome of testing to establish the structural integrity. Since then there has been an incredible on-again, off-again programme, punctuated by speeches in Australia ranging from defensive enthusiasm to exasperated criticism. When John Gorton took over as Prime Minister in January 1968 he said it was 'too late to cancel', and late in 1969 (just before the wing came off) the RAAF agreed to take the aircraft subject to various guarantees on WCTB life and modification cost. But in February 1970 the protracted delay caused by the decision to test every airframe made some sort of alternative inescapable and the RAAF arranged to lease 24 F-4E Phantoms costing $34 million for two years and $12 million a year thereafter. By March 1970 the F-111C programme was practically dormant, except for intergovernmental exchanges. By this time the purchase price had escalated from $A112 million to $A334 million, of which $A207 million had been paid. Whereas most of the price was supposed to be met by an $A80 million Ex-Im Bank loan at 4 per cent, an additional $A75 million borrowed in February 1969 carried interest at 6 per cent. In May 1970, after years of negotiation, Australia secured the right to cancel without losing her capital investment, in determining the detailed specification of the RAAF aircraft, and of having the option to sell them back (for $A120–140 million) to the US Air Force. I still do not know who has paid for the dismantling, modification and storage. Not until mid-1973 were the first F-111C aircraft reassembled and ferried to RAAF Amberley to equip the F-111 Conversion Flight and No. 82 Strike Wing (a small wing indeed, compared with those of the USAF which number 72 F-111s each).

When I wrote this chapter, early in 1973, the first F-111C crews (who were not necessarily the sons of the first ones appointed ten years earlier) were just re-starting the process of conversion at Nellis. The Australians are in the difficult position of not wanting to remember the F-111's troubled past, but I hope they do not try to pretend it never happened. The excellent Melbourne magazine *Aircraft* recently reported 'Rarely in history has so much balderdash, clap-trap and sheer stupidity been displayed over any single item. Never before have so many laymen usurped the role of aeronautical expert and combat pilot. And never have so many people been so wrong.' The writer even suggested the campaign against the F-111 was a matter of 'Communist smear tactics.' I'll let my readers judge the validity of this.

In the original TFX planning there were crucial compromises to try to be clever, but not too clever. Although the avionics was a central factor in establishing the mission capabilities, the stern requirement of high availability and low maintenance burden biased the systems in favour of state-of-the-art. For example, GD even specified an analog computer, which by 1962 was regarded as a quaint tool for data processing, although making sense in some other applications. From the outset the Air Force sought to introduce updated avionics; in fact I suspect they had nagging doubts that they ought not to have settled for the original avionic configuration. By 1963 a 'Mk II' avionic specification had been agreed, for introduction when its development permitted, which was expected to be at the 100th aircraft in 1968. Primary flight instrumentation, mission and traffic control (new name for communications, navigation and identification) and even penetration aids (what today is called 'defensive avionics') were not grossly altered, but the fourth element, firepower control, was started again from scratch.

Probably the most important Mk II advance, apart from getting IBM to produce a modern digital computer, was that the original attack radar was replaced by the radically newer APQ-130 multi-mode radar by Autonetics (now North American Rockwell Electronics), who were also awarded the Mk II systems-integration contract estimated at $60 million. The APQ-130 does all one would expect. It can map the ground with photographic sharpness, even at the low grazing angles of tree-top TFR flight, can pick out moving targets from a stationary background, has enormously better performance in heavy precipitation or against countermeasures, and can provide a beam for radar semi-active AAMs such as the Sparrow. Obviously, practically every module in the Mk II system is solid-state microelectronics which, apart from being very compact, uses much less power, generates less heat and doesn't go wrong in the way earlier electronic devices do. The new systems are linked to new cockpit displays of which the major items are the horizontal display by Astronautics Corpn. and the vertical situation and twin head-up displays by Norden division of United Aircraft.

Altogether the Mk II is exactly what the F-111A ought to have had, and could have had by first delivery of user aircraft in the autumn of 1967. Most of the technology was in production in 1960 for the Minuteman ICBM. But nothing ever seemed to go right for the One-Eleven. Autonetics encountered a heartbreaking series of problems with the Mk II avionics, was unable to prevent massive escalation in cost, and seemed to lose a month on schedule with each month that passed. The 'prototype F-111D', a converted A model, did not fly until 2 December 1968, when the whole system was meant to be standard in production aircraft. In March 1968 the DoD had accepted the situation and announced the F-111E as an interim aircraft incorporating the redesigned engine inlets but retaining the old avionics (except that one much-criticised feature, the manual scope camera, was replaced by an automatic strike camera, and the countermeasures were augmented). The E, easy to introduce, came on to the production line early in 1969 after the manufacture of 159 of the F-111A. Whether or not 159 is much too high a number is something one can argue about endlessly.

While GD made 94 of the E model, Autonetics finally cleared the Mk II avionics at the startling price of $2·2 million per installation, the R&D having soared from $60 million to $280 million by the spring of 1969. Delivery of 96 of the correspondingly costly D model began, interspersed with Es, in the autumn of 1970 at aircraft No 216. By this time there were wings of the A model at Nellis and at Cannon AFB, New Mexico, and a wing of the E model at Upper Heyford, England (quite a contrast with 1942 when I trained there in Wellingtons). The D at last entered service at Cannon in October 1971. The Air Force has for years toyed with buying a small force of RF-111D reconnaissance aircraft fitted with cameras, radar and IR sensors in the weapon bay, replacing the Gatling gun usually fitted there. The installation cost no less than $118 million to develop but, at the time of writing, it has flown only in the eleventh F-111A, converted in 1967 and flown on 17 December of that year, with excellent results.

There are two other active F-111 versions, but before dealing with them I must relate how Britain in 1965 thought the F-111 'the obvious choice' and in 1968 decided instead to accept cancellation charges. The RAF had been given a verbal assurance they would get the F-111 in place of TSR.2, and it was because of this that they did no more than go through the motions of evaluating the Buccaneer 2*, the swing-wing Phantom S and the Spey-Mirage. Through the summer of 1965 there were arduous discussions concerning the extent of fitting British hardware to the RAF version, called the F-111K, and of participating in the F-111 manufacturing programme. It was soon accepted there were no bits of F-111 that could reasonably be made in Britain, not even in return for a British buy of 50 aircraft, but the possibility of fitting the Spey 25R engine was probed in depth. I was assured by Pratt & Whitney this would 'result in a degraded flight performance', but I doubt that it could have been any worse than with the early TF30. Indeed a Spey F-111 would certainly have been more powerful and might have worked very well, but this all took place just when the Spey was in mismatch problems with the Phantom. British Defence Minister Denis Healey said he was 'personally strongly in favour of retaining the US engine and avoiding such problems'; he said this at a time when they were practically tearing their hair out at Fort Worth over exactly the same trouble! Healey had been told by Fort Worth there was 'only one mission profile where the Spey shows to advantage';

if GD had waited another two weeks they might have thought the Spey a potentially good thing and advised differently, with possibly far-reaching consequences.

When the British government cancelled TSR.2 they secured an option to purchase the F-111 on favourable terms. The option expired on 31 December 1965. On 13 December, at Healey's request, President Johnson extended the option to the following 1 March to allow Britain to complete its defence review. On 9 February 1966 GD president Roger Lewis, and Fort Worth division president Frank Davis, came to brief MPs in the House of Commons Committee Room 10, with the Palace of Westminster electrical engineer hired by GD to organize the energy supply. The audience were not used to such streams of highly technical data, and some found the bit-rate rather too high for their brains. I doubt if MPs had ever before heard such a detailed and exact briefing on a current aircraft programme, although it goes on all the time in the US. So impressed were they, it was no surprise that in his Defence Review of 22 February Healey announced 'to bridge the gap until the AFVG . . . it has been decided to buy 50 F-111A aircraft . . . no other aircraft can be available by 1970 to match the performance. . . .' (Little did he realize that this was to prove the last vital nail in the AFVG's coffin, and to confirm to de Gaulle that Britain had no place in Europe.) Later he said the initial order was for ten, the balance being contracted for in April 1967. There would be a 'ceiling price' of \$5·95 million 'covering production costs and a contribution to American R&D . . . which will be met by credit terms spread up to 1977. . . . The ceiling price will be agreed as soon as practical for the changes . . . which will include a British communications fit.' Hardly any Britons bewailed the apparent need to buy the foreign marvel, but some were incensed at what was being done to the Queen's English; 'Pardon me,' said one, 'while I throw a British communications fit.'

The agreed basic 'ceiling price' of \$5·95 million per aircraft was a bargain, and turned out later to be well below the price of any other type of F-111 (although I am not certain just what a ceiling price is, because the same figure was quoted to the Australians who have already paid more than \$12 million per aircraft). This was especially remarkable in view of the fact that the K was to have portions of the Mk II avionics, the strengthened gear, larger wheels, tyres and brakes, and other improvements. It was not surprising that indefatigable Senator McClellan wanted to 'ensure the British aircraft are not sold below cost.' McNamara later revealed that there had been 'most tortuous negotiations' with the British. 'The British government insisted on a fixed price. We did not have the legal authority to provide a fixed price . . . because we did not have a fixed-price commitment from our contractors. It was a most difficult negotiation to work out a formula acceptable to both governments.' To make it even more difficult the British wanted to 'offset' the cost of the F-111 by getting a reciprocal sales deal. As Mr Healey put it: 'The F-111 buy' will be 'paid for by British sales to the United States. . . . We have set ceiling totals for sales which together will cover the total cost of the F-111A.' As none of these sales had actually been made, this seemed rather like counting chickens before they were hatched. During the Defence Debate in March 1966 Fred Mulley, Minister of Aviation, added a new factor: 'Total dollar cost of the F-111A has been given as £260 million over ten years, corresponding to $725 million. We have the agreement of the United States that it will buy directly British equipment to the value of $325 million and that it will co-operate in sales to third countries . . . similar to that we have recently arranged with Saudi Arabia to the value of $300 million—covering the whole dollar cost of the purchase of these aircraft over the ten years.' I don't know whether these two sums were meant to add up to $725 million, but the Saudi deal had an export value of $210 million, not $300 million, and the US, in the shape of Lockheed and Raytheon, hardly 'stood aside'; in any case even Mulley said 'American assistance on the Saudi Arabian deal would have no influence whatever on any F-111 purchase by HM government' (whatever that meant).

In the same Defence Debate Healey announced the 50 RAF aircraft would cost £280 million over ten years (£20 million more than the cost given by his colleague a few minutes earlier) and that most would be based at Singapore, with some at Bahrain, Gan and Masirah, and 'if we were working with the Australians, Darwin and Cocos.' On 29 April 1966 the Military Aircraft (Loans) Bill allowed HM Treasury to lend £430 million to the Ministries of Aviation and Defence and borrow the appropriate number of dollars from the US. Tory spokesman Robert Carr said he was 'unable to oppose' the bill because there was now no source of RAF aircraft except the United States and to oppose would be to deny the nation essential weapons, 'however much we may detest this bill . . . which commits Britain to a vast expenditure on American military aircraft paid for on the never-never up to 1978 . . . and is never taken into account in our balance-of-trade figures.' When the Chief Secretary to the Treasury said the Bill provided for the sum to be spent on US aircraft over the six years ending 31 March 1972, Carr jumped up to ask if this sum was not £660 million. Merlyn Rees, RAF Under-Secretary, said £660 million was 'the total; the £430 million is the amount borrowed from the US government at $4\frac{3}{4}$ per cent', with interest exceeding £20 million a year even on these terms.

On 12 May my noble lords Kinnoull and St Oswald challenged the government with some fearsome words: 'compressor stall', 'drag' and 'weight escalation', which they had found in the American newspapers. RAF Minister Lord Shackleton told them not to worry about some small technical problems, and pointed out that the price Britain would actually have to pay might 'very well be less' than $5·95 million. But the commotion over the F-111 could practically be heard across the Atlantic. Soon Whitehall had to point out that the troubles affected 'only the F-111B and the FB-111' (the latter had not then even been built); 'the F-111A, on which our aircraft are based, is relatively unaffected.' On the BBC-TV programme '24 hours' Robert Carr probed Healey, to be sharply told 'Our version of the aircraft has nothing to do with the US Navy aircraft, and you ought not to try to pretend that it will be subject to development problems.' So much for commonality, or common-sense. On 16 November Healey announced 'The operational requirement for the F-111K is in all respects lower than the requirement for aircraft ordered by the US government . . . in all respects the performance of the K is superior to the requirement of TSR.2.' And he assured Enoch Powell that the 'total cost of the aircraft, as we buy it in its British configuration, will be about £2½ million.' In a written answer on 1 February 1967 he gave the 'total capital cost of the whole programme through the first five years of operation' as 'of the order of £135 million' (he did not explain why this, which included the purchase price, was less than half the figure for ten years). He said in the same month Britain might have to bear about £15 million in R&D charges, including the bill for the reconnaissance pod derived from the EMI installation for the Phantom.

On the last possible day, 31 March 1967, Britain signed for the main batch of 40 Ks, with delivery of the 50 to be made between April 1968 and January 1970. The ten-year programme cost was again given as £280 million, of which £240 million would be in dollars; Healey said he was adding in 'something over £100,000 per aircraft' to bring costs up to 1967 prices. In the Defence Debate on 1 May MPs were apparently startled to be told the '15-year programme cost' would be £336 million—'far above anything previously quoted' said Eric Lubbock, apparently not noticing that the MoD had switched to a 15-year reckoning.

On 15 September 1967 a protectionist Congress rejected a big offset deal involving surface ships for the US Navy. This embarrassed the DoD because, even though McNamara had had to overcome British ineptitude and disorganization to get the offset system working, there was a tacit assumption the deals would go through. My own view was that the Americans used the notion of an offset programme, and the big surface-vessel contract in particular, as bait to ensure Britain would really buy the F-111. Like a man chasing a girl, one never knew who was snaring whom. In any case it was soon evident Mr Healey's $325 million shopping list was by no means the *fait accompli* that it was presented as to the British public. In fact there was never any agreement to buy anything. All the agreement of 26 February 1966 provided for was that the DoD would 'search out and select items of defense equipment and supplies that appear to be competitively obtainable from the UK . . . and to evaluate . . . without imposing any differential under the Buy American Act or the DoD Balance of Payments Program. . . .' The $325 million began to evaporate as Healey admitted in a TV broadcast 'If the whole offset deal were to be ended we would consider cancelling the whole F-111 deal . . . although this would mean abandoning those elements of our defence and foreign policies which depend on this type of aircraft.' Until this moment I had fondly thought one's defence procurement was matched to one's needs, rather than the other way round!

I was scarcely reassured when I picked up a piece of news-tape on 14 October and read that John Stonehouse, Minister of State for Technology, had climbed out of an F-111A at Fort Worth and pronounced the view that 'The greatest thing about it is the ferry range, which means the 111 can be deployed throughout the United Kingdom' [*sic*]. And on 13 December it was apparent something had gone wrong with the ceiling price, because Healey announced that the cost to December 1976, a mere nine years, would now be £425 million. Devaluation had raised the dollar part of the total from £310 million to £360 million, but nobody explained how it had jumped to £310 million in the first place. Roy Mason tried to make out that the increase was due to arbitrarily adding £5 million a year for ten years, but the figures were 300 per cent larger than this. What was far worse was that it was soon obvious there was a crisis in the whole F-111K programme. On the first day of 1968 frantic talks in Washington screwed out of the Americans an offset deal raised from $725 million to $825 million (both figures are the total 'offset', not just the supposed US purchases but also the supposed sales to third parties), and DoD spelt out to Britain the consequences of cancellation. But cancel Britain did, Prime Minister Harold Wilson—who in 1965 had personally described the F-111 as 'a bargain'—claiming that the cancellation in January 1968 would 'save about £400 million between now and 1977–78, allowing for likely cancellation charges.'

Reasons given for the cancellation varied. The mass media hovered between 'US refusal to quote an overall cost for the order' and 'a drive to make Great Britain solvent.' Not one of the supposed reasons mentioned technical shortcomings. On 20 February DoD estimated cancellation charges at $130 million (£54 million), yet some clever negotiation (that a bright journalist might care to probe one day) brought the figure down to less than $30 million! On top of this, the DoD was going to inflict a 'penalty' of $129 million in planned offset sales, but I am assured that this was never done. The US also ceased to 'support' Britain in selling to third countries, but this was never more than a vague notion that would have collapsed as soon as a big US manufacturer considered he could be hurt by it. In 1969 the House of Commons Estimates Committee said that 'non-delivery of US equipment to the Army and RAF' (a delightful way of putting it) would probably 'cover the MoD share' of F-111 cancellation charges. This brought to an end the most remarkable series of negative procurement decisions in the history of any nation.

When Britain cancelled, hardware for all 50 aircraft had been made or ordered, 19 were on the assembly line and the two K flight-test aircraft were almost complete. The first two were re-designated YF-111A and cannibalized for spares. The components of the following 48 were used in manufacturing a new version, the FB-111. The original notion of a tactical fighter implicit in the TFX designation seems far removed from a strategic bomber, but in 1965 it was evident that, if the F-111 could be brought successfully out of its morass of weight, drag and thrust problems, it could form the basis for a useful machine for SAC. On 10 December 1965 McNamara announced that the FB-111A would replace the 345 Boeing B-52C, D and F aircraft and the 80 B-58s of Strategic Air Command. GD had conducted extensive studies of SAC versions of the F-111 but the FB finally agreed was a minimal modification, with a defence-systems operator replacing, rather than supplementing, the co-pilot, and virtually identical to the British K plus the bolt-on wing tips of the Navy B model. These modifications enabled the weight to be raised to a figure that is considerably over 110,000 lb to meet the required ranges and weapon loadings. In the nuclear role the FB can carry two SRAMs internally and four more under the wings. In the conventional role it can carry no fewer than 50 standard 750-pound bombs (which actually weigh 825 lb) with the wings at 26°. The knockers drew attention to the fact that in this condition, at military (non-afterburning) power, the aircraft 'could not clear the summit of Pikes Peak' at 14110 feet. This sounds disgraceful, but really doesn't matter. What does matter is that the FB can fly missions that SAC considers useful.

Indeed when the first FB was ceremonially accepted on 8 October 1969 the Commander of SAC, Gen Bruce K. Holloway (whom we met near the beginning of the story), said the aircraft would 'play a substantial role in contributing to the SAC mission of deterrence through the 1975 time period.' But although the FB began life as a known quantity, with practically all the worst problems visible at the outset, the programme has still been hurt by reduction in numbers and escalation in price; indeed you can't have one without the other. Originally the FB force was to number 210 aircraft, plus 53 for spares and attrition, making a total buy of 263 that McNamara thought would cost 'on the order of $1 billion and three-quarters.' After he left office the order was cut to 76, barely enough for two two-squadron wings, at a programme price of approximately $1·2 billion ($1200 million). On a cost/effectiveness basis this does not compare well with the B-1 (described in the companion 'Bombers' volume), provided that the latter can be produced for the estimated cost. But a bird in the hand is worth two on the drawing board, and the FB is a fully cleared weapon which in SRAM trials, against targets ahead, to the side and even to the rear, has launched missiles at all heights down to 300 feet with 'accuracy that bettered requirements by 51 per cent.' And, like its stable-mate the B-58, the FB did fantastically well on its first appearance in the SAC Combat Competition; two months after joining the command the two crews that entered came first in bombing and second in navigation and combined navigation and bombing. Hats off to the 509th BW at Pease AFB, New Hampshire; the second wing is at Plattsburgh AFB, NY.

Although the FB has slightly more power than earlier 111s, its TF30-7 being rated at 20350 lb, Pratt & Whitney took a long time to come through with a dramatically more powerful TF30. Although neither the original P-1 nor the P-3 met the chief propulsion demands of the requirement, and the massive rise in F-111 weight made it obvious that much more thrust would be needed, significant thrust-growth has taken ten years. At first the sharpest emphasis was on the Navy fighter, and it was via the more powerful P-12 for that aircraft that PWA derived the P-7 engine of the FB-111. But since 1967 PWA have been combining years of fundamental research in a very much improved engine, the TF30-P-100. This is not a book about engines, but anyone interested in modern engineering methods could do no better than study the P-100, what it is made of and how it is made. Its thrust in many F-111 flight regimes is 35 per cent greater than that of earlier TF30s, although it is the same size and weight, and has substantially lower specific fuel consumption.

The only tragedy is that, by the time the P-100 was nearing service clearance, the Air Force had little money left for the F-111, and the basic aircraft design was becoming somewhat dated. But the improvement in performance conferred by the P-100 engine, especially in field length, climb, acceleration and manoeuvre margin, is so great that GD were authorized to match it with a new model, the F-111F. This incorporates not only the obvious improvements, but also has most interesting structural revisions and an avionic system that provides nearly all the capabilities of the Mk II for half the price ($1·1 million instead of 2·2). Many airframe parts that gave trouble in earlier models are completely redesigned, and the wing pivots incorporate doubler plates of boron/epoxy composite laminates and fairings of carbon-fibre composite. GD had earlier made many experimental F-111 parts in advanced composites, including rear main-gear doors, wing trailing-edge panels, tailplanes and wing airflow-deflector doors, but the F is the first F-111 (and almost the first aircraft of any kind) to incorporate such construction as standard.

The F-111F is by a very wide margin the best of all the One-Elevens, and it is a mighty shame it came in so near the end of the programme. Originally the Air Force had planned to buy 219. Then cost-escalation forced a massive cut, to 98. Further rises in price left the Air Force with $566 million in 1970 and $283 million in 1971 but still $125 million short! The huge total of $849 million, which at the beginning of the TFX programme would in theory have bought 350 aircraft, actually sufficed to buy just 82 of the F model—even though this version came at the end of the learning curve when the unit price ought to have fallen dramatically. (It's a good thing the F has 'cheap' avionics!) The first F-111F blocks to come off the line temporarily had the P-9 engine, and entered service early in 1972 at Mountain Home AFB, Idaho, with the 347th TFW. Not until the 41st F was one delivered with a pair of P-100 engines, but now almost the whole force has been retrofitted with the new engine as a modification done at the home base. Lack of funds prevents the same thing being done with the British-based wing of E models, despite their big inlet ducts.

Towards the close of the Vietnam war the Air Force used the F-111 in anger for a second time. This time it was done with a big force of fully developed aircraft: two squadrons from the 474th TFW, the 429th and 430th, each with 24 aircraft. The 474th was the original Nellis wing, and its 428th TFS sent the six aircraft on the ill-starred Combat Lancer exercise. This time the effort lasted five months. In this period 74000 large bombs were dropped in more than 4000 combat missions, almost all of them by lone aircraft working at night and often in bad weather. This time the opposing radars and weapons were far more lethal. Time after time a late-model F-111 would need all its guile to stay under the probing electronic beams (the crew can tell when they are being 'looked at'), and six of them failed to make it. As Col William R. Nelson, 474th commander, explained, in this kind of operation you hardly ever get a clue what happened, so cannot guard against it happening again. A lone aircraft preserving radio silence far from friendly forces, and hugging the ground below all radars—not just enemy ones—is unlikely to be able to explain how it was lost. But Nelson made two important points when he finally returned to Nellis in 1973. One is that the One-Elevens needed none of the huge armada of helpers—KC-135 tankers, F-105 Wild Weasels, F-4D anti-radar attackers armed with Shrike and Standard ARM missiles,

EB-66 anti-ECM jammers, and fighters flying 'Mig-CAP' patrols—that supported the operations by earlier and more vulnerable attack aircraft. The second is that no other aircraft on Earth, according to Nelson, could have sustained the heavy attacks that were made by F-111s on one particular vital target surrounded by Hanoi city without a single bomb being put outside the target area. The operations of the 474th will probably remain a classic example of the deployment of modern attack aircraft for many years to come.

Unpredictably, the final new model of One-Eleven was an experimental one-off conversion with a supercritical wing derived from the NASA airfoil flown in 1972 on an F-8 Crusader. This conversion of an F-111 was done merely to explore the behaviour of the wing at different sweep angles, and not with a view to modifying any additional F-111 aircraft. So the programme was terminated at 550 aircraft, of which 525 had been delivered by February 1973. Soon the last of the first swing-wingers will go out of the great building in which were made 2743 B-24 Liberators, 124 B-32 Dominators, 385 B-36s, 116 B-58 Hustlers and sundry conversions including a batch of Canberras that would have horrified Teddy Petter. Hopefully Fort Worth will soon have another major programme, because it would be harsh for such a plant to have nothing to do but build bits of other people's aircraft. This programme could be the YF-16, a true 'fighter' weighing less than one-fifth as much as an F-111.

Memories of the One-Eleven vary. To the man in the street they revolve around bad news, with overtones of scandal. To Fort Worth and Hartford they certainly include problems, but now that the shouting has died down surely the thing that matters is that the men on the flight line and in the briefing room would not swap the F-111 for anything in the sky or on the drawing board; and it may be of significance that the F-111 was the only aircraft mentioned by the Russians at the SALT talks.

After so many words on politics and technicalities I feel like a breath of fresh air, and what better than to ride with author Ernest K. Gann and Tom Wheeler? Gann's tale—surely the best of 26 accounts I have read of flying, or flying in, the F-111—appeared in *True* magazine for August 1971: 'As you sink down from the heights, the mountains become ever more imposing and you remember a wager made the night before. If during the TFR run you manage to resist reaching for the stick and taking over from the automatic pilot, you will win two martinis . . . here are the 11000-foot mountains approaching from directly ahead at a mere 553 miles per hour and you are looking *up* at them from the vantage of 200 feet. You indulge in some erratic swallowing and glance furtively at Wheeler, who is not looking out at all but thoughtfully studying an old aviation chart, vintage 1935. . . . As if cushioned softly against the face of the mountain, the One-Eleven rises with the slope. . . . There is a saddle in the mountain ahead . . . trees higher than eye level, rocks, boulders, great chunks of very abrasive substance off both wing tips. Wheeler reaches for a knob. "Do you prefer your ride to be soft, medium or hard?" Your hand is curved like the talons of an eagle exactly one half inch ahead of the stick. . . . The One-Eleven slips through the saddle and starts down the backside of the mountain, still at 200 feet and just under the speed of sound. . . . Just as you are nearly resigned to continuing straight through the bottom of the valley on the direct route to Peking, the autopilot levels the nose and you slither across the rumpled surface like a giant manta ray seeking food.'

If I were a millionaire my executive ship would be an F-111F. Even in my tight little island I know some bits of territory I'd love to show Senator McClellan, preferably from 200 feet.

McDonnell Douglas A-4 SKYHAWK

THIS compact package of offensive power is my favourite example of what can be accomplished by a brilliant design and engineering team that has the leadership to run rings round a hidebound official specification. In 1951 the US Navy prepared a requirement for a tactical attack aircraft capable of carrying a 2000 lb bomb yet weighing no more than 30000 lb gross, with propulsion by two turboprops. Ed Heinemann could easily have set to work to meet it. The El Segundo (Los Angeles) factory of Douglas Aircraft, where he was chief engineer, could well have won with an indifferent aircraft that might have been phased out of the inventory by 1958 and forgotten by 1960. Instead, with immense foresight and courage, he steered his team along a totally different route. The resulting Skyhawk exceeded the specification by 100 knots in V_{max} and 100 miles in tactical radius while turning the scales at *under half* the specified weight. I do not believe such a thing had ever happened before, and I know it has not happened since. The result is that, as I write, Skyhawks are still coming off the production line after 23 years.

Going back 23 years we find the United States fighting a grim war in Korea with two sets of tactical aircraft, each of which was good in parts and bad in others. One set was piston-engined: Corsairs, Mustangs, Twin Mustangs, and Heinemann's own Invaders and Skyraiders. These could carry formidable ordnance loads from hastily-prepared airfields, fly long and arduous missions, loiter for hours in battle areas and make as many as a dozen runs at a ground target; but they were vulnerable, even to North Korean defences, and their pilots were utterly exhausted after sitting in their cockpits for, in the case of the Skyraider, as long as 12 hours (they literally had to be lifted out). The other set was jet-propelled: Shooting Stars, Thunderjets, Panthers and Banshees. These had plenty of flight performance, but they were severely limited in ordnance load, field performance and endurance. The Navy BuAer staff in Washington desperately wanted to launch a superior attack machine that could supplement or replace the Skyraider by carrying a big load faster. The twin-turboprop seemed the best answer, and I am sure they could have convinced me it was. Indeed, amazingly enough, 15 years later the United States found itself fighting the same sort of war over again and decided that what it most needed was—surprise, surprise—a modernized Skyraider with twin turboprops (p. 250)

As the designer of the Skyraider, Heinemann was expected to tender for the new requirement. His Skywarrior, described in the companion 'Bombers' book, was already under contract, and about half the BuAer staff regarded him as a dark horse who might try to sell them something dramatically unconventional. In fact he had spent the latter part of 1951 deeply engrossed in studies for an interceptor as a detailed exercise in the simplifying and lightening process that had come to be a central part of his professional life. By December of that year he had completed his big analysis of why combat aircraft had become so heavy, complex and costly that their operational effectiveness was actually becoming worse, partly because fewer could be bought and partly because they could not be kept serviceable. He never had any doubt that, whatever the mission requirement might be, the correct design approach was to conduct the most detailed investigation into every part, beginning with such things as electrical cable connectors and ending with the wing skins, to see which bits could be redesigned and which could be left out altogether. His philosophy was to make every item stand on its own feet and justify its inclusion. Not even the control column was taken for granted unless it could be shown there was no better pilot control device. The results were startling, because each pound saved could be multiplied by the basic growth factor, which, for a tactical jet in the 'rubber' project stage when engine size can be cranked up and down, was typically ten. This meant that a pound of weight saved on a cable loom saved ten pounds on the gross weight. Heinemann's preliminary investigation suggested that many pounds could be saved on dozens of items normally accepted without question, from the oxygen system to the ejection seat. As a vehicle for the study he chose a supersonic interceptor which, because of its incredible gross weight of only just over 6000 lb, had a thrust/weight ratio of 1·1:1 (better than unity).

All aircraft designers try to reduce weight, but Heinemann's study was unprecedented in its depth and ruthlessness, and in the context of Korea it seemed to be relevant to the superior aircraft the Navy was seeking. Just as the study was being finished, at the end of 1951, a top Navy official called on Heinemann, heard about the study and said 'You ought to give this pitch to Admiral Soucek'. The admiral, a former holder of the world altitude record (appropriately, gained over Washington), was head of BuAer. In the first week of 1952 the lean aircraft designer was ushered into the admiral's board room and found himself confronted by 50 of the top BuAer officers. But he warmed to his task, and held forth in a splendid and convincing presentation that lasted all morning. He felt good about the way it had gone over, and wondered if the immediate result would be a go-ahead on the proposed aircraft. It was Captain Epes, in the front row, who spoke: 'We just cancelled our requirement for interceptors.'

Such demolishing comments no doubt helped Epes, who is now an admiral, but in fact it was not meant to demolish. Every man in the audience was intensely interested and, although practically all were highly sceptical, they felt the man from California should be given enough rope to hang himself. Heinemann went home with authorization to come back in two weeks with his philosophy applied to an attack aircraft. Fourteen days and most of 14 nights sufficed to create the outline of the Skyhawk. Unlike the interceptor it was optimized to a single design point, for peak efficiency in high-subsonic cruise. The engine chosen was the British Sapphire, then just coming into volume production in the United States as the Wright J65, which was the most powerful and efficient turbojet available in 1952. All the ordnance was hung externally, and the wing was made so small it did not need to fold. Heinemann had a very clear idea of what he wanted to do: 'take the best engine I could get, stick a wing underneath and put a saddle for the jockey on top—and leave out the rest.'

But he found it difficult to communicate his enthusiasm. In the Navy there was no shortage of experts who made very unkind remarks about his 'irresponsibility', his 'unrealistic approach' and even about his enthusiasm. And even among his own design team in California there was a pervading feeling that, while trying to beat a specification was reasonable, what they were now trying to do was unreasonable. The 30000 lb weight limit was so ingrained in everyone's mind that not a few thought their chief engineer might be, to put it delicately, 'in need of a rest.' (In the most strict, literal sense this was undoubtedly true.)

So early one morning Heinemann locked himself in his office and didn't go home until he had prepared an outline drawing of the aircraft and drawn up a preliminary weight analysis with which he was satisfied (it added up to 12000 lb gross). The next day he called the whole project-design staff together, gave each a print of the layout, and delivered a brief address: 'I think this can be done. It will take a tough SOB to do it, and before you say it I will say it, I am he. I would like to have you all join my team. Anyone who doesn't wish to join, there is the door.' With this uncompromising introduction all the ingrained assumptions and beliefs flew out of the window, and nobody left with them. On the following morning Bob Smith, senior layout draughtsman, gave Heinemann a refined three-view which was soon the centre of attraction in Washington. The BuAer experts were reluctant to express their mind—with the exception of Cdr John Brown, chief of attack aircraft design and procurement. He was totally convinced, assigned himself Navy Project Officer and kept th concept sold when Heinemann could not be in Washington. But most oı his colleagues adopted a wait-and-see attitude. Heinemann was told to double the bomb load and add 100 miles to the combat radius. This put up the gross weight from 12000 lb to 14300. Douglas was then given an instruction to proceed with the design and mock-up, the project being called the A4D Skyhawk. Ben Collins was appointed the Douglas project engineer.

Despite the radical nature of the design, that original drawing is almost identical with the aircraft of 23 years later in wing and tail planforms and areas, engine location, fuselage arrangement, spar locations and other fundamentals. The only noticeable changes were to make the main landing gear retract forwards, instead of inwards, and to extend the rear fuselage when calculations showed the weight and losses of the longer jet-pipe would be more than offset by reduced base-drag. Today the Skyhawk is so familiar that it is hard to comprehend that experienced Navy staff were genuinely convinced it could never be built. It was not until several months had gone by, and Heinemann had submitted his detailed weight breakdown, that he began to receive quiet apologies from his critics. Then, once Soucek's organization had fully accepted the idea, the project moved fast. On 21 June an order was placed for an XA4D and a static-test airframe, shortly followed by an order for nine A4D-1s, each to have an empty weight of 8136 lb and a gross weight of 15000 lb. It was a negotiated contract, without competition. As Admiral Hayward put it, the success of the Skyhawk rested on 'trust and confidence', rather than upon the present-day procedure involving long periods of SOR, RFP and industrial competition.

Through the summer and autumn of 1952 the design went ahead rapidly. A team of El Segundo engineers went to Korea, studied the problems of operating attack aircraft from carriers and land bases, and came back with valuable data and ideas. The Mock-up Review Board convened in September, and by the following month all the refinements had been incorporated in the mock-up and the plant was fast being equipped with production tooling, the Navy having by now become so convinced of the rightness of the Skyhawk that the usual wait for flight-test experience before freezing the design was waived. In November manufacture of the ten airframes began, tooling was virtually complete in January 1953, the second Mock-up Review Board was held in the following month and the XA4D-1 was rolled out in February 1954. After considerable further engineering and instrumentation, Bob Rahn took it into the air at El Segundo on 22 June 1954.

Immediately attracting front-page treatment by the news media, the XA4D was called 'the Bantam Bomber' and 'Heinemann's Hot-rod', the latter being rather unfortunate in suggesting a stripped-down fast-landing aircraft quite unsuitable for the Navy's missions calling for heavy loads of ordnance. In fact the Skyhawk was no more stripped of essentials than was Petter's baby Gnat fighter of similar vintage. What Heinemann had done was take between 1000 and 2000 lb out of the dead weight and thus—by applying the growth factor—cut the gross weight from 30000 lb to 15000. To give an indication of how this was achieved, the avionics—communications, navigation and identification—were repackaged into a single unit, sealed and filled with clean nitrogen and coupled by a single multi-pin connector which could be undone in a few minutes. This saved 58 lb, which meant about 580 lb off the aircraft gross weight. Ultimately the savings were difficult to determine. It would have been easy to claim a saving of 500 lb through eliminating a weapons bay, thus cutting 5000 lb altogether; and by not using an afterburner the gross saving could be put at 7500 lb, but Heinemann would not have used one anyway. One valid saving, put at 205/2050 lb, was to use a.c. electrics; and another was the use of Douglas's own light ejector seat, which weighed only 31 lb compared with the 70 lb of contemporary designs, and gave Douglas a new product line which today is busier than ever.

One of the nicest parts of the whole design was the wing. While designers in Britain seemed to be having great difficulty in making good integral tankage, Heinemann simply made the Skyhawk sit on a box of fuel that happened to be shaped like a wing. While designers in Britain were bent on delta shapes, the Skyhawk wing was made a conventional shape with a low aspect ratio that happened to have its taper on the leading edge (not quite the same thing as the triangular delta). Best of all, the span was held to only 27 ft 6 in, so that wing folding was unnecessary (saving 200/2000 lb), and the 0·064 in skins were continuous from tip to tip (I cannot think of any contemporary aircraft where this was done). So were the three machined spars which Heinemann, in defiance of the experts, merely bent in order to avoid any joints. I am told that many A-4s returned from combat in Vietnam with 'two, or even three shear-webs cut through, and one A-4 has survived a 4 *g* manoeuvre with this damage.' It was to preserve the structural integrity of the wing box that the main gears were made to retract forwards, the legs lying under the box in light fairings and the wheels being ahead of it just behind the leading edge. Later, because swept-wing fighters had been scraping their tails, the Navy made Douglas lengthen the main legs; Heinemann regretted this, because it was quite unnecessary and reduced the allowable cross-wind component (and also the stability on rolling decks, though I never heard of a narrow-track, stalky Skyhawk tipping over). The Skyhawk wing box was a structural delight, and Heinemann actually exceeded the BuAer design load factor of 7 by choosing a figure of $7\frac{1}{2}$. This was the first time in history a manufacturer had asked for a higher load factor than the Navy; it was Heinemann's hedge against future weight increases—and how right he was! Behind the box he added simple split flaps, after looking carefully at more complex high-lift systems. On the leading edge he fitted automatic slats over almost the whole span—not for stability, as in the case of the Skywarrior, but because of the big increase in maximum lift coefficient. When Handley Page (who invented slats) saw this, on a wing of 4·5 to 5 per cent thickness, they at once sent over Doc Lachmann to find out how it was done, as related in the story of the Victor in the companion volume on bombers.

Rahn and his colleagues liked the Skyhawk very much. Despite the small overall size, the aircraft had a roomy cockpit and the range of vision was outstanding. Most aspects of performance and handling were good from the start, but quite a lot of aerodynamic development still had to be done. I don't suppose the design team has ever existed that could build a high-subsonic aeroplane and predict with certainty that it will behave exactly like tunnel models and give no buffet and drag problems. The Skyhawk's hydraulically boosted elevator and electric variable-incidence tailplane gave hardly any trouble, nor did the hydraulically powered ailerons. But there were three things that changed the detail appearance of the aircraft. Pulling g at high speed and high altitude caused buffeting and random wing dropping. Though this was in no way indicative of an incipient high-speed stall, it was most unpleasant and would have impaired the ability of the Skyhawk to tangle with enemy fighters or avoid them. Heinemann adopted the new cure of rows of vortex generators, or 'turbulators', which mix sluggish boundary layer with free-stream air upstream of the ailerons and keep everything nicely attached to the metal surface. He called these devices 'aerodynamic crutches', which is just what they are. The main row happened to lie along the trailing edge of the slat, and Heinemann used them because they were easy to apply and were unlikely to delay the programme.

The other two problems were at the tail end. Despite having lengthened the rear fuselage, Heinemann found the air was breaking away from the surface well upstream of the jet nozzle, causing violent buffet which at first limited speed to Mach 0·7. The swift cure was to reduce the boat-tail taper close to zero by adding extra volume above the rear end on each side of the fin, terminating in a large inclined crescent shape around the top of the jet nozzle. The original fix was bashed together in a matter of hours at Edwards, and it worked so well that nobody later got round to designing it 'properly' for production aircraft. The other snag was that, though directional control was good despite the absence of a yaw-damper, the rudder itself 'buzzed' very badly. I had not previously believed a hydraulically powered surface could oscillate this way—I fondly thought the incompressible fluid in the jack locked it solid—but seeing is believing, and the buzz was so bad that the prototype XA4D lost pieces of rudder skin! Again there was no time to take a pressure rake and design a 'proper' modification. Heinemann just remembered that when the trouble had hit North American a few months earlier the best cure had been to use a single-surface rudder, with the skin down the middle and ribs on the outside. This was tried on the Skyhawk and worked like a charm. It has appeared on every Skyhawk since. Heinemann told me 'You know, when I see that stuck-on bulge above the jet pipe and that single-surface rudder I feel slightly ashamed; if only we had had time to re-do these quick fixes in an elegant way!' Trouble is, he is an artist; if he were merely a businessman he would derive comfort counting the Skyhawks coming off the production line, quick-fixes notwithstanding.

As for the engine, there was never any doubt that the Sapphire was basically good, but its desperately hurried Americanization and mass-production had caused severe troubles to the J65-powered Air Force programmes, notably to the F-84F Thunderstreak. Heinemann was a bit put out when the first engines were found to give only a little over 7000 lb thrust instead of the 8000 lb promised, and he was even more hurt by a funding decision of the Pentagon that the Skyhawk production programme should use only J65 engines from existing Air Force inventory, many of them already used and reconditioned. Eventually the first engine was cleared at 7200 lb, and in the first production A4D-1 batch it was further raised to 7800 lb—still well below the UK Sapphire and with poor future prospects. Heinemann, like all good designers, liked to have a fall-back engine and a growth engine, possibly both the same, and in this case he had nothing in sight. In 1953 he had come to the conclusion the Rolls-Royce Avon was worth investigating. He visited Derby, England, and after long discussions with Lord Hives persuaded Rolls to consider having the Avon built under licence in the US. It should have been the most straightforward deal imaginable, and if the British firm's US licensee had still been Pratt & Whitney it might have come to fruition (though by this time Mr Pratt could do things for himself). Unfortunately someone at Derby had looked favourably on the approach made to them by Westinghouse, who saw Rolls as the best way out of their disastrous turbojet development problems. Hives had no option but to go and see Westinghouse, and propose that they should make an Americanized Avon. In fact Westinghouse had already begun studies for just such an engine, and Heinemann was led to believe he would soon get what he wanted. It was not until 1956 that he made the ghastly discovery that the Navy-funded Westinghouse XJ54 was not to be an Avon at all but a six-tenths scale, with a rating of only 6000 lb. Westinghouse had hoped to use this to replace their own XJ46 in such aircraft as the Cutlass and Sea Dart, fighters which by 1956 had been abandoned. So Westinghouse gained no production business—indeed they had to give up aircraft propulsion entirely—and Heinemann had lost three years and still had no Avon.

He made the best he could of the J65, and at least found ways of avoiding most of the troubles that were then afflicting the Air Force with this engine. One of the most serious problems was that when a new or reconditioned engine was first started the main bearings frequently failed completely, especially if the throttle was opened early. Heinemann's team concluded that oil starvation was the cause, and adopted the procedure of turning the engine by hand until there was no doubt that the main bearings were amply supplied; only then was the engine started. This completely eliminated the problem. Meanwhile, Wright Aeronautical were doing their best to up-rate the J65, and with the help of Armstrong Siddeley they succeeded in clearing the −4 at 7800 lb in 1955 and finally, in 1959, of reaching a useful 8500 lb thrust which earned them a big contract to rework every Skyhawk engine and bring it up to this standard. But long before this Heinemann had found an engine at Pratt & Whitney to replace the J65, as related later.

Even with the J65 the Skyhawk was no slouch. Douglas were contractually required to demonstrate the aircraft (in a dive, of course) at Mach 1·25, which they did. The first pre-production A4D-1 flew on 14 August 1954, and on 15 October 1955 one of the batch of eight, still with only 7200 lb thrust, set a new world 500 km closed-circuit record, at low level, at over 695 mph. At such speeds in dense air the shape of external stores is immensely important, and Heinemann was glad he had already, with the F3D Skyknight fighter, inaugurated a programme to provide the Navy with minimum-drag bodies. These resulted in the 'Aero-1A' family of shapes of 8·2 fineness ratio which for over 20 years have been scaled up and down to provide the outline for almost every US aerial bomb for external carriage, and every tank up to 450 US gal capacity. The low-drag stores have meant more to the little Skyhawk than to any other aircraft.

These bombs and tanks were ready when the A4D-1 was cleared for service with squadrons of both the Atlantic and Pacific Fleets on 26 October 1956. Production orders had been placed totalling 166 aircraft soon after the first flight. By 1955 these were supplemented by an order for the A4D-2, with single-point pressure fuelling and provision for a probe, and many other changes including a rear fuselage several hundred pounds heavier to make it much stiffer in torsion. In-flight refuelling was considered a rather unproven system when the Skyhawk was designed and it was not incorporated, but in 1955 Admiral Thomas H. Moorer (when I wrote this chapter he was chairman of the Joint Chiefs of Staff but he was then head of military requirements for the Navy) told Heinemann some of the aircraft would have to be tankers. After a very strong discussion that lasted far into the night Heinemann found an answer in true 'back of an envelope' manner. Next morning he appeared in the Pentagon with a drawing of a completely new external store that is today known the world over as a Buddy pack. He took a streamlined shape and fitted a windmill at the front to drive a hydraulic pump feeding a closed-loop energy-transfer system passing through the 300 US gallons of fuel to drive a hose-reel at the back. It could be hung on any 2000 lb bomb rack, of which there were three on the A4D-2. The Marines found Buddy-equipped Skyhawks could ferry non-stop across the North Atlantic, while in about 1966 an analysis of the technique credited it with saving 380 aircrew by supplying fuel at critical periods. Later, of course, other Buddy packs were developed, including some in the UK.

Between 1956 and 1961 El Segundo delivered 1000 Skyhawks, all powered by the J65 and incorporating progressive improvements. Under the new DoD numbering system the A4D became the A-4, and the most prolific sub-type became the A-4C (previously called A4D-2N), with more capable autopilot, terrain-clearance radar, LABS system, angle of attack indicator and other additions which put over 1000 lb on the equipped weight, from 8526 to 9559 lb, but so increased the all-weather capability of the Skyhawk that 638 were built and supplied to 23 squadrons of the Navy and nine of the Marine Corps. In fact, 'all-weather' is slightly overstating the case, but the A-4C marked the firm move away from the high-altitude mission with an atom bomb to the arduous low-level life with a massive load of conventional ordnance.

This in itself is no mean achievement, but Heinemann's beef that he had no growth engine ultimately helped produce further results. As early as 1955 the Navy BuWeps had decided to fund the Pratt & Whitney JT8 proposal for a scaled-down JT3 (J57), and by 1957 the resulting engine, the J52, was running on the bench. Douglas, who wanted to use four of these in their proposed DC-9 short-haul jetliner (nothing like the later aircraft of this designation), was awarded a contract for four A4D-3 (A-4D) prototypes with this neat two-spool engine, only to have it cancelled two years later, in 1959. It was not until 12 July 1961 that Douglas finally flew the first of the new family of P&W-powered Skyhawks, the A-4E. This had the J52-6 engine, which at 8500 lb gave no more thrust than Wright had finally wrung from the J65; but it had a substantially lower fuel consumption stemming from higher pressure ratio and component efficiencies, and the A-4E had a range increased by 27 per cent. It also had five stores pylons, capable of carrying a remarkable 8200 lb load; before entry to service in November 1962, this had been raised to 9155 lb or almost exactly the same as the empty weight. Maximum gross went up to a remarkable 24500 lb. The airframe and landing gear were locally strengthened, especially around the catapult hooks, and the operators of the C-13 catapults on the great carriers were rather glad not to have to reset their huge device to quite such a rock-bottom combination of speed and weight as they had had to do for the original Bantam Bombers.

By 1964 Douglas had at last accepted that it could see the end of the programme. While the J52 had added a welcome 499 A-4Es, the bigger and more powerful Grumman A-6 Intruder and the even newer VAX (which became the Vought A-7 Corsair) looked like taking all the future business. But before Heinemann left Douglas in 1960 he had completed advanced planning for a number of further developments. The first, which crystallized in 1964, found no takers. This was a substantially uprated Skyhawk powered by a Rolls-Royce Spey engine. This would have fitted the airframe beautifully and would have done wonders, especially in reducing field length and increasing range. Compared with the advanced A-4E, the Spey-Skyhawk would have carried a 4000 lb bomb load a radius increased from 200 nautical miles to almost 600. But Britain's adoption of the Spey as a military engine came too late for this proposal and also for the equally convincing Spey-Starfighter and F-100 of the same period. This was a blow not only to Rolls-Royce but also to Douglas, which by late 1965 was much in need of military business, but it was by no means the end of the A-4.

Indeed in terms of variants the family had scarcely begun. Today Douglas Aircraft is part of McDonnell Douglas. It has sold El Segundo and concentrated its aircraft at Long Beach where, amidst the big jetliners, the baby bomber still flourishes. From here have come: the A-4F, with increased thrust and many other new features including a camel-like hump containing relocated and augmented avionics; the TA-4F with a second cockpit with dual control at the expense of a lot of fuselage fuel but still able to fly six hours; the multi-role A-4G for the Royal Australian Navy; and the corresponding TA-4G; the A-4H (universally called H for Hebrew) and TA-4H for Israel; the cheap and simplified TA-4J trainer used in large numbers by the Navy, and as a Vietnam FAC by the Marines; the A-4K and TA-4K for the Royal New Zealand Air Force; the Marines' very fine A-4M, with the J52-P-408A rated at 11200 lb and many other improvements including the braking parachute first fitted to the New Zealand aircraft which allows full-load operation from rough

4000 ft strips; and the Navy counterpart of the M, the A-4N, or 'Skyhawk II', which tries to beat the Corsair by joining it, with Elliott HUD, Kearfott inertial platform and Lear-Siegler computer. In addition McDonnell Douglas have rebuilt 50 A-4Bs for the Argentine Air Force and converted many A-4Cs into the advanced A-4L model. Total output in mid-1973 exceeded 2700 aircraft.

Of course, the real test of the A-4 has been Vietnam, for which it has been much better suited than most other aircraft in the US inventory. Whether based on carriers or on advanced airstrips, in either case often under torrential rain or scorching heat, the serviceability has been better than that of any other US jet, with 95 per cent availability for weeks on end, and at a servicing load of no more than 12 to 15 maintenance man-hours per flight hour. Quite early in the war the Skyhawk showed it could take punishment when an A-4E flew back 230 miles after being struck by four 37 mm shells. Pilots instinctively like Heinemann's original decision in 1952 to dispense with heavy cockpit frames (to make the cockpit smaller on the outside but bigger inside) and put the strength into heavier skin which can stop rifle bullets. I recall the Marine lieutenant who had flown 150 missions on 'the Scooter' (as they call it) who said 'I love it. If you lose your airspeed indication you just crane your head round and fly until those slats are half out. Then you can't get into any trouble.' What is little known is that many late-model A-4s and TA-4s were flown in Vietnam by the Air Force, many of them carrying a target-designator laser.

Of course today's 'Scooter' is not quite what Heinemann had in mind with his 12000 lb bantam. Today's Skyhawk can carry exactly that weight of fuel, and when operating from a land base can tip the scales at 27420 lb. But this most emphatically does not mean the Navy were right all along with their original 30000 lb specification. Perhaps the only people exasperated by the Skyhawk are the press-release writers. I have a press release dated July 1956 stating that the Skyhawk is 'expected to continue in production until the end of 1957.' Another says it will 'continue to be manufactured until the end of 1962.' Another puts the date for final shut-down of the assembly line as 'the last quarter of 1965.' The current 'Jane's' says the Navy plans to build new Skyhawks 'until 1974', but the next edition of that great annual will give the news that the Skyhawk will continue in production for four further years.

In today's budgetary environment, people do not go on building expensive aeroplanes through mere habit. In the case of the Skyhawk they have gone on making it because, totally contradicting what all save Heinemann thought at the start, it has proved to have utterly extraordinary potential for development. To rival the Skyhawk the Sopwith Camel would have had to remain in production until 1940, or the Mosquito until 1963; if we include the R&D part of the programme the contrast is even greater. Altogether it's not a bad record for something the experts said could not be built at all.

Grumman A-6 INTRUDER

OF all the mistakes made by the people who buy modern military aircraft, I think the biggest is that they have spent billions on aircraft that were irrelevant and unnecessary, and bought so few of the useful ones that they have been overpriced and grossly overworked. The major nations have concentrated on mighty strategic nuclear bombers, on fighters and on day attack aircraft, because these are impressive, seemingly cost/effective and capable of being built with contemporary technology. In all the major conflicts since 1945 such aircraft have either not been used or else used in ways utterly unlike the mission the planners had in mind. In nearly all these conflicts surface forces have said 'I wish we had aircraft that could find transient, mobile, difficult battlefield targets on the ground, and clobber them—at any time of day or night, in any weather.' Invariably there have been no such aircraft, so instead the enemy has been hit by scores of giant strategic bombers putting down hundreds of tons of iron bombs in the hope that something might be hit, and by costly Mach 2 fighters that make gruelling attack runs over a co-ordinate point on the map strewing napes, bombs, retarded bombs, missiles, rockets and cannon ammunition—again in the vague hope that something might be hit. It is terrifying to the enemy, who sometimes is unlucky enough to get in the way. It is also terrifying to count the noughts on the bill, not just for the cost of the mission but for producing the wrong aircraft in the first place.

It is hardly a new argument. World War 2 threw up a prime need for aircraft that could find and strike unmapped surface targets at night or in bad weather, and TRE (later RRE) at Malvern and USAF labs in Ohio and Massachusetts devoted a lot of time to finding ways of meeting the need. It didn't call for special aircraft, just for lots of special equipment. In pre-1945 days such equipment was difficult to conceive, even more difficult to make and probably impossible to take to the point where it would stay reliable whenever it was wanted in a rough full-scale war. After 1945 everyone forgot about such mundane things and concentrated on nice flashy jet fighters and atom bombers that appealed far more to the politicians. Then along came Korea, and instead of lovely strategic scenarios it threw up nasty ground battles in pouring rainstorms in almost unmapped territory. The flashy new jets could sometimes take out a bridge —either by luck or by flying 500 missions—and then take it out again when it was rebuilt, but unless they found a truck or train silly or desperate enough to travel in broad daylight they were very handicapped in their efforts to help the men in the nasty ground battle. The USAF started a research programme to see what could be done to produce a useful strike aircraft. It discovered (again) that it was a problem not of aircraft but of equipment, and it set about creating the missing technology.

Then Korea faded, and attention returned to the more attractive things: supersonic bombers, fighters bristling with weapons and flying at Mach 2·5 and, above all, the absolutely smashing ICBM. A politician, nettled by such criticism, would retort that, even though such things were not wanted, they were necessary 'to keep the peace.' Unfortunately, they have not kept the peace. We have had fighting in Kenya, Malaya, Cyprus, the entire Middle East, India and Pakistan, Borneo, the Congo and throughout south-east Asia, involving more than a million Americans. In every case the prime need (and I am writing from the viewpoint of a military commander, not as a Christian) has been the same old need. Curiously, while dollars by the thousand million were poured into the exciting weapons, a few tens of thousands did find their way into the harassed little research teams at Hughes, Dalmo Victor, the US Naval Avionics Facility, Norden and, above all, Westinghouse and Texas Instruments. As a result the missing technology was gradually created.

Two of its first applications are the B-57G and the A-6. The former is a version of the 25-year-old Canberra (described in the companion book on bombers), and in 1971 it gave the US Air Force the capability it had so urgently sought when it put the Canberra into production in the United States just 20 years before. The A-6 is relatively new. It was designed in the second half of the 1950s explicitly to use the missing technology, which the US Navy hoped would no longer be missing when the time came to bolt it into the A-6. The result has been predictable. In Vietnam the A-6 was worked to death. It has been bought in such modest numbers it is very expensive; and it is so costly it has only been bought in modest numbers. Squadrons equipped with nine aircraft, when they could 'sure use a coupla dozen' (I quote), have—night after stormy night—hit Charlie in pinpoint attacks that often hurt worse than B-52 formations that darkened the sky. The operational load that was borne by this handful of squadrons was at times near the limit that can be sustained without exhaustion. And even though 90 per cent of the A-6 combat missions were in fact flown against previously selected targets—which could be held to knock my argument into a cocked hat—these aircraft introduced the long-wanted capability of finding unknown targets on the ground in all weathers and of then hitting them. So hats off to the US Marine Corps, who formulated the original requirement. The Navy, who grabbed the first deliveries, could so easily have settled for finding and hitting surface vessels, which is a thousand times easier and could be done in World War 2.

Probably more than any other story in this volume, the A-6 is a matter of systems, avionics, instruments, and high technology to cause a formidable and sustained headache to highly skilled supporting personnel on the ground or in a giant carrier. The fact that all this costly stuff is packaged into a flying machine might at times seem almost incidental, yet to the A-6 crews the aircraft itself is more than just the thing that holds the new systems together. It is efficient, immensely strong and, apart from the clever items, commendably free from snags. In many ways it is a remarkable achievement, because it has a rather old-fashioned airframe, no swing wing, no blowing, no bomb bay, and two of the straight-jet kind of engines that people used before the fan came along. It also has such a crowded interior the flight-refuelling probe had to be stuck rigidly on the outside, just as if it was a British aircraft. It may also surprise some to discover that this modest-sized carrier-based aircraft leaves the deck carrying an external bomb load greater than that of a Lancaster and about three times that of a B-17 Fortress.

Its closest parallel is possibly the Buccaneer (p. 17), but the differences are considerable. The British aircraft was started just over four years earlier, yet took so long to develop that, before the design was frozen, it had incorporated extremely important blowing systems that make an immense difference to its performance; and all the Buccaneers in service today have turbofan engines more powerful and more efficient than the turbojets of most A-6s. Yet the Buccaneer is effective only in striking a previously known land target; in Britain the aircraft that can find unknown land targets, at night or in bad weather, has yet to emerge.

An official account of US Navy and Marine Corps attack aircraft ascribes the genesis of the A-6 to 'the demands placed upon our military airpower during the limited-warfare conditions prevailing during the Korean War' and goes on to comment that, although there was an hourly need for a truly all-weather attack aircraft, 'the requirement and the state of the art were miles apart at that time.' What brought the two closer together was the unprecedented advance in avionics after the Korean cease-fire. (Curiously, wars often put a brake on research; nobody is interested in things that can't hit the enemy next week.) The foundation of the advance was immense improvements in radars, in their basic design, power, miniaturization, reliability and in associated cockpit displays. A second line of development concerned the use of an airborne digital computer to process the information from radars, air-data systems and other sources, and either tell the pilot the optimum answers or else take over the flight-control and weapon-release task itself. A third series of advances was made in new sensing systems entirely: infra-red, low-light TV and laser ranging.

By 1956 this strong tide of improving technology coincided with a requirement by Marine Aviation for 'a close-air support attack bomber capable of hitting the enemy at any time.' The Corps obtains its aircraft through the Navy, and accordingly BuAer sponsored a full-scale design competition, stressing the long-range low-level attack mission in all weathers as well as short-field performance in the Marine Corps land-based role. Even before the competition opened the Navy was a certain customer; indeed, it would be unusual for an advanced combat aircraft to be bought by the Marine Corps alone (it has happened with the AV-8A, but the Harrier was already fully developed). So by the time the RFP went out in May 1957 the new attack aircraft was to be equipped for carrier operation. None of the likely participants failed to enter: eight major firms submitted eleven designs, almost all specifying two engines and two seats.

The competition lasted from May until December 1957, and on the last day of the year Grumman's Design 128 was selected. Actual design, under the leadership of Lawrence Mead Jr and Robert Nafis, began early in 1958, and in March 1959 Grumman received the first CPIF (cost plus incentive fee) contract ever awarded for a major weapon system. It covered design and some fabrication but not the delivery of any aircraft; and this was again unusual, because by this time construction of a test batch was well in hand both at Bethpage and at the new assembly and flight-test facility at Calverton, some 45 miles further along Long Island. Indeed the hardware took shape at an amazingly early stage, because the first aircraft was being bolted together by the time the Mock-up Review Board was held, in September 1959, by which time the aircraft had been designed A2F Intruder. The hardware was at last placed under contract by a supplementary document of March 1960 covering eight service-test Intruders, four for delivery in that year and four in 1961. They were not designated with a 'Y' prefix but were treated as regular production machines. By the time this contract was signed the first off the Calverton line, where the Intruders are assembled on trestles high above the floor, had been practically completed. Test pilot Bob Smyth flew it on 19 April 1960, enjoying the experience, and ten days later the Navy officially accepted the aircraft. Soon afterwards the new numbering system turned it into the A-6A, and the first eight aircraft practically completed the flight test and development programme—apart from some parts of the avionics—by the time the 60-day Board of Inspection and Survey trials began in October 1962. Probably the key man in 1962 was Major Chuck Sewell of the Marine Corps, the A-6A project officer in the Flight Test Division at NATC, Pax River. At the end of 1962 the paper work again caught up with the programme with an order for 67 A-6As and 12 of a special ECM version, the EA-6A. The A-6A entered service on 1 February 1963.

For so complicated a box of tricks this timing was good. The design of the A-6 did not begin until the Buccaneer programme had been proceeding for four years (six years including the design competition), yet clearance for service came only six months after the British aircraft. On the other hand the Grumman design choices were often earlier in technology than those of Blackburn, and in many ways the A-6 is reminiscent of the Buccaneer as it was on paper in 1954 with no blowing and two turbojets tucked into the space under a large shoulder-high wing on each side of the fuselage like the original US jet (XP-59) of 1942. There was another point of resemblance: both aircraft were planned to use jet deflection. This was thrown out of the British aircraft long before the hardware stage, but it was actually tested on the first Intruder. The two 8500 lb Pratt & Whitney J52-P-6 turbojets (9300 lb J52-P-8A from 1962 onward) were arranged to discharge through long tailpipes extending back under the wing with the final 10 feet hinged to pivot down hydraulically through 23° for landing (and possibly for take-off also). It was found that full deflection, with full thrust and the airbrakes (just above the jet nozzles) fully open, reduced stalling speed by six knots. This was judged not worth the candle, and the production aircraft were merely given a fixed 7° downward nozzle cant. (Blackburn would have used just over 60°, which would have made a much bigger difference of some 25 knots.) Instead Grumman relied solely on an extremely robust high-lift wing. Most designers would accept that the low attack role calls for the smallest possible span and area to give the crew a reasonable ride and not overstress the airframe. Remarkably Grumman chose a span of no less than 53 feet, with no variable geometry except to the section profile. Over almost the whole span are hydraulic leading edge flaps and trailing-edge flaps of the single-slotted type, which somehow reduce stalling speed to a mere 87 knots. Lateral control is by 'flaperons'—narrow-chord spoilers ahead of the flaps with a neutral setting of 3° up. Other features include a slab tailplane, huge fin and small rudder, and unique wing tips which split open into very effective speed brakes used for high-speed deceleration, and which one hopes never function asymmetrically. The fuselage door-type brakes killed engine thrust at high rpm on the approach, but were deleted from all production aircraft.

Obviously area-ruled, the fuselage has a voluminous front, packed with electronic and human brains, and then tapers sharply to a very slender mid and rear profile. The area ruling took into account the carriage of bulky external stores on five pylons each cleared to a 3500 lb loading. The configuration looks odd, but has low drag, high cruise efficiency and provides space for 2080 gal fuel internally—substantially more than in the Buccaneer which has dry wings. As in the A-4 Skyhawk, the main landing gears retract forwards without penetrating the strong wing box, the wheels turning to stow obliquely between the wing and engine nacelle. On both sides ahead of the wing a large piece of engine nacelle hinges down to provide a neat flight of seven steps up to the broad cockpit, covered by a huge rearward-sliding canopy, where reclining Martin-Baker seats are provided for the pilot on the left and the bomb/nav slightly behind on the right. The crew seating permits 'a high degree of co-ordination and effectiveness' which, it is implied, is absent with tandem seats. Ahead of the cockpit is what it's all about: the black boxes.

When the eleven competing designs were being evaluated there was not a great deal to choose between them, but one big point in Grumman's favour was their apparent strength in avionic systems and their detailed presentation of the system proposed for the Intruder that was to enable it accomplish its mission. Right from the start the system rejoiced in the name DIANE, for Digital Integrated Attack Navigation Equipment. DIANE is still, as I have emphasized, the only thing I know that can find as well as hit land targets, apart from the little-used systems of the B-57G. Perhaps it was all planned a bit too early, and there is no doubt a vastly better system could be created today, but there's an old saying about a bird in the hand being worth two in the bush. I cannot refrain from expressing some surprise that BuAer, now Naval Air Systems Command, did not around 1964 find money for a really new airborne attack system that could do DIANE's job more fully, more reliably and generally in a way befitting the late 1970s, but Intruder crews would tell me to stop criticizing the best DIANE they've got.

It was originally built with no sensors apart from two radars, which at the time of entry to service comprised the Norden APQ-92 search radar and the much smaller APQ-88 track radar developed in-house by the Naval Avionics facility. The radar outputs are presented pictorially by the Kaiser AVA-1 analog vertical display indicator. Navigation is by combined inertial and doppler systems, terrain-following uses the Navy-developed APN-141(V) pulsed radar altimeter, countermeasures were incorporated from the start, and everything is tied together, and to the aircraft flight-control system, by a Litton ASQ-61 digital computer. These were the original building-blocks that provided the missing capability. Possibly the two key bits were the computer and the new cockpit display. The following is a quote from a Marine Corps introduction to the system: 'DIANE . . . enables the Intruder to perform either as an attack bomber or in close support of ground personnel; to attack a preselected target or a target of opportunity; to deliver a variety of special or conventional weapons; and to fly over any terrain in any weather and under varying tactical conditions without ever requiring the pilot to look at the ground from take-off to landing. Navigation is automatic, requiring only mode-selection and manual insertion of pertinent data. Flight control varies in degree from a non-automatic to a fully-automatic hands-off mode, but in all modes the pilot obtains accurate information about the tactical environment via the "highway in the sky" presentation on his contact analog display. (This represents a road along which the aircraft is centered. Clouds, terrain, etc., appear on the "highway" depending on what the conditions are outside the aircraft,* and the pilot flies accordingly.) The attack function is fully implemented by equipment for acquiring and tracking a target, solving ballistic equations and generating release signals. The capabilities . . . are based on avionic subsystems and aircraft sensors which continuously send inputs to the central computer. The computer processes these inputs and generates accurate solutions to the navigation, flight-management and attack-control problems. The results are presented either in the form of displays, or as control or servo signals affecting the operation of the aircraft. . . .'

At last, thanks in the first place to the Marine Corps, there was a real all-weather attack aircraft. But first deliveries went to the Navy, to VA-42 at NAS Oceana, Virginia Beach, on the Atlantic seaboard. Oceana was the first A-6 training base. Since mid-1963 it has borne a heavy burden teaching Navy and Marine Corps squadrons how to operate this complicated aircraft; and for the first ten years the training was very much a matter of life or death, because every squadron promptly went into battle in south-east Asia. I believe the Intruder is unique among modern military aircraft in that almost every example made has either fought in action or else trained pilots who have subsequently done so. In August 1966 NAS Whidbey Island, Washington, set up shop as the first A-6 training base on the Pacific coast, and several hundred A-6 crews ultimately saw action. First operational sorties were made by VA-75, the *Sunday Punchers* from USS *Independence*, in early July 1965. Since then many thousands of A-6 missions have been flown over Vietnam by squadrons based on most of the

**What the Marine Corps mean is 'depending on what mode the pilot selects'.*

Seventh Fleet attack carriers and by Marine Corps squadrons based at Da Nang and Chu Lai. The rest of the story is mainly one of fierce and arduous action, with overtones of improving technology.

From the start nobody had any doubt of the impressive value of the A-6A, but there were some substantial problems, and it would have been incredible had there not been. These centred around the airborne avionics, the maintenance workload and the way the aircraft was being used. Everything was accentuated by the fact that Vietnam is a long way from the United States and that operational units were committed to intense action for extended periods in a harsh environment with extremes of heat and cold and torrential monsoon rains. One ought not to use such things as excuses, because nobody would deliberately design combat aircraft that worked only when based on the maker's airfield in a mild climate, but to the dog-tired radar technician in a check-out van in South Vietnam they are real enough.

Dealing with the method of employment, the original idea behind the A-6 was that one or two aircraft would stand off waiting for a call for help from ground troops. They would then approach the designated area, search for targets and hit them. The targets might be single vehicles, soft-skinned or hard, or local fortifications or similar battlefield targets. A detailed study in the comfort of the Pentagon in 1963 decided nine aircraft per squadron was the best establishment, and this was the level at which the aircraft went to war. Predictably, almost all its missions were subsequently flown against strategic targets, the location of which was known beforehand and generally was far into North Vietnam. They have been used just like any other bomber, except that they have been particularly called upon to strike at night or in bad weather when the hundreds of other US strike aircraft suffered grossly reduced effectiveness or could not operate at all. Not until 1968 was each squadron able to deploy 12 aircraft which, allowing for about three aircraft unserviceable at any time, roughly added 50 per cent to mission strength.

Avionic problems have been protracted. Perhaps the most annoying difficulties at first were the same as those for the F-86D in 1951–53 and for AI-equipped night fighters in 1941: it was all just too much for mere humans to keep everything working properly. According to Rear Admiral David C. Richardson the serviceability of the A-6 in its 1965–66 season was not higher than 35 per cent. The MMH/FH, the number of maintenance man-hours per flight hour, was a figure consistently well above 100. All this reflected the rather early technology of the avionics.

A fundamental difficulty was that there were two radars, more than doubling the crew radar workload; and at first the hardware itself was inadequate. The APQ-88 track radar was redesigned by Norden and emerged in 1966 as the APQ-112, with many features intended to improve reliability. Even then the -112 needed circuit improvements to eliminate drift and jitter, improved gating to give sharper output at the different frequency channels, a new klystron tube and a ceramic thyratron instead of a glass one. This track radar was intended only for use against moving targets, such as a vehicle against a land background, but its performance in this mode was initially marginal—and before long everyone realized the B/Ns (bomb/navs) were hardly ever using it. The easier answer was to concentrate on the main search radar, the powerful APQ-92, removing the physical and mental strain of trying to use two radars at once and yielding results at least as good. Most B/Ns approach a preselected target with the APQ-92 set to 12 miles, and the computer can handle an attack from a radar-reflective offset point as much as 80000 feet away from the target. To improve the APQ-92 the external microwave source was replaced by an internal klystron, drifting circuits were redesigned, new longer-lived crystals were fitted, thyratrons were again made ceramic, the terrain-avoidance display was redesigned and the moving-target indicator was greatly improved and simplified. Today the search radar is a vastly improved multi-mode radar and the track radar has been eliminated, but a great deal can still be done. Doppler beam-sharpening is a natural, but this seems to be slow to leave the lab. (I apologise to readers who are not electronics buffs, but I did say the story was full of advanced technology.)

Norden, who make the terrain-following radar for the C-5A Galaxy, have been trying to incorporate some of this newer technology into the A-6 radars, and Sperry was brought in in 1967 to see how much of the defunct ILAAS (integrated light attack avionic system), originally planned for the A-7 Corsair, might be incorporated. The vital AVA-1 display has been greatly improved, both in reliability and readability, and yet it may be thrown out altogether in favour of a conventional head-up display (I think this would be a retrograde step, unless the A-6 is always going to be used against targets of known location). The terrain-following system has had a lot done to it, and the original minimum bad-weather height of 500 feet has come down nearer to 100 feet; certainly from 1966 onwards crews used to cross the South China Sea at 100 feet or less, and I don't blame them. As for the crucial Litton computer, this pacemaking firm must feel bad that the ASQ-61 was solemnly designed to the naval specification with a rotating-drum memory store, and even worse that Grumman replaced it with a solid-state core from their rivals IBM. Gradually solid-state components have been introduced into the A-6 avionics, and today the whole thing works quite well. Overall system reliability now runs close to 80 per cent. MMH/FH has come down, but is still high: many squadrons have only just managed to beat the 100 hours level. Even the Marine

Corps, who at least have much more space to deploy the complicated test and checkout gear, have not fared much better. The Corps magazine, *Leatherneck*, quotes WO Joseph G. Mates, of VMA(AW)-242 'The Bats', as reporting 'It takes at least 75 man-hours of maintenance for every hour a Bat flies—and that's not just changing spark plugs either.'

After this basinful of avionics it is a sudden change of key to record that the first three A-6s lost over Vietnam blew themselves up. Typical loads envisaged when the aircraft was designed comprised three 2000 lb bombs, or a 'special store' and two 450 US-gal tanks. In fact typical loads have been five 2000 lb, 15 1000 lb, 20 750 lb or, most often of all, 28 retarded 500 lb. With such loads all the aircraft would by now have been lost, had World War 2 ordnance continued to be used. Such bombs were still being used in 1965. In steep diving attacks the mechanical nose fuse became armed in about 0·7 second, and the several bombs released from an MBR (multiple bomb rack) tumbled into each other and, in the three cases mentioned, detonated directly beneath the aircraft. After a few anxious months in 1965–67 attacking straight-and-level, all Intruders were fitted with the Douglas-developed MER and TER (multiple-ejection and triple-ejection racks) with cartridge ejectors. So they were once more able to zoom up a mile or two from the target and then attack in a dive. In any case nearly all the 500 pounders today are retarded Snakeyes, with big cruciform speedbrakes that smartly pull the bombs back behind the launch aircraft. The A-6 is claimed to be 'the only aircraft in the US inventory that can carry anything in the Armed Forces aviation weapons without physically changing the . . . aircraft.' Actually it cannot carry air-to-air guided weapons except Sidewinder, and only recently has it been made compatible with the Standard ARM anti-radiation missile, and with the air-to-surface Condor; and I am sure it cannot carry SRAM or Hound Dog!

The version equipped to launch Standard ARM is the A-6B, all of which are converted A-6As. The next variant, the A-6C, is in my view closer to what the A-6A should always have been. It has two new sensors, developed under the TRIM (Trail/Roads Interdiction Multisensor) programme: an FLIR (Forward-Looking Infra-Red) and a low-light TV system, both of them housed in a big turret under the centre fuselage which, though faired in to look like a wartime H_2S, offers considerable drag and cuts the speed at low altitudes. These sensors enhance the ability of the aircraft to detect and acquire targets at night or in bad weather, which is what the A-6 was designed to do. Curiously these sensors were not in the original specification although they were well enough known in principle in 1956. The 12 A-6C aircraft were not ordered until 1968.

The next sub-type is the KA-6D tanker, with Flight Refuelling hose-reel pack and more than 20000 lb of transfer fuel. These aircraft, which can serve as long-loiter air/sea rescue control centres or as day bombers, are so far all A-6A conversions. The final attack Intruder, the standard front-line version, is the A-6E, with APQ-148 simultaneous multi-mode (nav/attack) radar, IBM '4π' ASQ-133 nav/attack computer and other improvements which include dual 30 kVA generators and self-contained waveguide pressurization and avionic ground air-conditioning. An A-6E can tote thirty 500 lb bombs to a target 350 miles away and spend an hour at low level in the target area before going home.

The EA-6A, mentioned much earlier, was a minimum-conversion A-6A tailored for the ECM (electronic countermeasures) role, retaining a limited strike capability. The 12 aircraft, included in the original production buy of 1962, all went to the Marine Corps, and by 1967 all of them wore the lightning-strike insignia for ECM missions over North Vietnam. There they used their 'more than 30 different antennae to detect, locate, classify, record and jam enemy radiation.' Externally obvious ECM gear is mounted on the fins, on the wing tips and in up to four under-wing pods each with a windmill electric generator. The EA-6A flew in 1963 but it was not until late in 1967 that the Corps really learned how to get startling results. They were used both as 'leadships' for other aircraft and as defence-suppression systems. It may have been their fierce, automated electronic activity that caused *Naval Aviation News*, reporting on A-6 missions, to record 'at the same time some Soviet-supplied SA-2 Guideline missiles, used by the enemy, were seen to make radical course deviations after launch, expending their energy through manoeuvring and falling harmlessly to earth.' ECM is intensely interesting, but classified.

So important is the ECM game that in 1966 Grumman received a prototype design and development contract for the EA-6B Prowler which is new from stem to stern. The nose is 54 inches longer to accommodate a crew of four, the right-seat man and the two new rear men being in charge of a fantastic ECM installation for which the prime contractor is Cutler-Hammer. All details remain classified, but I can record that the empty weight of the aircraft has risen from the 25980 lb of the final A-6E to no less than 34851 lb. Much of the ECM system is housed in five external jammer pods, but some tons of it fills the nose, wings and tail. Just as important as the avionic capability of the EA-6B, first flown on 25 May 1968, is the improved structure that comes with it. Grumman chose this variant to redesign the wing, because the increase in weight on the centreline—almost all the extra 9000 lb of equipped weight—posed a more severe fatigue problem. Although the original five-spar wing was amply strong and was tested to 4500 hours in the simulated attack mission, the actual life in Vietnam-type operations is unknown. But the EA-6B wing, the same shape but structurally altered, has been tested to a 6000 hour life with the full 18000 lb external load on the five stations. It incorporates provision for unspecified high-lift systems—almost certainly BLC blowing—should these be necessary to allow increases in weight to 70000 lb or more, and it also can have an additional weapon (but not tank) pylon closer to the tip. The Prowler's engines are 11000 lb J52-P-408s. Yet a further change in the EA-6B is a stronger nose leg, because much of the extra weight is well forward; this leg is also used in the A-6E attack version. A-6 nose gears are very strong; they were the first designed for the nose-tow system in which the catapult accelerates the aircraft by pulling on a link at the base of the nose leg, imparting a severe bending load.

I believe the EA-6B is the supreme example, surpassing even ASW machines such as the Viking and Nimrod, of the trend towards aircraft systems and avionics becoming more costly than the aircraft in which they are carried. It is difficult to get a meaningful figure because the small EA-6B procurement has been lumped together with R&D costs, but it seems a fair guess to put the price of the systems carried by the EA-6B at twice the price of the bare aircraft. The vote for the first eight of these Pandora's boxes was no less than $139 million! Such a price could serve an excellent purpose for humanity if it makes men return to fighting with bows and arrows. Even the 440-odd attack Intruders have cost more than $5 million each, including the Navy GFE, but in view of the burden they have borne this could be considered cheap. What was this burden like? These extracts come from 'Night Strike from the *Enterprise*' written for *NANews* by Lt Robert S. Owen USN:

'As we step out onto the flight deck a misty rain driven by 34 mph winds cools our faces and begins to dampen our clothing. The deck is lighted by an eerie moon-glow of red lights, but beyond that there is only the pitch-black darkness . . . the ordnancemen are completing the fusing of the bombs. All four A-6s on this launch have been loaded within the past hour with the same bomb load as mine—more than 80 500's, all loaded by hand by ten men. Like the plane captain the ordnancemen work 14 to 20 hours a day. . . . When at last I climb into the cockpit my B/N is already strapped in and is busily aligning his inertial platform. He's Lt jg Bruce Borchers and, as you will see, he's easily the coolest man in the world. . . . Although some say a monkey could run an A-6 system as long as everything works, when a component fails immediate response by a highly skilled operator is required to complete the mission. With almost no time for thought the engines are running, the system is checked out and we're taxying onto the catapult. Troubleshooters give us a careful check and the catapult officer is waving his green wand back and forth in a slow, rhythmic movement. . . . I switch the external lights on and wait. The green wand moves slowly down until it touches the deck. We are slammed back against the seat until the aircraft has accelerated from zero to 140 mph, into a huge wet ink bottle. "Wheels up and we're climbing; 170, flaps up; looks good." . . . Coast-in; Bruce says calmly "Feet dry". . . . My throat is awfully dry as I bank hard towards the target. I wish for 800 knots. . . . As we approach the target the flak gets more intense. Suddenly this monster I'm herding around begins to shudder and shake like a toy in a storm. The 85's are on us, but there's just a second to go to release. Bombs away and I break out so hard we nearly stall. They're not so close now but still shooting. "Which way out?" I glance at Bruce. He's quietly typing away on his computer keyboard, as a bright orange glow from our bombs illuminates the cockpit. . . . After what seems an eternity but is actually a matter of minutes we cross the coast. Happiness is feet wet. . . .' It was far from a push-over, even with all the avionics helping.

Vought
A-7 CORSAIR II

ITS pilots call the A-7 the Sluf, contracted from 'Short little ugly fellah'. Maybe this is what a Polynesian would say on first seeing one, but for hard-bitten and very professional Vietnam veterans to give an aircraft such a name shows that that aircraft must be treated with both affection and respect. I obviously have a soft spot for the earlier A-4 Skyhawk (p. 209), but that must not blind me to the fact that the short little ugly fellah. designed as its replacement, marks a tremendous advance in capability. Part stems from simply being later. Part comes from the more powerful and more efficient engine, the later A-7s having a basically British turbofan that Heinemann tried to get into the Skyhawk. But most of its improvement comes from the much more extensive avionics. Instead of being an aeroplane flown by a pilot who can drop bombs, the A-7 is an integrated system that can measure, integrate, correlate, make allowances and just about do everything but polish the windscreen. There still has to be a pilot, and it helps if he can see through the windscreen, but he is nevertheless given powers that a few years ago would have seemed superhuman by the neatly packaged avionics of this quite small and rather unimpressive-looking aircraft.

The genesis of the A-7 typifies the way a progamme may be made to move if it can stay out of the newspapers and the political arena. By the early 1960s the classic Skyhawk was considered rather dated. Certainly it was not expected to continue in production so long, and plans were drafted in 1963 to acquire a replacement, for both the US Navy and Marine Corps. The Navy BuWeps called the programme the VAL, for heavier-than-air (letter V) Attack Lightweight, and the OR was drafted on 17 May 1963. How little argument ensued is shown by the fact that the RFP was sent out on the 29th of the same month. Responses were received from Douglas, Grumman, Ling-Temco-Vought (LTV) and North American. The BuWeps evaluation was completed on 6 November, the Navy and SecDef reviews took place on 13–14 November, Congress voted funds on 8 February 1965, LTV were named the winners on 11 February, a contract was signed on 19 March, the mock-up review took place on 22 June and the first off the production line flew on 27 September 1965. Deliveries to a user squadron began on 14 October 1966, after very extensive testing at NATC and other establishments and at sea. For an extremely advanced attack aircraft, with a list of integrated avionics longer than my arm, I think less than 3½ years from drafting the OR to having an operational squadron rather shows up everybody else.

Of course a critic could claim the A-7 was not a new aircraft at all, but just a re-vamped F-8 Crusader fighter. In fact there is hardly a split-pin common to the two designs, and even the superficial similarity tends to vanish under detailed scrutiny. But the fact remains that Vought did start with the F-8, and had already studied the possibility of turning this Mach 1·8 fighter into a subsonic attack aircraft. Douglas had done extensive studies with improved Skyhawks, and had it not lost Heinemann to General Dynamics it might have won the VAL programme. In the event Douglas placed second, and Vought had a programme that promised to be worth a thousand aircraft for the first customer alone, thus again proving that in the US the big contracts are parcelled out in a way that keeps everyone happy. Curiously this is also the way that tallies with the best technical and cost submissions, which leads one to think that perhaps the quality of the submission reflects the bidder's need for the work. Vought once claimed the competition was won 'against long odds', but although the rivalry was intense the odds could hardly have been worse than 4 to 1.

Range was the crucial parameter, where the Skyhawk fell short. It was considered that a radius of 600 n.m. would enable a carrier-based strike aircraft to cover 'close to 100 per cent' of the world's likely regions of non-nuclear warfare. Other features of the VAL requirement were the ability to carry over 10000 lb of ordnance, and to fly three mission profiles with lesser loads: hi-hi-hi carrier attack and hi-lo-hi carrier attack with 1800 or 3600 lb of bombs over a combat radius of more than 600 n.m.; and a land-based close-support mission with 7500 lb of bombs over a radius in excess of 200 n.m., in all cases with allowances for sea-level loiter over target or over base. There were the usual calls for robust structure, ease of weapon loading, low maintenance requirement and so forth (including the first numerical requirements for reliability and maintainability ever written into a Navy production contract draft), but nothing about speed. This was in sharp contrast to the mid-1950s when subsonic aircraft seemed to be obsolete. Indeed, when in 1960 the Navy first began to want something with more range than could be wrung from the Skyhawk, they wrote a specification (VAX) which did call for particular supersonic capabilities both at altitude and on the deck. But it was at this time that Defense Secretary McNamara came into the Pentagon bristling with slide-rules, taking nothing on trust and generally calling for everything in uniform to go away and do its sums in greater detail. It was as a result of this that, in December 1962, the Sea Based Air Strike Forces Study Group—which makes a terrible acronym—began a marathon evaluation that investigated and priced a total of 144 different aircraft programmes, with varying avionic and ordnance configurations and assuming carefully assessed production rates for each aircraft company. McNamara made the sailors find out all sorts of things they had not known before; and in doing so they discovered that the VAX was going to take too long and be too expensive.

Moreover, they discovered a fact of completely fundamental importance that I do not believe anyone had previously fully appreciated: in the lo penetration mission supersonic speed is no advantage. The SBASF study proved this numerically, but the basic argument has been beautifully explained by Capt Henry Suerstedt, BuWeps, who was the A-7 Project Manager: 'If you were to take two ducks—one a sort of fat little duck that flies only at subsonic speeds and the other a larger and supersonic duck—and compare the two, the supersonic duck would always have to fly higher in order to keep from flying into the ground. Against a duck hunter in a blind having the same angle of sight in all directions, the time of exposure of the subsonic duck and the supersonic duck would be about the same. Both would have about an equal chance of being shot at the same number of times. Now the supersonic duck is a relatively rare bird and rather costly to develop in dollars and time, thus you could buy three or more subsonic ducks for the same price. Then, when three or more subsonic ducks are subjected to the same degree of exposure as a single supersonic duck, the probability of them flying successfully past the hunter would be far greater than the one supersonic duck getting past.'

So the Navy decided it wanted a fat little duck, and both the technical evaluation, begun on 12 August 1963, and the cost/effectiveness evaluation, begun on 3 September, clearly showed Vought's bird was fattest. The subsequent evaluation by the SecDef's office was primarily concerned to confirm the improvement that the A-7A would make over the current Skyhawk, the A-4E. This was done with no trouble at all, and it is not too unfair to Douglas to recall that the Navy summed up the comparison as 'The A-7A can carry more than twice the conventional ordnance load for the same distance as the A-4E, or carry the same ordnance load well over twice the distance.' Indeed, although considerably more expensive to buy than the A-4E, the A-7A promised to do so much more—quite apart from its enormously improved avionics systems—that the Navy said in 1964 it would 'provide more light attack aircraft striking capabilities for the dollar than any other aircraft in the world whether in the inventory or on the drawing board.' I believe this was a true claim, and I believe it is true in 1974, although one could argue endlessly about the merits of rivals with two crew, two engines and supersonic performance, or about short-range close-air support aircraft with hardly any avionics at all.

To win this extremely useful contract Vought had to submit to being screwed down to a very tight contract indeed, in a way that nobody had ever thought of when the same team won the F-8 Crusader contract just ten years before. Then Chance Vought had been part of United Aircraft, but Washington considered it undesirable to have this airframe company in the same group as Pratt & Whitney engines and so it was hived off, merging in 1961 with Ling-Temco Electronics. The LTE board chairman, James Ling, was cock-a-hoop at winning the A-7 because this removed any doubt that the new Ling-Temco Vought, the union of the aerospace and electronics companies, would be able to win major defence programmes. So pleased was LTV that it resurrected the name of the outstanding Vought aircraft of World War 2 and Korea, and called the A-7 the Corsair II. Much of the credit for assembling the VAL technical team and directing it with consummate strength goes to Paul Thayer, senior LTV vice-president, who had reached that position by surviving the nasty Cutlass tailless fighter when he was senior experimental test pilot at the old Chance Vought company. Most of the A-7A design came from the brains of another LTV vice-president, J. Russell Clark; Sol Love, who was Vought director of engineering and is today the company's president; and Conrad A. Lau, the A-7 programme manager. They had guided the swiftest genesis of any combat aircraft in the non-Communist world since World War 2. In an effective period of a year they worked away from the F-8 into a totally new aircraft for a totally new mission.

Compared with the F-8 it has a much newer engine. The VAL specification was predicated on the use of the Pratt & Whitney TF30 turbofan, which was already under intensive development with afterburner for the supersonic F-111 (TFX), modified for use without afterburner to give economical performance up to the top VAL speed of about Mach 0·9. The wing was kept at 35° sweep, but it was completely redesigned. It is slightly thicker, contains much more fuel in self-sealing integral tanks, has outboard ailerons driven by a triplex hydraulic system, large slotted flaps with spoilers just ahead of them, and leading-edge flaps from root to tip. The unique F-8 feature of being able to hinge the wing up into a high-incidence position, so that the aircraft can take-off and land with the fuselage level, was no longer needed with the stubby, subsonic, fully flapped A-7. The wing was provided with six stores pylons, supplemented by two racks high on the fuselage. The wing racks were provided with inbuilt hoists, driven by a large power tool clipped on by the ordnanceman to each pylon in turn. On each side of the engine air duct was installed a Mk 12 20 mm gun, with 250 rounds fed by gravity. Most important of all, waist-high panels (some of the 35 which form about half the skin area of the aircraft) along the fuselage gave access to avionics an order of magnitude later than those of the A-4E, including: Lear Siegler three-axis stick-steering autopilot; the new ILAAS (integrated light attack avionics system) instrument panel; Texas Instruments APQ-116 multi-mode radar; doppler, navigation computer and roller-map display (part of ILAAS); and a series of weapon-delivery systems including a computer, armament-station control unit and release programmer. Compared with what happened later this seems crude, but in 1963 it represented the latest thinking.

Altogether, although the A-7A was very much a 'state of the art' aircraft, considered by Capt Suerstedt to pose 'virtually no technical risk', its avionics even in its early days were sufficiently complicated to pose the risk of all kinds of trouble. And even with the modern technique of repairing avionics by smartly pulling out the faulty module and clipping in a new one, the company was bold to agree to an MMH/FH (maintenance man-hours per flight hour) of 11·5. To give an idea of how good this is, when the A-7 was designed there were several major combat types that had been in US service five years or more that had yet to get their MMH/FH figure below 75, and at least two were consistently over 100 (and one RAF machine was close to 200). Moreover, Vought's agreement to 11·5 was not just a brazen boast. According to the contract of 19 March 1964, Vought was to be penalized $50 per flight hour if the MMH/FH should be found to be 13, $700 per hour if it should be 17 and the entire cost of the aircraft if it should exceed 17. Imagine a British contractor agreeing to hand back the whole price of an aircraft just for not being able to get the MMH/FH below 18! There were other penalties too. Should Vought fail to deliver the first aircraft on time to NATC at Pax River it would be fined a cool $65000 per day until delivery took place. If the British government finally succeeds in eliminating competition in the British aircraft industry (by reducing the number of companies to one) they will find contracts of this kind rather difficult to arrange.

In the event, practically the only penalty Vought had to bear was that aircraft No. 1 came out nearly 600 lb over the guaranteed empty weight of 14857 lb, about 460 lb of the extra 'beef' having been deliberately devoted to making the wing strong enough for a structural ordnance load of 20000 lb. Has any aircraft previously been able to carry bombs weighing one-third more than its equipped empty weight? This capability is so remarkable that the penalty for exceeding the guarantee was not severe, the Navy taking the view that it would prove useful in assisting the natural growth process of the aircraft. With the original TF30-6 engine, rated at 11350 lb static thrust, the potential weight-lifting ability could not be used. The potential was gained by the combination of a high-lift wing (in turn needed by the low wind-over-the-deck requirement) and a very strong structure with an 8000 hour life in the most arduous combat usage.

From the outset the A-7 had been designed for minimum vulnerability to defensive fire. Critical airframe components were dispersed, vital systems were duplicated or triplicated, and much of the fuselage was armoured. Part of the weight overrun was due to the use of 0·375 in steel armour in front of the pilot and 0·5 in aluminium armour beneath him. But Vietnam experience had shown even this was not enough. What *Aviation Week* called 'primitive but effective techniques such as massing up to 1000 troops armed with rifles and light automatic weapons around likely ground targets to fire simultaneous volleys into the path of low-flying aircraft' demanded armour for the engine, several major systems and other areas. Not until the later versions of the A-7 was the much more effective boron carbide (HFC) armour introduced, which for a given weight gives about twice the stopping power of the original purely metallic plating.

The original contract of March 1964—a fixed-price one, like all subsequent A-7 contracts—bought much of the R&D and three complete aircraft. More would have been bought, but the programme had moved too fast for the Navy's funds, and they had no more money at the time! Soon money was found for four more, followed in the next fiscal year by a buy for a further 35. Throughout the development period, and so far as I know up to late 1973, the A-7 programme ran on or ahead of schedule. The first flight, on 27 September 1965, was 25 days early. Only a little over a month later, on 2 November, Vought invited over 1000 guests, from the government, armed forces, industry and the Press, down to Dallas to see the first two flight articles perform. It was an informative occasion. Director of flight operations John Konrad, who in 1955 had taken the first Crusader beyond Mach 1 on its maiden flight, rolled the first A-7A very rapidly three times in each direction while carrying 12 inert 500 lb bombs and six 250 lb. Colleague Bob Rostine used the second, clean, aircraft to sustain 4·5 g in a turn. It was small wonder that Navy Secretary Paul Nitze announced that the fourth A-7 buy would be for a real number: 190 aircraft, worth over $91 million.

While the Dallas plant got on with these, other irons were in the fire. Vought announced that it was hoping to sell other versions of the A-7 for different customers. The original A model was intended for the Navy, for use from carriers, and for the Marine Corps, who would use it with its arrester hook in SATS (small airfield for tactical support) operations. The A-7B would have the up-rated TF30-P-8 engine rated at 12200 lb. The A-7C would be a lengthened dual-control trainer. The A-7D would be a version for the Air Force, probably fitted with a 'short-stack' afterburner to improve short-field take-off and combat acceleration. There was also an export version. As the classified GFE (government-furnished equipment) would have to be left out, this variant would have no TF30 engine and would also lose several avionics modules. To replace the TF30 the British Rolls-Royce Spey appeared likely to fit admirably. Apart from needing a changed engine-mounting arrangement, the British engine was somewhat lighter and at least as good in fuel economy and thrust. With Navy blessing Vought sent salesmen to see everyone who wanted a good attack machine.

In the event, though several air forces and navies found the Corsair the best technical choice, nobody signed a contract. But the bringing together of the A-7 and the Spey was of far greater value to the programme than a few mere exports. It was the very essence of the A-7 programme that it should move fast and without trouble. Vought soon showed it could build the airframe on time, but poor Mr Pratt up in Connecticut was having a hard time with his engines. The massive consumption of the Vietnam war had come on top of unprecedented demands for Pratt & Whitney engines by the world's airlines, and by 1965 output finally and unmistakably failed to keep pace. Each day it was a case of deciding whether to annoy the airlines or the military—what an agonizing choice!—and, unlike the airlines, the military were able to think of second-sources. On top of this, the TF30 was giving trouble, and was beginning to suffer from the much greater and more public difficulties of the F-111 programme. So Allison division of General Motors at Indianapolis (now the Detroit Diesel Allison division), which had long been linked with Rolls-Royce in the aero-engine field, could not have chosen a more auspicious time to sit round a conference table and discuss the possibility of getting an Americanized Spey into the A-7 in addition to, or even in place of, the TF30.

At first the Spey was merely a means of providing an engine for possible export models, but by August 1965 Allison and Rolls had jointly schemed a developed Spey, with 35 per cent greater airflow, that appeared likely to meet the possible US Air Force requirement without needing an afterburner. Pratt & Whitney, already striving to improve the TF30 for the F-111 models, was under no illusions about the sudden emergence of this rival. It fitted the A-7 like a glove, and Vought was enthusiastic. By the end of 1965 the Allison 912 had been given the DoD designation of TF41, and teams at Rolls (where it was called the RB.168-62) and Indianapolis were fast turning it into an engineering design and test hardware (though the official history says design did not begin until June 1966). Moreover, during 1965 Britain had cancelled the last of its native military-aircraft programmes and replaced all of them with US products. There arose in Westminster a sudden intense interest in 'offset agreements' for the

Americans to buy British defence hardware in exchange. It was as if all the forces of fate were conspiring to push the TF41 into the A-7. In fact the mere existence of the TF41 would have got it into the Air Force A-7 anyway, but the political circumstances were ideal for the government in Washington to explain the adoption of a 'foreign' engine and the government in London to point with glee at a massive offset.

Interest by the Air Force in the A-7 was sharpened by the Vietnam war. As explained in the companion volume on 'Bombers', the USAF had spent billions on equipment for global nuclear war and almost ignored the lessons it had learned at great cost in Korea. So it went into action in Vietnam with supersonic fighters, such as the F-100 and F-105, and used them to stooge about at low level trying to drop bombs on scattered enemies in forests and rice paddies. Discovering that this was not a very cost/effective operation, it went to the other extreme and planned Co-In aircraft with straight wings and propellers. Rather to its chagrin it very gradually came to realize that the Navy's A-7 was superior to either a light turboprop or a Mach 2 fighter. Until 1966 a rival faction in the Air Force considered the trim little Northrop F-5 an attractive tactical machine, and pointed to the quite good performance of the special evaluation squadron sent to Vietnam, where 12 F-5s had flown up to 33 sorties per day (which in pre-Harrier days was considered good). But there is nothing like real warfare for making hard numerical data win over vague emotions, and the numbers showed that in a Vietnam-type conflict the stumpy, pugnacious A-7 won hands-down over the sleek, supersonic F-5. Air Force Secretary Harold S. Brown was an expert at this sort of evaluation, and he personally backed the range, endurance and ordnance load of the A-7. In February 1966 provision was made in the USAF funding for the acquisition of the A-7D with the 14250 lb thrust TF41 engine.

Immediately there was a political storm in Canada. The Canadian Armed Forces had just chosen the F-5, and Canadair was tooling up to make some. Mass media are seldom concerned to report the facts, which in this case were not difficult to establish, but merely to try to concoct a dramatic 'story'. The newspapers drummed up every argument they could find to suggest, variously, that the F-5 was no good, that the Americans had let Canada down, or that the USAF was picking an inferior aircraft (purely, according to one commentator, in order to please the British by using a Rolls engine). It was left to the Ottawa Defence Minister, Paul Hellyer, to pour oil on troubled waters by explaining 'We have an entirely different requirement . . . the F-5 is a versatile aircraft, which can operate without fighter escort.' They were words chosen to mollify his voters, but they offended people in Dallas (and in the USAF and Navy who have never used a fighter escort in all their A-7 operations). But all this was a silly side issue. The big issue was that the Air Force was, for the second time, going to buy a Navy aircraft; and it was going to do so with a different and more powerful engine.

The Air Force also had a few words to say about the avionics. Although the original VAL specification had seemed comprehensive, judged against the much older A-4, by 1966 the ILAAS programme had been superseded. The Air Force evaluated the A-7D against numerous much newer aircraft, both real and projected, with avionics of still later conception. Cutting a very long story short, the A-7D was bought with no fewer than 24 new items of equipment including the APQ-126 multi-mode FLR, an inertial navigation system, a new digital computer, special subsystems for new and forthcoming Air Force weapons, new ECM equipment, and a head-up display (HUD). The HUD, which projects symbols and numbers on to the windscreen in such a way that the pilot can both look out ahead and at the vital steering information without re-focussing his eyes, is a product of what in 1966 was Elliott-Automation and is now part of the British GEC empire. It really was an offset agreement, and a great breakthrough for a British company. But the TF41, as I have said, would have happened anyway, even though the news of the deal was deliberately put out by Washington in August 1966 in terms suggesting that the whole thing was arranged in order to buy British: 'To fulfil the associated US commitment to make $325 million in purchases from the UK over a period of years, we plan to use a version of the Rolls-Royce Spey engine in the USAF A-7 aircraft. The engines will be built in the United States by Allison, initially by using engines and components supplied by Rolls-Royce valued at approximately $100 million.'

But this was merely politically convenient. British MP Enoch Powell, who is nobody's fool, asked 'Is it not a fact that negotiations for the sale of these Spey engines have been in progress since long before the offset agreement was entered into; and that there is no reason whatever for connecting this sale . . . with the offset agreement?' Defence Minister Denis Healey replied that Mr Powell was wrong: 'Spey engines for the A-7 were one of the items jointly identified by the two governments, and without assistance from the government the deal which we now hope to go through would have had little chance of succeeding.' In other words it was part of the offset agreement, because Mr Healey chose to say so; in the same way the sale of Lightnings to Saudi Arabia was claimed to be an offset because instead of being beaten commercially the Americans were supposed to have 'stood aside' and let the British win. The notion of 'offsets' merely took away from Rolls-Royce the prestige they could have won with a superior product by making it seem that product-superiority played no part in the choice. Psn, as J. D. (later Sir Denning)

Pearson was known at Derby, called the TF41 'the biggest breakthrough Rolls-Royce has ever had', but to the British public, and to the official record, the TF41 was just an offset deal. So I'll close the argument by quoting what Lt-Gen Thomas P. Gerrity, then USAF DCOS for Systems, told me in April 1967: 'Offsets never entered into the deal at all until your government invented the idea. . . . Then our administration found this an admirable way of explaining contracts for a foreign-designed engine which have now run to $255 million and will go on for some time yet. The TF41 was a distinctly superior choice . . . Allison even bid us a lower price than the TF30.'

During 1967 the Dallas plant actually increased its tooling to build the A-7 faster, and by 1968 it was not unknown for four aircraft to come off the line in a single day. All were still of the A-7A type, of which 199 were delivered, until the first A-7B flew on 6 February 1968. By this time more than half the aircraft on the line were Ds for the Air Force. The first two of these were fitted with the same TF30-P-8 engine as the B model, because although TF41 development was running ahead of schedule Allison did not even run an engine until March 1968. To avoid a clash with the great ceremonial roll-out of the C-5A transport on 2 March (at least this was the reason Vought gave) the first A-7D flight was held back and finally took place on 5 April. Less than three months after the engine first ran in the US, a production TF41 was delivered in June 1968, and the first flight of the engine took place in the third A-7D on 26 September. The speed of the TF41 programme could have led to troubles, but, like the A-7 itself, it went fast and well. Pratt & Whitney, still under pressure from all sides, fought back doggedly with the TF30-8, by then a somewhat dated basic engine, and suffered one problem after another. Most of the worst difficulties were second-stage turbine failures. Finally, in March 1968, a fully modified -8 engine was put to an acceptance test to prove the design changes intended to cure this particular fault. The engine failed the test. The result was that the Navy rejected fifty A-7Bs, many of them still on the production line. A deeper result was that this hardened the Navy's resolve to emulate the Air Force and switch to the TF41.

From the start of the A-7D programme the Navy had been appreciative, if not envious, of this more powerful Air Force version with its continuous-solution navigation and weapon-delivery system, and it determined in 1967 to use the A-7D as the basis for its future buys, thus nicely returning the compliment the Air Force had paid it with the A-7D. Discussions with Allison confirmed that there was plenty of 'stretch' in the TF41. In planning the engine Allison and Rolls-Royce had modified the original Spey up to the airflow limit of the A-7 inlet duct, giving the engine a bigger fan but with fewer stages. They also followed the modern trend in eliminating intake guide vanes, although these may not be a bad idea in aircraft that penetrate at low level through flocks of birds (at least, so GE say, with the F101 engine of the B-1 bomber). From the start Allison began drawing projected TF41 models with higher airflow still, and with thrusts ranging up to around 20000 lb dry or 25000 to 30000 lb with full afterburner. For the initial Navy application they picked a slightly modified TF41 rated at 15000 lb, and started by an air-turbine hose instead of the self-contained gas-turbine starter of the A-7D. Designated A-7E, the new Navy Corsair closely follows the equipment specification of the A-7D, including the single six-barrel M-61 20 mm 'Gatling gun' which replaced the two older guns of the original model; but the 'fit' differs in the Communications, navigation and ECM areas, which reflect the compatibility of the E model with the carrier or SATS environment. Rather remarkably, the Navy managed to lop more than 1000 lb off the equipped weight, which in the D model had climbed to no less than 19665 lb. At the same time the gross weight with the powerful TF41 engine was allowed to rise from the original 32500 lb to 42000 lb, taking the A-7 way above the weight class of the original F-8 fighter and greatly extending the practical combinations of payload and range. Indeed the KA-7F, which was never built but was proposed as a replacement for the Skywarrior as the standard carrier-based air-refuelling tanker, would have carried no less than 31000 lb of fuel, 18600 lb internally and 12400 in four underwing tanks! Fuel would have represented 70 per cent of the take-off weight, and if Vought had built this version it might have had a go at the single-jet world distance record.

Already the Corsair has some very long flights to its credit, the outstanding example being the non-stop mission of two standard A-7Ds from Dallas to the Paris air show in May 1971 with two in-flight refuellings. Updated by radar, both inertial systems showed zero error on arrival at Le Bourget; without any correction the errors for the two aircraft would have been 10 and 12 nautical miles, which is excellent for a 5758-mile journey at about 400 knots. These D models had the prominent refuelling boom receptacle above the left side of the fuselage, but the first 27 were delivered with probes such as are standard on the Navy aircraft and are also fitted to many earlier TAC machines. Indeed the switch to the rigid boom was a rather surprising indication that the Air Force considers this method of refuelling preferable even for single-seaters, largely on account of its higher flow rate (thinks: so why not buy a fatter hose for the other method ?. Total deliveries of the D at the end of 1972 were 387; deliveries of the Navy variants comprised 199 As, 196 Bs, and 374 of the E type, the first 67 of the latter being delivered with the TF30-8 and the designation A-7C.

As related earlier, this designation of A-7C was originally allocated in 1966 to a proposed tandem-seat version, with a length increased to 48 ft 4¼ in and optional dual controls. Vought and its customers never doubted that most Corsairs would be single-seaters, but it seemed reasonable to investigate a two-seater to open up further possibilities in the fields of conversion training, mission training, bad-weather and special-combat missions and various other applications. The same thing had been doen in the Crusader programme, and the first TF-8A flew on 6 February 1962, but money for a production two-seat Crusader was one of many items thrown out of the FY64 budget by a surprisingly adverse Congress, and this project therefore withered. It was an odd situation, because the Navy wanted that aircraft, a batch had been ordered by the French and the R&D had been done. As it is, the lone TF-8A has done sterling work on all sorts of jobs at Pax River and the Navy still has nothing else like it. In 1966 it really looked as if the A-7C would fill the gap, but funds remained tight and Vought was too busy making single-seaters to do much pushing. But talking never stopped and finally, in November 1971, the Navy agreed to bail back (freely loan) an A-7E for a conversion funded by the company. Conversion was a big job. It involved adding 16 in ahead of the wing for the new dual-control cockpit, a second 18 in insert aft of the wing—which also tilted up the rear fuselage almost 2° to avoid scraping the tail end on landing—and a single side-hinged canopy over both cockpits, with ejection made 'through the glass'. A friend of mine saw the bits of what is variously called the Vought V-519, the YA-7H and the Corsair II-2 lying around in the experimental shop at Dallas in May 1972, and told me 'They'll never get it into the air on their target date in mid-September'. He was right; Konrad flew on 29 August. So far the two-seater has demonstrated performance and reliability very close to the figures for the A-7E.

Obviously the Corsair is a splendid basis on which to build. There is an outside chance we shall see developed versions for 20 years, because the notion that everything has to be supersonic has at last been finally demolished, and air forces are realising that buying a mere 600-knot aeroplane is no loss of face. I have not seen the pile of classified proposals LTV's Vought Aerospace Corporation has cooked up for future programmes, but they obviously include refined high-lift devices, more powerful engines (not only TF41 growth-versions but also engines from GE and Pratt & Whitney), more powerful guns, new sensing and aiming systems, new combat protection techniques and new airframe structures. But they have yet to become hardware.

Another version yet to reach fruition—although it exists as an off-the-shelf demonstrator—is the A-7G originally tailored for the Swiss. Since

1967 the Swiss Air Force had been looking for a new fighter/bomber to replace its aged Venoms. Remembering the terrible financial storm which blew up when they bought the Mirage fighter the Swiss took their time evaluating rival candidates. As they had £130 million to spend, practically everyone with a suitable product knocked on the door. The Swiss scarcely even considered the F-111F, Jaguar, Viggen or any Soviet type, and tried to ignore the Harrier on the ground that it was not in service when over 100 were with squadrons of the RAF and US Marine Corps. Repeatedly their Armament Group said it wanted the Corsair, even though—obviously making a very generous allowance for spares and support gear—the money would have bought only 60, fewer than for any rival type. The A-7G was a simpler aircraft than the later American Corsairs, but would have had an up-rated engine (probably the Allison 912-B28 rated at 17200 lb). For toting massive ordnance loads out of narrow valleys and delivering them with pin-point accuracy the A-7G was hard to beat, and came out technical winner. The runner-up, the Dassault Mirage-Milan, had the advantage of commonality with the only existing modern Swiss type but could not come anywhere near the Corsair in mission effectiveness because it lacked the black boxes. Nevertheless the French put up a terrific campaign to push the Milan and unsell the Corsair, which was knocked slightly off-course by the announcement that the French navy wanted to buy the Corsair. Eventually the Swiss decided to buy two batches of 30 rebuilt Hunters to help tide them over. This soothed Hawker, who knew the dice were so loaded against the Harrier that it could never win unless the Swiss realized that somebody might blast their nice Alpine runways.

As long as an air force has unblasted airfields, and a navy has unsunk carriers I know no tactical interdiction machine to surpass the A-7. Just what can it do? Compared with its predecessors it can lay down iron bombs with close to 100 per cent accuracy without demanding great pilot skill or experience and without exposing him to the risks of long and straight diving attacks to low levels. The stand-off capability enables attacks to be made on unseen targets, although the A-7 pilot ought to be able to see the ground. It is thus not truly an all-weather aircraft, except in the flights to and from the target, although it is at least as accurate as anything in World War 2 in level radar bombing from great heights. The rapid-fire gun has proved appreciably more accurate than had been expected in attacks on ground targets, and it is a useful tool in aerial combat.

As related in the final chapter of this volume, Vought declined to compete for the AX contract which has now resulted in the Fairchild A-10A, but took a great interest in the very powerful GAU-8A gun which that aircraft is expected to carry. Unfortunately the A-7 is not the easiest of aircraft into which to fit a GAU-8A gun, and I discount Vought's chances of going ahead with a new A-7 variant fitted with the gun low in the forward fuselage, an offset or twinned nose gear and side inlet ducts to the engine. GE have offered a shortened and rearranged GAU-8A which can be made to fit today's A-7, but as I write in mid-1973 this seems an unlikely match. On the other hand, a great deal continues to be done to improve the Corsair, partly because it is a first-rate combat aircraft and partly because the AX is making it fight harder.

One area in which improvements will probably continue as long as an A-7 is in service is sensing and display systems. It is simple to lay down basic laws about the equipment needed by modern attack aircraft. I doubt if anyone would deny that such aircraft need accurate data on aircraft velocity, rate (rotation about the three axes, or rate of change of velocity) and range to the target. For all except good daytime visibility conditions it also needs sensing systems capable of finding, and if possible of actually 'picturing', targets. Both the old and new A-7 radars are good, but it would be much better if the aircraft had either a FLIR or LLTV able to portray the Earth's surface ahead in fine detail—and, if possible, feed the information through the HUD to paint a picture by TV scanning (raster) techniques so that it can be seen by the pilot in the right place and at the correct scale. This is just what people have been trying to do, although the new package has to be carried externally in an under-wing pod. It looks as if the FLIR will win, and it will be very interesting to see just what kind of 'vision' it gives the pilot in otherwise blind conditions. Of course, infra-red is badly attenuated by cloud and precipitation, but the A-6 has done quite well with an early FLIR and I would judge it well worth having on both naval and land-based A-7s. If the reader can bear looking up yet further sets of initials, the A-7 could also be matched with TRIM or TRAM, but I think these things fit better into an A-6 or Canberra.

Such systems are conspicuously absent from the A-10A (p. 249). This rather crude, yet bigger and later, aircraft is not designed for the same job as the A-7: it is a close-support platform, whereas the A-7 is a long-range interdictor for use from better airfields well back from the battle area. On the other hand, it certainly competes with the A-7 for funds. In 1972 the A-7 appeared to begin to fade, with Senator Barry Goldwater asking that it should be placed on public record that it would 'not be procured instead of the AX'. Indeed, though in the 1974 budget the Navy put in $109 million for A-7Es, there was no Air Force buy at all. This made Texas Congressmen lobby pretty hard, and the sheer merit of the aircraft is likely to keep it in production until at least 1975. But in 1974 the fact must be faced that next year the Dallas plant that has made Corsairs faster than any other Western combat aircraft of the 1960s may have to run down. So the entire programme may have a life-span of barely ten years, in the final eight of which more than 1200 aircraft have been delivered on schedule. It is more probable that A-7 versions will continue in reduced-rate production for many years, especially as Congress has for at least two years been trying to get the A-7 procured in place of the supposedly inferior A-10A.

I have never heard a Sluf pilot speak of his stumpy, subsonic mount with anything other than warm satisfaction. In the March 1972 issue of *Air Force Magazine* Capt Thomas G. Ryan, of the 355th TFS at Myrtle Beach, S Carolina, wrote of it with unrestrained enthusiasm. There are probably still a few people who consider that a heavily laden subsonic bomber must need a fighter escort to penetrate contested airspace. If there are, Ryan has news for them; he feels he would have a good chance of taking 24 big bombs to his target even if he was jumped by enemy fighters on the outward trip. This is especialy interesting when it is learned that he came to the A-7 after having flown 141 combat missions over South Vietnam in the well-loved 'Thud'—the Mach 2 F-105D Thunderchief. Ryan recalled that he had known aircraft fitted with automatic weapon-release systems 'that sometimes did not perform as well as a skilled pilot using manual delivery. None of us was ready to concede superiority to The System (as the Sluf's avionics are known) without a shoot-off. . . . The big showdown was no contest. On my first mission to Avon Park gunnery range in Florida the range officer started to read the bombing winds to us, but our flight leader said "No thanks!" This surprised the range officer because manual bombing requires aim-point adjustment for winds, and the winds were 25 to 30 knots and 90° to our attack heading. We rolled in for high-angle bombing in sequence, and I can still hear the range officer's voice climbing higher with each bomb impact: "Bull's eye, leader . . . bull, two . . . BULL'S EYE, THREE . . . BULL, FOUR!!" Small wonder Ryan calls his A-7D, with its emphasis on cost/effectiveness, 'a silver lining in sometimes very dark clouds.'

Fairchild Republic A-10A

IN the winter of 1965–66 the US tactical airpower scene was interesting, to put it mildly. For four years the nation had been involved in an escalating war in South-East Asia. It was a singularly nasty and difficult war, rather like a second Korea and not at all tailored to the biggest and most costly weapons in the fantastic armoury the United States had created. Where airpower was concerned the prime need was for 'battlefield' type firepower, for close air support (CAS) of ground forces. To do the job the American combat units deployed an amazing diversity of equipment. Some of it was old, some new, and two very important types were shortly to enter service. In addition there were several conversions, modifications and radical lash-ups which were all intended to clobber Charlie as hard as possible. Visiting reporters sent back across the wide Pacific stories of supremely professional aircrew, of good and trusty equipment, of high morale and of no particular beefs apart from the climate. But inside the Pentagon, Air Force staff officers looked at the scene differently. How could they have got everything (but everything) so wrong (again)?

In Korea they had had masses of aircraft except ones suited to the CAS mission in Korea. This time, more than ten years later, they had attack aircraft by the hundred except any tailored to CAS missions in Vietnam. The Navy, Marines and Air Force had the A-4 Skyhawk, which was very good in many ways but had been around for more than ten years and was not designed for land use. The A-6 Intruder had marvellous black boxes and could do a pinpoint job in all kinds of weather, but it was in no sense a CAS aircraft; it cost millions of dollars and needed dozens of highly trained and dedicated men at good airfields or carriers to look after it. The A-7 Corsair, then being designed, promised to be very good and efficient; but like the A-6, it was packed with black boxes and was really a long-range interdictor. The F-4 Phantom was a great all-round performer but it was designed as a Mach 2-plus carrier-based fighter and was not remotely like anyone's idea of a purpose-built CAS aircraft. The A-1 Skyraider could tote lots of weapons under its 15 pylons but it had been designed before the Normandy landings in World War 2 and its ranks were being fast thinned by age and combat vulnerability. The B-26 Invader was even older, and the T-28 Trojan had originally been planned in 1948 as a trainer. The F-100 Super Sabre was of a different calibre; this had been the world's first supersonic military aircraft in 1953, but it was planned not for CAS but for air combat. The impressive F-105 Thunderchief was a Mach 2 fighter and interdiction machine, which like the F-100 needed good weather, acres of concrete and truckloads of dollars. The AC-47 (Puff the Magic Dragon) was a C-47 (DC-3) intended to fly left-hand circuits round ground targets whilst blasting them with gunfire from its left-side windows; this was not quite what Arthur Raymond had designed the DC-3 for 30 years previously. Cessna's neat little A-37 was really a jet trainer; although it had been souped up with twice the power and a commendable array of weapons under its beefed-up wings, it was limited in load, range and endurance. The new F-111, on the other hand, had lots of load, range and endurance, but was coming out at around $15 million a copy and was severely limited by weather and visibility in CAS operations. The B-57, developed from the British Canberra, was quite effective and had been financially written off the books long ago, but the ten years of hard work had made it structurally tired and thin on the ground. There were also attack versions of helicopters, and these were obviously fine if you could base them close by and afford costly attrition. Finally, there were many little STOL aircraft that were supposed to do a CAS job, from the Helio U-10 Courier to the brand-new, purpose-built (Co-In) North American OV-10A Bronco. These just lacked punch.

What a wealth of attack aircraft! No other country could deploy anything like it. Unfortunately not one of them had been designed for the job. So the Air Force generals got out sketch pads, again, and began drawing the sort of thing that seemed to be needed. They kept coming back to the old Skyraider. Really this was quite a good jumping-off point, because generals love the view from the cockpit when there are *seven* pylon-loads of stores inboard of each wing tip, plus something even bigger on the centreline. It also had four 20 mm guns, long endurance, could turn on a sixpence at 150 knots and absorb severe punishment. It appeared that what was wanted was a sort of 1966 Skyraider. The airframe had to be simple, cheap, strong (Americans always use the word 'rugged' here, though this word actually means 'rough, hairy and uneven') and combat-survivable. In other words it had to be designed to stay together when riddled with strikes up to at least 20 mm calibre. The wing seemed to need 1966-type high-lift devices to claw at the air and lift enormous loads out of short fields. Power apparently had to be turboprops, and there had to be at least two engines far enough apart for one of them to survive a direct hit on the other. And all the systems had to be cheap, reliable and 'combat-survivable'; so if a 20 mm shell blew off an aileron it didn't matter, any more than if it severed one lot of elevator controls or one set of hydraulic lines. Supersonic speed, solid-state computers, phased-array radars and inertial platforms were NOT wanted, thank you.

This was contrary to one of the most deeply ingrained beliefs about the world of aerospace, long cherished by the experts of the mass media. This belief is that one naturally strives for the mostest—not necessarily the biggest but certainly the fastest, cleverest and newest-looking. There is a tradition that US Congressmen want 'nothing but the best for our boys', and if one of them tries to economise on defence weapons he is likely to be taken apart in a thousand newspaper editorials. Likewise the Air Force general is commonly imagined as a belligerent monster who takes the cigar from his mouth and growls that he only has ten thousand bombers flying at Mach 2 when he needs twenty thousand flying at Mach 3. How far such mental images are from the truth is shown by the fact that, at the most trying time of the Vietnam war, the real-life generals were planning to fight the war with a propeller-driven aircraft that looked like a throwback to the days before Pearl Harbor. Exactly what it would look like none of them could tell—indeed, biplanes were examined as carefully as they had been in the Co-In programme five years earlier—because hardly anyone had ever tried to build an optimised CAS aircraft. The French, who have tried everything, built the Potez 75 in 1952 but this extraordinary piston-engined pusher was primarily for busting tanks with its 75 mm gun.

The real nigger in the woodpile was that the CAS mission had always been the 'easy' undemanding duty that could be flown by fighters and bombers when they became too old for anything else. The idea of creating a tailor-made CAS aircraft might almost have seemed an unnecessary luxury, but in fact the USAF requirement for an optimised design is one of outstanding technical interest. It happened to grow in an environment of unusually intense inter-service rivalry, great budgetary pressures and an Air Force smarting after the worst programme-management experiences in its history (notably with the F-111 and C-5A).

With the tailor-made CAS machine the Air Force wanted to accomplish several things at once. It wanted to knock out the efforts of the Army to try to protect itself with its own gunship helicopters. It wanted to secure CAS once and for all as a wholly Air Force mission, flown by fixed-wing aircraft. It wanted to arm itself with an economic and effective CAS machine, not only for use in Vietnam-type wars but also in Europe—where, after 1975, the very expensive F-15 Eagle (or whatever other fighter might be to hand) would not be available in large enough numbers to rule the skies and also provide CAS, and in any case would be hamstrung by European overcast weather. (So the F-15, unlike every other US day fighter since 1941, was not designed to be capable of flying a CAS mission; and this made a purpose-built attack aircraft vital.) Finally the Air Force wished to demonstrate, by setting modest targets in an unchallenging concept, that it really could bring forth a new aircraft roughly within the timescale and financial budget it had planned.

In retrospect I think the whole concept of what was launched as the AX (attack experimental) programme in June 1966 was 100 per cent sound. The strenuous efforts of the Army to deploy a force of Cheyenne gunship helicopters, and the slightly later interest of the Marines in the British Harrier, could easily have triggered off an AX programme in self-defence. It could have been that AX was merely a desperate bid by the men in light blue to cling on to a big and important area of airpower that other services seemed to be trying to take over for themselves. The Air Force is probably still the most powerful of all the US services on Capitol Hill, and would have to mis-play things pretty badly not to get its own way. But in fact I am certain the AX requirement would have been written in the same terms, and at the same time, even if no other service had been trying to muscle in on the CAS act.

During the summer of 1966 many organizations within the Air Force conducted studies, trade-offs, computer modelling and first-hand investigations in Vietnam to establish beyond doubt the sort of aircraft that was needed. These in-house studies continued long after the Chief of Staff, Gen John P. McConnell, had put his name to the AX requirement in September 1966. I doubt if the Air Force ever seriously considered making the AX a helicopter, although they continually studied fold-away rotors. The Air Force has a deep-rooted emotional link with aeroplanes, and helicopters tend to be things that the Army goes to war with because the soldiers are not allowed much else. In fact the only Army war aeroplane with much size and perfomance is the Grumman OV-1 Mohawk, and this is actually amazingly like the way the Air Force viewed its AX, although AX was to be rather larger. I remember Clinton Towl, board chairman of Grumman, telling me how Grumman had sincerely felt the Mohawk could merit evaluation in the CAS role, and how they had offered to do a cost-sharing exercise to build a fully equipped and armed CAS prototype which they hoped would appeal to the Army and/or Air Force. This was way back in 1961, when even the Co-In/LARA programme (which led to the Bronco) was only just beginning to be defined, and long before anything like AX had crystallised in people's minds. In the event, when the Air Force finally decided to invite submissions from industry, Grumman was high on the list.

Although the Air Force never for a moment anticipated any major technical, timing or cost problems with AX—in fact, it was hoped to give everyone a blissful holiday from such things—great care was taken to manage the programme correctly. At the go-ahead in September 1966 the subject of correct programme management was in the melting-pot. Defense Secretary McNamara was still in the saddle, and the proper procedure was supposed to be 'fixed-price total-package procurement' in which the customer delegated the whole development task to the prime contractor and left the contractor pretty much to get on with it. This had played a large part in the two huge management disasters I mentioned earlier, and right from the start there were many influential Air Force men who said 'With AX we ought to be able to afford to evaluate rival prototypes just as we did in the old days; then we will really be certain just what we are buying.' Thus, early in 1967 the long corridors of the Pentagon, and of Air Force Systems Command up in Ohio, carried the message of a new catch-phrase: 'Fly before buy.'

On 6 March 1967 the RFP was sent out for an AX design study; those who like the idea of a single 'nationalised industry' can ponder on the fact that this mailing was sent to 21 companies. On 2 May 1967 the Air Force did what might seem a strange thing. Instead of just waiting for the studies to come in, which would undoubtedly have resulted in at least 12 contrasting proposals, it chose four companies—Grumman, General Dynamics, McDonnell Douglas and Northrop—and awarded each of them a paid study contract. Bearing in mind that from the start it was considered AX would be a programme for well over 500 aircraft, this seemed to be paying the industry to do something it would do anyway, whilst deliberately restricting the number of participants. With a little more understanding of the programme I learned that the studies were not only concerned with the broad design configuration but called for in-depth research into exactly where you put the armour, how thick it should be and of what material, how the fuel tanks and piping should be arranged and protected, and in general how one could get the highest degree of structural and systems redundancy (so that parts could be shot out without affecting structural integrity or system response) for minimum weight and cost. It was a task for large computer studies because each optimised answer tended to affect all the others. It all served to underline how seriously the programme was regarded. Into AX the Air Force wanted to build 'everything we have learned about CAS in three wars'. The speaker was Lt-Gen Marvin McNickle, who in late 1968 was DCOS for R&D. He was one of the Top Brass who had become concerned at the fact that some USAF pilots were actually younger than the aircraft in which they were facing the enemy in Vietnam!

McNickle's successor, Lt-Gen Otto J. Glasser, recalled how the original studies had not completely discounted the possibility of V/STOL. He had read the study reports—prepared before he was given the R&D responsibility—and seen the reasons for supposing that V/STOL carries a severe 'penalty'. This leads straight into one of the two giant areas of debate that nobody who tries to build an attack aircraft today can escape. One of these areas is how many clever black boxes you fit The Air Force approached AX in a frame of mind which said 'Our creed is made up of four words: maneuverable, survivable, lethal and simple. Black boxes run contrary to this creed, so we will try and leave them out.' The other big argument concerns the field length. This is a very big problem indeed. In the case of black boxes you can always fit additional ones, and this may be done to the production AX as I shall describe later. But field length is fundamental to the design of an aircraft. It was absolutely crucial that the Air Force should pick on the right field length for the AX, because departing from this optimum distance appeared to impose crippling penalties. Too short a distance meant excessive installed thrust and/or complicated high-lift systems, in turn causing gross increases in complexity and degrading the payload/range performance. Too long a distance meant that the aircraft would not be able to operate at all, except from good undamaged runways.

Planners in air-conditioned offices can possibly weight the different variables in a sharply different way from the harassed soldier trapped in a foxhole and trying to summon help. The cool man with a slide-rule may well push the optimised point further and further down the scale of length and eventually decide the best distance is something like a mile. The beleaguered GI would prefer a true VTOL able to leap out of the next foxhole. Nobody doubts that full VTOL performance, if used, does mean less payload for a given installed thrust, and many would claim it also means a more complex aircraft (though there could hardly be anything much simpler than a Harrier). But this notion of 'penalties' is not the best way of approaching the problem. The Air Force appreciated this. In a big study called TAC 85, in 1971, it took a long look at likely operating environments for the AX. Much of the time was spent studying Western Europe, and it was concluded that after strikes on airfields, there would generally be 4000 feet of runway left in operation. Further studies showed what an attractive aircraft could be devised if 4000 ft was accepted as the ground roll at maximum weight. At reduced weight the same aircraft could get off in much shorter distances. After very long discussion this spread of take-off ground-roll distances—1000 to 4000 ft—was written in to the AX requirement.

I do not know the complete range of scenarios studied in TAC 85, and the document is classified. But the answers you get to a set of equations depend on the values you crank in to them, and the vision of warfare in Western Europe is utterly unlike the kind of war the US Air Force could find itself involved in. Western Europe is dotted with paved runways, and I am not in a position to disagree with the conclusion that there would usually be 4000 ft available within a few minutes' flying time (though it seems to me a grossly optimistic presumption). AX does not need a paved surface, and even though 4000 ft is more than three-quarters of a mile it is hard work clobbering an airfield so that no run of this distance is left on its surface. But what about other parts of the world where airfields are few and the terrain rugged? And what about the basic requirement that the AX was to be 'contiguous to the combat zone' and 'organic to the battle area'? AX is no long-range interdictor based somewhere hundreds of miles behind the battlefield. This is the job of such aircraft as the Corsair, Jaguar, MRCA and F-111. These aircraft can operate from 4000 ft strips—indeed, the Jaguar and MRCA need barely 3000 ft—even though they can be based a long way off. In contrast the AX was meant to be sited close by the army it was supporting, and in a modern war of movement this means that its base must move around with the battle. I have pondered at length, and argued with many responsible experts, on what sort of base one can reckon on using in order to fly CAS missions. Leaving Western Europe aside, the answer in a fluid war of movement in thousands of likely trouble-spots around the world is that you don't have much of a base at all. Suppose the enemy has air power, and can fly over looking for your aircraft? Suppose you have to move the base 20 or 50 miles every day? Suppose the enemy can hit the base with artillery or even mortar fire? This is when it pays hands-down to forget even about the S in STOL and come closer and closer to V.*

Suffice to say, in December 1968, after thousands of experts and lengthy computer studies had all made their contribution, the Deputy Secretary of Defense approved the concept-formulation study with a take-off ground roll of 1000 to 4000 ft, calling for a fairly level and smooth cleared strip much longer than this if it is surrounded by trees or other obstructions. The only proviso made was that the Air Force should 'study the possibility of making the AX cheaper by making it smaller'. Until then most studies had been of propeller-driven aircraft approximately in the size class of the B-57 Canberra, with weights in the bracket 40000–60000 lb and unit cost, allowing for R&D, of at least $1·5 million. By mid-1969 the 'baseline

---

**When the eventual winners of the AX contract reviewed this chapter they took strong exception to my argument, considering it 'a parochial sales-pitch for the Harrier'. It is not intended to be. My concern, in every chapter, is to tell it like it is. Time will show how far it will be possible to reduce the field-length of CAS aircraft while still keeping them simple and effective.*

AX' had come down to 35000 lb and the target cost to around $1 million. It was also at this time that the fanjet began to loom strongly upon the scene as a method of propulsion at least as attractive as the turboprop. To a considerable degree this was because engine designers had around 1965 at last got used to the idea that by-pass ratios could usefully lie in the range 5 to 10. Until then the giants of the engine world (notably excepting Bristol and GE) had for no very clear reason decided that by-pass ratios up to about unity were acceptable whereas anything much higher was not. Opening up the sights and making slim core engines drive large-diameter fans at one stroke improved the propulsive efficiency by 25 to 30 per cent whilst simultaneously reducing the noise and (a factor of military importance) generally making the engine more difficult to detect by its infra-red signature. In any case, propellers were heavy, unreliable, prone to damage (in the air or in a belly landing) and strictly limiting on flight speed. So by July 1969 most of the AX studies at Wright-Patterson AFB had lost their propellers.

In this the story parallels the search for a replacement for the DC-3, which began (even at Douglas) around 1937 and will probably go on into the next century. I have no doubt whatever that, quite apart from their vastly improved passenger comfort, the modern STOL transports with fan engines will set, or are setting, levels of total direct operating cost lower than they could if they had propellers. Rather to their surprise, the Aeronautical Systems Division at Wright-Patterson AFB found the same thing in their trade-off studies on the AX in 1968–69. Cost was from the start one of the dominating factors in this programme (however irrelevant this may be to the GI in the foxhole with his head down). From the viewpoints of both first cost and cyclic mission cost it began to look as if the turbofan-engined aircraft might be superior to the turboprop, apart from its other advantages.

Choosing the best speed for the AX was one of the fundamental problems faced by the writers of the operational requirements (or, in US jargon, who formulated the concept for the system). It really took the hardest of all schools, the Vietnam war, to drive home the lesson that an effective CAS mission cannot be flown at high speed. This is not to deny that many CAS missions actually were flown at close to the speed of sound. Many is the time an F-105 or F-4 was called down from his loiter height of 8000 or 10000 feet to lay down some napes or retarded bombs on a particular geographical location in fairly featureless terrain. If Charlie had betrayed the fact he had plenty of guns in the area, the attack might well be a single long pass, pulling up at over Mach 0·9. This is just what I would have done myself. My view would have been 'I'm not paying the bill for the ordnance, but I have a strong personal interest in getting in and out again in one piece.' As a result it was not unknown for the FAC to say something like 'Great . . . now if you could just put your next one about 100 yards closer to the north-east corner of the wood, roughly in line with the eastern edge and about half-way to an east-west line through the place where the trees seem to get darker on the other side . . . then you ought to be able to hit it.' The result was an F-4 jock, probably low on fuel and desperately trying to remember complex instructions, plummeting down for a second or third try and each time just failing to get the desired effect in the desired place.

With AX the Air Force finally decided to slow down, get lined up and try to achieve a bull's eye on every pass. In 1969 the speed was still 350–400 knots, but the following year 400 knots became the lower limit on maximum speed, perhaps because of the remonstrations of the jocks whose job it was to sit in thin-skinned cockpits in occasional close proximity to the enemy. Obviously there had been an utter revolution in thinking from the period not long before (indeed, in Britain it extended well into the 1960s) when the fact that an aircraft was subsonic was held by the military mind to provide a *prima facie* case for its replacement—or, if it was a new design, for refusing to buy it. Vietnam had shown what apparently some people had not previously realized: that, even if an aircraft can in theory fly at Mach 2·5, by the time it has started trying to hit targets on the battlefield it will only momentarily exceed Mach 0·8. Even a glamorous F-4 with all its ordnance in place is exceedingly subsonic, and when it spends time pulling sustained tight turns it will need full reheat to hold anything above 400 knots. So making the AX a 400 knot aeroplane is not as much of a revolution as it might at first sight appear. The fundamental difference is that, as it does not have to fly in the stratosphere at over Mach 2, it can be 'configured' (another lovely Americanism) for lifting enormous loads out of short fields. It has a big high-lift wing that gives it a very small radius of turn. Its ratio of thrust to weight can be 0·4 instead of something between 0·7 and 1·3. These were the keys to a very efficient AX.

This concept of a relatively slow combat aircraft is so unusual that it is worth emphasizing that the AX has been planned to be a very carefully optimised aircraft indeed. The fact that it has of necessity had to be developed in an environment of austerity must not be allowed to obscure this fact. It is all too easy to correlate financial stringency with the rather old-fashioned shape and low top speed, and—however much one may really know better—retain a few cells deep inside one's brain wherein is locked the belief that, if the US Air Force could suddenly afford $10 million a copy, the speed would be supersonic. This is totally wrong. The speed of the AX is as carefully optimised as everything else, and is considered the best for the CAS mission. AX pilots will not be second-class citizens. At the same time, the Air Force had to look very hard at their rating as an insurance risk. Even Vietnam was no picnic. The belief—quite widely held among many ordinary members of the public without particular left-wing convictions—that the US airpower was unfairly unleashed against almost defenceless, untrained peasants, quite unable to hit back, could hardly have been wider of the mark. The anti-aircraft defences in some areas were officially judged, by people who ought to know, as 'equalling in intensity anything experienced in World War 2' (though perhaps the accuracy, even when guided missiles were used, could fairly be described as patchy). The AX obviously had to be capable of meeting tougher opposition than this. Air Force Secretary Bob Seamans testified before Congress in 1969 that it 'will be designed from the first for high survivability in the anticipated ground-fire environment of the 1970s and 1980s.'

This is really the central issue around which the viability of the concept revolves. As a final decision on quantity production is unlikely to be taken before 1975 I suppose the AX must be regarded as a weapon not so much of the 1970s as of the 1980s and 1990s. By this time almost every likely enemy will probably have gone some way beyond the use of a few thousand riflemen firing in the general direction of the target, and even a few thousand riflemen showed themselves in Vietnam to be very discouraging to the pilot flying CAS missions. Perhaps the enduring memory one has of the earliest generations of surface-to-air guided weapon systems is that they looked much more lethal than they in fact were. They suffered from countless snags involving unreliability, long reaction time, inability to handle ECM, and many other shortcomings, and even as late as 1972 the US Air Force claimed that an average of 60 of the archaic SA-2 ('Guideline') missiles had to be fired for each American aircraft lost. Whether this was an accurate estimate or not, I do not think anyone would dispute that SA-2 is hardly representative of what an AX is likely to have to meet when it gets into service. So the question of vulnerability to defensive fire loomed overwhelmingly large in the AX concept from 1968 onward.

During 1969 the Air Force crystallised its thinking into a final draft requirement. While leaving the engine choice entirely up to industry, it generally considered the best answer to be two turbofans in the 7000–10000 lb thrust class. With a thrust/weight ratio of 0·4 these would match an aircraft with a gross weight of 35000 to 50000 lb. Thrust was to be adequate for take-off at maximum weight on a tropical hot day from an unpaved strip about 4000 feet long, and for sustained high-rate manoeuvres at speeds between 150 and 300 knots without losing height or speed. Fuel was to be adequate for a mission radius of 250 miles, with a corresponding loiter time over the battle area of 2 hours. Large and variable payloads were to be carried up to a limit of 16000 lb, and for use against hard-skinned targets the Air Force—having been deeply impressed by the execution of T-54 tanks by the 30 mm DEFA guns of Israeli Mirages in the Six-day War—decided to fund competitive development of a new gun which I shall discuss later. With maximum fuel weighing 10000 lb and full gun magazine the external load was expected to be 2500 lb. Means for accurate delivery of all weapons figured strongly in the requirement; indeed, I think if the Air Force had been asked in 1969 to pick a single word for the most important attribute of the AX it would have been 'lethality'. The need for high survivability against enemy fire might have come second, and another very important criterion was 'ease of maintenance for austere basing.' At the end of it all was the real challenge: AX had to 'possess all of these attributes at low cost.'

I will interject at this point a purely incidental fact that aircraft historians will find interesting. The AX had a precursor in World War 2, which had an extraordinary number of similarities. The Henschel Hs 129 was used in large numbers by the Luftwaffe, especially on the Eastern front, specifically to provide CAS to its ground forces. The Hs 129 was a twin-engined aircraft of moderate size, less than average power and quite low performance, but its manoeuvrability was good. The single pilot sat in the nose in a heavily armoured cockpit. Bombs and rockets could be carried under the wings, and a powerful gun was carried low on the centreline for use against armour. The aircraft was specially engineered for sustained operation from front-line bases, with unpaved surfaces and austere maintenance facilities. And the lower parts of the main gears protruded when retracted, to facilitate a wheels-up landing. It did a lot of hard work in many huge land battles, and even on occasion appeared with a battery of 75 mm recoilless guns firing downwards just aft of vertical and triggered automatically by flying low over a metal object such as a tank. But the Hs 129 could not live in a sky dominated by the enemy, and I do not believe it ever showed its face in Western Europe. Likewise I am sure AX pilots, despite their good all-round vision (something the Henschel pilots lacked), excellent power of manoeuvre and ability to survive damage, would find life hard if the enemy were to control the airspace.

McNamara moved from the Pentagon to the presidency of the World Bank on 19 January 1968 and his successor, Clark Clifford, was replaced by Melvin R. Laird on 20 January 1969. Laird, who had the massive advantage of long Congressional experience, set about whittling down the payroll in the Pentagon and reversing the McNamara policy of centralized control. In particular, he made it clear that he was not going to follow the McNamara doctrine of the Secretary taking all the big decisions personally. Indeed, in the matter of procurement he practically unloaded the whole subject on to his capable deputy, David Packard, who tried to make the system-acquisition process more flexible and, in particular, replaced the discredited 'fixed-price package' by a cost-plus-incentive-fee system. Under McNamara one imagines there would have been a great RFP competition, a giant fixed-price package awarded to a prime contractor and then, some time later, a feeling of foreboding in Washington while everyone waited for the storm to break. Packard would probably agree that the AX might have been acquired perfectly well by the McNamara doctrine, because the ill repute of the latter stemmed from its use with projects of extreme technical difficulty. At the same time there was by 1969 a powerful wish to do things differently and, insofar as this is possible with fast acquisition of new defence hardware, to avoid catastrophic trouble in programme management.

Basically, the new doctrine tries to preserve choices and options as long as possible, and to take decisions on the basis of visible comparisons. In the case of the Air Force's two biggest and highest-priority programmes, the B-1 and F-15, the astronomic costs totally prohibited any kind of evaluation of rival airframes. The answer here was to adopt a 'milestone' technique where each phase of the programme is funded only when the first has been shown to have been satisfactorily completed, or to have reached a stage where a swift completion looks attainable. Of course, as there is no fall-back programme one can always ask 'What happens if you run into big trouble?' The answer is 'It takes longer and costs more, but at least you don't have to modify a whole production line.' A further change under Packard is that the 'concept of concurrency' was modified if not abandoned. Concurrency means that all the new items needed for a system are developed simultaneously. Obviously this bears an increased technical risk. For example, to quote a gross example, it might be found that six avionics packages all turned out to get too hot and to need increased cooling-air supplies that had not been allowed for; whereas if the avionics were developed in advance the cooling airflow might be correctly predictable. On the other hand it is equally obvious that concurrency is to some degree inevitable. It would be ridiculous to hold up an aircraft programme for 100 years or so while all its bits were separately perfected one after the other.

Although it would be grossly misleading to suggest that the AX did not pose severe challenges, some aspects of it were deliberately made simple. It was hoped to be able to use an existing design of engine, even though it could be a fairly new one. The airframe was obviously going to be big and roomy, so that if an item of equipment turned out to be much bigger than expected at least it would still fit in. And to the maximum possible degree the Air Force wished to use off-the-shelf hardware, which at one stroke slashes costs and saves both time and technical trouble. Indeed the Air Force wished also to use off-the-shelf technology. In 1968 I was required to investigate in some depth the exciting new technology of composite materials based upon extremely strong and stiff fibres of carbon (graphite) and boron. These were then to be found on the laboratory benches of every major company interested in advanced aerospace structures. They were being used in the form of 'prepreg', or even as individually wound filament many miles long, to build up or reinforce test pieces or experimental structures that were not only much stronger and stiffer than any previous ones but also much lighter. The consensus of opinion was always 'It's very encouraging. What it really needs is a completely new programme for a military aircraft calling for great strength, long fatigue life and low material density. Then we shall have the budget and the opportunity to show what a revolution these new materials can bring.' With the AX there came the ideal programme—except that, to save money, the Air Force actually spelt out that the structure would be 'conventional'. Of course this does not preclude the introduction of advanced composite structure later on.

I have deliberately spent a long time discussing the technical background, because the AX, more than any other aircraft, illustrates how today the inexorable march of inflation makes one not merely run furiously to stay in the same place but, in some areas, deliberately run backwards. There is little point in developing a marvellous aeroplane if you cannot afford to put it into production. We have already got to the rather startling stage where one fine and efficient company, asked by the US Navy to build a further 48 of a quite small fighter already in full production at a contract price of $16,500,000 each, chose to refuse because it could not face the loss it would suffer (ultimately, after long litigation, it has agreed to go ahead and somehow absorb a loss of $105 million). As I can well recall the time when Spitfires were supposed to cost £5000—and early marks really didn't cost much more than this—we seem to be heading for a time when air staffs will ponder on the effectiveness of darkening the sky with a resurrected Sopwith Camel. Such thoughts were very much in the mind of the Air Force when on 6 April 1970 it received DoD permission to proceed with engineering development of the AX. From the start this had to be a vehicle that could be procured, deployed, repaired, and if necessary replaced, all in quantities which in today's context are very large numbers indeed. After months testifying before Congress that CAS was the job of the Air Force, and that the Army had no business to try to do it itself, it would not have looked too good if in some future war the Army had urgently called for CAS from the Air Force and been told 'Sorry, our AX is having a tyre-change.'

The numbers that the Air Force finally agreed were a programme of 600 aircraft and a unit price of $1·4 million, plus a contingency allowance of 15 per cent, reckoned in 'constant 1970 dollars.' In other words, if by the time the aircraft came to be delivered the dollar had fallen to half its 1970 value, the price could be $2·8 million. I suppose this is as fair a compromise as could be reached. A total of 600 aircraft would not have lasted a week in World War 2, and a large proportion of such a fleet would have been written off the books by a single attack on airfields such as the Luftwaffe mounted on 1 January 1945. As for the price, this is only about 50 times the price of a Mustang and 12 times the price of the first Skyraiders, so I suppose it is cheap. At least, it was the price that caused most of the furrowed brows in industry. I have bet a crisp £5 note that nobody will ever deliver an AX to the Air Force user squadron without having to go way above it. The winning contractor has accepted the bet.

Indeed it was mainly, if not wholly, on account of the price that half the 12 companies to whom the RFP for competitive prototype development was sent on 7 May 1970 declined to bid at all. Those who decided to try to make money elsewhere were Beech, Bell Aerospace, Grumman, LTV, McDonnell Douglas and North American Rockwell. The six who on 10 August 1970 chose to have a go were Boeing-Vertol (yes, with fixed wings), Cessna, Fairchild Republic, General Dynamics, Lockheed and Northrop. I have not seen all of the unsuccessful submissions—each proposal ran to just over 1000 pages—but doubt if they contained anything as odd as some of the candidates for the LARA (Co-In) contract early in 1964. On the other hand, I must confess to a strange feeling when I saw the artist's impressions of the two successful bidders, Fairchild Republic and Northrop, which Secretary Seamans announced on 18 December 1970. Both aircraft, respectively designated YA-10A and YA-9A, looked exactly like jet fighters of 1944–48. Indeed the Northrop design bore a superficial likeness to the company's own F-89 Scorpion, first flown in August 1948. The Fairchild, with its engines arranged Caravelle-style and blasting between twin fins, was certainly an uncommon shape but had actually been antedated by projects at Junkers and Messerschmitt in 1944.

When the Air Force chose these two finalists it announced 'Each company will design and build two prototype aircraft. A joint evaluation, which includes an assessment of competitive fly-off test program results and proposals for development and production, will be used to determine which company will be awarded the final AX development and production contract.' The prospect of a fly-off between rival prototypes made everyone feel excited. It had become a most uncommon thing, although the eventual winner recalled a 1956 fly-off of its F-105 against the F-107, and Convair did build a bomber to try and compete with the B-52—and Ed Heinemann thought there should have been a fly-off between his smaller and cheaper F3D Skyknight and the F-89 I just referred to. But before the war it was almost the universal rule, and on some marvellous occasions the lush grass at England's Martlesham Heath was blown by the slipstream of as many as five or six aircraft all striving for the same contract. But this new 'fly-off' was going to take place at Edwards, out in the vast Mojave desert and probably under a blazing sun. A fly-off is a stern test that in my view is very well worth its cost. Especially in the case of a CAS aircraft it enables a procurement decision to be taken on the basis of actual performance during sustained simulated CAS missions.

Col James E. Hildebrandt set up his AX System Project Office at the Aeronautical Systems Division at Wright-Patterson, and wondered whether he would later move it to Northrop, at Hawthorne, close to Los Angeles International Airport, or to their rivals at Farmingdale, in the flat countryside of Long Island about 25 miles east of New York City. The two companies strove furiously to beat each other yet outwardly remained friendly, and each took the rather nice step—without any pressure from the Air Force—of not only mentioning their rival in their press releases but even of repeating some of their rival's claimed design advantages! It may not be too indiscreet if I try and outline what each might have said to the Air Force.

Northrop's main line of attack was based on their heritage of trying to cut costs: 'We have a special interest in finding approaches which produce the required level of performance at reduced cost. This shows up right at the start; to produce our two prototypes and flight-test them we have asked for only \$28·9 million, whereas Fairchild have asked for \$41·2 million. Our A-9 is a conventional shape, whereas the A-10 is quite unlike any attack aircraft ever built. The A-9 is low slung, and apart from the rudder practically all its maintenance can be performed by men standing on the ground, whereas the A-10 will need ladders and workstands which will slow turnarounds and increase costs. We have a Large Amplitude Flight Simulator, the only one in the Western world, which we have used to the full, with additional help from Cornell Aeronautical Laboratory, to achieve superb handling characteristics and ensure accurate weapon delivery. On top of this we have incorporated unique side-force control (SFC) which enables a pilot to effect instant fine corrections to his lateral trajectory without having to bank. We have made our ailerons in upper and lower halves. To use SFC the pilot flicks open the upper half of one aileron, causing a large asymmetric drag force, and then neutralizes this with the rudder. The result is that he can adjust his attack trajectory from side to side in a way never before possible. Of course we have fully redundant flying controls and other systems, and we have encased the pilot in a veritable bathtub of aluminium armour up to 2 in thick which, allowing for the fact that much of it serves as structure, weighs 1200 lb. The fuel supply is duplicated, foam-suppressed and partly self-sealing. And it feeds the engine of our choice, the Avco Lycoming F102, rated at 7500 lb thrust initially and with promise of 7860 lb. Compared with our rival's engine the F102 is shorter and considerably cheaper; and, instead of being wholly new, it is based on the core section (gas generator) of the T55 turboshaft engine which has flown millions of hours in Vietnam. We calculate that the ten-year maintenance cost of the A-9, operating at a peacetime rate of 40 hours a month, will be $740,000. We do not believe anyone could equal this low figure.'

This sounds a powerful lot of reasons for choosing the A-9. But Fairchild Industries would have had a few things to say about the A-10: 'The division of Fairchild which has created the A-10 is the former Republic Aviation Corporation, which itself was formed in 1931 as Seversky Aircraft. For almost 40 years this team has been a non-stop supplier of more than 25000 of the Air Force's best fighter and attack aircraft. We have superior experience in this field, and we are confident we know better how to meet the Air Force's needs. We have built the first A-10 to be as representative as possible of a production machine, whereas Northrop have made their prototypes quite different (for example their prototype wing goes right through the fuselage, whereas in a definitive A-9 it would bolt on each side). It is true we asked for a larger sum to build our two demonstrators, but we think we have produced two completely equipped fighting aircraft, and we do not think Northrop has quite done this. Our odd shape is the result of very careful planning. Among many other advantages it puts the engines where they will ingest very little in the way of gun gas, gravel, dirt and other foreign material, yet where they can give 100 per cent performance whilst well separated from each other, or from the fuel (or from the pilot, who might get tired of noise after a long mission). The engine we chose, the General Electric TF34, is rated at 9275 lb thrust and enables us to design for low cost without worrying about aerodynamic drag. Far from being a 'new' engine, it is already qualified for the Navy Viking anti-submarine aircraft and is more fully funded than its rival. We have chosen a simplified, cheaper version of this engine. The rear engine location allows the A-10 design to carry heavy stores right across the centre-section of the wing, whereas the A-9A has to carry everything well away from the centreline (and, incidentally, we have 11 pylons, not 10). As drag is not a critical problem we have made our main gears fold into axial fairings from which the tyres protrude, and we believe an A-10 could make a wheels-up landing with virtually no damage. In combat survivability we believe we are second to none, and we have even put foam around the outside of our fuselage tanks as well as inside. Our twin fins are just part of the built-in redundancy, and we have made all the control surfaces, and their actuators, as well as the main legs and the engines, completely interchangeable left and right. Our offset nose gear provides for a gun installation which we believe will be superior. Our distinctive downswept wing-tips increase low-speed lift and efficiency. Finally we believe the A-10 is better equipped to meet demands for greater thrust, greater weight or a longer list of equipment items.'

Evaluation officers love nicely balanced decisions, and they could have fun with the two AX contenders. Neither was going to walk over the other. But were they really so close? I have a letter from a good American friend who commented 'With all other things being more or less equal . . . there is a breathtaking political battle going on in which Fairchild is waging a heated campaign stressing unemployment and the doom that will befall them if they don't win this program.' In my experience, unless there are technical reasons that are simply inescapable, contracts often tend to go to the home states of particular congressmen or to areas which are capable of being a political nuisance. Unfortunately for Northrop, neither they nor California could claim they would collapse if they lost the AX. Unfortunately for Fairchild the political situation was such that, if they won the award, few people unacquainted with the programme would give them credit for truly having the better aircraft.

Fairchild Republic really needed the AX very much; so did Long Island's aerospace industry, which only had one big aircraft programme left—and that, as mentioned earlier, had lost money and was going to lose another $105 million. In 1970 the v-p and general manager at Farmingdale, Donald J. Strait, saw AX as the only evident foundation on which to build the Republic Division's future. The splendid Thud (F-105) was merely bringing in an obviously limited series of modification contracts. The US/FRG, a swing-wing, jet-lift V/STOL fighter, had been cancelled before it became hardware (leaving behind an enduring belief at Farmingdale that V/STOL is 'complicated, expensive and not survivable in the battlefield environment', which it undoubtedly is if you choose to do it like the US/FRG). In 1969 the division girded its loins and made a mighty bid to win the F-15, but succeded only in being one of the three finalists. So, apart from subcontract work, it was practically AX or nothing. What did Farmingdale have going for it? Strait himself is not your average v-p, for a start. In addition to the expected managerial experience he has thousands of hours on all the division's fighters—P-47, F-84 and F-105—and has served as a major-general and head of the New Jersey Air National Guard and held high office in the Pentagon. But at Farmingdale he is better known as Head Tiger. Borrowing the concept of Kelly Johnson's

Skunk Works, which secretly built the Lockheed U-2 and A-11, the division set up an integrated task force called the Tiger Works to create the A-10. Under Strait came slightly lesser Tigers: Dr Norman Grossman, v-p engineering; Vincent Tizio, program director; and AX engineer Robert Sanator. Soon they were going at it day and night.

The first YA-10A, 71-1369, was ready for inspection by stockholders at the Fairchild annual meeting on 19 April 1972. Then it was dismantled, transported to Edwards and reassembled. Although it was carefully made as representative as possible of the production aircraft, and had further (geographically) to come, it beat its rival into the air. Early on 10 May the Republic division c.t.p., Howard 'Sam' Nelson, made a highly successful 43-minute flight. He called the odd-looking bird 'a beautiful machine to fly.' Undoubtedly he meant that it *felt* beautiful; in any case, from where he was sitting, you can't see much of it. A week later Northrop showed the first YA-9A to the press, but 71-1367 still had some ground-testing to do. It was 30 May before the Northrop director of flight test, Lew Nelson (no relation to 'Sam'), started the A-9A flight test programme. The second Fairchild aircraft flew on 21 July, and the second Northrop on 23 August. On 31 August the second Fairchild blew both main tyres on landing and went off the runway, but all four aircraft had completed Task 1—the contractor's basic flight programme to prove design figures and explore the flight envelope—by the first week in October. They had not tried to fly intensively, and each had averaged about 20 missions a month of 90 minutes each. On 24 October the Air Force took over. From then on it was pretty rigid, and no modification or repair was permitted unless demanded by reasons of flight safety (in which case someone would lose marks).

Minor deficiencies and problems naturally showed up in both types. Typical of these was the fact that, like so many other rear-engined aircraft before it, the Fairchild A-10A could not be stalled without making its engines swallow an ocean of turbulent air, which made the engines stall themselves. As a temporary but effective palliative a fixed slat was installed on the wing leading edge, and the wing root was modified with a fillet and a forward-projecting fence. A short stall strip was added to the leading edge outboard of the landing-gear nacelle to ensure that this part of the wing stalled first. Much later, in the spring of 1973, an aerodynamically actuated movable slat was fitted, and this was adopted as standard.

Task 2, in 'blue-suit' hands, involved 50 hours on each type (ie, 25 hr per aircraft) in performance test, 53 hours in weapons delivery and 20 hours in a TAC suitability test. The pilots, from TAC and AFSC, were assigned to a Joint Test Force under Maj George P. Lynch. Each pilot first familiarized himself with the mission procedures, using Cessna A-37Bs, and then flew first one aircraft and then the other, to eliminate possible bias due to any special pilot proficiency. Everything was fully instrumented, plotted by exceedingly accurate radar and recorded as digital data. Finally, after a brief Christmas vacation, the competitive evaluation concluded on 2 January 1973 after a week of intensive maintenance trials. It had been expected that the winner would be announced in March, but Fairchild was named as early as 18 January—at which everyone, so it seemed to me, said 'But of course'. To try to overcome this unsatisfactory state of affairs Lt-Gen James T. Stewart, Commander, Aeronautical Systems Division, AFSC, took the possibly unusual step of spelling out one or two reasons why the A-10A might just have been truly the better aircraft. He picked up several of the points I named earlier, then revealed the rather lower MMH/FH figure of Fairchild (a remarkable 8·1 against 10·5), emphasized that the millions of bits of weapon data had come out just about evens ('though at reduced levels of confidence the A-10A came out ahead') and then hit the nail on the head: 'At first glance it looked like Fairchild was just going to be more expensive to do business with . . . but . . . The Fairchild people had their eyes further downstream in the company's approach to a prototype model. We can do a great deal more with the Fairchild prototype than with the A-9A. The prototype-to-production transition will be much better with the A-10A.'

With the news came an award of a pre-production contract to Fairchild Industries worth $159·2 million for 10 aircraft and one worth $27·6 million to GE for TF34 engines. The documents contained options on a further 24–72 aircraft and 62–186 engines. The ink had hardly dried before a delegation from Connecticut, led by Senator Abraham Ribicoff, angrily pointed out the lower price of the F102 engine (which happens to come from Stratford, in Connecticut) and demanded a contract investigation. To my surprise the Air Force—who are not too eager to go through the TFX nausea all over again—not only gave an immediate public reply but stated that there would be 'a cross-over point in the production run where the overall cost of the A-10A will be less than for the A-9A.' But this was only the start of the in-fighting. Over the preceding 20 months a series of Congressional investigations and hearings into the CAS mission, and which service should provide it, had at one point brought the excellent A-7 Corsair (p. 234) much into the picture. It took no less a person than Sen. Barry Goldwater to get up and ask that it should be written into the public record that the hearings had not at any time suggested that the A-7 should continue to be bought in place of the AX. But as soon as the award to Fairchild was made public there was an air of hurt surprise in Washington that the Air Force should have seemed to rush ahead with the AX while both the Senate and the House of Representatives had big investigations into the CAS situation still uncompleted. In fact the chairman of the House Appropriations Committee, Rep. George Mahon, wrote to the Secretary of Defense, Elliot L. Richardson (who must by then have been in the Pentagon saddle all of a week), asking him officially to stay the Air Force's hand. Mahon happens to sit for Texas, where the A-7 is built.

What happened next was that the Air Force sent Mahon a previously classified computer study, centred on a war game called 'Saber Armor Charlie' in which nice battlefield targets, including plenty of armour, were presented for the attention of various existing attack aircraft and the A-10A. The latter 'proved to be better suited for the close-support mission' (this is news ?). But the special CAS subcommittee of the Senate Armed Services Committee—a body that general officers ignore at their peril—still considered the Air Force ought to have conducted actual fly-off evaluations between the A-10A and the A-7. Such a test would have been difficult to conduct in meaningful terms. According to a DoD official 'If a forward site in an austere environment was selected the A-7 would be at a disadvantage; if a rear-area runway 400 miles from the battle area was selected the A-10 would be hard pressed.' And there is more to it than this, as I shall outline at the end of this tale.

Vought, which makes the A-7, was one of the companies which in the summer of 1970 declined to fight for the AX business. But Vought was intensely interested in the new gun the Air Force wanted the AX to carry. Everyone knows how bitter experience in the early days of the Vietnam war made USAF pilots cry out for effective guns for use in air-to-air fighting, so that 20 mm Gatlings soon appeared on the F-4, A-7 and other attack and fighter aircraft, both as inbuilt equipment and as external pods. What was not so obvious was that there was also a cry for a gun capable of unfailingly busting armour. Charlie did not present too many hard-skinned targets, but the Air Force had no doubt that it ought to fund a new gun for air-to-ground use, just as it was funding a new one for use by fighters. The fighter gun is the GAU-7 (Gun Aircraft Unit) and it is a lightweight, rapid-fire weapon firing 25 mm caseless ammunition; in effect the 1-inch calibre shells are mounted on nothing but structurally robust propellant which is wholly consumed in firing. In 1970 the air-to-ground gun requirement was drafted, calling for a much bigger weapon firing 30 mm (1·18 in) ammunition at the highest possible rate and with the extremely high muzzle velocity of 3500 ft/sec, roughly 50 per cent higher than that of some aircraft guns. To get 50 per cent higher speed of flight not only reduces flight-time of the projectile, easing aiming problems, but also much more than doubles the impact energy of the projectile; thus, making many large assumptions, the penetrative capability of an armour-piercing round is more or less doubled. On the other hand it means about twice the quantity of propellant charge, and an extremely strong breech and barrel. This meant a completely new gun, the GAU-8, which was worked on by GE, Philco-Ford, General American Transportation and Hughes Tool.

By 1972 the first two companies were developing prototype GAU-8 submissions under $12·1 million Phase I contracts, and later in the year both began firing. The guns are formidable indeed. Both are Gatlings, but they use quite different principles and one has seven and the other six barrels. Each turns the scales at around 1500 lb, without its huge magazine of ammunition which can be consumed at either 2000 or 4000 rds/min. At present the ammo is aluminium-cased but, if the GAU-7 works well, it may be possible to make these bigger propellant charges caseless as well. AX was required to carry 1350 rounds of this impressive ammunition; by comparison a typical load for a fighter is 125 rounds per gun. GAU-8 prototypes were not ready during the fly-off between the two types of AX, so the 20 mm M-61 Gatling was used instead (to the tune of over 21000 rounds). Late in 1973 one of the GAU-8 models was to be chosen for possible production—a big shoot-off having started at Eglin AFB, Florida, on 15 January—and fitted into one of the two A-10As. Secretary Seamans had re-affirmed that the gun is 'not a pacing item in AX development', and it will not be until 1975 that a full-scale decision will be taken on quantity production of the A-10A and gun.

Vought's interest in the gun arose from the company's wish to fit it to the A-7. Indeed the A-7 had been one of the possible carriers when, in signing their two $12·1 million gun contracts, the Air Force had asked for preliminary designs for a GAU-8 pod capable of being attached to existing aircraft. The pod would be quite a package, and even with only 750 rounds it would weigh about 2500 lb. Moreover, while the F-4 could fix it under the centreline, the A-7 would have to sling it as a sidearm, or even latch it under a wing. As an alternative GE, whose gun has a linkless feed, offered Vought a smaller 500-round package that might conceivably fit inside a modified A-7 fuselage. But a gun of this power needs to be designed in from the start, slap on the centreline and not too far below the main axis of the fuselage. This is where it goes in the A-10A, and the nose gear is accordingly offset to the right (Northrop's gear was offset to the left, like that of a Trident airliner). A gun is a form of heat engine. It was Sir Peter Masefield who, when he was a young aviation writer in 1942, first used muzzle horsepower (MHP) as the best yardstick for comparing the effect of aircraft guns. MHP is the actual power developed at the muzzle, calculated from projectile mass, muzzle velocity and rate of fire. The MHP of a rifle-calibre Browning machine gun, such as was used by the Allies throughout World War 2, varied from 75 to 82. The MHP of today's GAU-8 is around 17,700, so even a brief burst will take a lot of knots off the airspeed.

Certainly the punch of the A-10A will hardly be in question, neither is its ability to drop things. And even with a single man aboard it ought to be able to take out a pinpoint target using just one of its possible load of six 475 lb TV-guided Maverick missiles. It is quite a big aircraft; in size it is rather like a Canberra standing on stilts. This makes it a very obvious target, even if it has smokeless engines, and the Air Force conducted extensive trials at Wright-Patterson in which various guns, including a Soviet-made 23 mm cannon, were used to pump shells at point-blank range into representative parts of the A-10A wing, fuselage, cockpit and other items while they were subjected to winds of up to 400 knots from a large jet engine. There is no reason to dispute the Air Force's findings that the eventual A-10A will be 'the most combat-survivable aircraft ever built'. On the other hand I must reserve judgement on just what this means in practice. In a companion volume dealing with bombers I often seemed to be expressing surprise that people went on for so long thinking that they could fly big bombers safely through defending missiles just by flying a bit higher. Those bombers and missiles were mostly of the 1950s. The A-10A is meant to live in the 1980s, when missiles will be deadly. If the Air Force finally decides not to build many A-10As it will probably be because they will be too vulnerable.

The A-10A is meant to live close above the ground battle, either stooging around at 150–300 knots looking for targets or engaged in multiple low-altitude passes knocking out one target on each run. In the absence of opposition it will undoubtedly do a fantastic job. It will be able to operate in the most rugged terrain (note correct use of 'rugged'!) in conditions of 1000 foot ceiling and 1 mile visibility, pulling fierce turns at maximum weight and laughing at most light AA fire of the type encountered in Vietnam. But I doubt that it could laugh at a Soviet 57 mm—a gun very effective in Vietnam—and even in 1974 there are many quite small guided-missile systems that ought (and a lot hinges on this word) to be able to knock down an A-10A without greatly disturbing its crew's poker game. For example the Rapier, a neat missile system easily towed by a Land-Rover, makes any bathtubs of armour and system redundancy seem rather pointless. If I may misquote Damon Runyon, 'It doesn't matter quite where you hit him; you seem to hit him all over.'

There is yet another factor I have purposely left to the end because it is again controversial. The Air Force hopes to use the A-10A with 'austere' avionics. This is an honest word, but when Secretary Seamans wrote about the programme he had a better public-relations sense and called the equipment 'simple'. Full details have yet to be decided, but it is not expected to include more than a simple HUD giving such basic parameters as airspeed, dive angle and height, and a simple weapon-control unit with optical (HUD) sight. In addition there would be a Maverick guidance box, possibly a controller for laser (smart) bombs, and ECM penaids. Space, weight, power and cooling capacity is being left for a wide range of other equipment including radars, IR and other sensors, and possibly a navigation system other than Tacan. Will the 'austere' fit be enough? If I were a potential enemy I would probably think the unmistakable silhouette of an A-10A a good reason for not being there at all in the daytime, but I might get up to all sorts of things on a foggy night. I hope the great German offensive in the Ardennes in the foul winter of 1944 has not been forgotten. All around were airfields packed with 'Jugs'—the fine P-47 Thunderbolt made by none other than the ancestors of Fairchild-Republic—and their pilots fumed and fretted and waited for the weather to clear so that they could at last give CAS to the hard-pressed US Army. Austere fits are fine for the Mojave, but in some parts of the world the human eyeball needs a lot of help.

I recently saw an article in which the view was expressed that the AX might be 'AX-ed' because it was 'so specialized' and would not sell outside the US. Apart from being untrue, this is beside the point. To the rather large body of fighting men in the US Army the A-10A might before long be the main thing between them and oblivion. As the Air Force has fought a long and bitter battle to keep the CAS mission as its exclusive preserve it can hardly now walk away from it, and in another three years it will have little but the A-10A with which to do it. Congress, as I write, is the scene of a surprising amount of in-fighting on behalf of the A-7, because people seem to find it difficult to understand that a 400 knot aerial trucking system might actually do a better job. Of course it could, for a third time, decide that aircraft tailored to limited ground battles are not as exciting as supersonic dogfights in the wild blue yonder. It could just as well decide to go out of business, because the CAS mission is the only one it is likely in the foreseeable future to have to perform in earnest.

I proof-read this book in March 1974. In April 1974 the A-10A successfully flying with the GAU-8A gun was to go through a competitive fly-off against an A-7D at Fort Riley, Kansas, surpassing the earlier fly-off against the A-9A. A fantastic measurement and data-collection system was to quantify and record everything that could be measured, as the rival aircraft made simulated attacks on American soldiers simulating Russians who were to fire back with simulated Gainful and Grail missiles. Accepting that Americans are even more like small boys than are most of us—or are more ready to admit it—and just love this kind of thing, this mighty fly-off is something new in history. It might even come up with the right answer, but I doubt it. There's an old proverb about lies, damn lies and statistics.